The Brain

BOOKS BY RICHARD M. RESTAK

Premeditated Man:
Bioethics & the Control of Future Human Life

The Self Seekers

The Brain:
The Last Frontier

The Brain

The Brain

Richard M. Restak, M.D.

BANTAM BOOKS
TORONTO • NEW YORK • LONDON • SYDNEY • AUCKLAND

THE BRAIN

A Bantam Book / October 1984

All rights reserved.
Copyright © 1984 by Educational Broadcasting Corporation and
Richard M. Restak, M.D.
Book design by Barbara N. Cohen.
Layout by Joyce Kubat.

Library of Congress Cataloging in Publication Data
Restak, Richard M., 1942–
    The brain.

    Bibliography: p. 363
    Includes index.
    1. Brain. I. Title. [DNLM: 1. Brain. WL 300 R436ba]
QP376.R46   1984   612'.82   84-45177
                    ISBN 0-553-05047-8

Published simultaneously in the United States and Canada

PRINTED IN THE UNITED STATES OF AMERICA

DW   0 9 8 7 6 5 4 3

To Jennifer, Alison, and Ann.

Contents

Acknowledgments

This book is an outgrowth and expanded interpretation of an eight-part public television series of the same name produced by WNET/New York for distribution by PBS. Because WNET always saw *The Brain* as a complex project entailing many forms of communication, a book related to the series and addressed to the general reader was always an integral component. I was delighted to take on this exciting task when Leonard Mayhew and other members of the station asked me to write the book.

The concept of the series was the brainchild of Richard Thomas and WNET's Science and Arts Programming Area headed by George Page, also the series' host-narrator. After carrying out the research and development phase and launching the production phase, Thomas returned home to England to pursue other projects. He was succeeded as Executive Producer by Jack Sameth, a thirty year veteran of television production. Richard Hutton, who had been a member of the team from the outset, continued as Series Science Editor. Hutton assisted me, with extraordinary dedication, in innumerable ways during the writing of this book. He was particularly important in helping to coordinate the book with the television series in terms of subject areas and emphasis. During the writing of this book I was in constant touch with the producers of all of the programs. In addition to Richard Thomas and Richard Hutton, who originally developed the series, I had steady contact with John Heminway, producer of four of the programs, DeWitt Sage, Robin Spry and Terry Landau. Linda Lillienfeld, assisted by Cathy Cevoli, saw to it that I had the interviews, transcripts and background memos that I needed to write the manuscript. She also researched and obtained the very important visual material included here. In all this work she was assisted with intelligence and energy by Benjamin Frank during the early stages and Kevin Wayne during the crucial last six months.

The Brain television series and educational program was made possible by the Annenberg Corporation for Public Broadcasting the National Institutes of Health and the National Science Foundation. The series was co-produced with WNET by Antenne 2 in France and NHK in Japan.

In addition I wish to thank the following neuroscientists for discussing with me their research projects: Roger Porter, Miles Herkenham, Frank Putnam, John Mazziotta, and Mortimer Mishkin. Special thanks are due to Dr. Paul McLean who offered many helpful suggestions on how the book might be improved so as to convey to the nonspecialist reader the excitement and challenge of contemporary brain research.

Finally, the writing of THE BRAIN would not have been possible without the encouragement of my editor at Bantam, Peter Guzzardi, his assistant Alison Acker, managing editor F.X. Flinn, my wife-researcher-counselor Carolyn Restak, and my wise and supportive agent and friend, Ann Buchwald. Last, but by no means least, the project was helped immeasurably by my secretarial research assistants, Mary Heamstead, Wilma Holland and "Vee" Riggs.

Richard M. Restak, M.D.

Introduction

Weighing less than sixteen hundred grams (three pounds), the human brain in its natural state resembles nothing so much as a soft, wrinkled walnut. Yet despite this inauspicious appearance, the human brain can store more information than all the libraries in the world. It is also responsible for our most primitive urges, our loftiest ideals, the way we think, even the reason why, on occasion, we sometimes don't think, but act instead. The workings of an organ capable of creating *Hamlet,* the Bill of Rights, and Hiroshima remain deeply mysterious. How is it constructed? How did it develop? If we learn more about the brain, can we learn more about ourselves? Indeed, are we anything *other* than our brain?

Some of these questions remain unanswered, others ("Is the brain the mind?") may remain forever unanswerable. But in recent years neuroscience has been making some remarkable advances. On the basis of what is now known, neuroscientists have begun to suspect that our very humanity may someday be defined by the chemical and electrical activities within our brains. But most of us recoil at the idea that our hopes, our dreams, our lusts, and our ambitions may someday be defined in terms familiar only to the neurochemist and the neurophysiologist. Our mind, our free will, our creativity—*surely* these things attest to the presence of something more than the gnarled mass of cells we call the brain.

In this book, based on the Public Television series *The Brain,* we will explore these questions and try to give you some feeling for the outer limits of our present knowledge about the brain, as well as what we can reasonably expect in the near and distant future.

Since the brain poses such a formidable challenge, neuroscientists are exploring it in a number of different ways. For one thing, they are hard at work plotting the connections between and among *neurons,* the brain's basic unit. But since there are between ten billion and a hundred billion neurons (no one knows precisely how many), it is obvious that a mere "wiring diagram" will not supply all the answers we seek.

Neurons communicate with each other through electrical and chemical messages. These messages can now be decoded. But as neuroscientists decipher them, they encounter the brain as paradox: those same neuroscientists are using their own brains to understand the brain. In a very literal sense, the brain is seeking to understand itself. This is a much more urgent goal than, say, learning about our most distant galaxies or peering into the subatomic world of particle physics. None of those inquiries can be satisfactorily answered until we understand *how* we understand. Just as our knowledge of other people is based on our knowledge of ourselves, "reality" is limited by our knowledge of the physical basis of all understanding, the human brain.

Here are some of the most exciting areas of brain research in the mid-1980s.

Vision and Movement. We humans are capable of prodigious feats of strength and power. Witness the hands of a championship boxer as they curl into fists and within split seconds land on an opponent's body with bone-shattering impact. The brain that directs this activity can also "program" movements of exquisite delicacy: the pirouette of a prima ballerina, the ever-so-brief contact between a piano keyboard and the fingertips of the concert pianist.

Every day each one of us carries out movements of incredible complexity. Even something as "simple" as walking engages our brains in a precise electrical and chemical repertoire. Each muscle must come into action at a specific moment. If the sequence is altered even slightly, we literally fall all over ourselves.

From the study of patients with "movement disorders" we learn a great deal about normal movement. The goal? To develop treatments for many of the nation's elderly who are afflicted with Parkinson's disease, a disorder that imprisons the affected person within the confines of a body that will no longer move as it should. From these studies neuroscientists are also discovering ways of improving athletic performance and reducing muscular tension, which leads to athletic injuries and permanent disability.

Is the eye like a camera? How is the complexity of the outer world suitably recorded and transformed within the brain? Neuroscientists are answering these questions by research directed along several fronts. In one of the most promising, electrodes are being implanted within cells along the brain's visual pathway. These electrical activity recordings reveal a system of incredible complexity. Even slight variations in the contour of an object within a person's visual field may bring into play a totally new population of brain cells. Research on vision and movement may make a philosophical contribution to such subjects as free will and the difference between instinctual and voluntary behavior.

The Brain's Underlying Rhythms. No living creature lives in a vacuum, and we are no exception. Our bodies are constantly influenced by cycles of day and night, seasons, tides, magnetic and gravitational forces, and, some claim, even such environmental forces as lunar phases. The human brain responds to these cycles by mirroring them with cycles of its own: sleep and waking, the ebb and flow of hormones, periodicities in our levels of alertness and competence. Even our emotions follow cycles that, when they go awry, can result in forms of mental illness. Neuroscientists are currently exploring how all these "biological clocks" are constituted, what winds them up, and how they run down.

Madness. Investigations by neuroscientists reveal that many forms of mental illness may result from alterations in normal brain functioning. A psychosis is often accompanied by shifts in neurotransmitter balances or changes in the brain's electrical patterns, which, when the patient improves, return to a normal pattern. Can mental illness be explained on the basis of changes within the brain? Neuroscientists are at the point where answers to such questions may soon be possible.

The Neuronal Basis for Learning and Memory. Brain research is raising the astonishing possibility that at the molecular level we may operate very similarly to such humble creatures as the sea slug. In all living organisms, memories may be stored within the brain according to their importance for survival. An animal "remembers" its predator and withdraws at the first sign of its enemy's approach. Memories are also laid down in tandem with the intensity of emotional experiences. As children, we don't have to be told more than once not to put our hands on a hot stove.

The Electrical and Chemical Brain. The lightning of a sudden thunderstorm has its terrifying equivalent in the human brain—an epileptic seizure. Even a slight electrical malfunction in the brain can make normal life almost impossible. This is the problem that many of the nation's two million epileptics face daily. From investigations into the brains of epileptics, neuroscientists are learning what it is within our healthy brains that limits electrical discharges and protects us from epileptic attacks.

Specialization Within the Brain. There is firm evidence that parts of the brain are at their best when engaged in certain activities. For instance, the left hemisphere is generally concerned with language and verbal reasoning, while the right hemisphere is more involved with spatial perceptions and emotions. But none of these rules is etched in granite. In fact, the number of exceptions is prompting neuroscientists to reevaluate their preconceptions about what goes on within the brain.

Endorphins: "the natural high." How does the brain respond when we're injured? There is evidence that it produces several chemicals which provide pain relief during times of extreme physical and even mental stress. These endorphins ("morphine-like substances") have their own receptors in the brain. By using their knowledge of endorphins, neuroscientists are developing pain killers which may be able to relieve pain without leading to addiction. Researchers also hope that their studies may lead to understanding what happens when a person becomes "hooked" on a drug, which in turn may make new, more effective, treatment possible.

Brain Activity Mapping. The brain uses glucose (sugar) and oxygen according to its activity at a given moment. Reading this sentence results in increased glucose and oxygen consumption in the visual cortex. Closing your eyes and thinking about turning the page sparks an increase in metabolic activity in the frontal areas of the brain. Since the advent of radioactive tracers (special procedures capable of tracking molecules of radioactively tagged glucose), brain activity maps have become possible. Maps can also be plotted for electrical impulses in the brain and, in the near future, for the brain's magnetic fields. We are fast approaching a time when it will be possible to observe physical changes within the brain in "real time," from moment to moment. But despite these advances, considerable disagreement exists among neuroscientists on whether it will ever be possible to equate a "disordered thought" with a "disordered molecule."

Consciousness. No one really knows what consciousness is. Its nature is perhaps the greatest mystery of the human brain. Neuroscientists are now attempting to solve this enigma by concentrating on what happens within the brain during altered states. For instance, although insomnia has claimed victims through the ages, neuroscientists have only recently learned of the complicated interplay of forces that must proceed exactly according to schedule if we expect to have a good night's sleep. Research on people with multiple personalities provides another avenue for understanding the brain's role in consciousness. Does a person with several different personalities exhibit distinctive patterns of brain activity for whichever personality is dominant at the time? If they do, then many of our concepts about who we are may have to be changed. Imagine the social and legal consequences. If a multiple personality commits a crime in one state of consciousness, how can that person be held responsible at a later time when another personality may be in command?

Although many other areas of brain research will be discussed throughout this book, the above topics convey some sense of how broad our canvas will be.

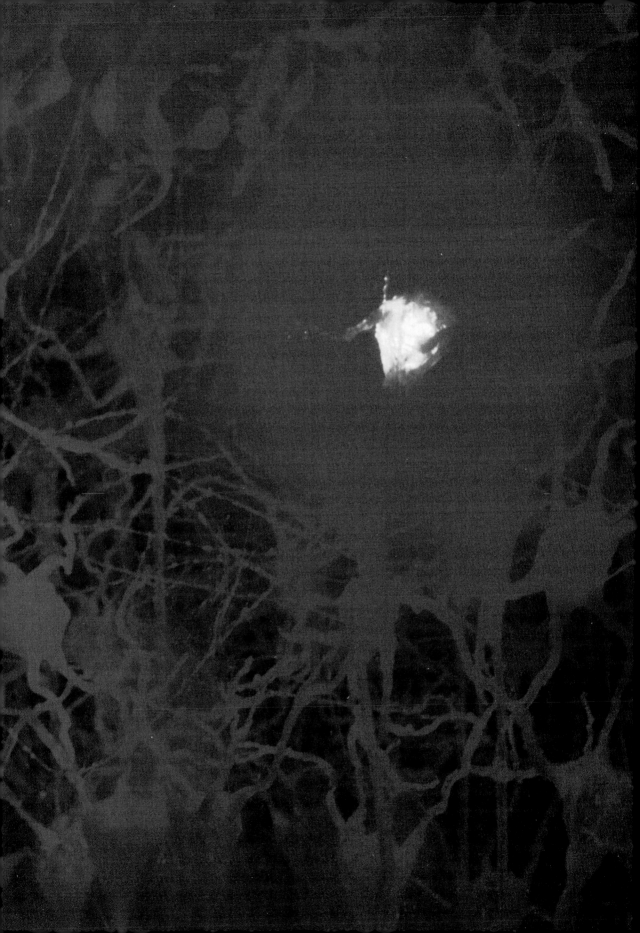

1.
The Enlightened Machine

Prior to any meaningful discussion of specifics, we need to get some rough grasp on what we mean by the word *brain*. Basically, what is a brain? Surprisingly enough, a straightforward definition of a brain is difficult to come by. Textbooks devoted to the brain rarely provide a useful definition. One of them begins: "The brain is made up of individual units—the nerve cells and the glial cells." But this is only a circular definition. The brain is a collection of nerve cells. Nerve cells compose the brain.

A more precise and encompassing definition of the brain can be found in the dictionary: "The portion of the vertebrate central nervous system that constitutes the organ of thought and neural coordination, including all the higher nervous centers, receiving stimuli from the sense organs, and interpreting and correlating these with stored impressions to formulate the motor impulses that ultimately control all vital activities, that is made up of neurons and their processes organized into layers and nuclei of gray matter and tracts, decussations, and fasciculi of white matter together with various supporting and nutritive structures, that is enclosed within the skull, being continuous with the spinal cord through the foramen magnum and with the cranial nerves through various other openings."

Although this definition is encompassing, it is also overwhelming. For our purposes, the brain can be defined

A neuron fires deep inside the cerebral cortex.

simply as the part of the central nervous system that is contained within the skull. The rest of the central nervous system can be found in the spinal cord.

If you lift the hard, bony canopy of the skull, you first encounter three membranes, each with Latin names: the outer *dura mater* (hard mother); the second, the *arachnoid* (cobweb); the third, *pia mater* (tender mother).

The *dura* is a hard, fibrous enclosing membrane just beneath the bony skull.

The *arachnoid* bridges the brain's many crevices, a fact some fanciful early neuroscientists compared to the vaulting of a spider's web.

The *pia* is molded with the firmness and tightness of a gymnast's outfit, designed to dip into every irregularity on the brain's surface.

Between the pia and the arachnoid flows cerebrospinal fluid, which winds like a vast network of rivers, filling every

The protective layers of the brain provide a superb defense against injury.

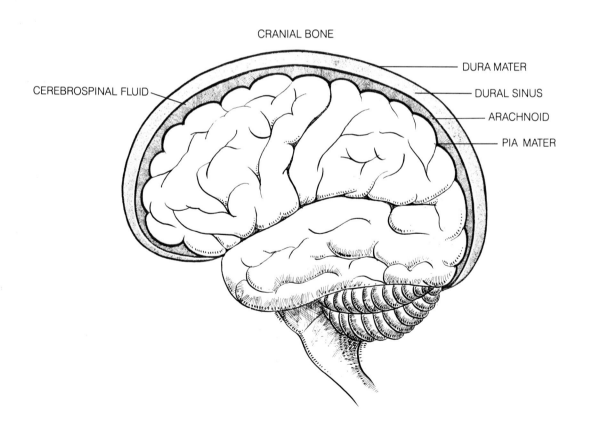

CRANIAL BONE

DURA MATER

DURAL SINUS

ARACHNOID

PIA MATER

CEREBROSPINAL FLUID

one of the brain's gullies. Even so, the total amount of cerebrospinal fluid in the brain is only about 120 milliliters, barely enough to fill a good-sized teacup.

In some areas the cerebrospinal fluid within this sub-arachnoid space (literally *under* the arachnoid) widens into miniature lakes. In other quarters the flow narrows into a system of canals. Imagine what it would be like to sail through this waterway. Every twist and turn of this minia-ture Venice would bring into view a new landmark, an area of the cortex bearing a name lovingly bestowed on it by some long-dead neuroscientist intent on achieving immortality. Many of these *gyri* (ridges) and *sulci* (valleys) bear names that trace as far back as the Renaissance.

For some reason no neuroscientist fully understands, we have two brains. Or to be more precise, our *cerebral hemispheres* look almost as if someone slipped a mirror down the center of our skulls so that one hemisphere reflects the other. Although detailed inspection reveals that

Although arbitrary, the "land-marks" of the brain are useful demarcations.

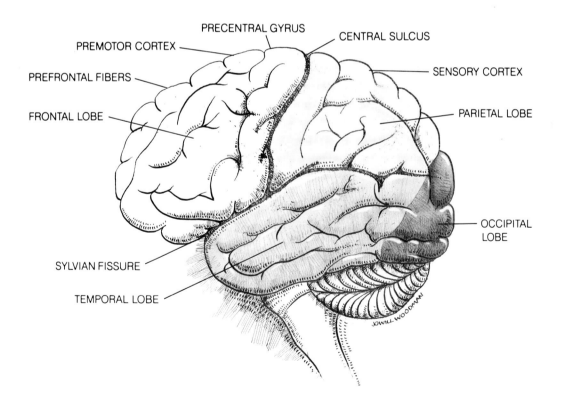

PRECENTRAL GYRUS

CENTRAL SULCUS

PREMOTOR CORTEX

PREFRONTAL FIBERS

SENSORY CORTEX

FRONTAL LOBE

PARIETAL LOBE

OCCIPITAL LOBE

SYLVIAN FISSURE

TEMPORAL LOBE

the two hemispheres aren't precisely alike, they are similar enough to the untrained observer that one wonders, "What could be the purpose of such an arrangement?"

Along the center of the brain lies a deep ditch—the *longitudinal sulcus*—running from front to back. A second sulcus—the *Sylvian fissure*—runs along the outer side of each hemisphere at about the level of the angle of the jaw. A less conspicuous furrow—the *central fissure*—runs downward from the top over the outer portion of the hemispheres, where it blends into the Sylvian fissure. Their importance derives from the use neuroscientists make of them: to divide the cerebral hemispheres into artificially separate territories.

The frontal lobe: everything in front of the central fissure.

The parietal lobe and occipital lobe: the cortical areas behind the central fissure, parietal coming first and merging into occipital.

The temporal lobe: everything below the Sylvian fissure.

On the "sail" through the subarachnoid space proposed a moment ago, our directions would read: Sail backward for the occipital, downward for the temporal, forward for the frontal, and upward for the parietal. But once you have entered these four basic "continents," you will find that each continent contains its own unique terrain. One sails to the Caribbean with the expectation of encountering islands, and the brain, too, has its own ecology.

The frontal lobe contains, from the central sulcus forward, the *precentral gyrus,* which is the primary area for movement of the opposite side of the body. Destruction to this area leads to paralysis. Farther forward is the *premotor cortex.* Here more complex motor movements are organized. Even farther forward are the *prefrontal fibers,* which exert an inhibitory control on our activities (such as telling us not to talk during a tennis match). With lesions in the prefrontal lobes we might act without inhibition until some outside agency took over the function of our prefrontal lobes (by whispering to us to shut up).

The parietal lobe contains the primary *sensory cortex,* the "feeling" part of the brain, which receives impulses from all the sensory receptors. Like a proper English garden, the parietal lobe is meticulously arranged, with each area of the postcentral gyrus corresponding to a particular part of

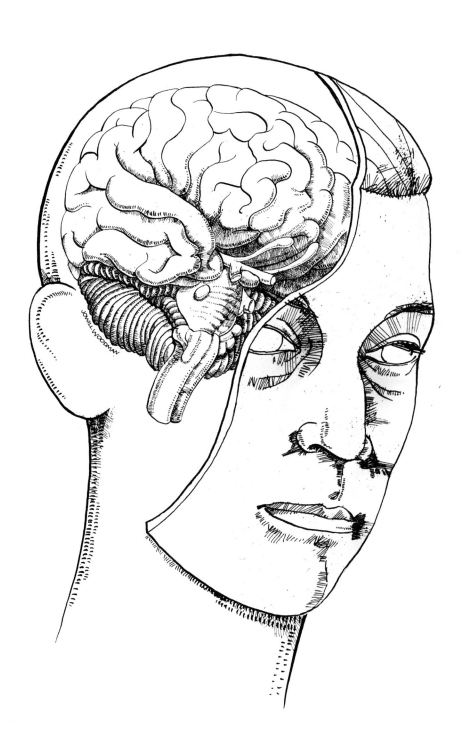

the body. This isn't to imply that "feeling" is confined to the parietal lobe. We can experience touch, pain, and pressure at areas lower down in the brainstem. But in such instances our localization is faulty. A patient with a parietal lesion will react to a pinprick in his or her hand, but the patient won't know that the pin is pricking the hand as opposed to, say, the foot. The parietal lobe has to be intact to do that.

Sailing downward from the central sulcus, we encounter the temporal lobe. This area is involved in *hearing* and *memory.* The senses of time and individuality are located here as well. *Déjà vu* experiences, in which we seem to be reliving an aspect of our past, can be elicited by electrical stimulation of the temporal lobe. But in some instances, stimulation produces just the opposite effect: a *jamais vu* experience, in which familiar things and people seem strange and otherworldly. In all, the temporal lobe is the most intriguing part of the cerebral hemispheres, largely because of its link with those underlying areas of the brain that we share with other species. Because of the temporal lobe's connection with the "animal brain" (*limbic system*), we are able to experience the emotions of fear, anger, lust, and even primitive forms of jealousy.

Somewhat behind the temporal lobe is the *visual center,* the occipital areas where incredibly complex transformations are wrought in the signals conveyed from our eyes by means of the optic nerves. A wound to the back of the head, if it shears off part of the occipital lobes, will leave the sufferer blind. In fact, it was the effect of missile and sword wounds that first alerted neuroscientists to the importance of the occipital lobes—one of the very few benefits ever to emerge from our ancient tendency toward war.

Two hemispheres and four lobes; separate continents bounded by three fissures. This is the basic organization of the cerebral hemispheres. But as every traveler knows, continents contain an infinite variety of customs and cultures; specifics are often less certain than geographers comfortably admit. Neuroscientists, too, have learned to be less dogmatic: depriving a laboratory animal of its vision by lopping off its occipital lobes is a long way from understanding how the brain enables us to appreciate Michelangelo's "Pietà." At various points throughout this book we will be amplifying our ideas about the cerebral hemispheres. But in the

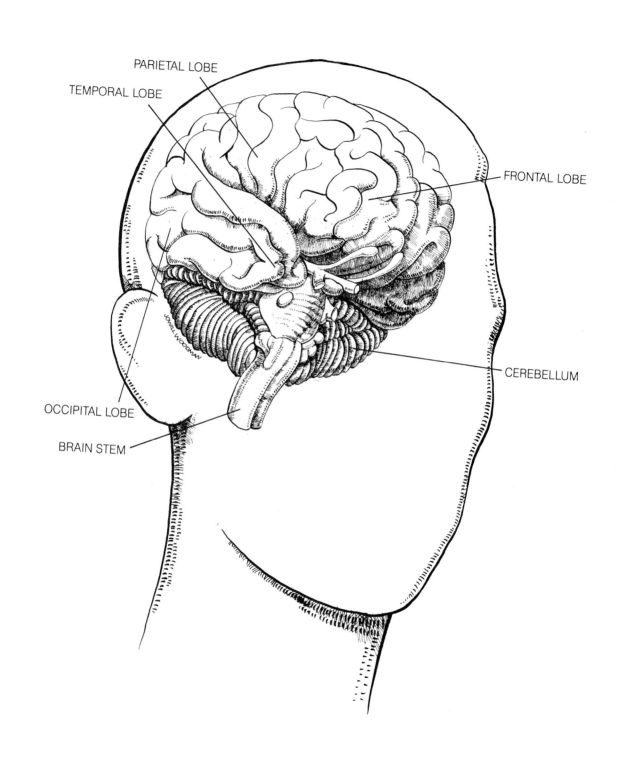

PARIETAL LOBE

TEMPORAL LOBE

FRONTAL LOBE

CEREBELLUM

OCCIPITAL LOBE

BRAIN STEM

meantime the cerebral geography we have described is useful as long as one doesn't lose sight of the fact that "the map is not the territory."

Our brain isn't simply the sum total of our cerebral hemispheres. Cats in heat, raging bulls, murderous jungle foragers—these creatures have brains, too. Their cerebral hemispheres, however, are poorly developed. In many organisms they are not developed at all. Would we be totally at the mercy of our instincts if we didn't possess cerebral hemispheres? The notion is far from absurd. Removal of our cerebral hemispheres reveals a series of structures very similar to those found in the cat purring at our feet or the pigeons we feed in the park.

Where the spinal cord enters the brainstem it expands into an inch of vital flesh, the *medulla.* Swallowing, vomiting, breathing, talking, singing, the control of blood pressure, respiration, and, partially, heart rate—these are the tasks carried out in this magic inch. Cut the brainstem below the level of the medulla and the blood pressure drops to zero, breathing ceases, and death follows within a minute or so. It is through the medulla that all of the nerve fibers from the cerebral hemispheres pass down on their way to the spinal cord. The crisscrossing of these fibers in the medulla is the reason why the two cerebral hemispheres wind up controlling the opposite sides of the body. Morphine and nicotine act within the medulla. The polio virus also once fashioned a home there. In the 1950s, patients with polio required an iron lung to do for them what their injured medullas could do no longer.

Just above the medulla is the second portion of the brainstem, the *pons.* Pons means "bridge," and this area of the brainstem contains a broad band of fibers that provides a neural link between *cerebral cortex* and *cerebellum.*

Above the pons and continuous with it is the *midbrain.* Smaller than the pons and medulla, it is the smallest division of the brainstem. Midterm, midyear, midnight—each of these terms implies a lack of completeness. So it is with the midbrain. Although the midbrain has none of the grandeur of the cerebral hemispheres, it is far more splendid than the medulla or the pons. Elementary forms of seeing and hearing are possible in the midbrain, thanks to four small *colliculli* (little hills) on its posterior portion.

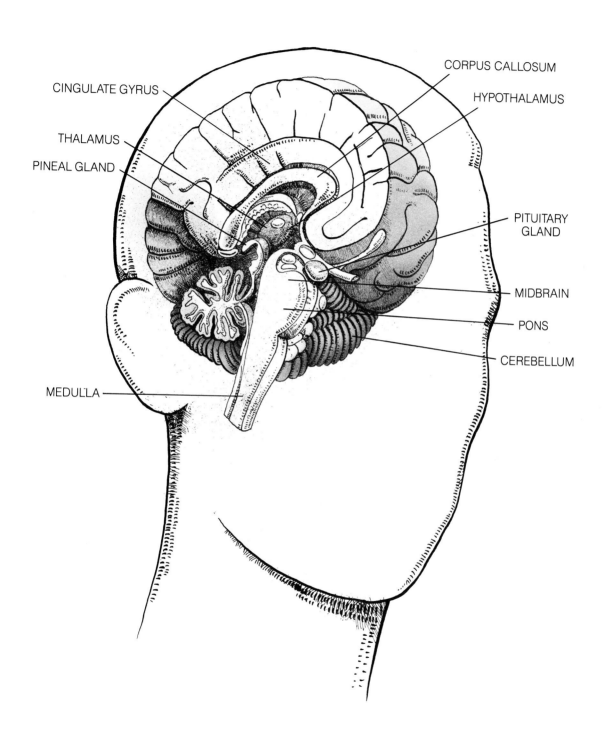

CORPUS CALLOSUM

HYPOTHALAMUS

CINGULATE GYRUS

THALAMUS

PINEAL GLAND

PITUITARY
GLAND

MIDBRAIN

PONS

CEREBELLUM

MEDULLA

Proceeding still farther aloft (moving in centimeters), we encounter the area known as the *diencephalon*, which includes the *hypothalamus* and the *thalamus*. The thalamus is a Greek term meaning "couch," and the cerebral hemispheres do rest comfortably upon it. All information must pass through the thalamus on the way to the Great Analyzer, the overarching cerebral hemispheres. Each of the senses, except smell, relays its impulses through the thalamus.

Immediately below the thalamus is the hypothalamus, the control center for food intake, endocrine levels, water balance, sexual rhythms, and the autonomic nervous system. Merely touching the hypothalamus with a soft sponge during surgery will send the temperature soaring or precipitate a coma in the patient more long-lasting than any mugger's blow to the skull. The hypothalamus is also the command center for a host of complex motivational states: fatigue, hunger, anger, placidity. Electrical stimulation of one part of the hypothalamus can send a cat into a frenzy of hissing, back-arching, and, if the opportunity permits, a slashing attack. Stimulation of yet another part and that same cat will come over and lick your fingers. In all, the hypothalamus is an orchestrator for the behaviors that accompany emotional states.

But is the cat who hisses and attacks after hypothalamic stimulation *really angry*? Further experiments on the hypothalamus, which we will discuss presently, suggest not. The rage response from electrical stimulation of the hypothalamus is a form of "crocodile tears": neuroscientists call it "sham rage" because it can occur without any provocation and disappears as quickly as it came. "Sham rage" also can occur in humans who launch aggressive attacks as a result of tumors within the fiber tracks leading down from the hypothalamus.

The weight of the hypothalamus? Four grams, less than one three-hundredths of the total brain. The surface area? Less than 1 percent of total brain volume. But despite its unimpressive physical dimensions, the hypothalamus is involved in regulating the body's most critical activities. The hypothalamus teaches us that the brain can't be understood simply by using calipers or scales.

Above and tightly interconnected with the hypothalamus is a rim of cortical structures, the *limbic system*. (*Limbus* is Latin for border or rim.) The limbic system, like the

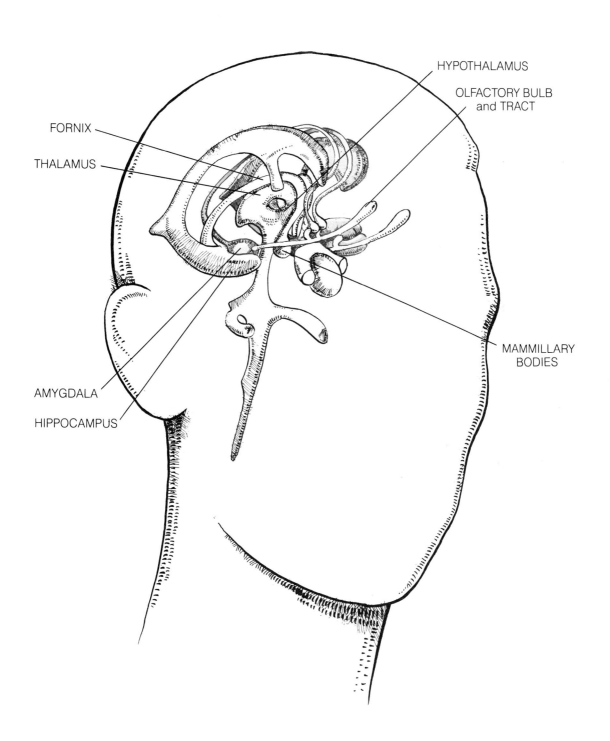

HYPOTHALAMUS

OLFACTORY BULB
and TRACT

FORNIX

THALAMUS

MAMMILLARY
BODIES

AMYGDALA

HIPPOCAMPUS

hypothalamus, is also involved in emotional issues. Separating the influence of the hypothalamus from the limbic system is like keeping a portrait in a frame while trying to remove all the canvas. James Papez, who first suggested that the limbic system formed a neural circuit for emotions, figured it out this way: A connection must exist between the cerebral cortex and the hypothalamus, since emotions reach consciousness, and thoughts affect emotions.

Think of it this way: Your apartment is cold because the superintendent let the heat go off. As a first step, your hypothalamus initiates a constriction of the blood vessels in the skin, thus preserving body heat. At about the same time, your cerebral hemispheres begin processing a series of logical inferences: The superintendent is in charge of the heating arrangements in the building. . . . He has failed in his duty. . . . The heat is now off, with the temperature rapidly falling within your apartment. Simultaneously, the limbic system is generating an emotional response to the situation: rage at the superintendent's carelessness, a determination to set things right. The interplay of the cerebral cortex and the limbic system generates a response aimed at raising the heat: You march down to the superintendent's office and give him hell.

Years ago, the popular analogy for the function of the human brain was that of a military hierarchy. The forebrain (or cerebral hemispheres) was thought to formulate plans and goals. The limbic system, via its connection with the hypothalamus, generated the necessary emotional vigor to carry out the goals. Together they relayed their "orders" to the brainstem—midbrain, pons, medulla—and, finally, to the spinal cord, the brain's foot soldier, whose task was simply to obey. But all analogies spring from the social values of the time. It is no accident that military analogies enjoyed their greatest popularity at the time of World War II. Today we are more pacifist in our approach (at least some of us are), and the concept of a tiny army inside our heads isn't enthusiastically received. Instead, we prefer the idea of a bureaucratic organization with several interlocking and interdependent hierarchies.

Whichever analogy you choose, someone must do the job of keeping everybody in contact with everybody else. In the army such people are referred to as "aides-de-camp"; in a civilian organization they are "public-relations specialists."

In the brain these supporting roles are played by a group of centers known collectively as the *basal ganglia*. Like public-relations people, the basal ganglia come to attention only when something goes wrong. Talk of the basal ganglia to a neuroscientist, and you are talking of glitches in systems that are expected to be running smoothly.

An inexperienced actor called on to portray an eighty-year-old man automatically slips into caricature: stooped posture, stiff movements, tremors of the face and hands, painfully slow thinking and speaking. In actuality, normal aging isn't accompanied by any of these things. The actor who portrays an aged person in this way hasn't done his homework. He has noted only the appearance of those elderly persons with disease, not normal aging, of their basal ganglia.

Kleinhirn is what the Germans call the cerebellum: diminutive brain. In weight, the cerebellum represents only one eighth of the total brain. Like the hypothalamus, its size belies its importance. Without the cerebellum I couldn't control the movement of my pen across the paper just now. You couldn't hold this book without dropping it. If you want to see the cerebellum in all its glory, go to the ballet, watch an international tennis star in action, study the hand and finger movements of a concert pianist. It was once said about a former President that he couldn't chew gum and walk at the same time. If this were true, his cerebellum was to blame.

There you have it: a rough but serviceable sketch of the principal areas of the human brain. As with any sketch, the details must be drawn in. Filling in those details has occupied thousands of neuroscientists from the seventeenth century to the present. Nobody has grasped the entire topography; nobody could; nobody ever will. But obviously we have to start somewhere. To recap briefly: Working from the ground up, the central nervous system consists of the spinal cord, brainstem (medulla, pons, midbrain, diencephalon), cerebellum, and cerebral hemispheres. The spinal cord is continuous with the medulla, the medulla is continuous with the pons, the pons is continuous with the midbrain, and the midbrain is continuous with the diencephalon. Arching over the pons and the midbrain is the cerebellum. Buried beneath the cerebral hemispheres and interconnected in an incredibly complex way with everything else are the basal ganglia. Encircling the upper brainstem and separating it from the arching expanse of the cerebral hemispheres is the limbic system.

Translated into functional terms, the brain is arranged like this:

The *spinal cord* receives all our information from the skin and muscles. It sends out motor commands for movement.

The *brainstem,* the extension of the spinal cord, receives information from the skin and muscles of the head and neck and is responsible for moving these muscles. The brainstem also contains the centers for our senses: hearing, balance, all of them except smell and vision. These two exceptions connect directly with the limbic system and the cerebral cortex, respectively, which is why smell and sight have such powerful effects on us. They report "directly to headquarters," as our military friends would put it.

The *cerebellum and the basal ganglia* together coordinate and modulate all body movement.

The *diencephalon* (thalamus, hypothalamus, and other structures) serves as a relay station for forwarding information (sensation) and movement. It also contains (within the hypothalamus) important control areas for integrating bodily processes that normally lie outside our awareness: temperature, blood pressure, heart rate, respiration, and so on.

The *cerebral hemispheres* concern themselves with our highest conceptual and motor functions.

Everything we will discuss in this book and everything that neuroscientists will ever learn about the human brain will be based on this fundamental arrangement.

Many of our insights into the nature of the brain began with the Greeks. The most astute observer was Galen, a Greek physician in the second century A.D. who learned about the structure of the brain by skillfully dissecting the heads of farm animals and apes. In his later years, Galen was appointed physician to the gladiators in his native Pergamon, an experience that provided him the opportunity to see firsthand the effects of injury on brain structure.

In his writings and teachings, Galen attacked the tenets of the philosopher Aristotle, who believed that the heart and not the brain was the center for human thoughts and

feelings. To prove his point, Galen carried out crude experiments showing that pressure applied to the brain can paralyze an animal while similar pressure on the heart had no such effect. Unfortunately, Galen's curiosity failed to inspire other Greeks, and his ideas of the importance of the brain were entombed with him. Little progress was made over the next thousand years.

To the ancient Greeks all living things drew their vitality from a *pneuma* (air) derived from the cosmos. Growth, movement, and ultimately thought were made possible by alterations of this pneuma. In humans these alterations came about by means of an elaborate system. Food, after ingestion and absorption within the intestine, was conveyed to the liver, where it was imbued with *natural spirit.* From there the spirit was conveyed to the heart, where it was endowed with *vital spirit.* Finally, this humoral potpourri entered the brain where, inside the ventricular cavities, it was converted into the *animal spirit.*

This concept that a substance, the animal spirit, resided within the brain and was distributed throughout the body by a vast network of hollow nerve fibers persisted well into the sixteenth century. Each of the ventricles was considered the repository of one or more brain functions.

At the beginning of the fourteenth century, medical schools in Italy began authorizing dissections of the human body. At first the procedure was restricted to a small number of professional dissectors who were allowed to pursue their craft only on specified occasions. For instance, the

University of Bologna allowed the annual dissection of one male and one female body. After a while the practice of yearly dissections gave way to more liberal policies until, eventually, the procedure was sufficiently widespread that even nonphysicians, such as the artist Leonardo da Vinci, could be found in dissecting rooms. (He claimed to have dissected more than one hundred bodies.)

Leonardo da Vinci, after making a wax cast of an ox brain in 1504, declared that the first ventricle was responsible for imagination and common sense, the second ventricle took care of reasoning, and, finally, memory could be confidently placed in the third ventricle. Others disagreed. They insisted that the first ventricle was closest to the organs of the five senses and, therefore, must be the ventricle of *sensus communis* (common sense).

By the seventeenth century, detailed descriptions were

Leonardo da Vinci was one of the earliest artists to recognize the importance of having first-hand knowledge of the texture of muscles and the arrangement of nerves for the accurate drawing or painting of the human body.

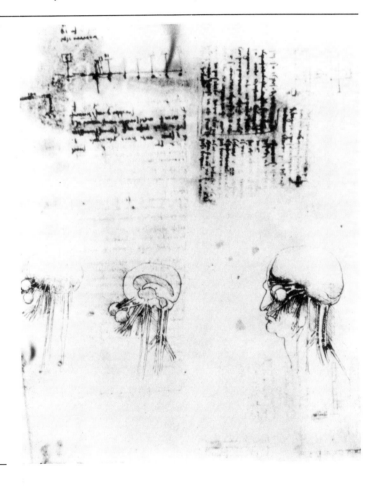

available of the general outline of brain organization gleaned from brains exposed after death. The brain being roughly the consistency of a soft avocado, a method was required to "harden" the specimen. At first this was accomplished by immersing the brain in vats of wine. At a later point, chemicals were added that softened some components while hardening others. Such procedures made it possible to trace fibers from their origin in the cerebral cortex down into the spinal cord, revealing that the brain is not a homogeneous structure but contains an overlying gray matter that extends over its entire surface. Beneath this is a large mass of white matter (nerve fibers) containing small islands of subcortical gray matter (the basal ganglia) deep within itself.

But despite these advances, considerable disagreement over the role of the brain in mental activity still persisted. The idea of the superiority of the heart held sway in some quarters. The reasoning went something like this: When the heart stopped, the body grew cold, implying that the heart generated heat. The arrangement of blood vessels emanating from the heart also encouraged the view that the heart was the repository of the soul. After all, *anima* is the Latin word for "soul," and the heart certainly looked like the *anima*tor of the body.

As late as 1616, William Harvey, the discoverer of blood circulation, was still equivocating on whether the heart or the brain was the more "honorable organ."

"The brain is deemed the prince of all parts," he wrote. "However, there is no disputing the heart because its sway is wider, for the heart is seen in those creatures that want a brain."

In 1664, Thomas Willis published his *Cerebri Anatome (Anatomy of the Brain),* illustrated by the future architect of St. Paul's Cathedral in London, Sir Christopher Wren. Willis and Wren formed perhaps the most extraordinary "team" ever to investigate the human brain. Willis's greatest contribution to our present-day understanding of the brain stems from his enthusiasm for exploring the brain through meticulous dissection. Wren, already at work on his plans for the Sheldonian Theatre in Oxford, had recently invented a method for injecting substances into the bloodstream of animals. This innovation, the forerunner of the first successful blood transfusion in humans, provided a practical method for revealing the inner blood supply of the

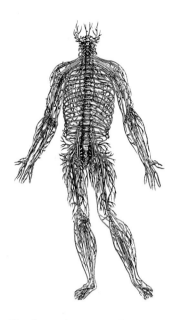

Vesalius, the sixteenth-century artist who made this woodcut for his great work, De Humani Corpus Fabrica *(1543), realized that the nervous system included not only the brain but the spinal cord and peripheral nerves as well.*

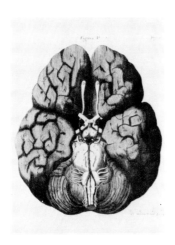

A view of the base of the brain by Christopher Wren. The accuracy of his work is impressive even by today's strict standards.

brain. Willis and Wren injected a preservative (most likely wine) laced with India ink into the blood vessels leading to the brain. The result was a stunning depiction of the course of the vessels. More important than the vistas achieved by this method (suitably preserved for posterity by the brilliance of Wren's drawings) was the change that Willis brought about regarding the most important parts of the brain. In 1664 Thomas Willis finally retired the fanciful notion of the preeminent importance of the ventricles rather than the brain substance itself. "And there yet remains that we speak of its ventricles. Since they are only a vacuity resulting from the folding up of its exterior border, I see no reason we have to discourse much of the office, no more than Astronomers are wont of the empty space contained in the vacuity of the Sphere."

Willis's emphasis on the brain substance rather than the fluid-filled ventricular cavities was the pivotal insight responsible for the development of modern neuroscience. Christopher Wren's sketches in *Cerebri Anatome* are incredibly accurate, even by the demanding standards of today. Unfortunately, Willis's description and interpretation of what he encountered fared less kindly at the hands of history. Some brain parts, such as the two cerebral hemispheres, inspired him to military analogy. "So the Brain, like a Castle, divided into many Towers or places of Defense, is thereby made the stronger and harder to take." Other analogies had a geographical flavor, such as his description of two brain portions separated by an artery, "like a Bounding river to both, distinguishing them as it were into two provinces."

Before criticizing Willis too harshly, however, it is worth remembering how every age develops its own metaphors of the brain. In the 1930s and 1940s the brain was compared to a telephone switchboard (the most advanced communication device generally known at the time). Today we speak of the brain as a computer. For reasons that we will explore in a moment, the brain isn't any more a computer than it is a castle or a pathway for animal spirits. The brain is, simply, itself. There is nothing remotely like it in the known universe, and we shouldn't limit our understanding of it by using simplistic analogies. The most famous example of the harm that can ensue was provided by the late-eighteenth-century neuroscientist Franz Josef Gall.

Gall believed that the brain was the instrument of the mind and, therefore, possessed a number of centers concerned with innate "faculties." He became convinced that these centers could be localized by touching protuberances on the skull. He traced this belief to a childhood observation that students with good memories often had "prominent eyes." Gall was "seized with the idea" that mental faculties could be identified by certain physical characteristics. In support of his theory, Gall visited hospitals, schools, prisons, and asylums—anywhere he could locate individuals with exceptional talents or disabilities. A person with a deformed or misshaped skull was of particular importance to Gall. Throughout his lifetime Gall clung to the belief that

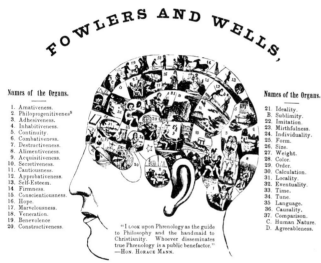

In the nineteenth century, phrenologists were active in the major cities of Europe and North America. For a fee they would feel your skull, gauging your innate capacity for "amativeness" or "secretiveness."

FOWLERS AND WELLS,

Names of the Organs.

1. Amativeness.
2. Philoprogenitiveness
3. Adhesiveness.
4. Inhabitiveness.
5. Continuity.
6. Combativeness.
7. Destructiveness.
8. Alimentiveness.
9. Acquisitiveness.
10. Secretiveness.
11. Cautiousness.
12. Approbativeness.
13. Self-Esteem.
14. Firmness.
15. Conscientiousness.
16. Hope.
17. Marvelousness.
18. Veneration.
19. Benevolence
20. Constructiveness.

Names of the Organs.

21. Ideality.
B. Sublimity.
22. Imitation.
23. Mirthfulness.
24. Individuality.
25. Form.
26. Size.
27. Weight.
28. Color.
29. Order.
30. Calculation.
31. Locality.
32. Eventuality.
33. Time.
34. Tune.
35. Language.
36. Causality.
37. Comparison.
C. Human Nature.
D. Agreeableness.

"I LOOK upon Phrenology as the guide to Philosophy and the handmaid to Christianity. Whoever disseminates true Phrenology is a public benefactor."
—HON. HORACE MANN.

PHRENOLOGISTS,
142 WASHINGTON ST., BOSTON,
308 BROADWAY, NEW YORK,
231 ARCH ST., PHILADELPHIA.

OUR CABINETS OR MUSEUMS
Contain Busts and Casts from the heads of the most distinguished men that ever lived; also Skulls, human and animal, from all quarters of the globe—including Egyptian Mummies, Pirates, Robbers, Murderers and Thieves; also numerous Paintings and Drawings of celebrated Individuals, living and dead. Strangers and citizens will find our Phrenological Rooms an agreeable place to visit.

PHRENOLOGICAL EXAMINATIONS
AND ADVICE, with Charts and full Written Descriptions of Character, given, when desired. These MENTAL portraits, as guides to self-culture, are invaluable.

THE UTILITY OF PHRENOLOGY.
PHRENOLOGY teaches us our natural capacities, our right and wrong tendencies, the most appropriate avocations, and directs us how to attain self-improvement, happiness, and success in life.

VALUABLE PUBLICATIONS.
FOWLERS AND WELLS have all works on Phrenology, Physiology, Phonography, Hydropathy, and the Natural Sciences generally.

Santiago Ramón y Cajal, the Spanish neuroscientist and artist who combined his talents to produce the first accurate representation of the neuron.

Camillo Golgi, the Italian neurohistologist who in 1906 shared the Nobel Prize in Medicine with Cajal.

examination of a skull was tantamount to looking at the underlying brain. On the basis of thousands of observations of "skull bumps," Gall conceived the pseudoscience of phrenology. He argued that all of the faculties of the mind, even such things as intelligence and moral character, were controlled by separate "organs" or "centers" within the brain.

Today, of course, we recognize all this as nonsense. Palpation of skulls tells us little about the underlying brain; many mentally retarded patients have large heads, and genius cannot be correlated with either brain size or brain shape. Unwittingly, however, Gall brought about the biggest change in attitude about the human brain since Thomas Willis's recognition of the importance of brain substance compared with the underlying ventricles. After he conceived phrenology, more restrained neuroscientists took the helm from Gall and began formulating our present understanding of brain organization. But to do this, it was first necessary to explore the brain's fundamental unit: the neuron.

"The aristocrat among the structures of the body, with its giant arms stretched out like the tentacles of an octopus to the provinces on the frontier of the outside world, to watch for the constant ambushes of physical and chemical forces." In these words Santiago Ramón y Cajal, nineteenth-century Spanish artist and neuroscientist, described the nerve cell. The inspiration for his poetic eloquence was the discovery in 1871 that neurons could be selectively stained with a special silver preparation. Although the method picks out only one in a hundred cells, it nonetheless encrusts the entire neuron body along with all its processes.

In the early days of *neurohistology* (the study of the microscopic architecture of the brain) there were heated arguments about whether nerve cells were separate from each other or whether all the cells of the brain were connected to a network or reticulum. Another famous neuroanatomist, Camillo Golgi, supported the latter theory. Cajal favored the view that neurons were separate from each other. At night, after many hours spent staring into a microscope, he sketched his observations of the neurons on a drawing pad he kept by his bedside. His drawings, preserved today, show the neuron, "aristocrat among the structures of the body," as a separate structure. Eventually Cajal was able to demonstrate to everyone's satisfaction the existence of a gap (*synapse*) between nerve cells, forever putting the "network" theory to rest.

A nerve cell consists of a cell body containing the *nucleus,* a long fiber (the *axon*), and a varying but extensive number of branching fibers (*dendrites*) that reach out toward other nerve cells. The functional role of the dendrite is to provide an increase in the surface of the neuron and thereby enhance the receptivity of the neuron to the influence of other cells.

A nerve impulse is conveyed from the nerve body out along the length of the axon, where it terminates on varying numbers of dendrites or the cell bodies of other nerve cells.

Two neurons in synaptic contact.

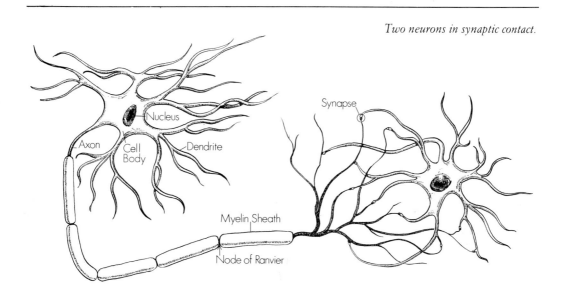

Each of the at least ten billion neurons in the human brain may have over a thousand synapses—points of contact between nerve cells. With some cells within the cerebral cortex, the numbers may approach two hundred thousand connections. The total number of connections within the vast network of the brain's neuronal system is truly astronomical—greater than the number of particles in the known universe.

But anatomical connections between nerve cells fail to provide a sufficient explanation for how the brain works. What kind of "message" is conveyed along the nerve fibers? How is information transferred within the brain? Again,

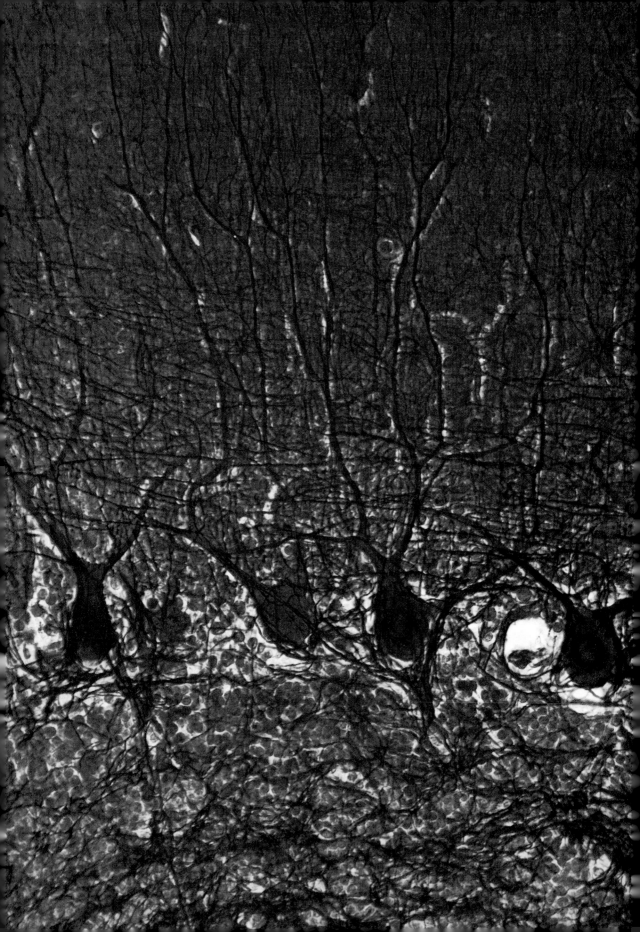

history provided two points of view. On the one side stood those who were convinced that neurons communicated with each other by electrical impulses, a specific form of "animal electricity." Those in the opposing camp favored a chemical transmitter. At this point we know both sides were partially correct. Communication within the brain is *electrochemical*. We have arrived at this insight by a series of observations on *epilepsy,* an ancient affliction that for a while was named the "Sacred Disease."

This spectacular Cajal stain of neurons within the cerebellum clearly shows the cell bodies and branchlike dendrites. Estimates of the total length of dendrites within the human brain exceed several hundred thousand miles.

The first epileptic attack one witnesses is not likely to be soon forgotten.

One moment all is calm. Then, suddenly, everything comes apart. Chaos ensues, terror, horror. Some spectators turn away, others want to help but don't know how, still others stare transfixed. A fall; abrupt unconsciousness perhaps heralded by a scream; jerking, violent contraction of the body; more noises, more jerking, and then as suddenly as it began, the seizure is over. The typical epileptic attack lasts only a few seconds, almost always less than a minute.

To date, neuroscientists aren't sure why seizures occur in some people and not in others. There is a strong suspicion, however, that the cause of epilepsy lies buried deep within the brain and may involve a subtle alteration of the brain's structure.

An interesting historical narrative could be written with epilepsy as the centerpiece. Alexander of Macedonia was said to have the disease. This may have been one of the reasons for his charisma. Most Greeks considered epilepsy an affliction imposed by the gods; other Greeks were more cynical. "It seems to me that the disease is no more divine than any other. It has a natural cause just as other diseases have. Men think it is divine merely because they don't understand it. But if they called everything divine which they do not understand, why, there would be no end of divine things." This remark was made by Hippocrates, the Father of Medicine.

Later periods had equally bizarre ideas about epilepsy. For instance, it was commonly believed that the moon had an influence on the recurrence of attacks, with the greatest number of epileptic episodes occurring during a full moon. Human blood was considered an effective antidote. The historian Pliny the Elder described epileptics seeking relief from their affliction by sucking blood from the mouths of dying gladiators.

The Greek physician Galen believed epilepsy resulted from stagnation of the cold humors (phlegm and black bile) within the ventricles or cavities of the brain. The tendency for epileptics to fall precipitously to the ground stimulated one observer to introduce the term *caducus* (falling one), and soon after, the disease was referred to as *passio caduca* (the falling sickness). Based on these observations, a specific cure was suggested: the use of mistletoe. Claims for this remedy depended on the natural history of the leaf. In autumn it clung to the trees and didn't fall to the ground like other leaves.

Understanding epilepsy proceeded pretty much along these lines over the next millennium. During the Renaissance, epileptics were burned to death as sorcerers. The "villains" were renamed several hundred years later in Salem, Massachusetts, when epileptics were burned at the stake because of their alleged association with "witches" and "devils." Not until the mid-seventeenth century was anything proposed that even approaches our contemporary understanding of epilepsy. But before that could happen, mankind had to become aware of electricity and its role in biology.

The existence of an animal capable of producing an electric current had been known as far back as the Egyptians. Fishing scenes depicted on the walls of Egyptian tombs regularly featured views of the Nile electric catfish, which was capable of producing a shock of over 450 volts. The nature of the electric fish's power, however, had remained mysterious.

The essayist Montaigne was one of the first to comment on the "numbing" produced by the discharge of the electric fish: "The torpedo has this quality, not only to benumb all the members that touch her, but even through the nets to transmit a heavy dullness to the hands of those that move and handle them. . . . This is a miraculous force."

The response of living tissue to electricity was first demonstrated in the late eighteenth century by an Italian anatomist, Luigi Galvani. According to legend, he made his discovery by means of a series of experiments, some of which were performed in the unlikely atmosphere of dinner parties prepared by his wife, Lucia. One after-dinner "experiment" consisted of placing a dissected frog on the table with a wire extending from its head to a metal rod on a balcony. Another wire extended from the frog's foot to a nearby well. This rather bizarre arrangement was hastily put together just before an impending thunderstorm. When lightning flashed, the frog's muscle twitched—much to the mystification and wonder of Galvani's guests!

Luigi Galvani conducting one of his famous experiments with frog muscles. Although the brain generates a weak electrical current which can be detected by an electroencephalogram (EEG), it is no longer believed that electricity is "stored" within the nerves.

In another experiment, Galvani cut off a frog's leg muscle and placed the attached nerve against the cut surface of another muscle. The second muscle twitched. Galvani concluded that something similar to the electricity of lightning was contained in nervous tissue. He called it "animal electricity." He assumed that the brain was the source of the electricity within the body and that this force was stored within the nerves for later distribution. This idea was in line with the thinking at the time: Electricity is a subtle fluid that "flows." Not until the construction of the first galvanometer in the 1820s was it possible to confirm the presence of a weak electrical current in brain tissue.

Details of the generation and the propagation of current awaited the discovery in the 1930s of a peculiarity of the anatomy of the squid, an aquatic animal found in the Atlantic Ocean.

The swimming structure of the squid, an enlarged tubu-

a

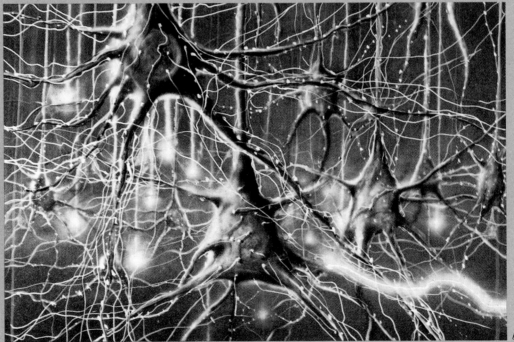

b

Artist John Allison's rendering of a look inside the neural network of the cortex (a). A signal from one neuron is transmitted electrochemically to another (b), and the nerve cell fires (c), sending the signal on to the next neuron in the network (d). The small white nodes are synapses, gaps between cells.

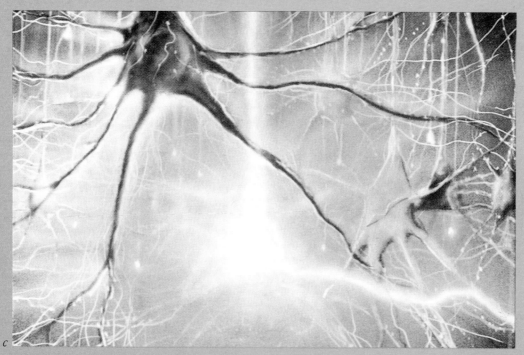

c

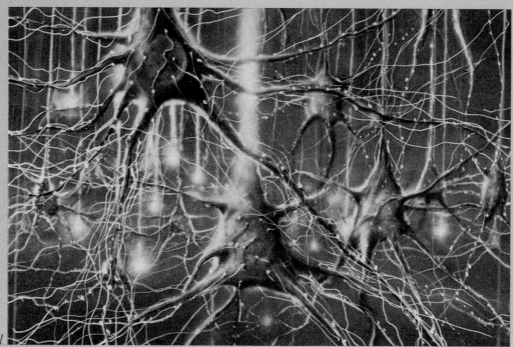

d

lar appendage, consists of a giant axon several times larger than the biggest human nerve fiber. Insertion of electrodes into the squid's axon revealed that at rest, the neuron has separate charges across its external membrane: positive charges on the outside and negative charges on the inside. All communication between nerve cells results from altering this basic resting potential. For example, touch is transformed by receptors on the skin into electrical energy in the following way: Depression of the skin receptors releases the electrical energy, which runs along the length of the receptor. This "generator" potential is a purely local affair that fades in intensity as distance increases. It also varies in size and length according to the intensity of the original stimulus. A light touch generates a weak signal, greater pressure over a larger skin area produces a stronger generator potential. If the resulting potential is sufficiently large, it will trigger an *action potential,* which is propagated at a faster rate without any decrease in electrical energy as it proceeds along the nerve fiber. The action potential, the basic mechanism of communication within the brain, allows impulses to be transmitted over great distances at high speeds. Whether the local generator potential succeeds in eliciting an action potential depends on whether a certain critical level of excitation is achieved.

No one neuron is exactly the same as another. They differ in shape and in the particular thresholds required to fire. The neuron switches itself on only when its particular resting threshold is exceeded. If the stimulus is too weak, the neuron will not generate its action potential. Some of the neuron's dendrites make activation less likely. Other dendritic connections are "excitatory," tending to contribute toward the generation of an action potential. In some cases the number of excitatory and inhibitory influences just balance each other, and the neuron remains in its resting state.

So far, the propagation of information within the brain seems very similar to the connections within a computer: one cell tied to another by a cablelike network of interconnecting fibers. But the analogy with a computer soon breaks down. The nerve signal must cross a gap about a millionth of an inch wide, the synaptic cleft. It is at the synaptic cleft that the message from one nerve cell is converted from an electrical signal to a chemical one.

There may be from ten trillion to one hundred trillion

synapses in the brain, and each one operates as a tiny calculator that tallies signals arriving as electrical impulses. If a sufficient number of signals arrives along the first neuron, it releases a chemical, the neurotransmitter, that has been stored along the presynaptic membrane in the form of vesicles. These vesicles, the structural units of neurotransmission, are released in small packets.

Imagine the presynaptic membrane studded with release sites with vesicles milling around nearby in random motion. With the arrival of the action potential, the vesicles release their store of neurotransmitter into the synaptic cleft. The transmitter then crosses to a specialized receptor on the postsynaptic membrane of the second cell. There another computation is performed. The arriving packets are assigned to particular receptors on the postsynaptic membrane. Each neurotransmitter has its own receptor and will not accept a substitute: acetylcholine has its receptor, while norepinephrine has yet another. In this manner the message code within the brain is converted, as it moves from one nerve cell to another, from electrical into chemical and then back again to electrical signals.

Neurotransmission is a far more complex process than mere nerve "stimulation." Every signal sent across the synapse to another nerve cell is not necessarily an order to fire. The signal may involve an inhibitory neurotransmitter that makes the second cell less likely to fire. Indeed, inhibition rather than excitation is the hallmark of the brains of more sophisticated organisms. If more than a tiny fraction of our billions of neurons fired at once, we would suffer a prolonged epileptic convulsion. One of the ways of managing epilepsy consists of increasing the amount of inhibition within the brain.

Another order of complexity is provided by the redundancy that exists within the nervous system. Many cells may cooperate to process certain signals. The loss of a fraction of these neurons may have no discernible effect. The loss of a few more may produce only minor modifications. Eventually, the loss of a certain critical number of neurons impairs the brain's capacity to process the incoming signals.

Neurons also participate in many different processes. For instance, neurons often fire spontaneously, resulting in unpredictable releases of packets of neurotransmitters across the synaptic cleft. Although these random events have little

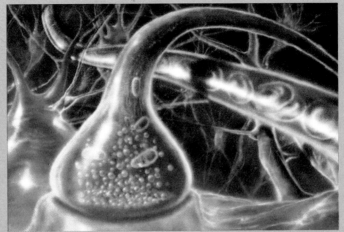

a

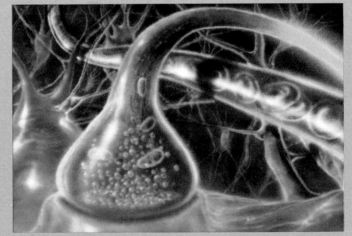

b

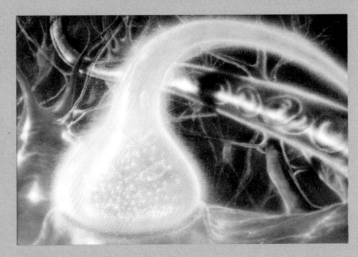

c

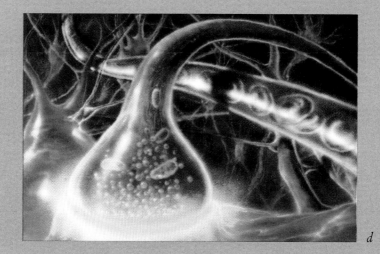

d

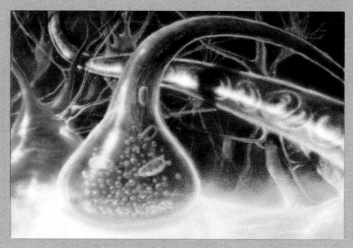

e

The artist's rendition of a neuron's axon extending toward a nearby cell, forming the synapse (a). As a signal (b) reaches the end of an axon (c) it triggers the release of neurotransmitters across the synapse (d), which in turn causes the receiving neuron to fire (e). The reddish tube depicts a nearby capillary carrying oxygen-rich red blood cells.

The artist's illustration of the synaptic gap (a). As chemical neurotransmitters are released by the nerve fiber (b), the gap fills (c) and the receptors on the dendrite are activated (d). The full signal is received (e) and the signal continues on its way (f).

a

b

c

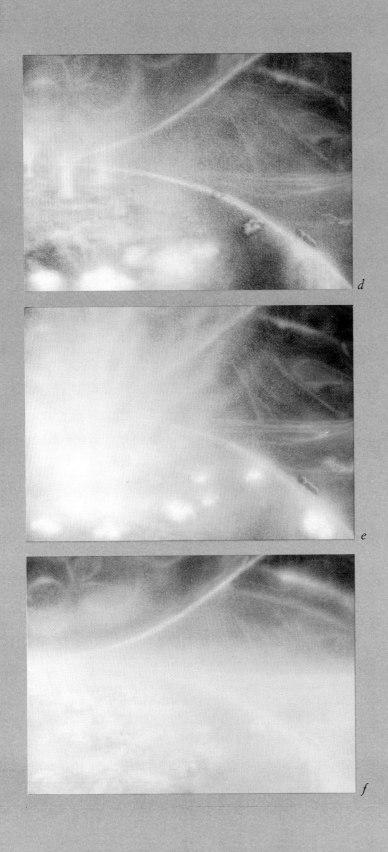

d

e

f

effect on overall brain functioning, they nevertheless illustrate the delicate balance within the brain. As a result, the passage of neuronal impulses is a mixture of the predictable and the unpredictable, the stable and the unstable. The situation is very similar to that which occurs in classical as opposed to quantum physics.

The ordinary world of sensory perception follows fairly fixed rules that are adequately described by classical physics. At the submolecular level, however, predictability is stymied by the inherent randomness of submolecular particles. In the brain, overall functioning can be fairly adequately described, at least for some of the simpler processes, such as elementary sensations. This can't be done, however, when an observer wishes a more encompassing "window" on brain activity aimed at identifying the participation of millions or billions of neurons at one time.

To this extent the structure of our brain faithfully corresponds to the complexity of our mental functioning. Some of our actions require split-second responses: withdrawal of our foot from the tack left on the bedroom floor. Others may require a lifetime of cogitation: Einstein wrestling for over thirty years in search of his unified-field theory. In between, we find gradients of force, power, delicacy, and savvy: the knockout kick of the karate black belt, the delicate precision of the watch repairman. A brain must be capable, on the average, of an incredible range and variety of responses. We have to know when to start, stop, measure how much, how little, how often, how strong, and how weak. As a result, the largest nerve fibers conduct impulses at one hundred meters per second, close to two hundred miles per hour. Other fibers move more slowly, twenty-five to thirty meters per second—well below the fifty-five-mile-per-hour speed limit. Even at its fastest, however, brain transmission is slower than jet plane travel, transmission over cables, and electronic transmission. In comparison to these, the brain's own products, the brain itself is slow—marvelously, agonizingly, frustratingly slow. But it has to be so our thoughts don't get too far ahead of us, so we don't undershoot the contraction times of our muscles and fall over our own feet. The brain's responsiveness is geared to the "average expectable environment," which changes from age to age. The brain must therefore be capable of responding to the threat of a tiger about to pounce from the high grass, while at the same time it must be able to manage the notice accompanying the paycheck: "We regret to inform you that your services are no longer required."

Felicity, anger, humor, the correct response at the right time—the brain must be capable of it all because, simply, all this is part of the human condition. It is not unreasonable to expect that the vast range in environmental demands would correlate to the organization of our brain: fast-conducting fibers, slow ones, neurochemicals that excite, neurochemicals that inhibit, other neurochemicals that act as facilitators, still others that act in ways we don't yet understand.

How could an organ such as the brain, which contains between ten billion and one hundred billion cells, ever develop from a single cell, the egg? Some flippantly respond that it is all genetically programmed, forgetting for the moment that a program is a meaningless term without a programmer. But there are additional difficulties with the "it's all in the genes" approach to brain development.

The number of neuronal connections in the human brain is perhaps 10^{15}, while the total genetic information is only about 10^5 genes. Clearly there must be some contributions from both the internal and the external environments. Recognition of this fact immediately gets us into the nature-nurture problem, that vexing dualism that runs throughout all our thinking: hereditary vs. environment; free will vs. determinism; and, since Descartes, the brain vs. the mind. In our enthusiasm for tackling these conundrums, we shouldn't forget that the brain is first affected by the same processes that, starting from conception, influence the growth and development of other bodily organs.

Nothing very brainlike can be found in the human embryo until about three weeks of age. After that, the brain, along with the rest of the central nervous system, starts unfolding from a sheet of cells surrounding the embryo. This sheet, the neural plate, is 125,000 cells strong, quite a jump from the original single cell formed by the fertilization of an egg and a sperm. In comparison to the final 10- to 100-billion-cell goal, however, 125,000 cells isn't even close. But one shouldn't be too quick to judge potential. In the beginning Chartres was only a few stones piled on top of stones.

The *neural plate* folds into a hollow tube called, appropriately enough, the *neural tube.* From the hollow end of this structure emerge the three most powerful prominences in the charted universe of the brain: the precursors of the forebrain (our cerebral hemispheres), the midbrain, and the hindbrain (pons and medulla). The neural tube (also called the *central canal*) is retained throughout life and forms the brain's *ventricular system.*

Remember those balloons that inflated to take on the shape of a rabbit, or some other animal dear to our childhood fantasies? Before blowing air into the balloon, it was difficult to imagine that the flat surface could ever look like much of anything. Think of the brain's form as that balloon. Its final configuration, however, is dependent not on the expansion of the central canal but on the growth of neuronal and supporting cells. In our balloon analogy, it would be as if the outer membrane started to thicken and grow out of proportion to the inner cavity until, eventually, the cavity was much diminished in size compared to the balloon's outer walls. The brain cells lining the walls multiply and expand upward, outward, and downward, with the central canal simply tracking along to form the interior of the new territory.

The brain's growth and final form depend on brain cell multiplication, a process that races on during the nine months before birth at about 250,000 new neurons per minute.

In the earliest developmental stages, embryonic cells are free to become components of skin, muscle, or other body areas. For instance, if cells from part of the embryo destined to become brain cells are removed and placed in a different region of another embryo, they will be transformed into cells appropriate to that region. What was once destined to be a neuron may thus be transformed into a cell that will line the intestines. But if the same operation is performed only a few days later, it won't work: transposed nerve cells can grow up only as nerve cells no matter where they find themselves. This process of "commitment" results from the influence of one or more chemicals released from a layer of the early embryo.

Neurobiologist Eric Kandel speaks of two competing theories of the growth and development of cells in the human brain. On one side are the "strict constructionists,"

25 DAYS   35 DAYS   40 DAYS   50 DAYS   100 DAYS

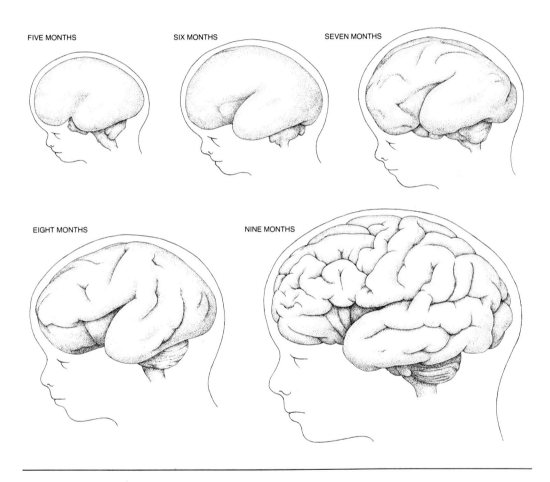

FIVE MONTHS   SIX MONTHS   SEVEN MONTHS

EIGHT MONTHS   NINE MONTHS

The human brain shown in its developmental sequence starting at twenty-five days and progressing through birth. Early in our brain's development, the neural tube expands to form three prominent structures, the hindbrain, midbrain, and forebrain. As the cerebral hemispheres develop from the forebrain, the midbrain unites it with the hindbrain, which develops into the pons and medulla.

who believe in the existence of an "extensive genetic and developmental program in synapse formation." To these scientists, the complexity of the human brain, the precision of its neural connections, and the incredible rapidity of brain development all suggest a genetic program. But for reasons we have already mentioned—the number of nerve-cell connections as compared with the modest number of genes in human cells—the "strict constructionist" view leaves a lot of unanswered questions about how the human brain develops.

On the other side of the aisle are the "loose constructionists," who favor only a limited developmental program. This theory harkens back to views held half a century ago, when psychologists insisted on the importance of the environment in stimulating brain development. Although this sounds very reasonable and appealingly democratic, it leaves open the question of why the brain develops fairly uniformly despite vastly different environments encountered by people in different parts of the world. Barring environmental extremes (starvation, poisoning, oxygen deprivation, and so on), the neuropathologist performing an autopsy in New Delhi can expect to find the same brain organization in his cadaver as would be found by his counterpart whose autopsy experience doesn't extend below Fifth Avenue and Forty-sixth Street in New York. If the environment is so important, why are all brains organized pretty much along the same lines?

The "strict" vs. "loose" constructionists' views of brain development constitute only another example of the debates that have arisen over the centuries since people first became curious about how the brain works. At one time neuroscientists argued over which was more important, the brain or the heart. A bit later others were divided on whether the neuron is a single cell or part of a vast network. Looking back now, it becomes obvious that each of these intellectual contests was not resolvable because, in a way, each side was correct. Granted that the brain is the seat of the "mind," heart stoppage for more than a few minutes renders the brain-vs.-heart question academic, of little interest to anyone other than the pathologist carrying out the autopsy. Although it is true that neurons are separate, it is also true that they ramify into interactive patterns of incredible complexity.

Why then do neuroscientists, past and present, tend to put forward one-sided theories, attacking the opposition and advocating explanations of the brain that in their less-impassioned moments they would acknowledge as oversimplified? The answer to that question would take us far afield, into the thorny areas of Nobel prizes, grants, departmental chairmanships, egos, perks, the drive for power, and so on. Brain scientists are no different from the rest of us. They want to be right; they want to be first; they want people, particularly their peers, to think well of them.

In 1906, Santiago Ramón y Cajal and Camillo Golgi shared the Nobel Prize in Physiology and Medicine. The subject of Golgi's acceptance speech? What else but a harangue against Cajal's individual-neuron theory, spiced with barbs at Cajal himself. If there is a lesson to be learned from Cajal, Golgi, and other "advocates," it is that when controversies exist about the brain, the truth usually incorporates something from both sides.

What we need is a unified theory of brain development, a theory that contains aspects of both the "loose" and the "strict" constructionists' views. In the absence of such a synthesis, neuroscientists can do little more than describe as accurately as possible exactly what takes place during brain growth.

The first step in a succession of stages involves the proliferation of cells from the neural tube. They may be either neurons or the supporting *glial* cells that make up the greatest proportion of cells within the human brain. At maturity, the glial cells will be concerned with exchanging nutrients and maintaining an optimal distance between neurons.

As a general rule, neurons within the brain don't remain at their site of origin lining the neural tube (the future ventricles) but migrate to a final position that is sometimes a staggering distance away. They do this by extruding a part of their cell body, the growth cone, out into the surrounding environment. This cone pushes aside any intervening obstacles and starts the cell on its way. The cells in the cerebral cortex are guided in this migration by special radial fibers which span the distance between the proliferative area along the neural tube and the final destination within the cortical plate. This migration is exquisitely timed and controlled. For instance, those fibers that arrive first form one layer, while later arrivals occupy berths closer to the cortical surface.

After migration, the neurons enter the next stage: growth and maturation. Some neurons are destined to become motor cells, others are sensory cells, and still others—the vast majority—are the uncommitted cells that will serve to connect motor and sensory neurons. In line with these functional differences are variations in the rate of growth.

Within the cerebral cortex the larger motor cells mature first, followed by neurons involved in local circuits (interneurons). In contrast to the comparatively short period required for the birth of a nerve cell (about the first hundred days in the human brain), maturation may extend over a lifetime. The maturation of cortical neurons is associ-

Neurons migrate from their initial position along the ventricular wall to their final destination in a highly organized fashion. Those that arrive first form one layer, while later arrivals assume places closer to the cortical surface.

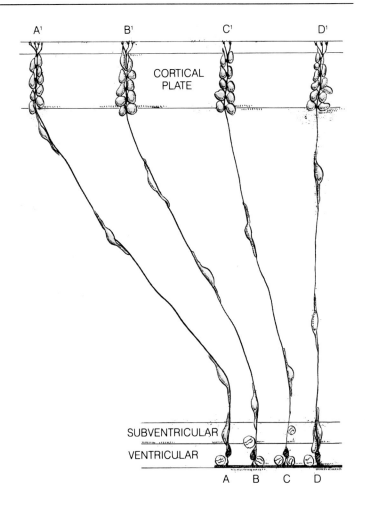

ated with the formation of cortical circuits. The formation of these synaptic connections is a competitive process.

"The competition of organisms for survival in the external world mirrors a competition in the inner world among neurons to fashion the circuits that will be the most effective in the external world," according to Gordon M. Shepherd, professor of neuroscience at Yale University.

With the formation of synapses, brain organization shifts toward patterns consistent with the "loose constructionist" view mentioned earlier. Increases in the number of synapses are associated with corresponding increases in the complexity and number of dendritic spines. This process is dependent on environmental stimuli. If the brain is deprived of environmental stimulation, the number of spines and, by implication, the complexity of synaptic connections is reduced. For instance, raising an animal in darkness reduces the number of synapses in the animal's visual area. Even more dramatic are the differences in brain organization that can be found between animals raised in deprived vs. enriched environments. Merely adding a few toys to play with, or mazes to run through, leads to an increase in the number of synaptic contacts as well as a thickening of the animal's cerebral cortex. A similar relationship can be found in the wild: Domesticated animals have thinner cortical layers compared to their counterparts in the forest, an observation first made by Charles Darwin.

The dependence of brain development on environmental influences should come as no surprise. Even casual observations of animals and humans reveal that an enriched, stimulating environment is conducive to mental agility. Each synapse can be considered a component of an interior world wherein neurons interact with each other in ways dependent on the brain's developmental history, its experiences, the richness of the outside environment, and the variety and complexity of sensory experiences. Throughout life—not just during the first few months—the brain's synaptic organization can be altered by the external environment.

The weight of the human brain at birth—the brain lifted out of the skull of a stillbirth and placed on a scale—is about 350 grams. After one month of life, it is 420 grams. At one year, it is half the adult weight of 1,400 grams. By seven years of age, the brain is almost adult in weight and size. From here on in, brain development doesn't depend on any further increase in the size or the formation of additional neurons. There aren't any more: neurons cease to divide any more after birth. But since neurons do die off over a lifetime, living, in a sense, involves doing more and more with less and less.

As with any complex process, brain development and maturation can break down at various stages. From the studies of these "breakdown products," neuroscientists are able to learn about what goes on during normal development. In *mongolism* (Down's syndrome), the dendritic spines are tiny, thinner, and fewer in number—a clue that the configuration of dendritic spines can serve as a rough indicator of the complexity of synaptic organization.

More efficient brains are characterized by a richness of neuronal interaction and a multiplicity of synaptic connections. Does this mean that the brain of a genius can be distinguished by its neural organization? At this point the answer to that question is a firm no. Present techniques don't allow such a distinction. There are also reasons to believe geniuses will never be distinguishable from the rest of the population simply on the basis of examining their brains. The "genius" of a Vincent van Gogh is far different from the "genius" of an Albert Einstein. Painting involves different brain areas than those required for higher mathematics and physics. It is likely, but far from proven, that if brain organizational differences exist, they would involve variations in cortical interactions within specific areas. In other words, the ability to visualize in three-dimensional space is likely to be associated with an enhanced synaptic complexity within areas of the brain involved in visual experience. An alternative explanation of "genius" might concentrate on variations in the organization of the association areas— those portions of the cerebral cortex not directly related to sensory or motor functions. Finally, "genius" may not be a matter of organizational differences in the cortex at all but rather be dependent on factors having to do with neurochemical transmission.

The power and majesty of a violin concerto depends less on the violin than it does on the violinist. As long as the violin is well chosen and reasonably well tuned (the "average expected environment"), the violinist determines the quality of the final production. Throughout our study of the human brain we will repeatedly encounter this dualism of form vs. function, structure vs. activity. The brain is a physical structure of daunting complexity, a veritable Chartres erected upon our shoulders. But it is also the home for a dazzling interplay of activity: electric codes, neurochemical messages, and tiny but powerful electromagnetic fields. Which of these is most important for brain organization and development? One might as well ask, "Which is most important to the *Brandenburg Concerto:* Bach, a Stradivarius violin, or the concert violinist of your choice?"

2.
Vision and Movement

If you open up a television circuit from camera to screen, nowhere will you find a miniaturized image of the world. And if we crack a skull to examine a brain, all we discover inside is a pinkish organ with the texture of an avocado. In both cases objects in the environment are not actually taken up into the television or the nervous system, but they are transformed instead into symbolic representations: glowing dots on the TV screen, or actively functioning neurons within our brains.

Any further attempt to equate vision to television runs into a problem. Much of what we "see" derives its importance from the meaning it may have for us. A traffic light suddenly changing from green to red at an intersection isn't simply a shift from one color to another but a command that orders us to stop. Movement in the high grass of the Serengeti plains may be only the wind, but it may also be the only warning we will have of a lion preparing to pounce.

A correct explanation for vision, therefore, must provide for the symbolic aspects of our visual perceptions. In a phrase, there must exist symbols within our heads capable of representing the things we see, symbols that are as unlike the things they represent as the color red is from the implied command that we bring our car to an immediate stop. Vision—in fact, perception in general—relies upon converting objects in the environment into symbolic representations encoded within the activity patterns of neurons within our brains.

A moment's reflection will reveal other striking differences between TV images and the visual images we form

The neural network at rest. This condition might exist in the visual cortex at a time when the eyes are closed.

within our heads. Put at its simplest, what we see is often dramatically different from what we have before our eyes. The fun of "fun houses" comes from distortions created by the skillful deployment of mirrors. Optical illusions such as those seen here illustrate the point that we don't simply detect patterns of light and dark; we discern objects, which, if we are not careful, may turn out to be strikingly different from the object that is actually there. Furthermore, a change takes place when we become aware of the existence of an optical illusion. Suddenly we are able to see what is "really there." Some illusions, however, don't lose their capacity to fool us even when we know them for what they are. The wife/mother-in-law illusion, for instance, succeeds despite our best efforts to maintain one version in our minds. Illusions such as those that appear in the works of M. C. Escher remain illusory despite the most painstaking inspection. Such examples indicate that our eyes do far more than simply feed back a picture to our brains.

Some optical illusions, such as those by artist M.C. Escher, retain their capacity to confound even when carefully scrutinized. In the lithograph "Ascending and Descending," monks move along a never-ending staircase.

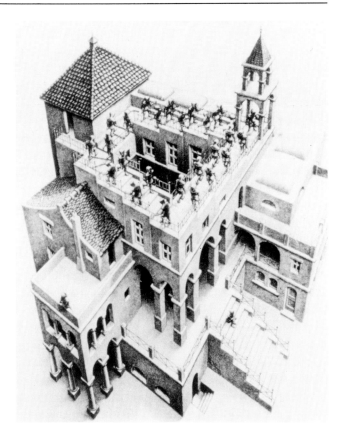

Vision might be more precisely described as a form of decoding. The eye absorbs light and, by means of special cone cells in the retina, distinguishes different wavelengths corresponding to color. Behind the retina, visual pathways in the two eyes cross with the inner fibers, passing to the opposite side—a shift that makes stereoscopic, three-dimensional vision possible. Finally, the visual stimulus is conveyed along several way stations until it ends up in the *striate* (visual) *cortex* at the rear of the brain. Within this pathway, light (specifically a narrow band of electromagnetic radiation) is transformed into electrical and chemical signals. Inverted by the lens of the eye, the final product is an upside-down image encoded within the neuronal networks of the brain. Deciphering this code has proved one of the most challenging and rewarding endeavors of modern neurobiology.

As a first step in decoding the visual process, consider for a moment some of the things that take place when we see. For one thing, our visual apparatus works best when dealing with contrasts. A white tennis ball that comes to rest against a white picket fence is likely to remain undiscovered. This everyday observation received experimental support in the 1950s with the discovery that cells within the retina respond to the contrast between points of light rather than the absolute light intensity of any one point. Based on this discovery, neurobiologist Horace Barlow put forth the theory—at that time quite extraordinary (and impossible to prove)—that single neurons within the visual cortex are capable of detecting features in the form of shapes, patterns, and colors.

In their Nobel Prize-winning research, David Hubel and Torsten Wiesel confirmed that neurons within the cerebral cortex of cats respond specifically to geometric features of visual input: straight edges, light or dark bars, and so on. It was hoped that by extending it a bit further, the feature-detector theory of vision would provide an explanation of how we see, based on a hierarchy of neurons encoding increasingly abstract as well as increasingly meaningful visual information.

With the development of single-cell recording techniques, research into how cells respond to events and people in the environment took a quantum leap forward. This method made it possible to impale a single neuron with a recording

The wife/mother-in-law illusion can be seen either as an attractive woman wearing a fur, her head turned away to the right, or as a gnarled old woman looking down to the left.

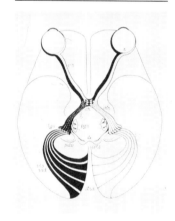

Our binocular, three-dimensional vision is made possible by optic nerve fibers crossing within the brain, as shown in this diagram.

electrode and monitor its response to different objects in the environment. At one point neuroscientists joked about the existence of a "grandmother cell," a particular neuron that came into play whenever we encountered our grandmother.

But there are problems with a visual theory that postulates a specific cell for the millions of objects and people we encounter over a lifetime. Our grandmother doesn't look exactly the same when she has a new hairdo. Suppose we see her walking a half block ahead of us on the street. How long does it take us to identify her from the rear? Recognition under such circumstances doesn't depend on the activation of a "grandmother cell." More likely it depends on flexible neuronal patterns interacting with each other in ways that enable us to extract the essence of "grandmotherness."

Artists have thought along these lines for years. For instance, English artist Anthony Green thinks of vision this way:

"Every object that one remembers, I think, one remembers at its most personable. Legs are leggy. Forks are forky. Newspapers are newspapery. And I think this is a facility that we have within us. That we file them under what I call the personality of that object. Take a fork, for instance. It is no good painting a picture of a fork if it looks as if it is made of India rubber. A fork is a hard thing, and it has a certain shine to it, which gives it its personality. It has got three or four prongs on it. It is forky. This applies to ears, noses, mouths, whiskers, doors, whatever you want."

In the past two decades neurobiologists have been thinking about the "forkiness of forks" and the "legginess of legs." This area of research, formally known as the "object-recognition problem," is based on the assumption that if we can screen out of the ongoing background of neural activity only those aspects having to do with, say, "grandmother" descriptions, then perhaps this knowledge can be encoded within a machine. The end result might be a prosthetic device for the blind or, sad to report, an improved weapon that could be mounted on a tank to make split-second decisions regarding the "friendliness" of neighboring soldiers and tanks.

More recent research directed to solving the "object-recognition problem" is based on a different and, to my

The Visual Experience: A Sunday Afternoon

How is vision processed within the human brain? Two theories are presently providing valuable insights into the mechanism of how we see.

The first, the work of David Hubel and Torsten Wiesel, postulates that every image we see is built up out of a multitude of bars, edges, and lines. "It might seem a real surprise that the cells of the striate cortex have this preference for lines because, after all, it is obvious that we don't see lines all the time. We see objects," says Wiesel. "But if you think of it for a minute, you realize that objects themselves consist of light-dark contours, and what the visual cortex is doing is asking 'Is there a contour, and if so, what is the direction of that contour?' So it really isn't lines that are being detected; it is contours and their directions. And that is probably sufficient information to tell you all you need to know when you look at a scene."

The second theory is the work of a team of scientists, headed by Dr. Russell De Valois at the University of California in Berkeley. Using radioactively tagged glucose, Dr. De Valois has shown which cells are most active during visual processing. Instead of just responding to lines, bars, or edges, some cells, according to Dr. De Valois, respond to quite different kinds of stimulation. "What about more complex patterns like the ripples on a swimming pool, or a waterfall, or a cloud, or a human face? It is very difficult to see how one could break down these very complex patterns into something like stick figures with identification of the edges and the location of edges. On the other hand, you can break down a pattern of any degree of complexity into its individual components, in terms of variations across space, or various frequencies."

It is important to note that Dr. De Valois' findings do not contradict the Hubel and Wiesel theory. Rather, Dr. De Valois' work goes a bit further: Some nerve cells are sensitive to frequencies of light, or differences in texture or tone, as in the subtle effects of sunshine on water or the prismatic swirl of texture—edges seem not to be the key features in these instances.

The same effect is at work when we look at the painting below, which appears continuous although it is actually made up of many individual daubs of paint.

Georges Seurat's "Sunday Afternoon on the Island of La Grande Jatte."

way of thinking, more realistic approach to how we see. Imagine, for instance, a cartoonist who does a rapid free-hand sketch of my grandmother. How much distortion can he introduce into the sketch before I finally lose the ability to recognize her? No doubt this may depend at least partly on how much actual experience I have had with my grandmother, how often I have seen her both in the flesh and in pictures. But regardless of these variables, the brain must be capable of encoding a *structural* description of my grandmother's face. This description must be superimposed upon an even simpler structural description: faces in general.

The question of how much distortion can be introduced before a face is no longer recognizable is not without practical implications. Plastic surgeons who deal with severely traumatized patients encounter this problem daily. They are constantly striving to keep from making changes so drastic that we lose the ability to recognize that person by sight alone. There seems to be a configuration of facial features (size of the nose, shape of the chin, thinness of the lips) that *taken together* make it possible to recognize an individual despite variations in time of day, distance away, aging, and so on. Expressed a bit differently, we arrive at a theory that is very similar to the principles of Gestalt psychology: "The perceptual whole is more than the sum of its parts." In other words, in visual perception parts are not treated as separate entities; rather, they interact to produce a gestalt.

For instance, if I take a photograph of your mother-in-law and draw a pair of horns on the top of her head, I have produced a devil, which, for me, is quite a different gestalt. Depending on your experiences with your mother-in-law, you may, however, claim that little change has been effected (which only goes to prove that gestalts can differ significantly from one person to another based on their own personal experiences). Putting aside these rather idiosyncratic gestalts, most people agree that there is a particular configuration of parts that conform to the gestalt of such things as chairs, or tables, or football stadiums. It's not that the individual parts can't be modified, sometimes extensively, but a certain number of features are necessary for general agreement that we are dealing with a chair and not a ladder.

Take something as simple as the letter *L,* for instance. A single letter would seem at first glance to provide a model of simplicity. An *L* is an *L* is an *L*, to paraphrase Gertrude Stein. But as a glance below will illustrate, an almost infinite number of variations are possible for the letter *L*. This is a strong argument against the view that somewhere within the brain resides a cell specialized for the recognition of the letter *L*. It would be impossible to arrange a cluster of photoreceptor cells that would activate only when *L* was present. There are simply too many variations possible for

A few of the infinite ways of forming the letter L. Our ability to recognize the letter in such a variety of designs makes it unlikely that such perception depends upon a specific L-recognition cell or cluster of cells.

the letter *L*. It is obvious, therefore, that an understanding of vision requires an examination of systems simpler than our own, systems less involved with symbolism and logic. A prime candidate is the horseshoe crab, an animal that has remained unchanged for millions of years.

Early research on the horseshoe crab was performed at Rockefeller University and presently continues under the leadership of Dr. Ehud Kaplan. Although the horseshoe crab possesses several pairs of eyes, only one pair is of immediate interest: two large, compound-faceted eyes along the sides. By careful dissection, it is possible to trace the full extent of the horseshoe crab's *optic nerve,* a barely visible, cobweblike strand running from the eyes to the brain. In an experiment performed during the filming of *The Brain,* the nerve was draped over an electrode capable of detecting electrical signals carried by the nerve. These were amplified and played over a loudspeaker.

When a strong pencil-beam of light was focused on one part of the faceted eye, the firing rate of the optic nerve immediately increased—a neat demonstration that the eye works by converting light impulses into electrical impulses. But when more light was added by turning on the overhead lights, the firing rate decreased. Does this curious result imply that the eye of the horseshoe crab responds better to dim light than it does to bright? Refining the experiment revealed what was really going on.

If a shadow is moved gradually across the eye, a volley of electrical impulses is recorded just at the moment the edge of the shadow crosses the eye. Bright light leads to a decrease once again in the firing rate of the nerve. As it turns out, the eye doesn't respond to light or dark, but reacts strongly to the junction between them.

In the wild, light and dark boundaries signal the edges of objects or telltale features. A lion crouching in the grass may be revealed only by patterns of light against a dark background. Successful camouflage depends on merging with the background to such an extent that telltale edges can't be discerned.

Human vision is postulated to work along similar lines. When we look at a photo of ourselves, our eyes respond to the edges on the photograph. Recognition of one's grandmother in a photograph, therefore, doesn't so much depend on the activation of a "grandmother cell" as it does on the recognition of edges arranged in a configuration of light and darkness that corresponds to one's "grandmother."

Certain processes seem universal enough for us to assume reasonably that they operate in all visual creatures no matter how simple or complicated the organism. Eyes respond to edges. Electrical signals leave the eyes by the optic nerve and then travel toward the brain. On their path, they stop at way stations (the *lateral geniculate,* or the *superior colliculus,* or in some instances both) before finally reaching the visual cortex. In organisms that have two cerebral hemispheres, each hemisphere receives half the image. Somehow the halves are joined up, and we "see," say, a face. How is this face, the common product of our visual system, encoded within the brain?

Encoding takes place according to a series of rules in the brain. For instance, visual stimuli are grouped according to proximity. The rows of dots in the illustration on page 60 are experienced as three *pairs* of dots rather than simply as six dots. If a series of dots is compressed together from top to bottom, a column is seen. If they are compressed from side to side, the dots appear arranged in rows. In each case the same number of dots is present, but their arrangement appears to differ. This process of grouping occurs according to a series of unwritten and, for the most part, unrecognized rules of perception. As we look at the dots, our eyes and brain extract a pattern from the arrangement of the dots, a pattern that is then given a name: a row, a column, and so on. It is important to emphasize that these perceptions are not dependent on language. A young child who has no experience with rows or columns and can't verbally distinguish between them will, nonetheless, perceive the cluster of dots in the same way.

To some extent these rules governing our perception provide support for the ideas of the philosopher Immanuel Kant. He believed that space, even time, are general aspects of awareness that exist prior to any specific perceptions. To the categories of space and time he later added number and quantity. All of these, according to Kant, are the mind's—we would say the brain's—own contribution to perception. Put in more neurobiologic terms, our brains are "prewired" to perceive the world in certain ways.

In Cambridge, Massachusetts, at the Massachusetts Institute of Technology, scientists have been working in recent years on computer simulation of normal vision. The principle behind their research is that a computer can be taught to extract and encode certain features of the environment in a way similar to the "groupings" made by our own visual system. These scientists are pursuing several avenues of research: color, motion, and three-dimensional stereoscopic vision. The inspiration for this research was David

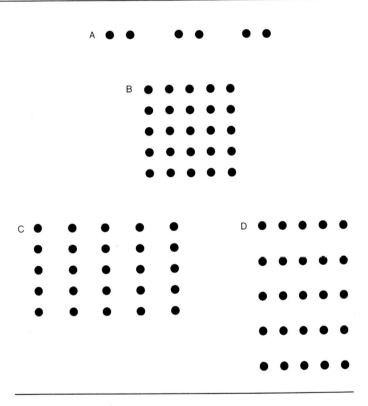

The dots in this diagram are all the same size, but we "see" them differently: Group A as three pairs; Group B as either columns or rows; Group C as a set of columns; Group D as a set of rows.

Marr, a young computer scientist who died of leukemia in 1981. But Marr's work continues today, thanks to his students at M.I.T. who are fired with Marr's own enthusiasm and sense of excitement.

Even at this early stage of research, it is obvious that the computer can be taught to recognize "groupings" in a way very similar to the way our brain does. For instance, when we "saw" a row or column of dots, something within our brain not only recognized the dots but also discovered a structure, a unifying cluster of features. In computer terminology we transformed raw visual data into symbolic representation somewhere within the neuronal networks within our brain. Computers are already capable of responding to motion, neatly separating figure from background. A row of dots moved in a certain way is perceived as a three-dimensional object instead of simply as dots on a flat surface.

The diagram seen below shows the ways in which a computer is capable of extracting the contours of a chair. In this illustration, taken from David Marr's earlier work, elements with similar orientations are collected together. Each cluster is then grouped as a unit and transformed within the computer into a suitable symbolic representation. These components of the figure are converted into digital information, which is stored and can later be extracted. Similar to the way our eyes and brain grouped together the dots into rows, columns, and pairs, the computer is programmed to recognize "perceptual" features that can later be organized into a high-level symbolic description.

Can a computer fail to recognize an object? Can it be

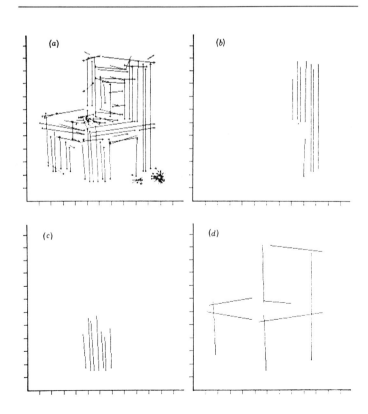

fooled? Of course—in the same way that our eyes and brain can be fooled by an optical illusion. Both computers and people go about making sense of the world by employing a "best bet" strategy in any given circumstance. The context often provides clues to what is before our eyes. When the context doesn't help or the clues are sufficiently ambiguous, as they were in the optical illusions mentioned earlier, all kinds of strange perceptions can result.

Seeing is like weather forecasting. First a considerable amount of data is gathered and encoded into several different categories: temperature, humidity, barometer readings, wind direction and speed, even air contamination as measured against a purity index. In a similar way the eye gathers several kinds of data: light, color, motion, depth, and so on. Just as wind and temperature aren't directly collected or stored, so there is no color, motion, or even light inside the brain. Instead, these qualities are transformed into codes or symbols that represent the incoming information. At a high level of coding, all the weather information is consolidated into a "weather report," which is a synthesis of all of the data, a symbolic representation of the rain or sunshine we are likely to encounter.

Each sensory system is restricted to a relatively small set of physical stimuli to which it is especially sensitive. The eye is responsive to electromagnetic energy within an extremely narrow band: wavelengths of about 400 to 700 nanometers, with really clear vision limited to 500–560 nanometers. We don't see everything out there, only those aspects of "reality" that conform to the physical limitations of our visual system. Thus we have real constraints on how we "see": a narrow "band-pass sensitivity" to radiant energy coupled with a tendency for grouping visual images according to such things as contrast, proximity, and so on. These observations are combined with texture, movement, and perhaps other so far undiscovered contributions to make "seeing" possible.

When you recall a person or event, the mental "picture" you see in your mind's eye can be rotated or turned—in fact, seen from any angle you wish. In addition, that visual image is assimilated into the brain in ways that aren't strictly visual. For instance, after seeing an object, we form a definite impression of how the object feels, or how heavy it may be. Practical jokers have a lot of fun based on the tendency

As described more fully at the bottom of the page, a simple experiment using several coins shows how various senses combine to create our "visual" impressions of day-to-day objects.

of our brains to associate visual images with how much something weighs. Rocks made out of Styrofoam give the visual appearance of weighing several hundred pounds, yet they can be easily picked up and safely thrown toward someone—to their great surprise!

Infants only a few weeks old will put up their arms and hands to defend themselves against an approaching object. How do they learn without experience that defense is necessary? Although neuroscientists don't understand the details, it now appears that integration of sight, size, and texture are present almost from birth. This suggests an exciting possibility. Could it be possible to bypass the initial input from the eye and pick up on the process farther "upstream," somewhere farther along the visual pathway to the brain? Would vision result? At first such a question seems ludicrous. Vision is vision. How can a person experience vision without employing the eye? The possibility of vision mediated by receptors other than the eye can be rendered less fantastic by a few simple experiments demonstrating the basic unity among sight, sound, and touch.

Gather together several coins, including a nickel, a quarter, some pennies, and some dimes. Put the coins inside your pocket and reach in, extract and identify each of the coins by manipulation alone. Only after you have made a firm identification is it fair to look at the coins to check your accuracy. You will find the task easy.

Now do the experiment slightly differently: Set the

coins flat on a table or other firm surface, close your eyes, and touch the tip of your index finger to the top of the coins. Don't pick them up, just touch their tops. You will find that you will be unable to separate the nickels from the dimes or the pennies. Don't take my word for it, try it. What accounts for this discrepancy?

In each of these two situations we are using the word "touch" quite differently. Only in the second situation—the coins aligned on the table—do we rely simply on touch. With the coins in our pockets we *manipulate* them—turning them, rolling them between our fingers in a process known as *haptic touch*. Manipulation leads to a perceptual unity composed of pressure, movement, resistance, and position of the objects. We build up a kind of three-dimensional re-creation of the objects in our brain, which allows us to identify them correctly. But touch alone provides very little information.

Identification of coins by manipulation, cross-checked for accuracy by visual inspection, is an example of cross-modal transfer of sensory information. It is possible to build up a fairly accurate "vision" of how something "looks" by modalities other than vision. In the final analysis, however, vision determines how large something really is. A dental cavity impresses us as a huge crater when discovered by the tip of our tongue. When we run the end of our finger over it, we usually can barely feel the cavity at all. Only later in the dentist's chair, when we can see the cavity in a dental mirror, do we feel properly informed about how large the cavity "really is."

But the relationship of vision to manipulation provides the most compelling example of cross-modal transfer. A skilled "card shark" can locate a card simply by running his fingertip along the deck until he detects a marked card that extrudes ever so slightly from the rest. The next time you agree to flip a coin to decide something, be sure to check that your opponent doesn't catch the coin between his thumb and index finger. After only a few minutes of practice most people can learn to make almost instantaneous identifications of "heads" from "tails."

This capacity to employ alternative means of sensory identification is by no means confined to magicians, ventriloquists, and professional gamblers. Optacon, a tactile reading aid for the blind, takes advantage of the capacity of the fingertips to make finely honed spatial discriminations. A blind person's reading ability is truly impressive when his or her fingertips are employed. This ability is drastically reduced when areas of the finger other than the tip are used. Variation in the sensitivity of the hand results from differences in the density of receptor units. The density is highest in the fingertips and decreases proportionately as one nears the wrist. In general, sensory discrimination is highest in those areas of the body that contain the most receptors, which is why the tongue and the fingertips are more "sensitive" than the back of the hand or the soles and heels of the feet.

As we will discuss in later chapters, cortical maps can be drawn representing the percentage of cortex devoted to a particular area of the body. The hand (particularly the fingertips) and the tongue have far more extensive cortical representation than would be expected on the basis of size alone. The hand, for instance, has a much greater area of cortex than the back of the arm or the small of the back. This is why we can often readily identify an object when it is placed in our hand but have to guess blindly about it when the same object is placed on our back or pressed against our arm.

When you identify a penny by holding it out of sight and rolling it between your fingers, activating your skin receptors has made it possible to form a visual image. Clearly, receptors for touch and manipulation must somehow be combined in the brain with visual receptors to provide this unity in perception.

Consider what happens when you both see and hear someone crossing a room. The visual image of the person moves across your retina and undergoes profound changes in size, shape, and orientation. The acoustical image also varies. As the person moves farther away, the intensity of the sound of his or her shoes becomes fainter, and if the person is moving to one side or the other from you, the sound may shift from the right to the left ear or vice versa. Yet what is seen and heard is not a cacophony of images and sounds but a unified perception: the *person,* a specific and recognizable person crossing the room. How can we account for this steadfastness of perception in the face of varying and shifting sensory inputs? This is one of the unresolved mysteries of the human brain. There is no doubt,

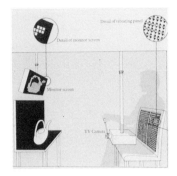

The apparatus used by the blind philosopher Guarniero to "see."

however, that unifying factors exist and that they can be recruited in visual substitution devices to help patients such as Professor Gerard Guarniero, philosopher, who has been blind since birth.

The visual substitution device used by Professor Guarniero employs a TV camera that the professor holds, training it on the object he wishes to "see." Light from the object then enters the camera, where it is fed to an array of blunt pins placed along Professor Guarniero's back. In the presence of light, or contrast, a pin will vibrate. Even though the vibrating pin feels like a tingle on the skin, it is perceived as a visual image by virtue of the fact that Professor Guarniero is operating a hand-held camera. In a way the brain is fooled, since cameras ordinarily convey impulses that our brains convert into visual perceptions. But if the output of the camera is used to stimulate the skin, the result is interpreted as a visual image rather than a touch.

"When I first started using it, it felt as if the images that the television camera were picking up . . . were on my skin," recalls Professor Guarniero. "But afterwards the *felt* quality of the sensations diminished to a point where the things that I was seeing with the system really didn't feel as if they were on my skin anymore. All of a sudden I had acquired a new sense because before I had always been restricted to feeling things, and, suddenly, I could perceive objects that were far away."

Professor Guarniero's sensory substitution experiences raise several intriguing philosophical questions. If "visual" perception can be modified through tactile stimulation of the skin, does this mean that neurons in one part of the brain can be recruited under the proper circumstances to carry out different tasks? Aristotle suggested as much: "For the perception of magnitude, figure, roughness, smoothness, and sharpness and bluntness, in solid bodies, is the common function of all the senses, and if not all, then at least the common function of sight and touch."

Aristotle was unaware of the importance of the human brain, and, therefore, he based his theories on observations of his own sensations. He recognized, for instance, that things such as shape and number are appreciated by several senses: We can see or touch two objects, hear two sounds, and so on. This ability of the different senses to appreciate such things as number, duration, and intensity depends, Aristotle claimed, on the existence of a *sensus communis,* a Latin term from which we derive our "common sense."

Aristotle's *sensus communis* can be translated into neurobiological terms by viewing perception as a *process* consisting of patterned activity in a large number of interconnected nerve cells. No single perceptual feature or quality can be explained solely on the basis of a small set of specialized neurons responding invariantly. Instead, neurons chatter and babble to each other in a complex network, the total of which provides us with a uniformity of perception—a *person* walking across the room rather than a shifting mélange of sounds and visual patterns. Further, it seems likely that this integration of multisensory information begins within the sensory systems themselves. For instance, in cats, the cells in the *superior colliculus,* a primary visual receptor, respond to auditory stimulation as well. Pure tones, tonal sweeps, and even just plain noises activate these cells. In fact, 80 percent of the cells in the deeper layers of the superior colliculus that maximally respond to light also react to sound and touch. Cells that perform double duty can be found in the visual cortex as well. Electrical stimulation of cats' *inferior colliculus* (an important way station in the auditory pathway) results in movements of the eyes and of the pinnae of the external ear.

In each of the examples just given, the cells, on the average, were much more sensitive to their primary modality (vision in the visual cortex and sound in the auditory cortex), but nonetheless they would discharge if other stimuli such as touch were sufficiently intense. Such findings suggest that a sizable portion of nerve cells are mediators of common sensory properties: shape, size, motion, rest, and perhaps even number.

Both skin and visual receptors in the cerebral cortex, for instance, are most sensitive to lines and edges and specific orientations. Objects placed on the skin are most easily identified when the contours of the edges of the objects are indenting the skin. This is strikingly similar to the "feature detectors" in the visual cortex where lines of a specific orientation are most easily perceived. Could edge sensitivity in specific orientations be the common property responsible for the function of sight and touch?

Or take something such as *contrast.* All sensations are most accurately perceived when they are strongly contrasted

by their background. The beam of a flashlight is instantaneously detected in a darkened room, whereas the same beam of light will go unnoticed in midday sunlight. The fall of a tree in a forest can be heard for miles on a quiet day but passes unnoticed during a thunderstorm.

Intensity is another common quality that extends across different senses. Schoolchildren, when requested to match colors to sounds, routinely associate violet and blue with low-sound frequencies and green and yellow with high-sound frequencies. The philosopher John Locke described a "studious blind man who bragged one day that he now understood what scarlet signified, upon which his friend demanded to know what scarlet was. The blind man answered, 'It was like the sound of a trumpet.'" Does the color scarlet resemble in any meaningful way the sound of a trumpet? The poet Algernon Swinburne thought so: "Like fire are the notes of the trumpets that flash through the darkness of sound."

Other poets and composers were also convinced of a fundamental unity between light and sound. In the eighteenth and nineteenth centuries multimodal concerts were held regularly and employed music combined with lights and sometimes odors as well. In 1725, Louis-Bertrand Castel invented the world's first color organ with a keyboard in which each key, when depressed, produced a colored light along with a musical note. The culmination of multisensory music was probably Alexander Scriabin's "Prometheus," written for piano, chorus, and color organ. I mention these historical oddities because they illustrate how the notion that different neurons may under the proper circumstances respond to more than one sensory input was anticipated hundreds of years ago.

Infants only a few days old show a remarkable selectivity when reaching for objects. If two balls are displayed, one small in size and graspable by the infant's hands and the other too large for easy grasping, infants will routinely reach for the graspable ball. Visual information regarding size appears to correlate with touch and feel prior to any contact. And infants only a few hours old will turn their heads toward the source of a sound, a neat demonstration that the translation of sensory information from sound to sight occurs prior to experience. But what happens if vision, sound, and touch report contradictory information? In situations where different sensations conflict with each other, how does the brain resolve the conflict?

An experiment aimed at clarifying these points was carried out during the filming of the show on which this book is based. The subject was Susannah Fiennes, an art student who, it could reasonably be inferred, is specifically trained for looking and seeing. What would be the effect on Susannah of placing before her eyes a pair of inverting lenses that turn the world upside down for her? Actually, since the lens at the front of Susannah's eye inverts everything before the image is relayed to the brain, inverting lenses should do no more than make everything right side up from the beginning. What effect would this have on Susannah's visual perception of the world around her?

Initially, Susannah's world appeared upside down. She was unable to pour milk from a jug into a cup. "I couldn't coordinate my two hands at all, because I couldn't see my hands. . . . Everything was completely opposite. It was just very strange."

But by moving around in her strangely inverted world, cautiously relearning the positions of her hands and her feet, Susannah was able to try writing her name by the third day. The effort, however, was a failure. Four days later, after additional attempts at learning to live with the lenses (walking, riding a bicycle, performing household chores, and so on), she tried again. This time she was successful. Over the space of a week, Susannah Fiennes was able to learn to match her altered visual information with her patterns of movement. Her *exploration* of the world around her made possible a reorganization of touch and movement that brought them in line with her new and profoundly altered visual perceptions.

Vision is thus married to movement. Susannah Fiennes literally had to relearn how to coordinate information from her different senses. Since vision is preeminent, she first "saw" the world as upside down and was promptly immobilized by the resulting confusion, disorientation, and mild panic. But, like the infant playing with a ball in her bassinet, Susannah was soon able to coordinate what she felt with what she saw. After a while the world began "making sense" for her once again. One can speculate that vision

We seem to find it natural to associate sound and light; a "red-hot" jazz trumpet, for example, elicits different emotions from a saxophone playing "the blues."

After two days of wearing inverting spectacles, Susannah Fiennes tried printing her name, first with her eyes closed (top two versions). She did the third version so that it looked normal to her. The final attempt, four days later, was to write correctly while looking.

and movement realigned themselves, this time according to a different set of rules.

The exact details of what went on in Susannah Fiennes' brain remain speculative at this point. It is clear, however, that her visual input eventually was integrated into her total interpretation of the world around her, much as Professor Guarniero's vibrating pins became a "visual sensation." Both Susannah and Professor Guarniero illustrate how the brain is able to utilize different sensations to build up a coherent reality. It does this by combining input from the various senses, oftentimes correcting for visual distortion by touch and manipulation. Vision is thus only a portion of our total exploration of the environment. We are not only creatures who see, but we also move in response to the world around us. These two separate processes—vision and movement—thus form an interrelated whole. Having concentrated on vision, let us further explore the mechanisms inherent in movement.

Essentially, all movement is mysterious. If we analyze walking, for instance, it soon becomes obvious that it involves a motor program that comes into action sometime immediately after we have made the initial decision to move from one spot to another. Although we "will" the initial act of walking, we have very little to do with the practical aspects of how this activity is carried out. This becomes intuitively obvious whenever one tries consciously to think about the ways one moves one's feet in, say, dancing or tennis. A clumsy performance can almost be guaranteed whenever we attempt to bring under conscious control something that usually proceeds automatically. This one piece of supporting data hints at the existence of a central program for this activity located somewhere within the nervous system.

Fifty years ago Soviet scientists isolated a segment of the brainstem, the *mesencephalic locomotor region* (MLR), which, when stimulated, produced normal walking movements in cats. This demonstration was particularly eerie since in these cats the brainstem had been surgically disconnected from the upper parts of the brain. With increasing rates of stimulation, the cats shifted from walking to trotting to galloping. These variations in the cats' movement seemed not to depend on anything other than the number of stimulations to the mesencephalic locomotor region.

Neuroscientists now believe the MLR is a command system for locomotion but does not itself contain the central programs for walking. Proof for this came from experiments in which only the spinal cord is connected to the limbs, having been surgically isolated from the rest of the nervous system. In these experiments the cats' legs can be made to walk at a rate dependent on the speed of the treadmill. This takes place even with cats who had the operations isolating their spinal cords performed at only a few weeks of age. On the basis of experiments such as these, neuroscientists are confident that the central program for walking is within the spinal cord. But this is only part of the story.

It is obvious that walking in the real world is different from walking along a treadmill. There are variations in terrain. Walking up a hill requires a different repertoire of muscle movements from walking down that same hill. Walking against the wind blowing on Chicago's Lakeshore Drive requires that we look out for our balance long before we even think of beginning to move forward. Analysis, even that carried out from the informal vantage point of a sidewalk cafe, reveals characteristic ways of walking that are as individual as fingerprints or electroencephalographic patterns. Students of *kinesics*—the study of basic units of body movement within the process of human interaction—suggest that the way we walk can reveal important clues to our psychological makeup, such as whether we are happy or depressed. Our language supports this claim: we "leap for joy" when we are happy or "plod along" when we are feeling down. The psychiatrist Wilhelm Reich even based his method of "character analysis" on observations of the way patients moved. For these reasons, it is obvious that the study of cats walking on treadmills after undergoing operations that isolated their spinal cords is unlikely to tell us much about our own walking, to say nothing about the marvelously coordinated movements of a ballet dancer.

This is not to say that automatic walking does not exist in humans. Studies of newborn babies by Professor Sten Grillner and his associates at the Karolinska Institute in Stockholm show that a capacity for walking is present at birth—therefore, it is inherited rather than learned.

Before birth a basic walking pattern is imprinted upon our nervous system, a pattern we learn to use when we can walk unassisted for the first time. A three- or four-year-old girl, unlike an infant, can support all her weight on her legs so that other movements (swinging of the arms and so on) can come into play at the same time. But her brain may still be partially dependent on inherited patterns of movement. Her walk continues to exhibit a number of "baby" features—her toes touch the ground before her heels, for instance.

Built-in patterns of movement—dependent upon intrinsic motor patterns—can be seen throughout the animal kingdom. The gait of a horse was first photographed a century ago by Eadweard Muybridge. He showed for the first time the order and movement of the horse's legs. Prior to Muybridge's photos, horses were drawn in a "rocking

One of Eadweard Muybridge's famous sets of photographs showing the movements of a horse.

horse position," with both forelegs and hind legs fully extended. Actually, as Muybridge's photos proved, the horse moves its legs in different time rhythm. The legs of a walking horse (or of a man, for that matter) operate on a pendulum principle—each leg, once raised, swings without effort into the next stride.

Some movements require only a very simple sequence of neuronal connections for the movement to be complete.

The classic "knee jerk" is a closed loop operating between the receptors in the knee and the spinal cord. When the doctor taps the patient's knee with a reflex hammer, the knee automatically "jerks" outward. This is an example of a reflex, since it occurs as automatically and predictably as a fire after a lighted match touches a bale of dry hay. With increasing numbers of neuronal connections, reflexes become less automatic. Consider, for instance, a decision to walk away from a boring movie. How many neuronal connections are involved in such an act?

In recent years, neuroscientists have shifted their attention from single-reflex movements like the knee jerk to immensely complicated motor acts involving conscious decision. Consider the following experiment by NIH neurophysiologist Edward Evarts.

A monkey is first prepared for brain recordings by placing a closed recording cap over an opening in its skull. A microelectrode is then inserted into a *single cell* within the monkey's motor cortex. With the monkey restrained in a chair, it is then given the task of holding a handle in a set position. By means of fruit-juice rewards, the monkey is then trained to respond to either a red or a green light. Red means "Get ready to pull" the handle. Green signals "Get ready to push" it. More important than the monkey's motor performance (the actual pushing or pulling of the handle) is the electrical activity within the single cell. The cell increases its discharge in response to the instruction to "pull" but decreases it in response to "push." Moreover, these changes in cell activity occur *before* the actual motor responses (pushing or pulling). In other words, the single cell alters its firing rate before there is any indication of which way the monkey is going to move the handle. To this extent the activity of the single motor cell is entirely internal: it occurs before the handle is moved and well in advance of any tension in the monkey's muscles, which ordinarily would precede the movement of the handle. How is this possible?

Evarts explains his results as proof for "centrally programmed" patterns of movement. The light served as a stimulus for the brain to "set up preparatory states for a particular direction of centrally programmed movement." But the single cell was only one component of this circuit. What were the other components, and what happened between the "internal response" and the monkey's actually

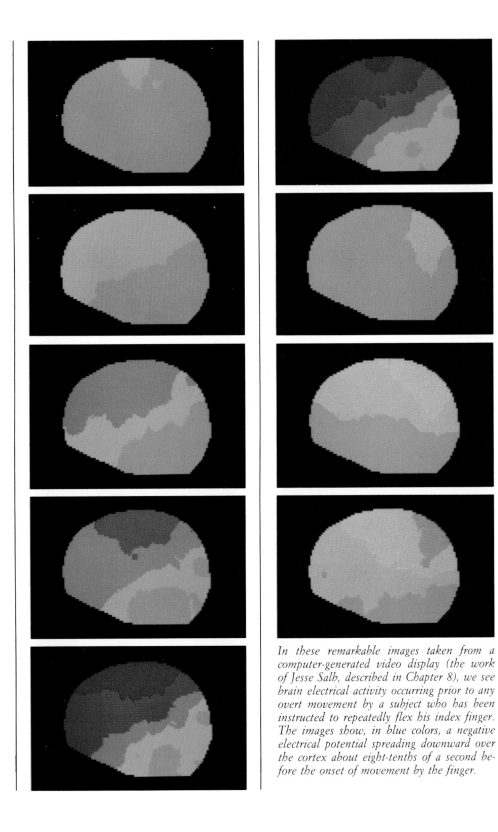

In these remarkable images taken from a computer-generated video display (the work of Jesse Salb, described in Chapter 8), we see brain electrical activity occurring prior to any overt movement by a subject who has been instructed to repeatedly flex his index finger. The images show, in blue colors, a negative electrical potential spreading downward over the cortex about eight-tenths of a second before the onset of movement by the finger.

pushing or pulling the handle? To get sufficient perspective to answer such a question, we'll need to review some earlier research on how the brain controls movement. Like much of the really important information on the human brain, the history doesn't extend back very far.

During the Prusso-Danish War of 1864, German physician Theodor Fritsch observed, while dressing a head wound, that touching the cerebral hemisphere produced twitching on the opposite side of the body. He discussed this finding with Eduard Hitzig, a medical practitioner in Berlin, and together they decided to test Fritsch's observation experimentally. Since neither physician had access to a laboratory, they carried out their experiments on Frau Hitzig's dressing table. Despite the crudity of the experimental procedure, the results agreed with Fritsch's original observation: Electrical stimulation of the cortical surface in dogs produced muscular contractions in the muscles on the opposite side of the body.

Fritsch and Hitzig suggested, on the basis of their observation, that parts of the body are controlled by areas on opposite sides of the brain. The Greek physician Hippocrates had suggested something along the same lines when he noticed that a sword wound to the side of the head in a soldier produced paralysis of the opposite side of the body.

Although Fritsch and Hitzig's discoveries were the first scientific demonstration of what we now call cerebral localization (different parts of the brain are responsible for specific activities), the two men failed to realize the full implications of their findings. It fell to a contemporary of theirs, John Hughlings Jackson, to amplify a series of chance observations of his own into a theory of brain function that still is operational today.

Jackson was a peculiar, aloof man, with a background unlike that of any neuroscientist before or after him. The son of a farmer, Jackson was largely self-taught. But he was a keen observer with intense powers of observation and, as fate would have it, a wife afflicted with a form of epilepsy that today bears Jackson's name.

Jacksonian epilepsy is marked by seizures in restricted parts of the body. Characteristically, the seizures start in the hand and pass upward to the wrist, elbow, shoulder, and eventually the face. The seizure then passes to the leg on the same side, where it may terminate.

Based on observations of his own wife's seizures, particularly their tendency always to "march" in a specific way from one body part to the other, Jackson arrived at a pivotal theory of brain organization. He suggested that the cerebral cortex is organized into different sectors, which provide the motor power for different body parts. He was the first to suggest that the brain possessed an internal geography all its own. During his wife's epileptic seizures it was likely, Jackson claimed, that the epileptic discharges moved from the hand area up to the wrist area and then to the shoulder, and so on. Since the pattern never varied, it suggested that the organization of the brain is quite regular, with some areas in close proximity (wrist-hand), while other areas are more widely separated (wrist-foot).

The existence of a "motor cortex" responsible for movement was a revolutionary idea at the time Jackson first suggested it. Based on autopsy examinations of the brains of patients who had suffered from strokes or tumors, neuroscientists were convinced that the cerebral hemispheres were responsible for *thoughts*. But now all that had to be changed. "There seems to be an insuperable objection to the notion that the cerebral hemispheres are for movement," Jackson wrote. "The reason, I suppose, is that the convolutions of the cortex are considered to be *not* for *movement* but for ideas."

To John Hughlings Jackson, brain activity was not sharply divided into automatic and voluntary. For instance, during one of his wife's seizures, her hand would be shaking uncontrollably, yet she didn't lose consciousness. Although she "willed" to stop the seizure, she couldn't do it. In this instance, the epileptic seizures inactivated the motor control centers for the hand. As a result, only "automatic," involuntary, and clumsy motions of the hand were possible. After the passage of the seizure, however, the hand would gradually recover function and, after a while, would be capable of carrying out all its former activities.

Sixty years later, Jackson's ideas were confirmed by Canadian neurosurgeon Wilder Penfield, who electrically stimulated the cortex of patients undergoing neurosurgical operations. He found, as Jackson had suggested, that the brain was organized along functional lines. This was a stunning confirmation of Jackson's observation that the epileptic seizures he observed followed a definite pattern.

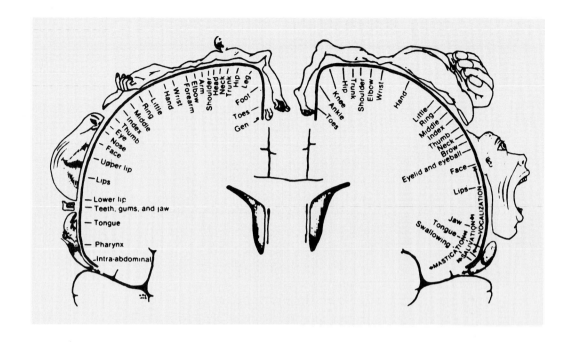

Penfield's operating room "experiments" also made possible the construction of a *motor homunculus,* literally a cartoon of the body surface drawn to scale and representing body parts aligned not according to their actual size but rather to the extent to which they are involved in skilled movements.

If Jackson had accomplished nothing further than articulating the principle of cerebral localization, he would be considered today as one of the great innovators in our understanding of the human brain. But Jackson accomplished much more, as the result of what was, for a physician, an unusual interest: philosophy. Early in his medical career, Jackson had come under the influence of the British philosopher Herbert Spencer. Jackson took from this experience a firmly entrenched belief in evolution, a belief he later incorporated into his own theories about the brain. For instance, he regarded the brain as organized along a hierarchical scheme, with lower centers gradually developing and merging into higher, more complex structures. Searching for a metaphor by which to describe his ideas, Jackson hit upon another of Herbert Spencer's concerns, the social system.

Jackson compared the brain to a government that can endure only by suppressing lower, less legitimate sources of

This motor homunculus makes the important point that our brains are organized according to the sensitivity and complexity of our body parts; the hands and fingers are represented over a wider brain area than the hips or legs.

authority, such as insurrectionists, anarchists, and so on. But if the government falls, then these "lower" forms of control take command. In this analogy the higher centers exert an inhibitory force on the lower centers that becomes obvious only if some catastrophe occurs to the higher centers. Jackson's breakthrough rested on his suggestion that *inhibition* rather than excitation is the hallmark of the healthy brain. As it turns out, only a small number of the total neurons in the brain "fire" at any given moment. Many of the remaining neurons are actively inhibited by other neurons.

Perhaps it is appropriate that John Hughlings Jackson, with his abiding interest in philosophy, should have stimulated neuroscientists to tackle a series of profoundly disquieting philosophical questions.

At the basis of Western philosophy is the belief in freedom of the will. If I decide to move my hand, I move it. If I don't want to move my hand, I keep it still. But during an epileptic seizure, my hand may move despite my best efforts to contain it. My hand may also be paralyzed for a time after the seizure, not responding to my wishes, hanging limp and useless at my side. When I decide to pick up my pen and write this sentence, where in my brain does the impulse originate? The search for an answer has stimulated neuroscientists along innumerable paths of investigation as well as into several blind alleys.

Think back for a moment to the experiment of Edward Evarts that I described a few pages earlier. A single motor cell in the brain of a monkey was observed to discharge in advance of any externally observable motion by the monkey. This was an example of motor activity that remained entirely *internal*. Evarts' speculation regarding a central motor program leaves unanswered the question of the origin of the monkey's decision to push or to pull the handle.

To gain insight into the brain mechanisms underlying coordinated action, Evarts extended his method of single-cell recording to include not only the cerebral cortex but the basal ganglia and cerebellum as well. The basal ganglia consist of a series of structures beneath the cortex and deep within the substance of the brain. These ganglia (a nineteenth-century term signifying large groups of neurons) are interconnected not only within their own network (*putamen, caudate, globus pallidus, subthalmic nucleus, thalamus*) but in addition form two-way connections within areas of the cerebral cortex and brainstem. Fibers are also thought to project to the cerebellum, which in turn activates various parts of the basal ganglia.

The illustration seen below gives some flavor of the richness and complexity of cortical-basal ganglia-cerebellar connections. But we still haven't answered the question of where in this interconnected system a motor act originates. The obvious choice appears to be the cortex. After all, it is the originator of motor cells that, when stimulated, lead to movement. In addition, as we saw in Evarts' first experiments, cortical cells were observed to fire just prior to the monkey's "decision" to push a lever. (I have used quotation marks around *decision* to convey the uncertainty concerning the process going on in the monkey's brain. Certainly pushing or pulling a lever is not quite the "decision" we associate with, say, our deciding to go to law school.)

As it turns out, the "decision" to push or to pull a lever is accompanied by discharges in *all three brain areas:*

Interior view of the brain showing the major components of the basal ganglia.

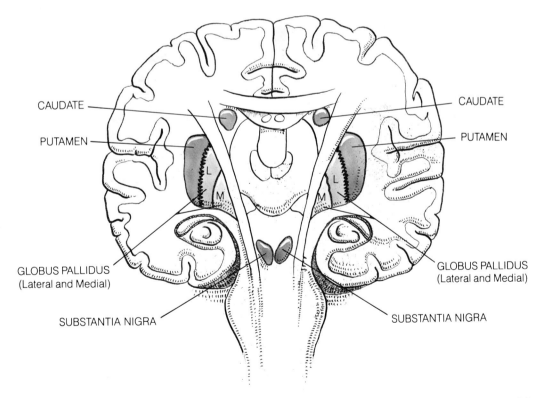

CAUDATE

PUTAMEN

GLOBUS PALLIDUS
(Lateral and Medial)

SUBSTANTIA NIGRA

CAUDATE

PUTAMEN

GLOBUS PALLIDUS
(Lateral and Medial)

SUBSTANTIA NIGRA

cortex, basal ganglia, and cerebellum. Furthermore, these discharges begin well in advance of any observable movement. In short, there isn't any "executive center" from which a motor program originates and then spreads to additional brain areas. Instead, the impulse is *distributed* throughout widely separated areas of the brain (cortical, subcortical basal ganglia, and cerebellar connections). This is a truly remarkable concept that literally blows the roof off our simplified conceptions of brain organization.

Evarts' work forces us to free ourselves from the concept that higher functions (decisions, acts of will, and so on) reside exclusively in one location, such as the motor cortex. Instead, the cortex interacts with centers throughout the nervous system, many of which can be identified in the brains of creatures existent since prehistoric times. "Thus the mammalian motor cortex, phylogenetically a new part of the brain, is subject to the same laws of reflex action that characterize the brain's older components," says Evarts.

As an example of what is meant by a distributed system, consider my act of writing this paragraph. Since I am right-handed, I am holding my pen with my right hand. This brings into action a group of muscles in my right hand, forearm, and shoulder. These are correlated with the muscles of my neck, which have to be turned at a certain angle so that I can see the paper in front of me. But suppose yesterday I had injured my hand carrying out a karate maneuver. Several alternative writing programs are available to me. I could, if I wasn't in too much of a hurry, simply switch to my left hand. If this didn't work out, I could fetch a typewriter and "pick" at the letters with my left hand. I could also dictate to a stenographer or into a tape recorder for later transcription. Each of these methods of "writing" the paragraph employs completely different brain areas. The unifying element in these different activities is, of course, my *intention* to write the paragraph. My purpose, in other words, provides the underlying theme upon which countless variations of brain activity may be played out. Something like writing a paragraph includes both stereotyped muscle actions (after all, there are only a few truly efficient ways of holding a pen) along with voluntary components that can't be localized in any meaningful sense at all. The intermingling of voluntary and reflex activity lends majesty and power to the human brain. We are not simply reflex organisms (after all, I can decide that today I don't fancy writing a paragraph at all and may return to my karate), nor are we totally unrestrained in our behavior (if I am going to compose a paragraph, there are only a limited number of ways I can go about doing it).

The brain, it seems, is organized along functional lines, depending on goal and purpose. An attempt to localize the area in the brain responsible for this sentence is like trying to catch one's own shadow. The purpose is the product of a distributed system in which the newer parts of the brain (such as the cerebral cortex) are coupled with the phylogenetically older brain areas (subcortical basal ganglia).

The importance of these older, "lower" areas of the brain can be seen in illnesses such as *Huntington's chorea,* which produces a series of random movements (for instance, the patient's arms and shoulders may writhe without stopping). Each component of these movements could, under the proper circumstances, be purposeful. In Huntington's, however, the patient isn't "willing" the movement but rather is the helpless victim of his or her own muscles. One of the areas affected in Huntington's is the caudate nucleus, a component of the basal ganglia.

Hemiballismus is another neurologic illness marked by involuntary movements. A patient with hemiballismus will without warning execute a motion that, to all appearances, looks exactly like a pitcher throwing a baseball. Unlike a baseball pitcher, however, the patient with hemiballismus does his or her best to inhibit the motion.

In Huntington's chorea and hemiballismus the involuntary aspects of movement have wrested control from the will. The individuals affected are beset by a series of embarrassing actions that are beyond their capacity to control. In a way, the sufferers become spectators of their own motor programs, which, like monsters in a horror movie, have taken on a life of their own.

Further proof of the importance of "lower" brain areas in willed movement was provided in 1982 by a twenty-five-year-old Frenchman living in Paris. The victim of accidental carbon monoxide poisoning, the man regained consciousness but was left with a tragic impairment: a complete loss of the powers of self-activation. If left to his own devices, the man would remain in bed all day, neither moving nor speaking. But if anyone spoke to him or merely

CAT Scanner (Computerized Axial Tomography)

Conventional X rays possess several limitations. An X ray doesn't provide a three-dimensional image. Nor does it distinguish from each other two structures which are of the same density. To get around these limitations, the *computerized axial tomography scanner*, or CAT scan, was developed. This technical advance makes it possible to "unpeel" the brain in a computer-assisted reconstruction. To do this, the patient's head is inserted into the "hole" of a special doughnut-shaped scanner. Above the head, an X-ray tube rotates along a circular path. With each sweep of the rotating scanner, X-ray beams are emitted which pass through the head. The brain tissue absorbs the radiation according to the density of its different components. (White matter differs from gray matter; normal brain tissue has a different density from diseased brain tissue.) Once the X-ray beam has passed through the brain, it is picked up by sensitive crystal detectors that convert the beam into electronic signals. The computer then performs an elaborate calculation involving the amount of radiation originally emitted by the X-ray tube minus the amount striking the detectors. This difference represents the radioactivity absorbed by the brain. By varying the angles of the original X-ray beam, it is possible to obtain additional layer by layer scans of the brain tissue as "seen" from different angles.

Although the CAT scanner represents a tremendous advance in terms of visualization of brain structure, it doesn't provide information regarding brain function. To this extent, the CAT scanner is a static rather than dynamic image. To study the living brain in its variations over time, it is necessary to use a PET scanner which measures brain *activity* rather than, simply, brain architecture.

This CAT scan shows a large tumor with irregular borders (arrows) surrounded by fluid (open arrows); the growth paralyzed the patient's left side. These images show the brain as seen from above looking down on to the top of the skull.

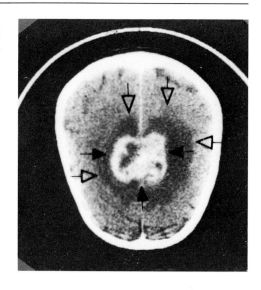

touched him, he sprang into normal physical, intellectual, and emotional performance.

Interviewing this patient revealed that in periods of inactivity his mind was actually overflowing with thoughts and impulses he couldn't put into action. Helpless to resist these obsessions, he literally sat immobile for hours, going over in his mind a series of repetitive thoughts that ceased only when someone spoke to him or physically stimulated him.

The CAT scan of this patient revealed a lesion in the globus pallidus, an area of the basal ganglia not usually associated with willed movement. In this instance destruction of the globus pallidus robbed this unfortunate man of vital control over his life: He literally couldn't spontaneously carry out actions or express ideas. What makes this tragic patient most interesting for our purposes is the proof he provides that without the aid of the basal ganglia the desire to carry out certain movements results in nothing at all.

In 1976, Dr. H. H. Kornhuber, a German neurophysiologist, recorded EEG signals from points on the scalps of healthy volunteers. These *electroencephalograms* were recorded while the subjects carried out a series of tasks. During the most interesting of Kornhuber's experiments, the subjects were requested simply to flex their index finger. There were no restraints or specific stimuli. Instead, they flexed their fingers whenever they chose to do so. Movement of the finger was electronically recorded to provide a precise indication of the instant of movement. By means of computer averaging to eliminate the spontaneous background "noise" of unrelated events within the brain, it was possible to isolate those brain potentials that were specific to the act of moving the finger. The most important questions were: Can an electric signal be detected prior to finger movement? If so, where in the cerebral hemisphere does the signal emanate?

Kornhuber discovered that a change in brain activation occurs 1.5 seconds before the raising of the finger. In addition, this *readiness potential,* as it is called, is not limited to the cortical area usually associated with finger motion. Instead, the readiness potential can be recorded over the surface of *both* cerebral hemispheres.

The Kornhuber experiment provides proof that a considerable degree of brain processing has already taken place prior to the moment when movement occurs. While a simple response to a stimulus ordinarily takes about 0.1 second, brain activation preceding the movement begins, in the form of a readiness potential, 1.5 seconds before we consciously start to carry out the act.

Several intriguing suggestions are raised by the Kornhuber experiment. First, we may have to revise the old idea that the brain follows the mind's commands and produces movement. During these brief but vitally important subfractions of time, the brain is formulating and starting to carry out a "motor program." To this extent, large areas of the brain are operating prior to movement—in fact, prior to the conscious act of the will involved in initiating the movement. This is a paradox only if one insists that the mind is somehow separate from the brain and that the relationship of the two is similar to that of a commanding officer and his or her subordinates. This conceptual problem disappears, however, if we recognize that in a very meaningful way *we are our brain,* or in the words of brain researcher Eric Harth: "The power of determining one's own behavior is not the power of one entity (the mind) over another (the body), but the influence the brain has on itself."

A second implication of the Kornhuber experiment is that it corroborates Evarts' notion that a specific movement doesn't originate in only one area of the brain. "Whenever motor acts or perceptions have been properly analyzed, they have been found to have involved a very large number of neurons in different parts of the brain. For this reason it also seems likely that conscious awareness as a process necessarily implicates a vast number of cells from different sites," states Nobel Prize–winning neurophysiologist Ragnar Granit.

Although the cerebral cortex is undoubtedly the predominant area for elaboration of the conscious experience accompanying movement, the original impulse to move can't flow into action without internally generated motor programs, themselves dependent on contributions of brain areas deep below the cerebral hemispheres. Although I can consciously will the act of picking up the pen, the mechanism by which the act is done must forever remain outside my conscious awareness. This inability to get into conscious contact with "motor programs" has philosophically intriguing implications for theories of free will. In this instance, I can't "will" the particular configuration of muscle contractions that come into play when I write my name. I can decide only to write my name and let the act unfold according to its own inscrutable ways. We now know that these ways include feedbacks from the cerebral cortex to the sensory areas of the cortex, downward into the thalamus, with contributions from the subcortical centers, notably the basal ganglia.

The degree to which this processing can be brought into conscious awareness is minimal indeed. In fact, we are capable of knowing very little about ourselves when it comes to the mechanisms of how will is converted into specific movements. Nevertheless, we are only truly ourselves when we act. Thus contemporary brain research has quite a bit to offer, not so much in the way of solving certain philosophical and psychological puzzles as it does in demonstrating that philosophy and psychology have been asking the wrong kinds of questions.

There is no center in the human brain responsible for willing movement any more than there is a center in the brain of a swan responsible for the beauty and complexity of its flight. To this extent the belief that we can truly come to understand ourselves through the study of the brain makes sense only if research is directed toward revealing how purpose can be encoded within patterns of neuronal organization eventually expressed in movement. This organization includes multiple centers and levels of the brain. How they are related, the degree of their mutual influence, and the means by which movement eventually comes about remain unsolved puzzles. The first step toward solving them, however, is to realize that the boundaries between involuntary and voluntary movements are not as clearly demarcated as we have been led to believe.

It is fascinating to realize that many of our most conscious activities, even those activities for which we take the most credit (such as our tennis game), have large involuntary components. And there is good reason to believe that on the whole we are better off carrying out many of our movements without the involvement of consciousness.

Taisen Deshimaru, a Japanese martial artist, has this to say on techniques of attack: "There is no choosing. It happens unconsciously, automatically, naturally. There can be no thought, because if there is a thought, there is a time of thought and that means a flaw. . . . If you take time to think 'I must use this or that technique,' you will be struck while you are thinking."

A similar reliance on the automatic is found in tennis, ballet, football, and boxing. Indeed, the excitement surrounding any sporting event often narrows down to the question of whether the athletes involved are sufficiently trained to respond appropriately to any contingency. When we talk of a player "choking," we are referring to his tendency to hold back, hesitate for only a fraction of a second, enough time to lose the opportunity for victory. Although the mental qualities of the accomplished athlete are currently the subject of much speculation, rarely does the commentator zero in on unconsciously directed *involuntary movement* as the distinction between the superstar and his or her more pedestrian counterpart.

Contemporary brain research provides proof for this view of the importance of "motor programs" for the athlete—a view that can be traced at least as far back as the 1890s. Here is what A. T. Dudley had to say at that time in "The Mental Qualities of an Athlete," an article in *Harvard Monthly*:

"Here is the distinguishing feature of the good player: the good player, confident in his training and his practice, in a critical game trusts entirely to his impulse, and does not think out every move. . . . The first-rate player is not trying to reason, but acting as impulse directs, is continually distinguishing himself, and plays the better under the greater pressure."

To bring together what we have discussed about vision and movement, consider some of the things going on in the brain of a star athlete. Consider a performance by world champion diver Greg Louganis.

A successful dive by Greg depends on the precise execution of a series of muscular movements, each exquisitely timed to combine visual, motor, and sensory cues instantaneously. Even a slight variation in motor sequence can result in crippling failure, perhaps even death. In performing this complex maneuver, the diver has no time to think out when and how each arm or leg is moved. Nor can the rapid shifting in eye, hand, and leg movements be consciously coordinated. An "automatic program" is required that, after a period of training, coordinates the necessary movements without the slightest hesitation. To accomplish this remarkable performance, a remarkable organ is employed: the cerebellum.

Although the cerebellum is part of the human brain, it has its own distinctive arrangement of brain cells. It has other unique features as well. It contains complete motor and sensory representations of the body. Damage to this delicate structure doesn't produce muscle weakness or any

Greg Louganis begins a world-class dive from the high board (continues next page).

perceptible change in sensation. Instead, a person with an impaired cerebellum loses the ability to do such a seemingly simple thing as walk a straight line; in fact, the patient may appear drunk, even though he or she has had nothing alcoholic to drink. If cerebellar disease is extensive enough, the patient may not even be capable of sitting without support. Eye and hand movements lose their coordination, so that a simple gesture such as reaching up to scratch the tip of the nose may result in a powerful and misdirected punch in the face.

In a phrase, the cerebellum is responsible for coordinating muscle tone, posture, and eye and hand movements. To do this, the cerebellum receives sensory information from every part of the body. This information is then synthesized into body maps at the cerebellum's anterior and posterior ends.

The anterior lobe of the cerebellum may be damaged by

the cumulative effect of alcohol over many years. Since this area is concerned with leg and trunk stability, the typical alcoholic stumbles around and cannot sit straight in a chair. If damage is located more laterally, then the hand and arm on one side of the body will swing wildly off target whenever the patient attempts anything with this extremity. Slight damage to the arm area of the cerebellum produces subtler changes. A patient once described his problem with his right cerebellar hemisphere in these words: "The movements of my left hand are subconscious, but I have to think out each movement of my right arm. I come to a dead stop and have to think before I start again."

It would be a dull world indeed if every activity, no matter how trivial, had to be shunted through consciousness before it could be carried out. But we are spared this boredom thanks to our cerebellum, which plays a large part in "programming" the details required for the automatic

execution of skilled movements. Without a cerebellum Greg Louganis would never be able to make it up the ladder, much less stand, perfectly poised, awaiting a signal to dive.

As Greg awaits the moment to begin, his cerebellum is receiving impulses from sensory channels throughout the body along with information from the cerebral cortex. Scientists believe that even the intention to perform a movement, particularly something as complex as a dive, involves activation of motor association areas in the cerebral cortex. From here, impulses are first sent directly to the lateral cerebellum, where a "program" is written and transferred through at least one intermediary, the thalamus, back to the cerebral hemispheres, in this case the motor cortex. The motor cortex corresponds to the executive in an organization who issues orders but often leaves the moment-to-moment implementation of those orders to subordinates. In this analogy, the role of the "subordinates" is carried out by a different, more medial part of the cerebellum that is kept informed of the commands of the motor cortex that shape the movement from moment to moment. Oftentimes adjustment must be made depending, in the case of Greg, on the tautness of the board, its degree of "give," and the "feel" of the situation.

But since few of us have much experience with high diving, let's switch for a moment to a more common example of cerebellar control, a tennis game. During an interview, Dr. Masao Ito, a Japanese expert on the cerebellum, formulated some of the things that must be going on within the brain, particularly the cerebellum, during a rigorous tennis match.

"The cerebellum is assisting the tennis player in many ways. First of all, when the player sees the ball flying to him at a distance, he must work out very quickly where and when the ball will be in his corner. This prediction may be done by the cerebral cortex. But the very quick swing of the racket to the future position of the ball must be performed by the cerebellum. Running, jumping, and swinging must be well coordinated. This entire function is the work of the cerebellum. Hitting the ball in a desired direction must be done by very skilled finger movements. And this skill, too, must have been acquired by the cerebellum through practicing, by means of its learning capability. In all these ways the cerebellum contributes mightily to tennis playing. And the various roles are probably carried out by different areas of the cerebellum, which, in fact, has many functional units."

Both the human cerebellum and cerebral cortex (as pointed out by John Hughlings Jackson) operate by dampening out unwanted discharges to enhance more appropriate patterns of neuronal firing. These neuronal patterns are programmed via the cerebellum, which, according to Dr. Ito, functions like a computer assisting an airline pilot during flight.

"A pilot operates a jet plane by controlling rocket engines with the aid of a computer," according to Dr. Ito. "In our movements the cerebral cortex, just like the pilot, controls numerous muscles with the aid of the cerebellum, which is our biological computer. However, if you compare a human to a robot, you can see that robot movements are rather clumsy compared to human movements. This is because the robot has a single computer, while the human being has as many as thirty thousand computers in the cerebellum."

As an example of the kinds of activities performed by the cerebellum, try this simple test. Hold your index finger in a vertical position about six inches in front of your face and begin moving your hand from side to side as fast as you can. The finger becomes nothing more than a blur, doesn't it? Now try holding the hand and finger steady while vigorously turning your head as fast as you can. Much less blurring, right? The blurring is largely prevented by means of the *vestibuloocular reflex* (VOR), which extends from the *vestibular center* in the inner ear and acts to maintain the eyes on a fixed target when the head is rotated.

A racing driver entering a hairpin turn, for instance, may have his or her head tossed to the right or to the left. This must be instantaneously corrected if visual blurring and an accident are to be prevented. The rapid refixation of the eyes is controlled by a small area of the cerebellum. This drives the eyes back to their original position, thus fixing the image in the visual field.

In experimental animals, Dr. Ito and others have located a smaller area within the cerebellum that is responsible for the vestibuloocular reflex. If this center is destroyed, animals lose the ability to compensate accurately for rapid head movements. Things become blurred in the same way our

finger looked blurred when we moved it rapidly in front of our face.

The importance of maintaining a stable image of the world varies from person to person. Although the survival of a racing driver depends on it, other occupations make comparatively humble demands on the VOR. Reading this paragraph, for instance, demands that your eyes be capable of scanning from line to line. As you finish one line your eyes rapidly shift leftward and drop down one line. Some individuals with reading disabilities have great difficulty doing this. In fact, they do it much better with one eye than with two eyes operating simultaneously. For this reason, this particular type of reading disability is improved by encouraging the student alternately to patch one eye at a time.

Slow-motion film analyses of birds walking reveal that their head is held almost perfectly motionless while the rest of their body moves in various postures and positions. Presumably this arrangement allows the birds to remain maximally sensitive to movement without themselves having to remain motionless. This fine tuning is made possible by connections to the vestibular center.

Maintaining balance, whether it be a bird walking on a tree branch or Greg Louganis jumping from a high board, depends on several different kinds of sensory information. Signals are relayed along axons from special sensors in the joints, skin, and muscles. Vision is also important for the sense of orientation in space. If you doubt this, see how long you can stand on one foot with both your eyes closed! Overall, though, these separate components aren't sufficient to keep the brain apprised of different alterations in the environment.

Over several million years of evolution special organs have, therefore, developed. A gravity detector, the *otolith,* is present in the lower brainstem of all vertebrates. Attached to it are one or more canals, known as the semicircular canals, to detect rotation. Together these structures form the *vestibular organ,* which is responsible for conveying information regarding orientation into the brainstem. In the course of evolution, the vestibular organ gave rise to an outpocketing, which became the organ of hearing.

The *vestibulospinal system* consists of fibers projecting to the muscles of the neck, trunk, and limbs. These reflexes act as stabilizers. During normal activities, the vestibulospinal reflexes are responsible for the corrective movements that continually restore the head to its original position. Connections are also made among the vestibular nucleus, the brainstem, the ocular muscles (via the vestibuloocular reflex, VOR), and the cerebellum (*vestibulocerebellar tracts*).

For years neuroscientists speculated about what would happen if the various vestibular channels were exposed to the experience of total weightlessness. In such a setting normal clues regarding direction and gravitational pull would be absent. How would people experience such an environment?

The next time you go to an amusement park, observe the average age of people on some of the wilder rides. As we grow older, most of us are less tolerant of sudden changes in the position of our bodies in space. This partially accounts for the fact that acrobats and high-wire artists tend on the average to be quite young. Children also enjoy spinning, rotation, and swinging—motions that many adults, particularly older adults, find extremely uncomfortable. Based on such considerations, neuroscientists had grave reservations about the effects of space travel.

Would the astronauts develop symptoms of motion sickness? The question was far from academic. If the astronauts couldn't tolerate the profound changes in orientation brought about by space travel, the whole space program would be jeopardized. (Have you ever tried working or even functioning at a tenth of your efficiency while in the throes of motion sickness?)

About half of all astronauts have suffered the symptoms of "space adaptation syndrome," characterized by nausea, vomiting, and general malaise. Within two days the symptoms disappear. NASA has established a special project to research the syndrome.

Fortunately, the vestibular system has great flexibility, and the astronauts experienced few difficulties accommodating to their new environment. Here is a description of the experience of weightlessness by Dr. Joseph Kerwin, the first physician astronaut, who was aboard *Skylab II* in 1973:

"I would say there was no vestibular sense of the upright whatsoever. I certainly had no idea where the earth was at any time unless I happened to be looking at it. I had no idea of the relationship between one compartment of the spacecraft or another in terms of 'up or down.' . . . Whatever you think is up, is up. After a few days of getting used to this, you play with it all the time. . . . It is a marvelous feeling of power over the space around you. Closing your eyes made everything go away. Then your body became a planet all to itself, and you really didn't know where the outside world was."

The ready adaptability of the astronauts in a weightless environment is a tribute to the plasticity of the human brain. Space travel was a totally new experience. Despite the stresses, the vestibular system adapted and, even more importantly, reoriented itself upon reentry.

Testing the astronauts upon their return to earth revealed difficulties with such routine tasks as standing on narrow rails with one's eyes open. With eyes closed, the performance was even worse. In all cases, however, performances returned to normal after a few days. Such results indicate that postural mechanisms are affected by prolonged periods of weightlessness but that things return pretty much to normal after exposure to normal gravitational fields. The process is similar to what happens when you step ashore after a few days aboard a ship. For the first few hours you experience fleeting sensations of movement on "dry land." But after a time period ranging from a few hours to a few days, the vestibular system and its connections adapt themselves, and once again the ground begins to feel firm beneath your feet.

Coordination of vision and movement is one of the miracles of the human brain. When the brain misfunctions, however, terrible things can happen. Consider the experience of the late comedian Terry Thomas, a man who once made the whole world laugh. Then, one day, Thomas's doctor told him he had *Parkinson's disease,* an illness marked by a deficiency of *dopamine.* Under ordinary conditions, dopamine acts as a messenger between brain cells (a neurotransmitter). When one cell communicates with another, a tiny "squirt" of dopamine is released into the cleft between the cells. It is then taken up by a special dopamine receptor on a second cell, and as a result the second cell is activated.

When dopamine is absent, as with Terry Thomas, things go terribly wrong. Many cells can't be activated, and as a result, they don't fire. This has specific and unfortunate effects on the patient with Parkinson's disease. Movements

Popular Questions About the Brain

Q: *Is it true that we only use 10 percent of our brains?*

A: The claim that we use only 10 percent of our brains probably originated from observations that people can recover from damage to large areas of the brain without noticeable effect on their behavior. However, it is also true that destruction of even a small proportion of other brain areas (such as the visual area) can have a devastating effect.

No one really knows how many neurons are contained within the human brain. For this reason alone, it is impossible to determine what percentage is used at any given time. Present technology is also insufficiently developed to measure the massive number of neurons involved in even the simplest activities. The honest answer to the question is: We just don't know.

Q: *What is the relationship of intelligence to brain size? Is the brain of a genius bigger than the brain of an average person?*

A: There is no evidence that "bigger brains" are associated with superior intelligence. In fact, we sometimes see just the opposite: Some forms of mental retardation may be associated with larger brains.

Q: *Is it true that every time you take an alcoholic drink you kill one hundred thousand brain cells?*

A: Alcohol as a neurotoxin (killer of brain cells) remains controversial. With the exception of absinthe, no popular alcoholic beverage has ever been convincingly demonstrated to be a neurotoxin. There is no doubt, however, about alcohol-associated damage to the brain. For instance, alcohol provides calories, which reduce a person's appetite. Therefore, many alcoholics ingest a deficient diet. The absence of B-complex vitamins leads directly to brain cell destruction, particularly in those areas concerned with memory and coordination. If the alcoholic can be persuaded to eat normally, a diet supplemented by vitamins, it seems that many pernicious effects of alcohol can be avoided.

Continued ingestion of alcohol, particularly in large doses, also brings about metabolic changes in the brain. The abrupt withdrawal of alcohol leads to a withdrawal syndrome—the DT's. It is likely that repetitive episodes of the DT's will produce brain damage.

begin to slow up, a tremor often appears, and one appears to slouch forward. Loss of elasticity and mobility of the major joints follows rapidly.

"The best parts of me now are my earlobes," Thomas once stated with wry humor. "They are still firm and muscular. But the rest of my body is all affected in one way or another by this syndrome."

Terry Thomas described in poignant terms what it is like to maneuver through a doorway a body afflicted with Parkinson's disease: "It was as though one's feet are glued to the ground. I tried tricks like dancing through, and sometimes they would work. And then one says, 'Well, that's good, that's settled,' and the next day you do it, and you fall. Fall on your arse."

For a while it seemed that a cure for Parkinson's disease was possible. In the late 1960s, scientists synthesized a chemical precursor of dopamine: *L-dopa.* It was found that if a patient with Parkinson's disease took L-dopa in high enough doses, many of the symptoms remitted. But, unfortunately, most of the improvements haven't been sustained. More and more of the medicine has been required to accomplish less and less.

In addition, flooding the brain with L-dopa is like trying to improve the public transportation system in a major city by giving everyone his or her own bus. In no time the highways become clogged with vehicles that interfere with the transportation of private cars, motorcycles, and so on. Too much L-dopa might interfere with other neurotransmitters in the same way that every person having his or her own bus would interfere with transportation. There are also other problems.

The drug's effect often wears off, sometimes at the most inconvenient time, leaving the patient literally frozen into a state of immobility. L-dopa also has profound effects on mood. Depression and inexplicable elations can interfere with sleep and mental stability. Finally, there is the suspicion—although at this point it is only that—that the drug may even be speeding up the destruction of cells in the brain that produce natural dopamine. For these reasons, scientists have been searching for ways to deliver a *tiny* dose of dopamine to the specific areas where it is needed.

At the University of Lund in Sweden, Dr. Anders Bjorklund has succeeded in transferring dopamine cells from an embryo of an unborn rat into an adult rat. He begins by surgically dissecting a portion of the midbrain that contains the dopamine-producing cells. The cells are tightly packed. In an area half a millimeter wide, there are more than thirty thousand dopamine-containing cells.

"The idea is to have these dopamine-containing nerve cells replace the ones damaged in the adult-operated animals, and in this way, hopefully, restore the motor function of these animals," Bjorklund commented during the filming of "The Brain."

After gathering the dopamine-producing cells, Bjorklund implants them into rats. Several of these implants have successfully reversed the rats' motor abnormalities, providing the equivalent of a "cure" for an illness in rats very similar to Parkinson's disease in humans.

"The important knowledge I think we have gotten from these experiments is that embryonic cells that are taken out at a very early stage of their own development can carry out their developmental programs in the new environment of a damaged brain," Bjorklund states.

It is important to point out here that neither Bjorklund nor anyone else in the world is carrying out a "brain transplant." Instead, only a part—albeit an important part—of the brain is being transplanted from one animal to another to make up for the inability of the damaged brain to produce a neurochemical, dopamine. Not that the procedure is without philosophical and ethical problems. For instance, some people already object to tampering with the brain, since it is the structural underpinning for the mind and perhaps even the soul.

"On that issue, I think it is important to realize that already today we accept manipulation of the nervous system," says Bjorklund. "Every drug that has action on the function of the brain is a way to manipulate it. And in many ways it may be a much more uncontrollable form of manipulating our minds than cell implants would ever be."

Bjorklund is quick to point out that transplants aren't necessarily a "cure" for Parkinson's disease. There are still too many uncontrollable variables. Where are the dopamine cells that will be used for implantation? How will transplant "rejection" be managed? Already two patients have undergone cellular implants. Nils Bergendahl says that while the operation didn't help very much, he would be willing to try again if his doctors asked him. Greta Skoglof feels that she can move about better now and on the whole feels her operation proved successful. These two severely impaired human beings, the first people ever to submit to the brain implantation operation, are helping researchers understand how movement is mediated in the brain and what happens when this incredibly complex system breaks down.

More extraordinary than the breakdowns and the neuroscientists' attempts at repair, however, are the marvelous performances of the brain when it works right: Picking up a glass of water or, like Greg Louganis, executing a perfect dive from a board 33 feet above the water.

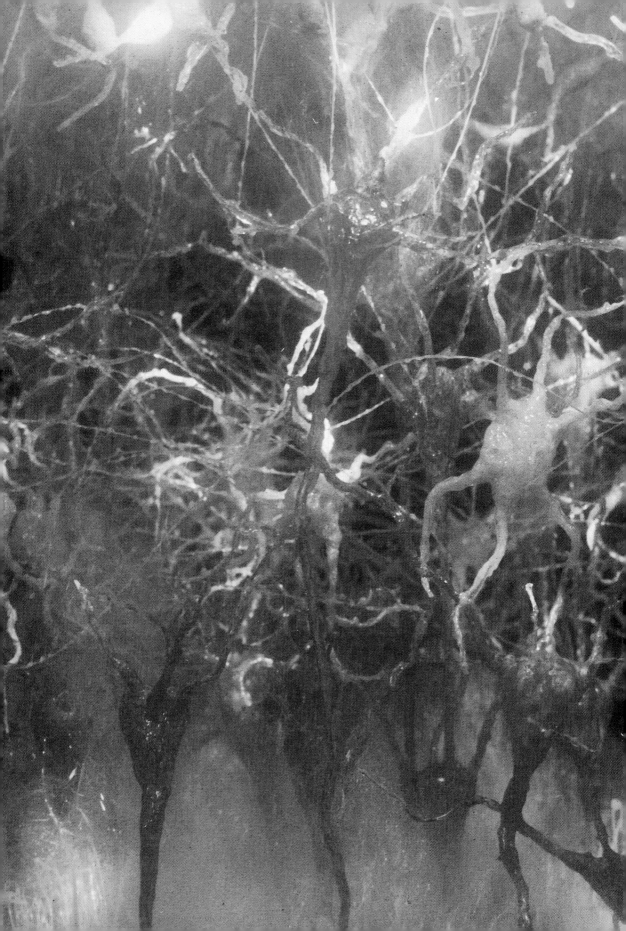

3.
Rhythms and Drives

The human brain is at once the most powerful and yet most helpless of biological organs. Although the brain can fashion vastly complicated theoretical systems of philosophy and physics, it is also profoundly affected by its internal and its external environments. If the levels of oxygen or glucose (sugar) within the blood decrease, the brain will cease to function. The brain, along with all living things, must also accommodate itself to an environment punctuated by powerful rhythms: day and night, summer and winter, high and low tides. In recent years scientists have discovered that one way the brain may do so is by fashioning powerful rhythms of its own.

It is now clear that these rhythms are crucial to adaptation. Disruption of these rhythms in humans, as we shall presently see, leads to serious consequences, ranging from a falloff in work productivity to sterility, even to murderous rage.

The most powerful environmental influences on biological rhythms are planetary movements. The rotation of the earth on its polar axis gives rise to the dominant cycle of day and night (the *circadian,* "about a day," rhythm). The revolution of the earth around the sun results in the progression of the seasons. The more complicated movement of the moon in relation to the earth and sun gives rise to the lunar month, and gravitational effects of both the moon and the sun produce tidal cycles.

Work carried out over the past quarter century has established that these four rhythmic environmental events have produced within all living organisms adaptations in-

An inhibitory neuron fires in the cerebral cortex.

Elephants testing strength.

volving self-generated biological rhythms. These rhythms often can be recognized by the changes they bring about in behavior.

- Every year, alerted by variations in water pressure related to tidal rhythms, a silver-green, six-inch-long fish common to the San Pedro region of California swims to the coast during the highest possible tide. Carried to shore on a wave, the California grunion mates, has her eggs fertilized by the male, and deposits them just below the sand. The fish then swim back to the ocean. Two weeks later, again at high tide, the eggs hatch and are carried out to sea.

- The breeding season in the Siberian hamster coincides with variations in the size of the male's testes, which grow and shrink every year in lockstep with springtime and fall. Some male ducks demonstrate changes in genital size even when kept in total darkness or constant light. Sheep kept in continuous light for three years breed at the same time as their counterparts raised under natural light conditions. These ducks and sheep possess a built-in sex-

Salmon leaping over a falls to reach their spawning grounds. In many species reproduction proceeds according to a "script" dictated by the genes of the organism.

ual rhythm. They have incorporated external environmental rhythms into their own genetic program.

• Many of the world's species of birds are migrators, flying unerringly to the same geographical location year after year.

• Tiny submicroscopic dinoflagellates flash on and off in the ocean according to a specific schedule.

• Plants move in clear concert with the cycles of light and darkness.

The most important external cue leading to the establishment of biological rhythms is light. Animals tend to be either diurnal or nocturnal, dividing their periods of rest and activity along the lines corresponding to dawn and dusk. Light in the form of shorter daytime hours tells the bear to begin its preparations for hibernation long before evenings turn chilly. In spring, light triggers the production of hormones in prairie dogs, thus beginning their cycle of reproduction. In nearly every land animal, light is the major *Zeitgeber* ("time giver"), with temperature a distant second.

Within the brain, various biological clocks respond to the passage of time. Some correspond to such powerful environmental rhythms as day and night.

In humans the situation is, of course, far more complicated. The development first of candles and then of electricity freed us from dependence on time cues provided by the sun. We have, in fact, so thoroughly removed light as an important variable in our lives that scientists believed for a time that light had little impact on our internal clocks and that, instead, sleep provided the critical cue. That is no longer the case. Strong light is now accepted as one of a huge number of external cues that may entrain, or modify, our internal rhythms.

One way of thinking about rhythms is to imagine gradually slowing down a piece of music until all you hear are incomprehensible sounds. Let's say you were listening to "The Star-Spangled Banner" and that over the course of several minutes all you heard were a few long, drawn-out notes. You would certainly not be aware of the fundamental rhythmicity of our national anthem, which would make it impossible to recognize.

In a similar way, most of us are not conscious of the intrinsic rhythms of our daily biological processes. But when we measure and chart some of these rhythms on a graph— such as a graph of our daily temperature or even of our sleep patterns—it is like speeding up the music. Suddenly we hear the rhythm and recognize the notes as part of our national anthem.

Imagine what it would be like if you could reduce a typical twenty-four-hour day into just two minutes. Think of it as looking at yourself in high speed, first playing, then eating, then sleeping or working. If you did this, let's say by having somebody videotape your whole day and then time-compressing it, you would probably begin to recognize the basic rhythms of your life. But you would notice that the time frames of these rhythms vary. Some last for seconds, others minutes, hours, days, weeks, and even longer.

Blood pressure shows as much as a 20 percent fluctuation during different times of the day and night, with the lowest blood pressure in the morning and the highest during the afternoon.

The number of white cells, the infection fighters within the blood, may vary by as much as 50 percent from one time to another. Such a fluctuation has practical implications: A drug that has the undesirable side effect of lowering the white-cell count may result in an overwhelming infection if given at the wrong time of day.

Cancer drugs in mice have been shown to vary in effectiveness, depending on when the drugs are administered in relation to cellular rhythms. Human cancers, too, have been observed to respond more favorably if radiation is administered when the tumor reaches its daily temperature peak.

Weight gain and loss often depend on when food is taken. It is a basic tenet among diet therapists around the world that the heaviest meals should be taken early in the day. The maximum weight gain occurs when heavily caloric meals are ingested late in the evening. Our ability to handle alcohol varies along similar lines: A drink early in the evening is less "intoxicating" than one consumed after midnight.

Although the existence of *ultradian* (more-frequently-than-a-day) rhythms isn't in any doubt, there is considerable confusion about their meaning. What is the "reason" behind the shorter, ultradian rhythms occurring in a range, say, between twenty minutes and six hours?

Dr. Serge Daan, of the zoology department of Groningen State University in Haren, the Netherlands, has studied short-term activity rhythms and believes many of them are phase-linked to eating and metabolic demands. Food may be scarce or abundant, depending on environmental circumstances. Grazing animals, therefore, stand to benefit from a regular rhythmic pattern of stomach filling, which protects them against scarcity. In addition, food may be difficult to process if all of it is taken at one time.

An even more intriguing explanation for ultradian rhythms concerns the existence of predator-avoidance patterns. In voles, Daan's area of special expertise, food-gathering carries with it the risk of death from animal predators. Since the risks may vary according to unpredictable factors, it's a good general strategy for all the voles to adhere to a fixed temporal schedule from day to day. In this way "safety in numbers" makes it less likely that a particular vole will be killed.

"A vole, taking his meal at the same time of day as his conspecifics [other voles], may have a slightly smaller chance of predation than if he chooses a different time," says Daan. "The rhythm may be the organism's way of guaranteeing that several variables of physiological and motivational state will reach appropriate levels in synchrony, which may contribute to an optimal coordination of behavior. . . . This may be one explanation of the circadian regulation of meals in voles."

In another field study conducted on the western coast of Spitsbergen, Serge Daan observed the patterns of three-week-old guillemots (diving seabirds) who jump from their breeding ledges on the cliffs to reach the sea. Even under conditions of constant daylight, the jumps occurred within a four-hour cycle. This period corresponded to the time when the foraging activities of predators (four varieties of arctic fox) were at their lowest, a time when earlier "guillemot meals" were still being processed within the foxes' intestinal tracts. The foxes were simply less interested in more guillemots.

In essence, Daan discovered that a behavior (the guillemots jumping into the sea) was phased-linked to occur during the period when the risk of death was at its lowest. How was this rhythm established? Where in the guillemots'

The meadow vole.

genetic program does such wisdom reside? And how is this transcribed into a message within the brain that alerts the newborn guillemot when it is safe to jump? Such questions are unanswerable now but are extremely intriguing.

The occurrence of such "reasonable" and even "intelligent" behavior suggests the presence of a "mind." Certainly, if you look at it from the point of view of the best course of action under the circumstances, the guillemots' behavior could hardly be improved upon. In fact, if you were put in the same situation of having to travel over treacherous terrain, you would do well to obtain the kinds of data the guillemot already has grasped intuitively. Who are my enemies? How can I best avoid them? Does the young guillemot therefore possess a rudimentary form of consciousness? We will return to this intriguing speculation later.

Imagine yourself standing in a room with hundreds of clocks all ticking independently of each other. The ticking creates a cacophony, jarring the ears and nerves. Now imagine the introduction of a kind of master clock that synchro-

Guillemots on the Farallon Islands.

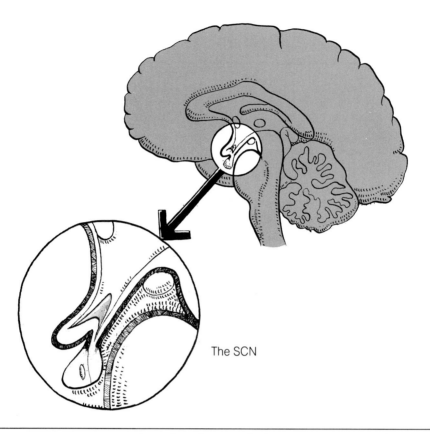

The SCN

The suprachiasmatic nucleus (SCN), nature's master clock, is located within the hypothalamus.

nizes the chaotic rhythms into one, much as a master program of a player piano sets in motion the cyclical melodies and themes that form a complete musical composition.

Researchers believe they have found such a "master clock" in a tiny center in the hypothalamus of most mammals, called the *suprachiasmatic nucleus* (SCN), an identifiable group of neurons comprising one of twenty-eight different nuclei in the hypothalamus. Two characteristics make it highly likely that the SCN is the "master clock." First, it has a clear, coordinated rhythm of its own, an endogenous rhythm it can maintain even as the tissues around it begin to lose theirs. Second, the SCN is the receiving station of information flowing from the eyes to the hypothalamus, a nerve pathway that carries information about environmental conditions of light and darkness to the brain.

The SCN in man is buried deep in the hypothalamic tissues rather than on the surface (as in, say, the rat). But even granting the existence of the SCN in humans, the puzzle of what purpose it serves is far from solved. Dozens of researchers around the world are currently struggling to discover what bodily processes are rhythmic and, in addition, how they are controlled. In the course of their work, they are amassing evidence suggesting that humans and other animals have not one but several *oscillators*.

Writing as far back as 1960, neurobiologist Colin S. Pittendrigh concluded: "We are forced, in fact, to abandon our common current view that our problem is to isolate and analyze 'the endogenous rhythm' or 'the internal clock' and are faced with the conclusion that the organism comprises a population of quasi-autonomous oscillatory systems."

What neurobiologists have discovered in the ensuing near quarter of a century supports Pittendrigh's view that different oscillators exist in different parts of the brain. Thus, if a master control like the SCN exists in man, it may directly control only certain rhythms, while at the same time acting as a coordinating oscillator, directing and unifying the actions of several other oscillators that are functionally connected to it.

But how many different rhythms exist within the human brain? What is their purpose? How are they organized? The breakthrough in our understanding of rhythms came when researchers began studying their subjects under conditions of sensory isolation. One of the clues that it is time to go to bed, for instance, is the setting of the sun and the arrival of darkness. But suppose a person is in a room where there are no windows or clocks? Suppose there aren't any clues when it is time to eat, work, or relax?

The first attempts to create such an artificial environment were carried out in the 1960s in an underground bunker in Munich, Germany, and in deep caves in France. Today, more sophisticated studies on the body's rhythms are carried out in aboveground laboratories and soundproof isolation chambers. Here, scientists concerned with bodily rhythms can monitor their subjects' cycles and can even modify the cycles by making judicious changes in the experimental situation.

When placed in these sensory-deprived environments, subjects exhibit free-running rhythms that approximate the twenty-four-hour cycle but differ from it to a greater or lesser degree according to species. Humans, for instance, exhibit rhythms that average about one hour longer than the usual twenty-four-hour cycle.

After a period of isolation from the usual time cues most human beings settle into a twenty-five-hour period of rest and activity. In most instances the metabolic and behavioral cycles of the body keep in step. But not everyone exhibits a twenty-five-hour cycle. Some subjects shift into forty-eight- to fifty-hour cycles—twice the normal rhythm— staying awake and alert for from thirty-three to thirty-six hours and resting between fifteen and twelve hours. In most instances this doubling of the length of the "typical day" passes unnoticed. This happens even with experienced cave experimenters such as Michel Siffre, who in 1962 and again in 1972 spent six months in a cave.

Michel Siffre at the conclusion of a six-month cave experiment.

"I was thinking that since I was a scientist, I could better control my data and reactions. And, in fact, I could not. I became confused between the twenty-four-hour cycle and the forty-eight-hour cycle."

But Siffre wasn't the only experimenter who doubled his sleep-waking times. In 1966, a two-pack-a-day smoker participated in a cave experiment. After shifting to a forty-eight-hour rhythm, the experimenter continued to smoke two packs, only the time period was now two packs every two days (forty-eight hours) instead of every one day! Although at first glance this might seem a neat way to cut back on the number of cigarettes smoked, cave experiments exert far too many other stresses on physical and mental health for them to qualify as substitutes for Smokenders. For instance, Siffre now feels that it took five years to recover from the psychological effects of his cave experiments: the complete isolation, the silence, the drifting in and out of sleep without time cues, the panics. He compares the experience to the technique of brainwashing, wouldn't repeat his experiments now for "one million dollars on the table," and warns that by isolating a person from his usual time cues "you can break a man completely."

Our usual rhythms of wakefulness and sleep, centering around twenty-four hours, seem to exert a stabilizing effect on our physical and psychological health. A disruption in this rhythm may come as a result of different body rhythms breaking free from their usual synchrony and taking on a new pattern, much as a symphony musician would eventually do if separated from his orchestra during a performance by a thick wall.

A similar shift occurs whenever researchers try to switch their subjects to a day longer than twenty-seven hours or shorter than twenty-three hours. Soon other rhythms normally synchronized around a twenty-four- to twenty-five-hour cycle desynchronize from their rest-activity rhythms. As a result of such studies, researchers have concluded that under normal circumstances our usual rhythms are easily capable of deviating from our internal twenty-five-hour cycle to the environment's twenty-four hours—a change triggered by such things as temperature, light, mealtimes, work schedules, and, not to be neglected, social cues. (If I find myself standing outside my girlfriend's apartment holding a bottle of champagne and a dozen red roses, the "nine o'clock" reading on my watch is more likely to refer to evening rather than morning.) But there are limits to the brain's ability to alter body rhythms. If a more drastic change of, say, five hours is demanded as a result of transatlantic travel, the synchronization breaks down and one or more "subordinate" oscillators in the body break away to establish rhythms more consistent with their own internal signals.

Jet lag is at least partially explained as the result of our internal clock "remembering" that it is bedtime back home. For this reason, international travelers who fly across time zones make accommodations for the changes. If important decisions must be made, they give their internal rhythms a few days to adjust to changes in environmental cues that can affect such things as mental alertness and mood. (After a five-hour time-zone change, it takes, on average, three days for all of the "body clocks" to be reset to the new local time.)

Most of us can classify ourselves according to whether we wake early and do our best work in the morning— "larks"—or whether we are "owls," who find it hard to start the day, but once we get ourselves together can work even into the wee hours of the next morning. Such differences in life-style correlate with both personality and body temperature.

The "lark," it turns out, is usually more introverted and shows an earlier temperature rise in the morning. The "owl," in contrast, is more extroverted and maintains his or her body temperature at a slightly elevated level later into the evening. But whether we are "owls" or "larks," we all experience a "postlunch dip," a slight falloff in our mental alertness at about 1:00 P.M. This time lag in mental performance seems to have nothing to do with what we eat for lunch. In fact, it happens even if we skip lunch entirely. Nor is it correlated with the one- or two-martini lunch, since teetotalers are just as susceptible as those who get slightly "smashed."

While we are on the subject of alcohol, there is also a circadian rhythm in the rate at which our body metabolizes the stuff. If alcohol is consumed earlier in the evening, it disappears from the blood more quickly. Between 2:00 and 7:00 A.M. alcohol is metabolized at the slowest rate. This is also the period when most of us are asleep and mental activity is at its lowest ebb. But if we are awake, we can count on the alcohol remaining in our blood the longest and thereby most adversely affecting our performance (another good reason for not drinking and then driving after late-night parties).

Mental performance is also correlated with body temperature. As we saw with the "larks" and the "owls," body temperature does not remain at the proverbial 98.6 degrees. It varies by about 0.5 degree Centigrade (1 degree Fahrenheit) over twenty-four hours, with the lowest temperature in the early morning. This has relevance, once again, to when we are best able to engage in certain activities. Performance and tests of mental arithmetic or reaction time are at their poorest in the early morning, which happens to correspond to when our body temperature is its lowest (except in the case of some "larks"). Does this mean that a lower body temperature "causes" mental efficiency to nosedive? Not exactly. The notion of one thing "causing" another, while it is a useful explanation for understanding why mechanical gadgets break down, has limited use when dealing with the human brain. It is more helpful to think of the rhythms of body temperature, mood, sleep, and alertness as closely interrelated. Knowing something about how they interrelate allows us to act more "rationally" when we plan our lives. Research indicates, for instance, that workers who have just changed their shifts do poorer work and are more susceptible to injuries than those who maintain a steady schedule.

The greatest disrupter of our natural circadian rhythms is the industrialized, urbanized world most of us inhabit. For instance, during the past hundred years, a mere instant on the evolutionary time scale, major changes have taken place in the schedules of the U.S. work force. One out of four men and one out of six women in the United States now has a variable work schedule, including both daywork and nightwork. Part of the reason stems from the need for round-the-clock operations in many industries, where an eight- or twelve-hour "downtime" would reduce productivity to unacceptable levels. With an increase in the number of people living in cities, the demand has risen for workers who are willing to adapt themselves to changing schedules. Emergency police and fire services must be ready at any time to respond to natural or manmade disasters. Unfortunately, both the workers and their employers have forgotten our dependence on those natural rhythms to which the brain has trained itself over millions of years.

"What has been forgotten in this headlong pursuit of progress is a lot of our history. We have evolved, like all other living organisms, on a periodic planet, a planet in which the sun is up and out during the day, and it is dark at night," according to Dr. Charles Czeisler of Harvard University and the Center for Design of Industrial Schedules in Boston, Massachusetts.

Czeisler goes on to point out that virtually all known organisms from simple-celled plants to mammals and humans exhibit prominent daily cycles or rhythms in virtually all physiologic functions. "Now what happens when we try to upset the applecart and sleep during the daytime and work at night is that we throw all these functions completely out of whack.

"A shiftwork schedule can wreak havoc on physiological timing systems that control the release of hormones, control the timing of when we sleep and when we wake, even control the timing of when we feel alert and when we feel ready for sleep," says Czeisler. Many shiftworkers report that they feel "lousy" most of the time, cannot function at work, and have difficulty staying awake on the job.

"When they get home and they are exhausted and would like to sleep, they find that they can't. It is because they are trying to sleep at a time of day when the body is trying to wake them up. The internal alarm clock is basically 'going off' at the time when they are trying to go to sleep. Later they find themselves trying to work at the time that their body is trying to put them to sleep. With frequent shifts in work schedule, they never have time to adjust to their shifts because it takes the body at least a week to adjust to an eight-hour time-zone change."

Significant differences exist in the tolerance people have for working or sleeping on abnormal schedules. When schedules entailing shiftwork were first adopted by the munitions industry during World War I, eight times as many nightworkers developed stomach ulcers as their day-shift counterparts. Ensuing studies over the years have failed on the whole to demonstrate differences quite that dramatic, an effect many experts on circadian rhythms attribute to the process of self-selection in any shiftwork. Those who find they can't cope with night-shift schedules simply switch to other jobs. Although such self-selection makes it difficult to draw firm conclusions about humans, animal studies leave little doubt of the harmful effects of abnormal work and sleep schedules. Laboratory animals subjected to a six-hour phase shift of their light-dark cycle every week (which cor-

responds roughly to a rotating shiftwork system) show a 20 percent reduction in their life expectancy.

There are plenty of reasons in humans, as well, to suspect that shiftwork takes a physical and a psychological toll on workers: insomnia, gastrointestinal problems, tension within the home, irritability, and depression are common among shiftworkers. Over 80 percent report that it takes from two to four days or more for their sleep schedules to adjust to the rotations. Twenty-five percent of the workers interviewed by Dr. Czeisler in a potash plant in Ogden, Utah, confided that they were *never* able to adjust. In an attempt to improve matters, Czeisler was asked to design a more sensible work schedule for Ogden.

As a starter, Czeisler rearranged the workers' schedules so that the weekly shift rotations were lengthened to once every three weeks. In addition, he altered the rotations so that work hours would follow the natural circadian rhythms of the brain. Since the brain operates on a twenty-five-hour rather than a twenty-four-hour cycle, it is more natural to conform to a schedule that calls for the worker to shift forward rather than backward. For instance, an 8:00 A.M. to 4:00 P.M. schedule is best followed by a change to 4:00 P.M.

Dr. Charles Czeisler on the site of the Ogden potash plant.

to midnight, not 12:00 midnight to 8:00 A.M., as usually happens in most factories.

"Day shift to night shift to evening shift is one of the most common schedules in the United States for people who do rotating shiftwork," says Czeisler. "And that schedule turns out to be very disruptive to the various systems which time the release of hormones, which time the daily changes in body temperature and alertness, which time the very sleep-wake cycle itself, because the natural tendency of those systems is for the sleep time to drift to later hours."

Czeisler's suggested changes involved nothing more elaborate than providing a work schedule that worked *with* rather than *against* the circadian rhythms. The result for

Work schedules that account for our body's natural rhythms lead to increased productivity. Abrupt shifts to night-time work can result in higher numbers of accidents.

that potash plant has included greater worker productivity and a decrease in personnel turnover. Three out of four of the workers reported they prefer the new shift rotation, while 27 percent claimed improvement in their health (fewer visits to doctors, fewer colds and other illnesses).

"One might ask, 'What did we learn about the human brain in Ogden, Utah?'" says Czeisler. "And what we learned was that you can't ignore a basic area of the brain that is controlling the timing of an intrinsic physiologic function like when we sleep and when we wake. Here in Ogden, Utah, we learned that you have to keep in mind how the brain functions in controlling when we sleep and when we wake in setting up any kind of round-the-clock schedule for continuous operation."

Airplane disasters, misjudgments in Pioneer space probes, acts of medical malpractice, ship collisions—these are just some of the catastrophes that can be directly traced to errors in judgment associated with alterations in circadian rhythms. But the most famous instance of a circadian rhythm disturbance that may have caused a disaster was the nuclear accident at Three Mile Island.

At about 4:00 A.M. on a March morning three operators in the control area of the nuclear power station made the first of several mistakes. Fourteen seconds into the accident one controller failed to notice two warning lights. A few seconds later, all three failed to notice that a valve that should have closed had stayed open. Later, investigators of the Three Mile Island accident placed the blame squarely on the operators, all of whom were involved in a work schedule that could be guaranteed to disrupt one or more of the circadian rhythms. The time of 4:00 A.M. also corresponds to the time of least efficiency and alertness for most people, a fact that the commission investigating the accident was aware of, at least implicitly.

"Throughout the first two hours of the accident, the operators ignored or failed to recognize the significance of several things that should have warned them that they had an open valve and a loss-of-coolant accident." The commission concluded that "except for human failures, the major accident at Three Mile Island would have been a minor incident."

Since circadian rhythms exert such a powerful influence on our behavior, it should come as no surprise that research scientists have recently discovered that the rhythms also influence certain forms of mental illness.

It has been known for centuries (in fact, as far back as Sir Robert Burton's *Anatomy of Melancholy,* published in 1621) that many depressives suffer most in the morning. Suicides occur commonly in the early hours. (Ernest Hemingway, who suffered from cyclic depressions, shot himself in the chill dawn hours.) Now scientists of the clinical psychobiology branch of the National Institute of Mental Health in Bethesda, Maryland, think they know why mood disorders display such diurnal variations.

Under normal conditions our dominant circadian pacemaker utilizes such environmental cues as sunlight to make the necessary adjustments that bring us into synchrony with the external, twenty-four-hour, day-night cycle. Dr. Thomas A. Wehr believes that this process is out of sync in patients with certain forms of depression. Rather than just speculating, however, Wehr and his colleagues at the NIMH tested their theories by studying their depressed patients' sleep-waking rhythms within the sleep laboratory.

In normal sleep, episodes of *rapid eye movement* (REM) sleep occur about every 90 to 120 minutes during the night. The REM periods themselves last 10 to 60 minutes and are followed by *nonrapid eye movement* (NREM) sleep for another 90 to 120 minutes; then the process repeats itself. Typically, the longest REM sleep periods occur late in the night. This concentration in the latter part of the sleep period results from a circadian rhythm whereby REM sleep is maximal near dawn. In certain depressive reactions the normal nighttime pattern is reversed: Increased REM activity occurs early in the sleep period, and in contrast to what is encountered normally, the first REM period may be the longest. In manic patients the findings are just the opposite—it takes longer than normal for REM sleep to begin.

A dramatic example of this phase shifting in REM and NREM sleep was discovered from the study of a fifty-seven-year-old woman with alternating periods of *depression* (low mood) and *mania* (heightened mood and affectivity). In this patient, sleep onset and the appearance of the first REM period progressively changed according to her mood at the time. In the depressed phase of her illness, REM came on early, and it appeared at a later time when she shifted into a manic state. These changes in REM onset and mood were paralleled by corresponding advances and delays in the timing of the circadian temperature rhythms, which reached its maximum five hours later in depression than in mania.

Wehr's treatment consisted of waiting until his patient was in the midst of a depression and at that point altering her sleep pattern. On four different occasions approximately two weeks apart, the patient was put to bed six hours earlier. Two days after the first six-hour shift (the sleep time had been advanced from the normal 11:00 P.M. to 7:00 A.M. to a new 5:00 P.M. to 1:00 A.M.), the patient's depression cleared up completely. But two weeks later she relapsed. A second six-hour phase advance (a bedtime period from 11:00 A.M. to 7:00 P.M.) produced a similar improvement.

According to Wehr, his patient's improvement resulted from a sudden alteration in the internal phase relationships between the sleep-wake cycle and other circadian rhythms—a situation reminiscent of the jet lag that accompanies eastward travel. His patient's relapses, in turn, resulted from the reestablishment of the disturbed internal-phase relationship.

Left at this, the treatment would seem self-evident: Simply put patients to bed six hours earlier each time they become depressed. Wehr tried that, but with disappointing results. After a third and yet a fourth six-hour phase advance, the patient remained deeply depressed. Temperature data suggest an explanation for these failures.

Although the patient's circadian temperature rhythm advanced along with the first two advances in the sleep-wake cycle, it became delayed after the third and fourth shifts. The advance of one rhythm (sleep-waking) coupled with the delay of another (temperature) in response to a schedule shift resulted, Wehr believes, in the reestablishment of the same pathologic phase relationship between temperature and sleep that characterized depression. "We are presently exploring the idea of combining shifting the timing of sleep or the amount of sleep with drug treatment because we hope that we can get an immediate response with sleep deprivation, which only takes one day to work, and a sustained response by adding drugs. Together, these two avenues of approach may provide the patient with a sustained recovery," Wehr said.

Studies at the NIMH and elsewhere suggest that at least some of the symptoms of depression and mania may be due to changes not just to sleep and temperature but in the timing of other circadian rhythms as well.

There are twenty-four patterns of secretion for *growth hormone, thyroid stimulating hormone* (TSH), *adrenocorticotrophic hormone* (ACTH, which stimulates the adrenal to put out cortisol), and *testosterone* (the male sex hormone), to name but a few. Each of these hormones has its own rhythm, reaches a peak at certain hours of the day, and then drops to a low point from which the level rises once again. It is thought that the secretion of these hormones is linked by mutually interacting rhythms that, like the individual musicians in a symphony orchestra, can lose their sense of time, each in his or her own way. In depressives, the twenty-four-hour secretion of cortisol, for instance, occurs during the first half of the sleep period—just the opposite to what happens in those not suffering from a depressive disorder.

Nor are circadian rhythms restricted to hormones. Studies of the neurotransmitters within the brain, notably *norepinephrine* and *serotonin,* follow clear-cut circadian rhythms as well. These cycles, which have been discovered only within the past two decades (the first studies on circadian rhythms date only as far back as the 1960s), provide an explanation for observations about disturbed behavior that can be traced back to antiquity.

- Mania and depression in women often occur in relation to their menstrual cycles, an observation that has already gained credibility in the courtroom via the defense of premenstrual tension syndrome (PTS).

- As many as one third of those suffering from cyclic depressions or mania demonstrate an annual or a seasonal pattern. In the days before circadian rhythms were understood, these mental alterations were informally referred to by psychiatrists as "anniversary reactions." Many elegant psychological theories were spun to account for why certain patients suffered mental relapses at certain seasons of the year. It is now thought more likely that relapses are linked to seasonal rhythms and the duration of daylight.

The Bear That Became a Butterfly

Pat Moore suffers from seasonal depression. Every winter she loses interest in life, spends more time sleeping, is less energetic and less motivated. "I was always under the impression that my grandfather must have been a bear. I did the equivalent of gathering nuts, only I ate, gained weight, went to sleep through the winter, I woke in the spring a little bit grumpy. Now I have turned into a butterfly, and I have never seen a bear yet that turned into a butterfly!"

Pat's transformation came about by means of changes in the brain induced by decreasing amounts of daylight. During the prolonged darkness of winter, when the nights are longer, signals are sent from the hypothalamus to the pineal gland. Melatonin is then secreted. In winter, when the level of melatonin is high, Pat experiences a kind of hibernation. In the spring, when the level of melatonin drops off, Pat lightens up, becomes more motivated, and turns into her "butterfly."

Dr. Norman Rosenthal, a psychiatrist at the National Institute of Mental Health, has studied more than seventy patients with symptoms of winter depression. He reasoned that if sunlight could suppress melatonin, altering seasonal rhythms, then something as simple as a bank of high-intensity, full-spectrum lights (grow lights) might help patients with symptoms like Pat Moore's seasonal depression. To test this hypothesis, Pat Moore awakened at 4:00 A.M. and sat in front of the lights for about two hours each morning. Within three days her depression lifted. "The lights have taken me out of hibernation. I feel like something has been turned on in my brain that says I am awake, it is time to live." The regular winter use of grow lights puts Pat Moore's hypothalamus, and hence her moods, into a summer schedule.

Pat Moore

If you put your forefinger just above the bridge of your nose, you will be separated from the hypothalamus and the *pituitary,* which dangles from it, by only a few inches of bone (this location is responsible for the pituitary's name, a distortion of the Latin word for nasal secretion). In naming the pituitary, the anatomist Vesalius assumed that it discharged mucus. Instead, the pituitary discharges far more important substances: the hormones that control the *endocrine system* and that are responsible, in large part, for the maintenance of the body's basic rhythms mentioned earlier.

Our knowledge of the hypothalamus has emerged over the centuries in piecemeal fashion. In the mid-nineteenth century a pathologist personally examined thirty thousand brains and noted that any abnormality within a specific section of the hypothalamus was apt to be associated with an ulcer. Somehow the brain—at least that part of it known as the hypothalamus—correlated with what was going on in the digestive tract, several feet away. A curious idea.

Later another hypothalamic connection was observed in a patient who had gained an inordinate amount of weight while at the same time exhibiting a total loss of sexual desire. This was an even more curious correlation. Is the brain somehow related to sexuality?

During tuberculosis epidemics, patients who slipped into a coma were often found to have damage in the hypothalamus. But this wasn't properly correlated with wakefulness until later, when surgeons operating on the brain learned to their dismay that a slight tugging on the hypothalamus, even the gentle application of a tiny sponge, would plunge the patients into a coma from which they might never awake.

Digestion, body weight, appetite, sexuality, wakefulness—these are only some of the body processes that came to be associated with the hypothalamus. Blood pressure, pulse, and temperature also were affected if the hypothalamus were handled too insensitively during surgery. Neurosurgeons soon learned to move very carefully with their probes and scalpels. "The operation was a success, but the patient died" is an apt description of many otherwise competent operations in which surgeons have run afoul of the hypothalamus.

From observations of corpses, the sick, and the dying, from patients under the surgeon's knife—in this piecemeal fashion, a picture of the hypothalamus began to emerge. A small area, by weight only about one three-hundredth of the brain, the hypothalamus is involved in an astounding number of rhythmic bodily activities.

For years scientists have recognized that the hypothalamus exerts proprietary control over the pituitary. For instance, if the blood supply from the hypothalamus to the pituitary is cut off in an experimental animal, the reproductive organs atrophy and permanent sterility ensues. The same thing can happen in humans as a result of a stroke or an accident. From such observations we can conclude that something is being transported through the rich network of blood vessels connecting these two structures. But what is it, and how does it work?

The first breakthrough in this area came in 1971, when *gonadotrophin-releasing hormone* (GnRH) was identified as the specific chemical messenger in the hypothalamus. The discoverer, Andrew V. Schally, was awarded the Nobel Prize in Physiology and Medicine in 1977 in part for his finding that the hypothalamus secretes GnRH into the blood supply feeding into the anterior pituitary, which then releases its own hormones into general circulation to stimulate the testes in men and the ovaries in women.

Under ordinary conditions the hypothalamus in the brain, the anterior pituitary, and the *gonads* (sex organs) are engaged in a kind of three-way conversation. After unsuccessfully treating several patients suffering from sterility (resulting from hypothalamic lesions) with doses of gonadotrophin-releasing hormone, it was plain that things were a lot more complicated than anyone had anticipated. When GnRH was given, either continuously or via a series of infrequent injections, the normal patterning of the pituitary failed to reestablish itself.

The next discovery—by far the most critical in terms of practical application—was that the anterior pituitary secretes its hormones in a pulsatile, rhythmic fashion.

"The pituitary functions much like a strobe light, blinking on and off throughout the course of the day," according to brain researcher Dr. William Crowley. "And it is this rhythmicity that is essential for normal function. And, in addition, the hypothalamic message—this chemical message of the gonadotrophin-releasing hormone—must be applied in an intermittent fashion. To administer it in a continuous fashion, or to give it as infrequent injections, results in a nonphysiologic patterning of the pituitary and gonadal function. But to administer it like a strobe light in a pulsatile rhythm results in normal functioning of the pituitary and, in turn, normal functioning of the gonads."

Crowley had an opportunity to put these theoretical ruminations to a practical test when he encountered Mitch Heller, an engineer who wanted more than anything else to become a father.

"In 1978 I was involved in a car accident. A few months later I wasn't interested in sex any longer; I had lost all my chest hair," Heller recalled as he sat in Dr. Crowley's office at Massachusetts General Hospital in Boston.

Heller's difficulties stemmed from the failure of his hypothalamus to secrete GnRH, which Heller attributes, probably correctly, to the head injury he experienced in the car accident. What made his situation so unique and led to his referral to Dr. Crowley's unit at Massachusetts General Hospital was that, with the exception of his recently acquired sterility, Mitch Heller was perfectly normal.

"When he was first seen, it appeared that the defect was isolated to the reproductive hormone in the hypothalamus—that is, the gonadotrophin-releasing hormone," recalled Dr. Crowley.

"And that was extremely interesting, because all other hypothalamic functions were perfectly normal. He seemed to have an isolated defect in this area of reproductive function, which had, in turn, shut down pituitary secretion of gonadotrophins and had extinguished his gonadal-testicular function."

Dr. Crowley was well aware that simply providing Mitch Heller's pituitary with GnRH wouldn't be enough. If Heller were to realize his dream of becoming a parent, it was necessary to devise a way of delivering the GnRH according to the same rhythmic pattern that exists under normal conditions. Mitch still recalls Dr. Crowley's explanation of how, working together, they could restore the normal brain rhythm.

"The primary failure is that of a hypothalamus and gonadotrophin-releasing hormone. We have had a breakthrough in that area in the last decade in which that hormone is now made available by a research program that we are involved in here to treat patients. The advantage of that is that this hormone, when administered in the proper fashion, will stimulate your own pituitary to make your own gonadotrophins to stimulate your own testicle," Dr. Crowley said.

To mimic the brain's own rhythms, Dr. Crowley modified a device used for many years by diabetics to self-administer insulin. In Mitch's case GnRH rather than insulin was the operative chemical.

Dr. William Crowley, left, explaining the use to the GnRH pump to Mitch Heller.

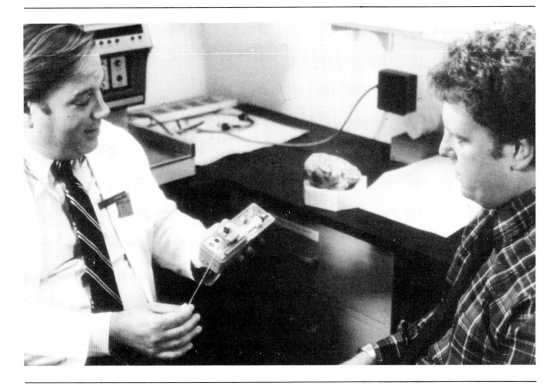

A syringe filled with GnRH was connected to a needle inserted just beneath the skin of Mitch's abdomen. The system was then connected to a small pump that delivered GnRH to the tissues just below the abdomen every two hours, both day and night. From there, GnRH was absorbed into the bloodstream and eventually found its way into the pituitary.

Since the hypothalamus secretes around the clock, it was necessary that the system be in place at all times. Mitch recalled the results:

Mitch with his wife, Debbie, and their daughter, Tovah.

"All of a sudden, two to four weeks after I had started using the pump . . . my interest in sex was back. I noticed a growth of chest hair was coming back as well."

Although this was encouraging, Dr. Crowley took a conservative approach and reminded Mitch that it took about seventy-seven days before the first signs of spermatogenesis would appear. Until then, assurances could not be made in regard to Mitch's main concern: "being a man again."

"After an analysis taken on the seventy-sixth day, they found some semen," Mitch Heller recalls; "it was very exciting." This was not nearly as exciting, however, as developments that occurred after five and a half months of treatment. The day after he was told his sperm analysis registered several million sperm, Heller learned from his wife that she was pregnant.

"And nine months later we had the most wonderful thing happen to us! We are extremely excited over Tovah. She is very special because she is the first child ever born under these circumstances and because we never thought we'd ever be able to have a baby."

The birth of their daughter Tovah was not only a milestone in the life of Mitch and Debbie Heller, it was also the first time scientists had ever been able to prove conclusively that sexual reproduction in humans depends on an inherent rhythmicity within the brain.

"The bottom line of all this research really is that the restoration of his reproductive function and behavior was tied intimately to the rhythms and the pulsatility of hormone secretion," said Dr. Crowley. "And in fact it seems that all restoration of reproductive processes hinges on the critical delivery systems of intermittent pulsatile or rhythmic hormonal presentation to the body."

Mitch Heller's case illustrates one of the ways in which the rhythmic processes within the hypothalamus can go awry, providing disruptions in both sexuality and reproduction. But most important of all, there is now hope that such technical breakthroughs as Dr. Crowley's "portable hypothalamus" may make it possible for other people to have an experience similar to Mitch Heller's on the occasion of the birth of his daughter.

"I was present at the delivery, although I didn't see much very clearly, because the tears of happiness were just totally filling my eyes as Tovah was born," Mitch said. "And there was immediate bonding, immediate love. And we knew that it was just one of the best things that had ever happened to us. We now had a daughter, and through the help of Dr. Crowley, we had created a life, just a beautiful, most perfect life."

The true story of Mitch Heller and Tovah epitomizes the kind of happy ending doctors and screenwriters dream about: science and medicine humanistically applied to bring joy into people's lives. The Hellers' happiness was made possible because of what neuroscientists have learned about the brain's inherent rhythms and how they can be modified. Over the years, some scientists have suggested that other aspects of our lives may follow a similar pattern. For instance, is there an inherent predisposition toward violence and aggression? Is there an "aggressive drive" that, like the "sex drive," might be modified by modifying some part of our brain?

In the 1920s Dr. Walter Rudolph Hess of Switzerland (no relation of the infamous Rudolph Hess of Nazi Germany) began a systematic investigation into the hypothalamus of cats. Hess's work, which won him the Nobel Prize in Physiology and Medicine in 1949, involved mapping the responses elicited by stimulation of 4,500 different sites in 480 cats, principally within the hypothalamus. The cats were fully awake and restrained only by connecting cables.

Initially, Hess and an American investigator, Stephen W. Ranson, who was working independently in the United States on similar research, were much concerned with locating sites within the hypothalamus responsible for blood pressure, breathing, and heart rate, as well as for the dilation and constriction of the pupil of the eye.

As his research progressed, Hess became more interested in more complex activities: temperature regulation, vomiting, sleep, and wakefulness. From here he began to stimulate his animals in a search for areas concerned with hunger, fight or flight, rage, defensive reactions, and so on. Late in his career Hess became convinced that stimulation of the hypothalamus was eliciting natural states.

He divided hypothalamic function into two separate systems, anterior and posterior. The anterior was responsible for restorative functions such as sleep and digestion. The posterior area was concerned with the regulation of the emergency responses required when an animal was threatened: an increase in heart rate, an elevation of the blood pressure, an enhancement of muscle tone—in fact, just about any bodily activity not ordinarily under conscious control but that might "aid the organism's greater success in its conflict with the environment."

But Hess soon discovered that stimulation of the posterior hypothalamic area brought about behavior that went far beyond the mere alteration of a few bodily functions. In his Nobel Prize acceptance speech Hess spoke of his observations:

"On stimulation within a circumscribed area of the *ergotropic* [posterior hypothalamic] *zone* there regularly occurs a manifest change in mood. Even a formerly good-natured cat turns bad-tempered; it starts to spit and, when approached, launches a well-aimed attack. As the pupils simultaneously dilate widely and the hair bristles, a picture develops such as is shown by the cat if a dog attacks it while it cannot escape . . . functionally, the total behavior of the animal illustrates the fact that, in the part of the diencephalon indicated, a meaningful association of physiological responses takes place, which is related on the one hand to the regulation of internal organs and on the other involves the functions directed outwards towards the environment."

In essence, Hess was suggesting that aggressive behavior could be elicited by electrical stimulation of part of the hypothalamus. Hess was not alone in his contention. A similar point was made by the Spanish neurophysiologist José Delgado. A handsome and brilliant brain researcher with a flair for the dramatic (he once stopped a bull in full charge by activating a radio-controlled electrode deep within the bull's brain), Delgado described in the early 1950s how cats reacted with fear after stimulation of several different areas in their brain.

Other researchers enthusiastically followed suit, and by the mid-1950s brain research laboratories around the world were jammed with electrode-containing rats, pigeons, chickens, rabbits, cats, dogs, guinea pigs, monkeys, dolphins, and even goldfish. Each researcher had his or her favorite experimental subject selected from this veritable Noah's Ark. Soon a firm body of knowledge was in place about the effects of stimulation on various parts of the brain. It was shown, for instance, that stimulation of the *reticular formation,* an extremely extensive neuronal network within the brainstem, produced a hyperalert animal. But if things went too far and the reticular formation was destroyed, just the opposite effect resulted: coma.

What interested the brain researchers the most, however, was that animals could be conditioned to avoid certain situations as a result of an aversive electrical stimulation.

Dr. José Delgado interrupting a bull's charge by means of remote-controlled electrical stimulation.

Rhythms and Drives

But this was only half of what we generally understand as *motivation.* What about forms of attraction, something positive to offset the avoidance behavior? Is it possible that animals might go out of their way to obtain stimulation in other brain areas? This curious idea that "pleasure centers" exist within the brain received experimental confirmation by accident.

Dr. James Olds of the Montreal University Department of Psychology was attempting to discover whether stimulation in the reticular formation resulted in aversive behavior. An electrode aimed for the reticular formation was accidentally bent during the implantation procedure, and it ended up a long distance from its intended site; the electrode lodged instead in the hypothalamus. The rat was then placed in a small cage. At this point the most peculiar things began to happen. These are Olds's exact words:

"I made the test in a relatively open situation, which permitted the animal to show both approach and avoidance. The rat was free to move around on a fairly large tabletop enclosure (three by three feet or more). A pair of stimulating wires was planted in the brain; it was aimed to affect the arousal or activating system, but it missed and landed in an area near the hypothalamus. I applied a brief electrical stimulus whenever the animal entered one corner of the enclosure. Surprisingly, the animal did not stay away from that corner, but came back quickly after a brief sortie that followed the first stimulation, and even more quickly after a briefer sortie that followed the second stimulation. By the time the third stimulation had been applied, the animal seemed indubitably to be 'coming back for more.'

"Later this same rat furthered my view that the electrical stimulation was rewarding by moving toward any part of the enclosure chosen by an independent observer, provided only that I turned on the switch whenever the animal took a step in the right direction."

It is fascinating to think that were it not for Olds's clumsy surgical technique we might have been spared Skinner boxes, behaviorism, and dozens of *New Yorker* cartoons poking fun at a whole generation of researchers who implied that human personality can be adequately understood by reference to rats running around in cages seeking out rewarding experiences via self-induced brain stimulation. Even our language would have been affected. For one thing, there would be no "rat race" to describe our occupational gripes. But Olds's failure to hit the target *did* occur. And its effect on brain research has been nothing less than staggering.

"In terms of dramatic impact and the amount of theoretical speculation and experimentation generated, no single discovery in the field of brain-behavior interactions can rival the finding that animals could be highly motivated to stimulate certain areas of their own brain," says neuroscientist Elliot Valenstein.

What is most important for our purposes in this chapter is the location within the brain of sites capable of eliciting both the "aversive" and the "reward" experiences. The latter sites tended to be in the lateral portions of the hypothalamus and the limbic system. The "punishment-aversive" system, on the other hand, is along points closer to the midline of the hypothalamus and its connection with the limbic system.

The suggestion that there is a balance in the brain between areas of reward and those of punishment has a faintly medieval ring to it—good vs. bad; the powers of light vs. the forces of darkness, and so on. If that sounds too fanciful, consider the words of the English philosopher Jeremy Bentham, who wrote in 1789: "Nature has placed mankind under the governance of two sovereign masters, pain and pleasure. It is for them alone to point out what we ought to do, as well as to determine what we shall do."

Whatever else may have influenced Bentham to make such an assertion, we can be certain that he didn't get his inspiration from brain research. In 1789 the most eminent brain researcher, Luigi Galvani, was totally preoccupied with studies of the muscular contractions of dead frogs. In a way, this suggests that social and political theories are miles ahead of the work of brain researchers. But I wonder if that is entirely so. I prefer to think of it in terms of a predisposition on our part always toward thinking in opposites: good and bad, painful and pleasurable, and so on. Since this is the way our mind works, these are the kinds of observations that come naturally to brain researchers: The animal must be either seeking pleasure or avoiding pain. Only years later, after the enthusiasm for "rat experiments" had died down sufficiently, were other brain researchers able to make a rather mundane but nevertheless extremely important

Since the pioneering research of Hess and Olds, scientists have continued to study the brains of cats and other animals by means of electrical implants. Here, in slides taken from the work of Dr. Allan Siegal, typical emotional display (hissing) is elicited by stimulating the hypothalamus (above). When the lateral hypothalamus is stimulated, the response is a quiet biting attack (below).

observation: If the animals are simply left alone in their cages (without interfering needles rammed into their brains) and if they aren't forced to press levers or engage in other circus tricks, the animals simply lead the lives of rats.

The concepts of reward and punishment, aversion and reinforcement exist in our minds and not in theirs. Our brains are predisposed to perceive, think, and act along certain lines because our brains are constituted the way they are. If our brains were constructed differently, we would think differently. If this sounds too theoretical, I can assure you it has practical applications: Think how many rats could have been spared the effort of stepping on pedals and pushing buttons just to prove that Jeremy Bentham was right.

Of the many brain-stimulation experiments that followed the work of Drs. Hess and Olds, the most interesting concerned aggression. Hess's original observation of a cat turning "bad-tempered" and then launching an attack represented only one form of aggression. If you have ever watched a cat toy with a mouse before killing it, you have witnessed the other form. You have also learned firsthand that aggression isn't always accompanied by spitting or hissing. Nor does the cat's back arch as if in a rage. Rather the cat stalking a mouse involves a more cold-blooded, calculated killing, termed by scientists "predatory aggression" or a quiet, biting attack.

In general, these two types of aggression are activated by different portions of the brain, with separate pathways extending from the hypothalamus down to the lower brainstem. Stimulation anywhere along these separate pathways elicits either a quiet, biting attack or transforms the cat into a raging, hissing ball of fur.

The hypothalamus is a regulator of the pathways subservient to aggression even as they extend down the brainstem. It in turn is regulated by parts of the limbic system above it. As we progress in the limbic system down through the hypothalamus and then farther downstream into the brainstem, the intensity of the stimulus required to elicit aggressive behavior begins to diminish. This hierarchical arrangement is reflective of the interconnectedness of neurons within the brain. As subsequent research showed even at the level of the rat, to say nothing of higher primates and man, there is no "aggression center" or "antiaggression center." Instead there is a network of neuronal connections, beginning in the limbic system and traveling downstream, that integrates and organizes aggressive behavior.

But the idea that specific brain areas are capable of producing predictable behavior on command died a slow death. Delgado's stopping of the charging bull, which comedian Tom Lehrer referred to as "a thousand pounds of angry pot roast," convinced some observers at the time that a center capable of inhibiting aggression had been found. In actuality, electrical stimulation of the bull's *caudate nucleus* was thought only to have brought about forced head turning. It is speculated that as its head was forcefully turned to the side, the bull became confused and slightly disoriented rather than less "aggressive."

When it comes to the more primitive drives such as aggression, the brain is like a mosaic in which only the complete aggregate of seemingly unrelated parts suggests the whole picture. If we think about it, that hypothesis makes a good deal of sense. Although a cat may react aggressively to rats, dogs, other cats, and teasing children, it reacts differently to each one. The character of its aggression changes according to the environment perceived by the cat. It does not merely flail at every noxious stimulus in the same way.

Investigation into drives such as aggression inevitably reveals a complex portrait involving brain pathways mediated by specific chemicals (neurotransmitters and neuromodulators); external sensory stimuli, which provoke the "aggressive behavior"; and complicated social hierarchies, which alter or altogether inhibit any expression of aggression.

In humans the picture also involves control and inhibition mediated by our cerebral cortex, principally the frontal fibers. There are customs and laws, spoken and unspoken prohibitions against the direct expression of aggression. Some people believe that our culture even provides ritualized, acceptable forms of aggression that help hold our own aggressive impulses in check. But for every exponent of this view you might meet at ringside on a Saturday night, there are dozens of others who consider boxing and other forms of ritualized aggression "dehumanizing" and more likely to *excite* rather than dampen our own aggressive impulses. Even the depiction of violence on television and in the movies may lead to subsequent violent behavior, according to a report by the National Institute of Mental Health.

"Watching violent programs at an early age is a better predictor of aggression or violent behavior when these young children become adolescents than almost any factor," according to Dr. David Pearl, director of the NIMH project on violence and TV.

Other studies point to a similar effect. In a study in London, England, of 227 possible causes of violence in society, television and movie violence was labeled as No. 1. Although this is hardly the place to settle the debate about whether observations of violence actually lead to violence, there is no doubt that violence persists in our society despite our best reasonable efforts to control it. One of the reasons might be that in some individuals the cerebral cortex exerts only a limited modulatory effect on the aggressive "drives." It must be remembered that the limbic system and its interconnections form the structural underpinnings upon which the cerebral cortex is imposed. We are not just thinking, reasoning creatures. We also *feel*. We experience anger, envy, hostility, and love. We often do what our best

Anger. When the forces of inhibition are relaxed by alcohol, people sometimes show an aspect of themselves that they later regret when "sweet reason" returns. The cerebral hemispheres are largely responsible for inhibition and their influence is diminished by alcohol.

judgment tells us not to do. It is also true that we are "reasonable" creatures, capable of language and symbolization, and it is certainly true that there are certain things only we can do. Have you ever heard of a chimpanzee filing for bankruptcy? But despite some of the marvelous and not so marvelous performances resulting from the contributions of our cerebral cortex, we remain dependent to a large extent on the underlying, more "primitive" parts of our brains.

Incidentally, some researchers prefer the term "ancient" to "primitive," and I think for good reason. The negative connotation doesn't fit the facts. The development of atomic weaponry, for instance, is the product of our "advanced" cerebral cortex. Yet thermonuclear war is more "primitive" than anything ever dreamed of by our "primitive" evolutionary ancestors, who engaged in warlike activity only for the short-term advantage of food or territorial appropriation. It is only the more "advanced" human beings who have harnessed their brains, via the cerebral cortex, to the task of utter destruction. Certainly there is no doubt that our aggressive "drive," if there is such a thing, is capable of a destructiveness of diabolical proportions. Therefore, it is reasonable that scientists continue to search for the brain mechanisms involved in aggression. Can we ever learn to harness our aggressive drives?

Unlike what we have seen in cats, where highly specific areas are concerned with different aggressive "styles," aggression in humans follows different patterns principally controlled by our cerebral cortex. Social and psychological factors play a key role. In some countries a man can justify murdering his wife by proving she was unfaithful to him. Some religions expressly forbid violence of any kind. But physiology also plays an undeniable if controversial role, as we see in those cases where people who have committed violent crimes within our society are found to have abnormalities of the brain. It is assuming a lot to claim that these abnormalities are *the* cause of the aggressive behavior. Still, in some cases there are tantalizing suggestions that human aggression is associated with certain specific abnormalities.

In 1980 in Sacramento, California, a twenty-one-year-old man, Mark Larribas, referred himself for psychiatric care because of his suicidal impulses. Two days earlier,

Dr. Paul D. MacLean
and the Triune Brain

If we remove the cerebral cortex—that part of our brain that has evolved over the past two million years or so—we essentially eliminate our humanity. Beneath the cortex is a brain that is not far different from that of a Bengal tiger, a French poodle, or an Arctic fox. We could, if we wish, remove even more to approximate the brain of a salamander or a rattlesnake.

Brain researcher Dr. Paul MacLean holds that we have three separate, intimately interconnected "brains" that reflect our ancestral relationship to reptiles, early mammals, and later mammals. The first, the R-complex (the "R" refers to reptiles), is an expansion of the upper brainstem. Within this complex are the neural mechanisms responsible for behavior involved in self-preservation and preservation of the species. By experimenting with the R-complex in animals as far-ranging as squirrel monkeys and turkeys, Paul MacLean has shown that it contains the programs responsible for hunting, homing, mating, establishing territory, and fighting. The second "brain"—the limbic system, which we share with all other mammals—deals with the emotional feelings that guide behavior. After destruction of part of the limbic system, young mammals "cease to play and there are deficits in maternal behavior," says Dr. MacLean. "It is as though these animals regress toward a reptilian condition."

The third "brain," the cortex, is most highly developed in humans. It is a kind of problem-solving and memorizing device to aid the two older formations of the brain in the struggle for survival. Dr. MacLean compares the cortex to a "computer" that can look into the future and anticipate the consequences of actions. The cerebral cortex furnishes us with our most human qualities: our language, our ability to reason, to deal with symbols, and to develop a culture. The prefrontal areas of the cortex are the most highly developed. Dr. MacLean considers the development of the prefrontal fibers the most auspicious turn of events in the history of biology. "It is this new development that makes possible the insight required to plan for the needs of others as well as the self, and to use our knowledge to alleviate suffering everywhere. In creating for the first time a creature with a concern for all living things, nature accomplished a one-hundred-eighty-degree turnabout from what had previously been a reptile-eat-reptile and dog-eat-dog world."

Dr. Paul MacLean

A sketch suggestive of the physical organization of the triune brain.

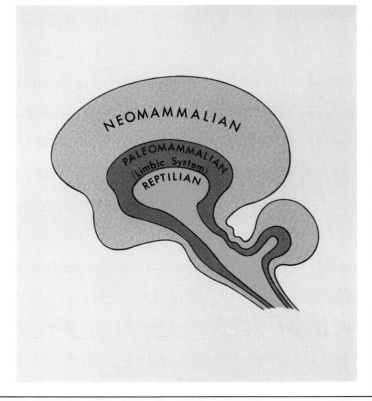

while baby-sitting with his girlfriend's two-year-old daughter, Larribas had lost control of himself in response to the child's "constant crying." Within seconds he flew into a rage, then beat and choked the child until she was unconscious. Similar episodes of loss of control had occurred in the previous year. On one occasion an argument with his wife resulted in an explosive fist-wielding assault that led to their marital breakup.

"When I hit my wife, it would be just like something I couldn't control. Like getting into a car accident on an icy road and the car loses control and there is nothing you can do to stop it. And then afterwards I would feel a lot of remorse, and I would find myself crying and begging her forgiveness."

When questioned about his temper outbursts, Mark Larribas had difficulty recalling the exact sequence of events. But he was aware of an increase in irritability, impulsivity, and sudden, often unpredictable, shifts in mood. Aside from these outbursts, Mark Larribas was described as easygoing. He held a steady job and maintained a good work record.

Based on the strange contrast between Mark Larribas's usual behavior and his angry outbursts, the psychiatrist in charge ordered a CAT scan of his brain, which showed a large lesion at the tip of his right temporal lobe. At surgery this mass proved to be a curable rather than a malignant brain tumor, and it was removed with remarkable results.

Over the ensuing two years of Mark Larribas's life, there have been no further outbursts—in fact, no impulsivity of any kind. He is now able to concentrate, and he tolerates frustration without recourse to violence.

The tumor in Mark Larribas's brain corresponds in location to areas from which aggressive behavior can be elicited in test animals after electric stimulation. Although there may be many social factors involved in Mark's case, his dramatic improvement after this removal, as well as the tumor's location, strongly suggest a correlation between the tumor and Mark's behavior. The psychiatrist who diagnosed Mark's tumor concludes: "The case of Mark Larribas clearly shows that the pathology of the brain can be associated with violent behavior. More fundamental, it seems to me, is the issue that the brain itself has the capacity for aggression and violence. Perhaps with different settings, different stimulations, different states of brain function, any of us could have done what Mark did." Although this conclusion is somewhat shocking, there are precedents for it.

Perhaps the most famous is the case of Charles Whitman, who in the 1960s climbed to the top of a tower in Austin, Texas, and began shooting at passersby. He killed seventeen people. Harvard neurosurgeon Vernon Mark believes there is a link between a brain tumor and Whitman's murderous assault.

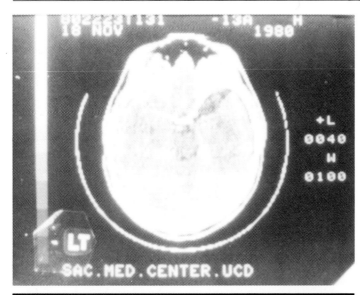

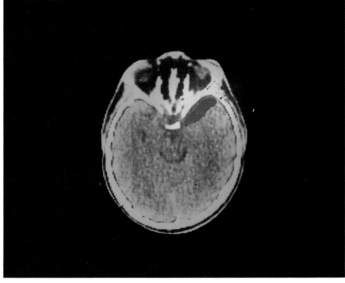

This CAT scan reveals the tumor that afflicted Mark Larribas. Below, the lesion becomes apparent to the untrained eye through enhancement techniques.

"Whitman had displayed a striking behavior change for the few months prior to the incident. He even went to see a psychiatrist. But in those days nobody thought in terms of physiological causes. A postmortem later showed that he had [a] brain tumor. But people were still reluctant to make the connection between the tumor and his violent behavior! Today we know better than that."

Dr. Mark is a specialist in violent patients, and he has learned firsthand how limbic system disease can stimulate violent behavior. "I once had a patient who tried to decapitate his wife and daughter with a meat cleaver. He was so violent the police had to bring him in wrapped in a fishnet. His family explained that his personality had started undergoing a change about six months earlier. And he had been complaining of headaches and blurred vision. A neurological exam showed that he had a tumor underneath the right frontal lobe pressing directly on the limbic system. We removed the tumor, and the patient had a dramatic reversal in behavior."

Outbursts of violence caused by abnormalities of the limbic system aren't all limited to brain tumors. Far more pervasive causes in contemporary America are mind-altering drugs. *PCP* ("angel dust") is associated with sudden impulsive outbursts. Such chemicals exert their primary effect on the hippocampus and cerebral cortex, sometimes leading to a massive discharge of aggression.

Although studies of the brain can tell us a lot about aggression, this *doesn't* imply that neurology has all the answers to why people are aggressive. But since the brain is the mediator of all behavior, it is important that we know as much as possible about its normal function. One way of going about this involves measuring the levels of brain neurotransmitters within aggressive animal subjects and then comparing the results to humans. Animal studies, for instance, show that a decrease in the neurotransmitter serotonin coincides with a rise in aggressiveness. An increase in norepinephrine and dopamine, two other major neurotransmitters, leads to the same result.

A study of twenty-six enlisted Navy personnel conducted in the 1970s showed that the least aggressive sailors generally had a higher level of *serotonin metabolites* (breakdown products) in their spinal fluid than those sailors given to fistfights, job conflicts, and so on. This suggested a possible approach to the control of aggression—the use of an agent capable of boosting serotonin levels in the brain.

Researchers over the years have reported that *Lithium,* a drug originally introduced for the treatment of gout, exerts a calming effect on aggressive animals. Putting Lithium into the water of Siamese fighting fish, or within the drinking water of male rodents, reduces aggressive behavior while it increases brain and serum Lithium levels. Similar results occur in mice, who, on the whole, become no less active than usual, only less aggressive.

Observations on the antiaggressive effect of Lithium aren't limited to laboratory situations but have been made in more "naturalistic" settings. Male rats, for instance, are extremely possessive and protective of homesites and will lash out at male intruders who dare to enter their lair. They lose this aggressiveness when Lithium is placed in their drinking water.

In an intriguing experiment, Dr. Michael H. Sheard, of the Department of Psychiatry in Yale University School of Medicine, administered a serotonin-lowering agent, *PCPA* (quite different from the notorious PCP), to a group of rats. This chemical depletes the brain supply of serotonin by inhibiting one of the enzymes involved in its synthesis. Rats treated with PCPA show a marked increase in aggression, which can be prevented if Lithium is given five days *before* the PCPA.

Based on findings in animals that Lithium is capable of inhibiting aggression, psychiatrists in several centers in the United States are administering Lithium to aggressive prisoners. There are several reasons for doing this. For one thing, Lithium is reasonably safe, if carefully monitored. Second, if similar effectiveness could be seen in humans, the benefits would be incalculable.

To test the effectiveness of Lithium, Dr. Joe Tupin, of the Department of Psychiatry in the University of California at Davis School of Medicine, selected twenty-seven inmates from the maximum-security prisons at Vacaville and Sacramento, California. All of the subjects, despite differing backgrounds, offenses, and reasons for referral to maximum-security prisons, shared two behavioral traits: (1) recurrent violence, both inside and outside prison, and (2) extremely rapid reactions of anger and violence to slight provocation.

Over the next nine months each of the prisoners was maintained on Lithium at a fairly high dose. The results showed a decline in disciplinary action for violent behavior. Among fifteen of twenty-two subjects, the number of disciplinary acts for violent behavior were reduced. Even more interesting than the decrease in violence, however, were the reports offered by several of the prisoners in Dr. Tupin's study. One man stated, "Now I can think about whether to hit him or not." Another said, "I have lost my anger." Each of the Lithium-dosed prisoners demonstrated an increased capacity to reflect on the consequences of his actions, a quality Dr. Tupin refers to as a "more reflective mood."

"In our society we are currently concerned about criminal assault and aggression. Certainly, this has been a major focus of the research I have done. With this research we can now understand parts of the brain, how medication may affect it, and can draw a hypothesis about the role of neurotransmitters in different functional areas of the brain and how it may cause or lead to specific kinds of aggression. In humans, almost always this aggression occurs as an interaction between brain disturbance, if it is there, and social situations. Either alone may be enough to cause aggression, but the focus of our concern is with brain dysfunction and disease," according to Dr. Tupin.

The key question remains whether Lithium or any other chemical agent is capable of extinguishing "aggressive behavior" in humans. There are several reasons that make this unlikely.

For one thing, experimental work has shown that aggression is not a unitary entity with a concrete existence. "The 'aggression' studied in different situations is not homogeneous," according to Dr. Paul F. Brain, of the Department of Zoology, University College of Swansea. "It consequently seems most unlikely that one will find a common underlying physiology for these behaviors which conserve offensive/defensive or even predatory functions. Most current workers recognize that 'aggression' is the result of value judgments supplied to the output resulting from the complex interplay between biological, situational, and experiential determinants."

Added to the neurobehavioral factors is the ambivalence in our society about aggression. Although we all fear physical assaults and look for innovative ways to protect ourselves against muggings and other violent crimes, we are also insistent that our lawyers be aggressive on our behalf. We are willing to pay high prices to attend professional football, boxing, or other sporting events in which aggression is an essential ingredient for success. And who would employ a sales force or hire a public-relations firm that isn't aggressive? Despite our most vehement claims to the contrary, we wouldn't want to eliminate aggression from our lives entirely, even if we could. This ambivalence shouldn't discourage us, however, from trying to *understand* aggression. And one of the most promising corollaries of investigation is the role of sex hormones in aggression.

Centuries ago farmers were aware that belligerent male animals could be calmed by castration, which, as we now know, eliminated the source of the male sex hormone testosterone. Castration also can be employed to prevent the appearance of aggression in animals at particular times. Male mice, for instance, begin fighting around the time they become sexually active (thirty-five to fifty-five days of age). Castration at birth prevents the onset of this aggressive behavior. Injections of synthetic or natural *androgens* (sex hormones), particularly testosterone, will restore aggressiveness. Based on findings such as these, some researchers have studied testosterone levels in groups of people recognized as aggressive.

The study of testosterone levels in university wrestlers found that winners had higher levels of the hormone than losers did. A similar study of aggression in hockey players noted a correlation between serum testosterone levels and ratings of aggression as determined by coaches and other players. But by far the most intriguing findings came from monitoring the testosterone levels among prisoners confined for aggression-related offenses.

Testosterone levels were measured in three groups: aggressive, nonaggressive, and socially dominant (manipulative and self-assertive but not given to physical violence). The plasma level of testosterone in the nonaggressive group was no higher than is found in the normal population. The aggressive group had levels almost double those found in normals and far in excess of the levels characteristic of the manipulative, socially dominant, but nonaggressive prisoners. On the basis of such findings, should society reintroduce castration as a means of curtailing violence? There are several reasons why this is a bad idea.

Putting aside the ethical and legal issues involved in performing a mutilating and irreversible operation on a human being, there is little reason to believe castration would "cure" aggression. Humans and nonhuman primates are as much dependent on learning and social variables as they are on precise hormonal levels. Although it is true that we are strongly influenced by our hormones and their rhythmic fluctuations from day to day, we are also able to use our cerebral hemispheres to control and even to counteract these rhythmic hormonal variations.

The powerful forces of society and our ability to exert conscious control over our environment free us from the overt domination of nature. But our conscious thoughts and actions are constantly modified by a barrage of signals from internal sources. Our situation is very similar to that assigned us by some of the medieval theologians, who placed man somewhere between angels and beasts. We have a limbic system; we are affected by rhythmic waves of hormones throughout our body; we have centers within the brain from which hatred and aggression can be reliably elicited. To this extent we are beasts. But with the development of the cerebral cortex, it became possible for love, altruism, and a sense of community, trust, and integrity to enter mental mechanisms for the first time. Like angels we are capable of "pure thought"—if by that we mean that ideas and concepts can exert a powerful force in determining the course of our lives. What makes our situation so unique and, I would argue, superior to that of either angels or beasts is the peculiar blending of the most primitive and most sophisticated possibilities within a single organ, our brain.

Simone de Beauvoir once said: "We are the beings whose nature it is to have no nature." She was wrong. We have a "nature," and it is provided us by our genes, our brain, and the society in which we find ourselves. We are also very much under the control of internal and external rhythms by which we must learn to live. Our lives are dependent on learning to exist within the constraints imposed by sleep-wakefulness, activity, growth, sexuality, and even aggression—all created within us by the rhythms of our brains. Fortunately, neuroscientists are finding new ways of overcoming some of these constraints. Thanks to the new discoveries about the brain discussed in this chapter, patients such as Mitch Heller and Mark Larribas are no longer at the mercy of rhythms and drive. To this extent, the study of the human brain is true humanism: knowledge about the brain leading to an increase in freedom and self-understanding.

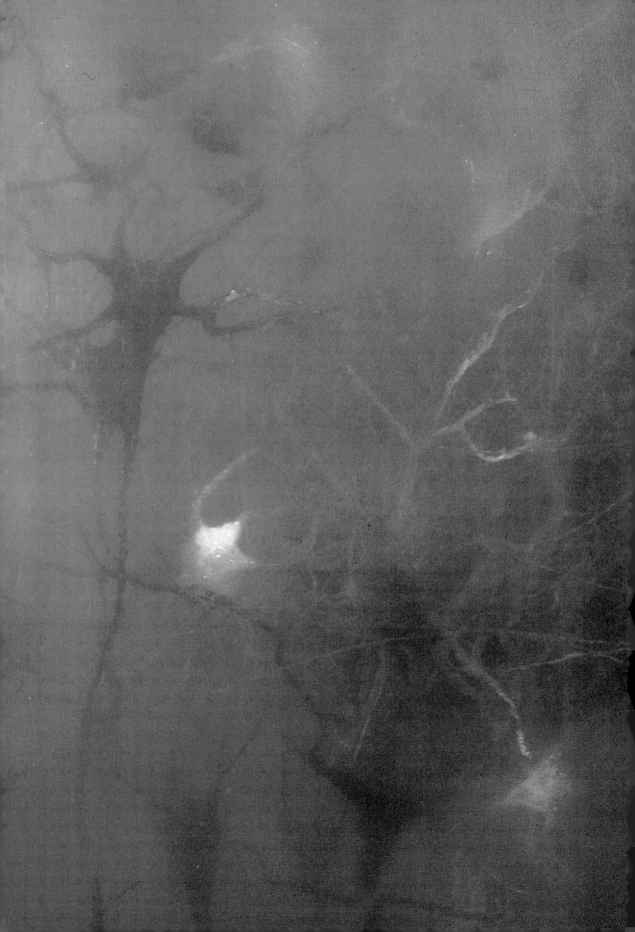

4.
Stress and Emotion

On September 13, 1848, a work crew on the Rutland and Burlington Railroad was blasting rock out of a gorge in Cavendish, Vermont. The crew's foreman was Phineas Gage, an energetic and capable man of twenty-five, well liked by his men and respected by his employers.

At 4:30 P.M., Gage was charging a hole drilled in the rock, filling it with gunpowder in preparation for blasting. His men worked behind him, loading rock on a nearby platform car. With the powder in place, Gage picked up a specially made tamping iron, a heavy rod three and a half feet long, flattened at its business end and pointed at the other. Gage then instructed his assistants to pour sand in the hole to trap any sparks set off by the iron as it descended toward the powder.

A few seconds later, Gage heard a noise behind him and turned slightly to his right. His assistant, also distracted by the sound, hesitated before pouring the sand. Unaware of this, Gage turned back to his task and let the tamping iron drop into the charged hole. As it descended, the tamping iron scraped the shaft and struck a spark, which ignited the powder.

Gage's tamping iron shot out like a cannon ball. It struck Gage beneath his left eye, tore through his skull and frontal lobe, and exited near the midline, just above where hair meets forehead. The iron flew fifty feet into the air before landing in the dirt, covered with blood and brains.

Gage himself was catapulted up into the air and backward, landing on the ground with a hard thud. Almost immediately his body began to shake in a convulsive seizure.

Drugs such as Valium (shown in blue) work in the brain by changing its chemical "soup," thus altering activity within the neural network.

Gage's crew, meanwhile, stared in horror at their supervisor, certain he could not possibly survive such an injury. But within minutes the crew witnessed something unbelievable: Gage began to speak. Suppressing their shock and disbelief, his men placed Gage on a nearby oxcart. Moments later, with Gage sitting upright, holding his head in his hands, they were on their way along the three-quarter-mile route to the Adams Hotel in Cavendish.

On arrival at the hotel, Gage astonished his men even further by stepping from the cart and sitting in a chair on the hotel's piazza, still holding his head.

Within a few minutes the local doctor, Edward H. Williams, reached the Adams Hotel. When Gage saw the doctor, he looked up from his chair. "Doctor, here is business enough for you," he said. Within several minutes a second physician, John Harlow, drove up. The medical men were as incredulous as the spectators, who, by this time, were lining up to stare at Gage. It hardly seemed possible that anyone could survive such a devastating wound. But Gage was not only alive, he was also sitting up in a chair, challenging his doctors in a good-humored way to do something to help him.

With some assistance, Gage walked up three flights of stairs to an attic room, where his wounds were cleaned and dressed. Detached bits of brain, bone, and skin were removed from the wound area. At one point Dr. Harlow passed the full length of his index finger into the wound without meeting any obstruction. As late as ten o'clock that evening the bleeding still continued, and the doctors feared that perhaps the blood loss could never be stanched. Nevertheless, Gage declared that he would be back to work within a few days. Then Gage became delirious, his temperature rose, and for the first time since the accident he talked "out of his head." But as the blood loss ceased and his temperature dropped, Gage became rational once again—a state of affairs the doctors attributed to liberal doses of calomel, castor oil, and rhubarb.

Over the next several weeks Gage's progress was slow but steady. By the sixty-seventh day after the accident he started wandering around Cavendish, buying supplies, and preparing for a trip to visit his mother in Lebanon, New Hampshire. But while Gage's physical recuperation was almost complete, his personality had undergone a profound

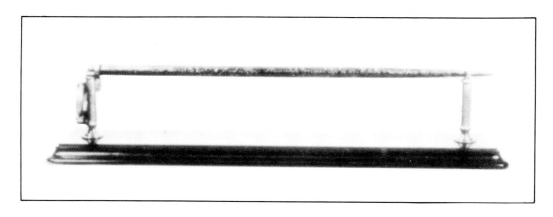

alteration. Dr. Harlow's notes provided the first indication of the change.

October 15th (32nd day) . . . *Intellectual manifestations feeble, being exceedingly capricious and childish, but with a will as indomitable as ever; is particularly obstinate; will not yield to restraint when it conflicts with his desires.*

October 20th (37th day) . . . *Sensorial powers improving and mind somewhat clearer, but very childish.*

November 15th (64th day) . . . *Is impatient of restraint and could not be controlled by his friends. . . . Yesterday he walked half a mile, purchased some articles at the store, inquired the price, and paid the money with his habitual accuracy; did not appear to be particular as to price, provided he had the money to meet it.*

Years later, Dr. Harlow had gained sufficient perspective on Gage's personality transformation to summarize his impressions: "The equilibrium, or balance, between his intellectual faculties and animal propensities, seems to have been destroyed. He is fitful, irreverent, indulging at times in the grossest profanity (which was not previously his custom), manifesting but little deference for his fellows, impatient of restraint or advice when it conflicts with his desires, at times pertinaciously obstinate, yet capricious and vacillating, devising many plans of future operation which are no sooner arranged than they are abandoned in turn for others appearing more feasible. A child in his intellectual capacity and manifestations, he has the animal passions of a strong man. Previous to his injury he possessed a well-balanced mind and was looked upon by those who knew him as a shrewd, smart businessman, very energetic and persistent in executing all of his plans of operation. In this regard, his mind

The tamping iron that struck Phineas Gage.

was radically changed, so decidedly that his friends and acquaintances said he was 'no longer Gage.' "

The rest of Phineas Gage's life was sad. True to his promise, Gage returned to his employers and requested his old job back. But his contractors, who once regarded him as a very efficient and capable foreman, now considered the "new Gage" unfit for the responsibilities of a foreman. They turned him away.

During 1849 and 1850 he was in Boston under the observation of a Harvard surgeon who made a name for himself describing Gage's wounds. Oftentimes during these visits Gage could be seen sitting at the entrance of the Boston Museum with the tamping iron resting between his knees.

Later, Gage hooked up with P. T. Barnum and performed in fairgrounds and circus tents around the country. He was a pathetic sight, holding in his arm the tamping iron responsible for the wound that had, for all intents and purposes, destroyed him. By 1851 he was working in a livery stable in New Hampshire. A year after that he drifted to South America, where he made his living as a coach

Gage's skull and death mask reveal the extent of the wound.

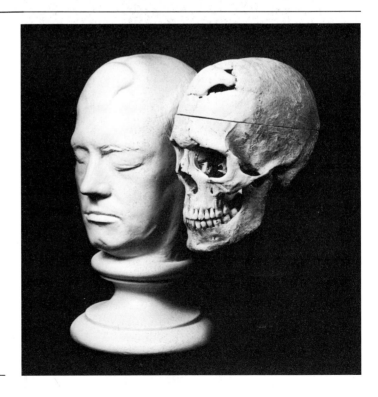

driver. Finally Gage returned to the United States, where he died in 1861, twelve years, six months, and eight days after the accident.

Although Phineas Gage was ultimately judged a "failure" by those who knew him, he bequeathed the world a much more bounteous legacy than a stretch of railroad: His injury and the effects it had on his personality provided the first clear indication of the delicate physical balance within the brain between thought and emotion.

Based on observations and writings about Phineas Gage by Dr. Harlow and others, neuroscientists in the 1930s began experimenting on the effects of surgical lesions on the frontal lobe fibers on each side of the brain. The most famous experiment was carried out by Yale physiologist C. F. Jacobsen on two fierce chimps, Becky and Lucy. After frontal lobe surgery (lobotomy) the chimps no longer reacted by scratching or biting when handled. When teased, the animals seemed not to care.

When Jacobsen presented his findings at an international conference, a visiting neurologist, Egas Moniz, decided to apply the same operation to agitated and violent patients under his care in Portugal. His decision to use human beings in surgery that was known to be safe and effective only with chimpanzees was possible both because of the similarities between human and primate brains and because of the looseness of regulatory control on experimental surgery in the 1930s. Today such an intrusive and irreversible operation would be unthinkable. But the operation was carried out, and the results were impressive. Patients given to excitement, agitation, and in some cases physical assaults on their keepers underwent a dramatic change. Like Becky and Lucy, in the wake of the operation they became relatively unconcerned about events around them, slow to anger, in fact slow to express any emotion. To this extent the early *prefrontal lobotomies* could be hailed as "successful."

On the whole, however, psychosurgical operations turned out to have exacted an unacceptable cost. Many of the patients were changed so utterly that their friends and relatives experienced difficulty accepting them as the same individuals they knew before the operation. But an even larger contribution to the decline of psychosurgery has been made by new discoveries about the frontal lobes and their connections with the rest of the brain.

In recent years the artificial division between thoughts and emotions has begun to give way. Anatomical studies reveal extensive connections between those parts of the brain traditionally associated with our emotions, the limbic system in particular, and the frontal lobes.

When the frontal lobes are damaged or destroyed, a person's ability to synthesize signals from the environment, assign priorities, or make balanced decisions is impaired. Once the frontal lobes disconnect from the rest of the brain, the limbic system is free to fire its messages of emotion. The control made possible by the frontal-limbic connections is weakened, and behavior becomes erratic and unpredictable. The exact details of just how this happens remain cloudy. What does become clear is that even tiny changes in the physical, chemical, and electrical state of the brain can lead to significant shifts in behavior. And since brain nerve fibers serve as conduits for neurochemicals and electrical impulses, damage to the frontal lobes can bring about chemical imbalances at far distant sites within the brain.

Common to all forms of frontal lobe damage are changes in the experience and expression of emotion. Although some patients, such as Phineas Gage, plunge phrenetically into endless rounds of oftentimes purposeless activity, others sit for hours suffering from what their neurologists refer to as "aspontaneity." This mélange of behaviors often is as perplexing to the neurologists who seek to understand the frontal lobe as it is to the patients themselves. "The clinical picture associated with lesions of the frontal region still remains the most baffling section of psychoneurology," wrote the late Russian psychologist Aleksandr Luria.

Part of the difficulty in understanding the frontal lobes derives from the mystery that surrounds our emotions. Why do we feel the way we do? Where do our anger, our infatuations, our griefs spring from? Such questions are unanswerable, even on the psychological level. For instance, it is impossible to experience an emotion in isolation. We can't experience the emotion of love unless we love someone or something. If we are angry, we have to be angry about something. This interpenetration of our emotions with the contents of our thoughts is mirrored, neuroscien-

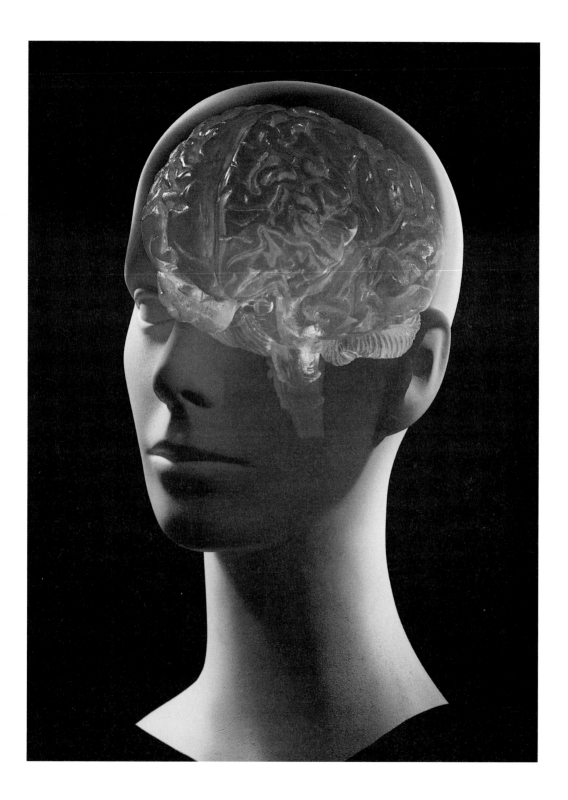

tists now believe, by extensive interconnections between the limbic system and the rest of the brain. What is needed now—and neuroscientists throughout the world are enthusiastically searching for it—is a practical explanation for the ways that our emotions go awry.

According to a currently popular hypothesis, the frontal lobes are responsible for controlling and shaping our emotions, which are largely the products of our limbic system. These two brain areas cooperate, and, together, they exert their influence on the hypothalamus, the area of the brain that controls the endocrine system and the autonomic nervous system.

Suppose you are reading this book late at night in bed while home alone. Suddenly you hear a creaking of the stairs leading up to your bedroom. Is there someone on the stairs? What does that *person* want? Within a split second the thought "I am alone . . . someone is there in the darkness" ricochets along frontal, limbic, and hypothalamic connections. If you elect to leap from your bed to investigate, fear is aroused via frontal-limbic connections, while the "program" for this action is formulated within the frontal lobes and their adjoining supplementary motor cortex. Finally, the hypothalamus springs into action, orchestrating a cascade of neurochemicals that will prepare the body for action.

The simplified behavioral sequence above—although helpful in some ways—overlooks several problems that are obvious to the careful observer of his or her own mental processes. Oftentimes fear arises before any definite idea is formulated. A startle response isn't, as a rule, associated with any mental content whatsoever. We jump as quickly when an impish child bursts a paper bag behind us as we would if exposed to a gunshot. Our heart palpitations also continue long after we have assured ourselves that we are only the victim of some childish prank.

In other cases, emotional distress often occurs out of the blue, seemingly unrelated to anything in the present. Every reasonably busy psychiatrist has patients in his or her practice who suffer from "panic attacks" or "free-floating anxiety."

On the other side of the coin are individuals who seem to be afflicted by a deficiency in emotional responses. They are fearless in situations that most people would find disturbing. Or they fail to experience pleasure when good things happen to them (anhedonia). Finally, as we will discuss more fully in Chapter 7, several million people in the United States suffer from disorders such as depression and mania who often have no objective reason why they should feel as badly as they do.

It is obvious that our thoughts and our emotions are not as easily separated as we commonly believe, nor do they follow a single, prescribed track. The way we feel influences the things we think about and vice versa, which is a natural consequence of the extensive connections in our cerebral cortex, particularly between the frontal areas and our limbic system. We are not mere logic machines, nor are we simply bundles of unrestrained emotions. We are a mixture of both, although on occasion the balance can be tipped toward one side or the other.

With Phineas Gage, the scales were tipped by the extreme stress of a brain injury. The same result can also be brought about by powerful, shocking, or horrifying experiences. The common denominator in each of these experiences is *stress*, which leads to a skewing of the balance between our thinking and our emotions. Indeed, it is from the study of stress that neuroscientists have learned a great deal about how our brain can malfunction.

The most universal form of stress is pain. No one can ever remain permanently free from the stresses of pain. It is part of the human condition. In the words of the nineteenth-century English poet Francis Thompson:

> *Nothing begins, and nothing ends,*
> *That is not paid with moan;*
> *For we are born in others' pain,*
> *And perish in our own.*

In an effort to understand stress, therefore, we should take a closer look at pain. As a starting point for an exploration of this research, consider again the example of Phineas Gage.

One of the most remarkable aspects of the Phineas Gage tragedy was Gage's response to his mutilating and, presumably, painful accident. But on this point all the witnesses are in perfect agreement. Gage didn't seem to be in pain and conversed calmly, even humorously, with his crew and the doctors who had come to help him.

Over the ensuing 136 years there have been other examples of what scientists refer to as *stress-induced analgesia*. Soldiers wounded at Anzio during World War II demonstrated remarkable equanimity in the face of devastating wounds. And athletes injured in the midst of highly competitive and stressful sporting events have also commented frequently on the absence of pain. What is going on in these situations? How does pain work, and why?

We all agree that pain is beneficial in small quantities. If we touch a hot stove, it is the rush of pain from the tips of our fingers that stimulates us to pull away. The pain of a headache may provide us with the first early-warning signal of a brain tumor. If we were permanently free from pain, many of the things we take for granted, such as cuts, bruises, and burns, would require constant monitoring and attention. Paraplegics often can't feel pain in their legs, and their lives become a constant battle to remain aware of their anesthetic parts so they don't develop skin ulcers or allow their legs to be jammed or punctured.

When taken to extremes, however, pain can also be immobilizing. Some cancer patients lose their ability to tolerate pain. After a while their entire lives revolve around their pain and the drugs that only partially relieve it. It is this loss of control, this inability to tolerate pain without complaining that often frightens us as much as the pain itself. No one wants to appear scared in front of his or her dentist. No one wants to break down in the face of pain that can no longer be endured. But how much pain *can* be endured? How much is too much?

Doctors often refer to patients as having high or low pain tolerances. These references are often judgmental, sometimes not so subtle suggestions that those with a "low pain tolerance" somehow aren't trying hard enough to fight off their pain. It has even been suggested that there are racial and cultural differences in the ability to withstand pain. All these speculations lead to difficulties, since pain is an intensely subjective sensation. Who are *you* to tell *me* that I am not in pain?

In recent years neuroscientists have made great strides in understanding the brain mechanisms responsible for pain.

They have also learned that pain can be eliminated, or at least modified, by altering certain chemicals.

The delicate balance between our perceiving too much pain and too little is largely controlled by (1) *substance P,* a neuropeptide found virtually wherever primary pain fibers extend, thought to be crucial in the transmission of pain signals from the skin inward to the spinal cord and (2) the *natural opiates,* comprising at least eighteen different substances within the body that, in several instances, are far more powerful than any opiates derived from plants.

The first step in experiencing pain takes place in the vast network of free nerve endings interlaced throughout the surface of the skin. As a result of tissue damage (pressure, a burn, a cut, and so on), a chemical is released into the surrounding area. The pain "message" is then carried along nerve fibers that conduct the impulse at varying speeds. Rapidly conducting fibers are responsible for our ability to instantly remove our hand from a hot stove. The dull, aching pain that persists at the end of our fingertips, sometimes for hours, results from the activity of slower-conducting fibers. They are also responsible for the chronic, unremitting pain that tortures some patients afflicted with incurable cancer.

Once inside the spinal cord, the impulse responsible for pain is conveyed toward the brain, finally terminating within the thalamus. Actually, fewer than 50 percent of the fibers ever make it to the thalamus. A large proportion terminate at the brainstem, in the *mesencephalic central gray matter.* This tiny, barely visible site is a central converging point for pain impulses. After electrical stimulation of their mesencephalic gray matter, laboratory animals can be operated on without anesthesia. But this pain-free state is highly selective. Touch and temperature sensations within the anesthetic area remain intact. Only pain is eliminated.

The discovery of a small area within the brain concerned with pain was one of the first clues that the brain exhibits selectivity in regard to pain. The vast majority of brain areas have nothing to do with pain perception; in most areas a neurosurgeon can electrically stimulate or even destroy brain tissue without exerting any effect on the patient's appreciation of pain.

Another clue to the brain mechanisms responsible for pain comes from the studies of *opiates*—drugs made from the poppy of Mesopotamia. Extremely small doses of an

A pain pathway: Nerve fibers near the surface of the skin send a signal along to the spinal cord, which in turn feeds the signal through the mesencephalic central gray matter and into the thalamus.

opiate can virtually eliminate pain for a short period of time. These amounts are much too small to exert their effect over large brain areas. Neuroscientists in the early 1970s therefore thought specific opiate receptors must exist in the brain that bring about *analgesia* (pain relief). But how could such receptors be demonstrated? And why would the brain contain a receptor for the extract of a poppy grown in Mesopotamia? Herein lies a compelling tale involving such unlikely elements as international teams of neuroscientists, Argentinian horses, and camels from Iraq.

In the early 1960s C. H. Li, a neurochemist at the University of California in San Francisco, began searching for substances produced by the pituitary, the tiny "master gland" that hangs from the bottom of the brain just above the roof of the mouth, like a ripe grape from a vine. One

ENDORPHIN MOLECULE

A modeling of beta-endorphin, the terminal part of the chain of amino acids comprising beta-lipotropin.

substance Li discovered he termed *beta-lipotropin* because it seemed to be involved in the metabolism of fat. (*Lipid* is a medical term for fat.) Unfortunately, the yield of beta-lipotropin was low. In an attempt to increase his quantity of the substance, Li hit upon the idea of extracting it from the pituitaries of camels. He selected camels because of their general body build: lean, hardy, and low in fat. Could the camel's leanness be the result of an abundance of beta-lipotropin?

To find out, Li asked one of his graduate students, an Iraqi, to pick up some camel pituitaries when returning from a trip to his home in Iraq. That summer the student returned with five hundred dried camel pituitaries stashed in his pocket. Li's analysis of the camel pituitaries turned up a surprise: no lipotropin. Instead, he extracted a new peptide that corresponded to the tail end of beta-lipotropin. (Beta-lipotropin is ninety-one amino acids long, and the new peptide, *beta-endorphin,* comprised the amino acids from position sixty-one through ninety-one.) Uncertain what conclusions to draw at this point, Li put the new compound on a shelf, and there matters stood.

In 1973 three research teams—headed by Lars Terenius in Sweden, Candace Pert and Solomon H. Snyder at Johns Hopkins in Baltimore, and Eric Simon at New York University—independently showed that morphine reacts with special receptors within the brain. Interestingly, these three researchers and their associates applied similar procedures in their quest for the brain opiate receptor. First they blended whole brains and separated out different parts by high-speed centrifugation. Samples were then incubated in a solution of radioactively tagged opiates. The binding that then occurred turned out to depend on the potency of the

various opiates administered. Those opiates with strong pain-killing and addictive properties had a strong affinity for the binding sites. Weak opiates either didn't bind at all or did so only at greatly increased concentrations.

The identification of a cellular brain component with an affinity for morphine and similar strong opiates immediately inspired a question: Why would the human brain contain a receptor for the extract of a poppy grown in Mesopotamia? The answer is the brain contains its own natural opiates.

In 1975 two Aberdeen researchers, John Hughes and Hans Kosterlitz, published a paper in the English science journal *Nature* describing a tiny, five-amino-acid molecule isolated from pig brains. They called it an *enkephalin* (meaning "in the head"). This peptide was similar to morphine in some of its effects. They hoped, therefore, that enkephalins might turn out to be useful as pain-killers without the addictive potential of morphine. When tested in animals, however, the enkephalins performed only marginally as analgesic agents (because they were rapidly broken down by body enzymes) and, what is worse, were highly addictive.

Meanwhile, back in San Francisco, Li discovered, to his surprise and excitement, that the enkephalin molecule was a small fragment of the substance he had abstracted from the camel pituitaries about a year earlier (beta-endorphin). This revelation stirred Li to take the chemical down from the shelf and reexamine it. Beta-endorphin might have some role in pain perception.

Further analysis revealed that although beta-lipotropin turned out not to have morphinelike effects, Li's mysterious peptide, beta-endorphin, did. When injected into the ventricles of the brain it is forty-eight times more powerful than morphine. An intravenous dose carries three times the punch of a morphine injection. It is also highly addictive.

Putting all this research together, neuroscientists were able to formulate a hypothesis about pain and the brain's response to it. The discoveries of the enkephalins and related chemicals suggest that the body contains a special chemical-control system aimed at dealing with pain and stress. Under normal conditions many of the body's own morphine receptors are occupied by these natural opiates. Narcotics relieve pain by occupying an additional number of the unfilled receptors. However, the administration of morphine or heroin reduces the amount of one of these natural opiates (enkephalins) produced in the brain. More receptors then become unoccupied, leading to an increased craving for additional narcotics. Eventually a situation exists in which the brain's own receptors are occupied by and dependent on narcotics. If additional narcotics are not available, the body undergoes a "withdrawal response."

Mood, too, may depend on the influence of natural opiates. We know that heavy concentrations of the enkephalins are found within the limbic system. The "high" produced by narcotics may result from occupying these limbic opiate receptors.

Under conditions of physical or mental stress, the pituitary releases a stress-related hormone containing beta-lipotropin. This substance modifies the body's response to pain. At the level of the spinal cord, enkephalin-producing neurons may block the action of substance P–containing neurons transmitting pain from the body. Additional pain modification is produced in fibers originating in the mesencephalic gray matter, conducted downward from this area to the spinal cord, where they activate enkephalin-containing neurons. The overall effect of these two separate influences is to lessen the experience of pain.

Neuroscientists are hopeful that further research into the body's own opiate system may lead to the development of synthetic pain-reducing agents that aren't habit-forming. So far this hasn't happened: Pain relief is inevitably associated with a tendency to take more and more pain relievers. In addition, there is a decreasing degree of pain relief with each dose. But one promising area of further research concerns the effects on pain perception by stress itself.

It has been known for years that exposing a laboratory animal to a novel stress situation enhances the animal's ability to endure pain. Repeated exposure to that same stress leads to a reduction in pain relief. Stress-related analgesia no doubt exists in humans as well. Variations in "pain tolerance" among different people under conditions of extreme stress may be the result of a special pain-relieving system. If so, this mechanism must involve far more than simply an increase in the production of endorphins or enkephalins. Stress often occurs far too quickly for the brain to increase the output of these substances.

Could stress-induced pain relief occur only under the most extreme circumstances? Support for such a hypothesis can be found in the letters and diaries of soldiers and adventurers throughout history. One of the most dramatic and convincing was provided by David Livingstone, who wrote in the 1850s of a lion attack twenty years earlier. It is a vivid account of how extreme stress can increase the body's tolerance for pain:

"I heard a shout. Starting and looking half-around, I saw the lion just in the act of springing upon me. I was upon a little height; he caught my shoulder as he sprang, and we both came to the ground below together. Growling horribly close to my ear, he shook me as a terrier does a rat. The shock produced a stupor similar to that which seems to be felt by a mouse after the first shake of the cat. It caused a sort of dreaminess in which there was no sense of pain nor feeling of terror, though quite conscious of all that was happening. It was like what patients partially under the

influence of chloroform describe, who see all the operation, but feel not the knife. This singular condition was not the result of any mental process. The shake annihilated fear, and allowed no sense of horror in looking around at the beast. This peculiar state is probably produced in all animals killed by the carnivora; and if so, is a merciful provision by our benevolent creator for lessening the pain of death."

Although pain is the most universal form of stress the brain is forced to deal with, there are other forms of stress to which the brain responds as if preparing for an equally unpleasant experience. Consider the following:

I wrote portions of this chapter while vacationing on Martha's Vineyard. A few minutes before sitting down to my desk, I had been reading an article in the *Boston Globe*. Several Massachusetts residents on the mainland had contracted eastern equine encephalitis, an often fatal and always severely damaging viral inflammation of the brain. As I began writing, I couldn't get my mind off a disturbing question: Could this mosquito-borne illness extend over to Martha's Vineyard? (The paper stated that all the cases so far had been restricted to the marsh regions south of Boston.) As I worried about this, I was also trying to ignore the itch from mosquito bites that formed a series of irregular "tracks" along my arms and legs. Could I have been bitten by a mosquito bearing this virus?

Suddenly I felt distinctly uncomfortable. I checked my

heart rate: eighty-six. My usual resting pulse is about sixty-four. Then I remembered the part of the article that quoted a public-health official on the likelihood of contracting the illness. "You would have to be either very, very unlucky or be bitten by a lot of mosquitoes to catch EEE." Suddenly I felt reassured. Two minutes later my pulse was down to seventy-two.

An experience such as I have just described is remarkable for all the exciting things that *didn't* happen. Someone watching me while monitoring my heart rate with an electrocardiogram would have seen a bearded man sitting and writing on a porch. Suddenly, without any observable change in his environment, the subject's pulse rate shot up. Then, a few minutes later, it returned to near its resting state.

The thought that I might contract encephalitis startled and frightened me. My accelerated heart rate was an outward manifestation of the inner distress I was feeling at the moment. I was undergoing, in fact, a *stress reaction,* which manifested itself in one way: the brief period of my heart racing.

The observation that a person's inner distress can be detected through observation of bodily responses can be traced back several thousand years. For example, ancient martial artists practiced breathing techniques so that slight fluctuations in the rate and depth of their breathing didn't betray fear to their opponents.

The most interesting question regarding stress reaction is this: How can a thought originating within the brain bring about an alteration in heart rate? Surprisingly, neuroscientists have been asking themselves this question for only a comparatively brief time.

By the early part of the nineteenth century, neuroscientists observed that the beating of a live frog's heart slowed up in response to electrical stimulation of the *vagus nerve* anywhere along its path from the brainstem to the heart. This response can be demonstrated just as nicely with a dead frog, whose heart will continue to beat in the laboratory as long as the heart is bathed in nutritive fluids. (The same holds true in humans, incidentally, which is why death is now defined by an absence of brain activity rather than by absence of a heartbeat.)

In 1921 a German scientist, Otto Loewi, carried out an experiment that has since been repeated thousands of

Dr. Otto Loewi established the connection between chemicals and the body's electrical activity.

times in neurophysiology labs around the world. Loewi was convinced that the instructions that slowed the frog's heart rate were issued in chemical rather than strictly electrical terminology. He believed electrical stimulation of the nerve brought about the release of a kind of "slowdown" chemical, which was the real cause of the heart's deceleration.

Although the theory was reasonable, Loewi couldn't come up with a precise way of testing it. How to separate the effects of electrical stimulation from the effects of his mysterious "slowdown" chemical? One night Loewi suddenly woke from a dream in which the answer to his dilemma was neatly set out for him. If there was a "slowdown" chemical released by the nerve, then some of it must end up in the nutritive fluid that surrounds the heart. Why not inject a portion of this into the fluid surrounding the heart of a second frog? Loewi got out of bed, dressed quickly, and went immediately to his laboratory.

First he stimulated the vagus nerve of frog No. 1 and observed, as expected, that the heart rate decreased. Loewi then drew off a portion of the fluid surrounding the first heart and added it to the fluid bathing the heart of the second frog. This heart also slowed down. Loewi was exuberant. He had proved beyond any doubt that it was a chemical (acetylcholine) that slowed the frog's heart and that the chemical was released in response to an impulse along the nerve.

Is there also a chemical that speeds up the heart? As it turns out, there is. If the heart is flooded with *adrenaline,* it will react in the same way it reacts when it is stimulated directly by the nerve.

Human nerves also employ a chemical to send "speed up" messages from the brain to the heart. But in our case the chemical is slightly different—*noradrenaline* (or norepinephrine), located principally in the *locus coeruleus,* a nucleus of the brainstem. Although the norepinephrine-producing cells in the locus coeruleus are few in number, repeated branching of these nerve fibers results in an extraordinarily complex net reaching into almost every part of the brain and spinal cord.

Did my rapid heart rate develop as a result of a chemical secreted in response to my fantasies about contracting eastern equine encephalitis? The answer is yes. A thought—in this case a fear—initiated a cascade of events which culminated in the release of stress-related neurochemicals. In response to the stress resulting from my hypochondria, norepinephrine was released by the nerve cells of my sympathetic nervous system and, ultimately, accelerated my heartbeat. In doing so, it was aided by epinephrine (adrenaline), a chemical sequestered within the adrenal glands. The nerves of the sympathetic nervous system stimulate the adrenal, which then secretes adrenaline, which circulates in the bloodstream and activates many of the same synapses as noradrenaline.

In the ensuing sixty-odd years since Otto Loewi's experiment, neuroscientists have formulated a useful metaphor for neurotransmission. They postulate that each chemical consists of a molecule of a specific shape, like a particular key. When these chemicals are released, they seek out a keyhole on the membrane of other nerve cells. These keyholes are also large molecules of a particular configuration. When the keyhole molecule receives the correct key, the receptors respond in a specific way. The noradrenaline key speeded up my heart rate during the short period of mental distress I was feeling. Other conditions of fear or stress would have brought about the same result.

In the jungle, survival depends on the proper functioning of the "fight or flight" response. As a deer grazes in open pasture, it must be responsive to the subtlest signals of its predator, the cheetah. Noradrenaline from the nerves aided by adrenaline from the deer's adrenal glands instantly speed up the heart rate and prepare the animal for the chase. A similar reaction is taking place in the cheetah. The pursuer and the pursued are both responding to stress. Whether the deer will escape or perish depends largely on the responsiveness of its brain and the effectiveness of its chemically mediated alerting and responding systems. In this instance, the stress response is beneficial and favors survival. But what happens when the world is no longer filled with enemies? When biological survival is not generally at risk?

Many components of the stress response in humans work to shorten rather than lengthen a person's life span. We usually think of stress in psychological terms but forget that psychological events have physical consequences. Entertaining certain thoughts can lead to a modified "fight or

A lion stalks its prey on the Serengeti Plain. In the wild, animals must respond instinctively to threats, or die. This "fight or flight" response is mediated by the brain and the endocrine system.

flight" response. This response is often inappropriate to the situation. Taking flight from the remote possibility of a mosquito-borne form of encephalitis has totally different consequences for survival than a deer fleeing from a cheetah. In one case the stress comes from an overactive imagination. The deer, however, is faced with a *real* threat to its life and must respond promptly if it is to survive at all.

Simply put, stress is any action or situation that places special physical or psychological demands on us. For an experienced sky diver, a routine parachute jump is far less stressful than parachuting out of a plane at night into enemy territory during war. During World War II, night bombing, the most dangerous combat activity (resulting in one casualty for every 160 hours of flying) was associated with the highest rate of neurosis, about 12 times the incidence that occurred among those merely performing training exercises. Such findings indicate that, in general, the more dangerous a situation is perceived to be, the greater the severity of the "stress" reaction. But a moment's reflection suggests that there must be other factors at least as important.

Jay Weiss, of Rockefeller University, and M.E.P. Seligman, of the University of Pennsylvania, postulated that one such factor is control: Being caught up in an uncontrollable situation is one of the most stressful experiences of all. To prove this, Weiss placed three groups of rats in adjacent shock compartments. One of the groups was able to terminate the shocks by turning a small wheel. The second group had no control over the shock situation. The third group, serving as a control, never received any shocks.

At the conclusion of the experiment, biopsies were carried out on the rats from the three groups. The non-shocked group was perfectly normal. The greatest numbers of ulcers were found in the second group—the rats who had nothing to say about when the shocks occurred and could do nothing about stopping the shocks.

To refine his observations and theories still further, Weiss designed a second study, which measured whether it is important to be able to predict or anticipate a stressful situation. Once again one group served as a control and received no shocks at all. The other two groups both received shocks with equal frequency; in one of these groups, however, the shock was announced via a warning buzzer. Weiss found that the group that was not forewarned—and thus could not predict when the shock would occur—suffered the greater number of ulcers.

Neuroscientists believe a similar situation exists in humans. For instance, it is commonly believed that an executive responsible for the operation of a huge organization is more likely to suffer a "stress reaction" than one of his subordinates with more limited responsibilities. Nothing could be further from the truth. The degree of control the executive has over his organization serves as a buffer against a stress reaction. His subordinates don't have the authority to set policy, hire and fire, or change corporate direction. As a result, the subordinate is more likely to suffer stress reactions: develop an ulcer, come down with a headache, or suffer from high blood pressure.

In 1974, Metropolitan Life Insurance Company examined 1,078 men who held the highest executive positions in the *Fortune* 500 companies. Their mortality rate was 37 percent lower than that of other men of the same ages. In another study of executives, certain attitudes came to light that seemed to offer protection against stress-related disorders.

The executives felt a sense of purpose, they enjoyed challenges. Most important of all, they believed they were in control of their lives.

Some people actually thrive on stress. Dr. Joel Elkes, emeritus professor of psychiatry at Johns Hopkins Medical School, postulates that for some people "Extreme stress produces a pleasurable arousal, followed by a feeling of release." After a while these individuals also come to enjoy the surge of adrenaline that accompanies the stress response. Without it they are bored, dissatisfied, and unhappy.

Stress can become an addiction in some people: a little bit produces a craving for more and more until, eventually, the situation gets out of control. What is worse, there is no way of telling at what point additional stress will lead to a breakdown. "It is unclear what an individual's stress tolerance may be," according to Dr. Paul J. Rosche, onetime president of the American Institute of Stress. "For this reason it is impossible to advocate stress as a means to better health." Dr. Rosche is convinced that job satisfaction and peer approval are important factors in determining whether stress is beneficial or destructive. "The real secret to a long and healthy life is to enjoy what you are doing and be good at it. It is not to avoid stress," says Dr. Rosche.

Experiments on the control and prediction of stress highlight the remarkable ties between psychological and physiological factors. What we think, our fears, our anticipations, our all-too-human tendency to prefer the quick and the easy to the painful and the unexpected—all these factors contribute to whether we are likely to experience a "stress reaction." In general, both animals and humans prefer warnings to surprise stress. We also prefer to choose when stressful events are going to occur.

Two highly stressful situations, the death of a spouse or the onset of a serious depression, are associated with an increased risk of cancer in humans. Recent research similar in design and scope to Weiss's original experiments suggests a reason why.

Steven F. Maier, professor of psychology at the University of Colorado, administered a series of shocks to two groups of rats. As in Weiss's experiment, only one group could avoid the shocks by turning a wheel at the front of their chamber. The second group just had to suffer through it. And suffer it did. Within a short period, the group developed a weakened immune system, making it less capable of fighting off infections. It was also less able to mobilize immunologic defenses against drugs that cause experimental cancers. Overall, Maier's findings provide some measure of support for the commonly held belief that a person's "state of mind" can weaken his or her ability to resist infection and, it now appears, make the person more likely to come down with cancer as well.

---

10 Most Stressful Life Events*

1. Death of spouse or loved one (immediate family)
2. Divorce
3. Marital separation
4. Death of a close family member
5. Major personal injury or illness
6. Marriage
7. Being fired or laid off work
8. Major change in health or behavior of a family member
9. Sexual difficulties
10. Gaining a new family member

*From *The Life Event Scale,* a measure developed by Drs. Thomas Holmes and Richard Raahe.

Obviously, mind and brain are not as distinct as some philosophers believe. Our "attitudes" are eminently important. We don't passively respond to events around us; we react to them. If too many things happen to us that are beyond our control, we may come down with a stress-related ailment (discounting for the moment such important factors as genetic predisposition for certain ailments, and the more controversial issue of whether some people will experience a stress reaction even under the most favorable life circumstances).

Stress also can account for less serious but nonetheless disabling reactions. Several moments before a performance, musicians and actors often experience a dry mouth, shaking hands, and slight feelings of constriction around the chest (symptoms of *stage fright*). Most of them are able to coun-

An antidepressant at work in the synaptic gap. As the neurotransmitters norepinephrine and serotonin are released, the drug blocks norepinephrine but allows serotonin to cross the gap and reach the receptor sites. The nature of the original signal is thus altered.

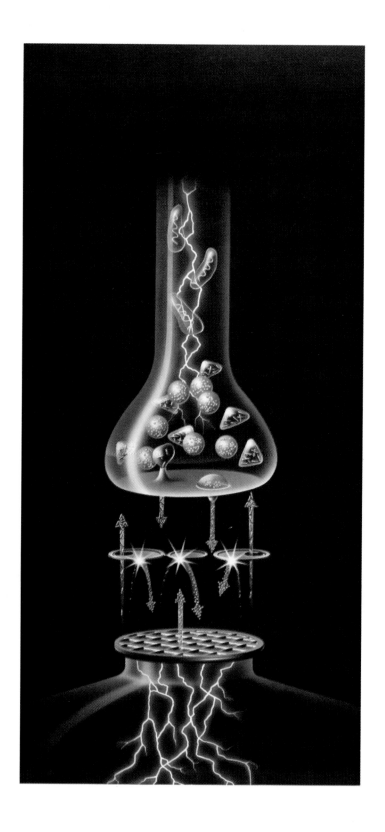

teract these feelings and proceed. Others continue to suffer, and in some cases such feelings can spoil a performance, even ruin a career.

For years neuroscientists wondered about the possibility of developing a drug that would short-circuit the stress reaction of stage fright without at the same time overly sedating the performer. Today the chemistry of stage fright is well understood. Messages from the brain pass down through the nervous system. The noradrenaline produced by this passage of nerve currents makes the heart beat faster; it also stimulates the adrenal glands to give off adrenaline, which pours into the bloodstream. It is the adrenaline, coursing through the bloodstream, that maintains the rapid heart rate and induces the trembling and sweating of stage fright.

Drugs are now available that fit into the adrenaline "keyholes" on the heart. These drugs, known as *beta blockers,* originally designed and still primarily employed to treat heart ailments, block the molecular keyholes. Since the keyholes are already filled, circulating adrenaline can't lock onto the receptor and speed up the heart. But, equally important, the noradrenaline signals coming down the nerves from the brain aren't affected. This creates a unique situation: The performer is fully alert and appropriately concerned regarding his or her performance, still "psyched up" to do as well as possible but no longer having to contend with the outward manifestations of stage fright—the racing heart and sweaty palms.

In the 1890s, William James, a psychologist and physician, and Carl Lange, a Danish physiologist, independently suggested that feelings are primarily physiological in origin. James maintained that "we feel sorry because we cry, not that we cry because we are sorry." According to James and Lange, emotions arise as a result of a person's perceptions of physical changes in the functioning of various internal organs: the rate of stomach contraction, heart rate, the dilatation and contraction of blood vessels. When beta blockers are administered to cure stage fright, the individual no longer experiences anxiety and stress, supporting James and Lange's argument. Could the opposite result be obtained by artificially injecting adrenaline (epinephrine) into a control subject?

In 1924, a French neuroscientist injected adrenaline

into 210 individuals of various ages and backgrounds. He asked each person to report what they felt. Almost three quarters of the volunteers reported one or more physical symptoms such as flushing, a racing heart, tremors, or a feeling of warmth. Only one quarter reported an emotional experience, and these were described by the researcher, Maranon, as an "as if" emotion. They told Maranon such things as, "I feel as if I were afraid," or, "as if I must cry." The emotions were tamed, unreal, almost as if they were occurring to someone else. It was possible, however, to elicit a "real emotion" if the subjects were psychologically stressed while under the influence of the administered adrenaline. Maranon described how this was brought about:

"One must suggest a memory with a strong affective force, but not so strong as to produce an emotion in the normal state. For example, in several cases we spoke to our patients before the injection about their sick children or dead parents, and they responded calmly to this topic. The same topic presented later during the adrenal commotion was sufficient to trigger emotion."

In the ensuing ninety years since the James-Lange theory of emotion was first elaborated, neuroscientists have moved from a peripheral to a more central theory of emotions. At this point the limbic system and its multiple connections within the brain seem more likely sources for normal or disturbed emotions. Use of antischizophrenic and antidepressant drugs relies on blocking central rather than peripheral pathways. Nevertheless, the demonstration that emotions can be altered peripherally by blocking the adrenaline receptors in the heart suggests that adrenaline, a product of the adrenal glands, interrelates in a complicated way with noradrenaline, a chemical released from the nerves, to produce emotions. If these are stress-related emotions—anxiety, fright, panic—the body as a whole can be harmed.

Lesser degrees of stress, however, can stimulate us to our best performance. The beta blockers have proved successful because of the *specific* effects they produce—cutting down on the action of adrenaline coursing within the bloodstream but not affecting the noradrenaline signals coming down the nerves from the brain.

Neuroscientists now believe that noradrenaline plays an important role in our general awareness. We tend to

Popular Questions About the Brain

Q: *Are the brains of left-handers organized differently from those of right-handers?*

A: Approximately 60 percent of left-handers process speech in the left hemisphere, just as right-handers do. The other 40 percent appear to use both sides. This dual processing enables left-handers to recover from strokes with greater facility than their right-handed counterparts.

About 90 percent of the population is right-handed. Humans are unique among all animals on earth in this way, since all other species show either no differentiation, or a fifty-fifty distribution prevails. Genetics seems to have little to do with whether a person is left-handed. Eighty-four percent of all left-handed children have two right-handed parents. At one time it was speculated that left-handedness resulted from brain damage at birth. Although this is no longer believed, no truly convincing theory has emerged to take its place. The origin of left-handedness remains a mystery.

Q: *Is it true that I.Q. tests are worthless in measuring intelligence? What does intelligence mean in terms of the brain?*

A: Traditional I.Q. tests often fail to distinguish people with low intelligence from the culturally deprived or poorly motivated. The Wechsler Adult Intelligence Scale (WAIS), for instance, calls for knowledge of specific facts, or an understanding of proverbs or breadth of vocabulary—three areas heavily interrelated with cultural and socioeconomic status.

Recent studies measuring the brain's response to simple tones and flashing lights indicate that individuals who score high in standard I.Q. tests take much less time to make judgments about such stimuli. "Were the two sounds you heard the same or different?" "Which of the two lines you saw was longer?" In general, the greater a person's I.Q., the less time it takes to process stimuli and make judgments. Similar findings are emerging from evoked potential studies. There is a strong correlation between the time required for a response (latency) and how well people score in I.Q. tests. Neuroscientists and psychologists are exploring the theory that I.Q. might correspond to rapid processing and low error rate within the brain: clever people may simply have better "connections" between their brain cells.

notice and remember events that occur when we are most alert and responsive to our environment—i.e., when our arousal level is at its peak. By contrast, when we are sleepy or bored we don't notice a lot of things and subsequently we exhibit faulty recall for these events.

Tests carried out at the University of California illustrate the effects of adrenaline and noradrenaline on the memories of rats. First a rat is given an electric shock at the moment it returns to its favorite darkened area of the cage. The next day it may or may not recall the shock, and it is as likely as not to return to its darkened lair. But if the rat is injected with adrenaline at the time of the electric shock, it will later avoid the darkened area. The adrenaline heightens the rat's level of arousal, makes it more susceptible to the unpleasant effects of the electric shock. It also may open the gates of memory so that particular events are more likely to be recalled. A trivial event, in short, is transformed into a meaningful and significant one.

Could human memory be improved through the administration of adrenaline or noradrenaline? Although the possibility is intriguing, there are several problems in this approach. For one thing, the dose would have to be carefully monitored to avoid precipitating an overwhelming stress or anxiety reaction. Too much noradrenaline can diminish memory as a result of central disorganization by panic or anxiety. Infusions of adrenaline can also be harmful to the body organs. Even if some of these effects are eliminated via beta blockers, no one at this point can satisfactorily predict the net effect.

With his first parachute jump, Tony Boucher, an electrical fitter from Luton, England, provided graphic proof of the effects of too much adrenaline. At first the jump appeared to have been successful, and Tony calmed down as he began his descent. But then his misinterpretation of some instructions from the ground caused him to panic. He opened his reserve parachute and was blown off course, eventually colliding with an airport building. (He suffered only a few scratches and a bruised ego.)

At the moment of Tony's panic, he appears to have forgotten his earlier instructions. He couldn't quite remember afterward exactly what happened and gave an unsatisfactory explanation for why he behaved as he had.

Animal experiments suggest an explanation for what

happened to Tony Boucher. It is likely that an overly generous outpouring of adrenaline interfered with his memory. He literally forgot his training at the critical moment and opened his reserve parachute. While he recalled the experience afterward on the ground, Tony's pulse rate jumped to 170. Describing the jump was almost as arousing as carrying it out.

Overall, stress response occurs along a continuum. At low and moderate levels it increases our alertness and preparedness. As the stress and anxiety mount, however, the sufferer experiences a further stress—witnessing the disorganization and deterioration of his or her own performance.

Consider a young nursing student preparing for an examination. To perform at his or her best, it helps to develop a mild state of aggressive preparedness. "I have to get psyched up for it" is a typical description of the process. This state of sustained mild stress facilitates recall. Memory channels are open and information is flowing. But if stress continues to mount, the student's performance starts to deteriorate. One is too anxious to take in new information. The dilatation of pupils makes reading more difficult. There is increasing awareness of the racing of one's heart and the uncomfortable sense of "tightness" across the chest. Difficulty recalling previously acquired information occurs when one suddenly finds he or she can't "concentrate." Anxiety grows and performance deteriorates further in response to the student's increasing disorganization. What can be done to halt this process before it becomes irreversible and the student flunks the test or, as in the case of Tony Boucher, the process results in a far more serious consequence.

One solution already mentioned is to take beta blockers, which cut back on the more physically unpleasant aspects of the stress response: increased heart rate, sweaty palms, etc. But for day-to-day use this isn't a sensible approach, for several reasons. Beta blockers are powerful drugs with potentially dangerous side effects. Besides, a dependency problem is likely to arise.

Sports medicine is providing more satisfactory solutions, along with new insights into how stress can be controlled, taking advantage of the power of stress to alert and prepare us without at the same time leading to a deterioration of our performance. Athletes have spoken for years of the experience of "choking," losing control as a result of heightened and uncontrollable anxiety. Only recently, however, have scientists started educating athletes about what is really going on. "Choking" is only another term for an uncontrolled stress reaction.

In a typical competitive sports situation—say, an important tennis match—it is necessary to gear one's stress response to a helpful level of arousal. Arousal, at an optimal level, is linked to two other internal functions critical to an athlete's best performance: concentration and self-confidence.

Concentration enables the trained athlete to screen out distraction, both from the environment (the roar of the crowd) and from within (awareness of his or her own level of tension, of a racing heart, and so on). But if an athlete becomes overstressed and gives in to the feeling of panic, then concentration is shattered. Thoughts begin to race in tandem with the rapid heart rate; attention shifts from the task at hand to a heightened and inappropriate awareness of one's own physical and mental state. As concentration further deteriorates, the athlete starts to lose confidence in his or her ability to perform. After all, if one can't control one's own emotional responses, how can a person possibly exert control over the competitive environment of a high-level tennis match? Eventually both concentration and self-confidence are thoroughly shaken, and the athlete may be psychologically and physically impaired—at least for the rest of the match.

The "panic" experienced by the athlete is another name for the "fight or flight" response. In both instances a delicate balance must be maintained between too little arousal and an overpowering, disorganizing panic. Is it possible that under the appropriate circumstances we can elicit the flip side of the "fight or flight" response?

The first clue to the presence of a "relaxation response" was discovered by the Swiss physiologist Dr. Walter Rudolph Hess, mentioned in Chapter 3. Hess found that sending an electrical current to one part of the cat's hypothalamus stimulated an increase in heart rate and pupillary dilatation, but stimulation to another part produced just the opposite. It is now known that relaxation can be deliberately induced by activities that decrease sympathetic nervous system activity by programming the hypothalamus to trigger lower blood pressure and a reduced heart rate—a decrease in sympathetic nervous system activity.

A relaxation response lowers oxygen consumption and carbon dioxide elimination. The heart and breathing rates simultaneously slow. An electroencephalogram reveals enhanced slow wave activity. Blood flow to the muscles is stabilized. In all, the state achieved is one of quiet, restful relaxation.

According to Harvard cardiologist Dr. Herbert Benson, "the relaxation response appears to be an integrated hypothalamic function response resulting in generalized decreased sympathetic nervous system activity."

Dr. Benson's research into what he termed the relaxation response indicates that the method has been used for centuries as a mainstay of both Eastern and Western mystic techniques. For instance, a fourteenth-century Christian treatise *The Cloud of Unknowing* describes a method of altering the state of consciousness toward "lower" levels. Through the elimination of physical activity and the exclusion of distractions and even thoughts ("beating down thought"), it proposes that an altered state of consciousness will be reached that will facilitate union with God. In the Zen practice of Zazen, the practitioner sits quietly following his own breath and ignoring all passing thoughts in order to focus the mind.

A similar focusing has been described in secular traditions as well. The poet William Wordsworth, for instance, believed that by freeing his mind from "little enmities and low desires" he could reach a state of mental equilibrium that he described as a "wise passiveness" or "a happy stillness of mind."

Impressed with the similarities among different religious meditation techniques, Dr. Benson attempted in the mid-1970s to isolate and organize the essential elements of the relaxation response. He reasoned that stress response starts in the cerebral cortex, which interprets present and past experience and defines what is and what is not stressful. The degree of stress can vary according to the meaning of the situation. Situation comedies regularly take advantage of the fact that interactions may shift from nonstressful to stressful ones according to the *meaning* of the interchanges. For instance, an office worker expressing candid opinions

Dr. Herbert Benson

about office policy to a newcomer he has casually encountered at the water cooler is likely to react with extreme stress when he finds out later that the newcomer is the recently arrived chief of his section. In this instance stress results from the change in meaning of the given experience. Meaning is primarily mediated by the cerebral cortex, which is intimately connected with the limbic system. The stressful response is then transmitted via limbic connections to the hypothalamus, the coordinator of the "fight or flight" response. Neurosecretory cells in the hypothalamus release to the pituitary mediators such as corticotropin-releasing factor (CRF), a remarkable chemical that triggers the stress reaction, complete with its characteristic high levels of norepinephrine and epinephrine.

The antidote to the stress response must alter the above sequence in one of several ways. "It may prevent the elicitation of the emerging response," says Dr. Benson. "At a cognitive level, the regular practice of a behavior such as prayer may change the perception of belief of what is a potentially stressful event, and as a result, the sequence of adrenal-cortical and medullary activation may be mitigated or may not even be initiated. In addition, regular elicitation of the relaxation response reduces the peripheral responsiveness to secreted noradrenaline: more noradrenaline is required to bring about an increase in blood pressure and heart rate."

Benson has incorporated separate components of many different historical meditation and relaxation techniques into a four-part instruction for the relaxation response. First, the subject sits quietly in a comfortable position with eyes closed. (The classical lotus position is optional. Not everyone is comfortable sitting in the position of the Buddha.) Second, the muscles throughout the body are allowed to relax completely. Next, the subject is encouraged to become aware of his or her own breathing. In rhythm with the breathing, a single word is silently repeated. For example, after one cycle of breathing in and then out, the word "one" may be silently rehearsed. With each cycle of the breath, "one" is repeated. This continues for about twenty minutes. Throughout the exercise, the subject is encouraged to maintain a passive attitude and not "try to relax," which is, of course, paradoxical. We can relax only by *not* trying to relax. In this way the relaxation response is similar to the mental state necessary for falling asleep. Our most determined efforts at falling asleep usually result in a sleepless night.

Application of the relaxation response has already brought about dramatic results among competitive athletes. In the face of mounting stress, the athlete is taught to sit on a chair or bench with a towel draped over his or her head. The neck and shoulders are allowed to relax; the eyes are closed; deep breathing is begun. By concentrating on the breathing, attention shifts momentarily from the tense and

Certain Zen techniques are very effective means of altering brain functions.

Jack Nicklaus

competitive atmosphere of the match to the internal "relaxed" state.

Between competitive matches, the athlete's relaxation response is combined with imaging techniques. The athlete is encouraged to review mentally the steps that have contributed to a successful performance in the past. Jack Nicklaus, in his book *Golf, My Way,* describes the process of relaxing and *imaging* a successful performance: "I never hit a shot, not even in practice, without having a sharp, in-focus picture of it in my head. It's like a color movie. First I 'see' the ball where I want it to finish. . . . Then the scene quickly changes, and I 'see' the ball going there—its path, trajectory and shape, even its behavior on landing. Then . . . the next scene shows me making the kind of swing that will turn the previous images into reality."

Nicklaus' imaging technique is the practical application of a comment made about a hundred years ago by Harvard psychologist William James. "We learn to skate in summer and play tennis in winter," said James. By this he meant that the integration of experience takes place slowly during periods of physical *in*activity. During periods of relaxation we can conduct mental practice sessions aimed at reducing the levels of stress that usually occur in competition. Mental rehearsal probably encodes a program within the cerebral cortex that can later be called upon *minus* the stress. One sports medicine instructor explained the process this way:

"Our brains do not store actual images. Sensory images are transformed into frequency patterns that are scattered throughout the brain. When we remember things, all we need is one image to reference the entire memory. In sports, this is what imaging is all about—creating vivid and accessible memories through physical and mental training and then using one shard of memory to reconstruct the total movement in a flash."

The cognitive therapist also encourages his or her patient to imagine in as clear and detailed a way as possible certain conflict-ridden situations. By mentally picturing a confrontation with the boss, for instance, the patient can be helped to formulate a response that will be less self-destructive. It is likely that such cognitive treatments reduce the heightened stress response that usually accompanies conflict situations. The *meaning* of the situation has been altered through prior rehearsal. By imaging, and formulating a successful coping maneuver, it is possible to maintain a level of optimal arousal rather than roller-coastering into panic and disorganized behavior.

At medical centers throughout the country, stress-reduction programs are helping patients with hypertension, muscle spasms, migraine headaches, and heart disease. Autogenic training, progressive muscular relaxation, Yoga, hypnosis, biofeedback—these heterogeneous approaches all aim at establishing the relaxation response. All of them modify the brain's reaction to stress. Zen master Katsuki Sekida explains Zen meditation along similar lines: "Zen is not in my view a philosophy or mysticism. It is simply a practice of readjustment of nervous activity. That is, it restores the distorted nervous system to its normal functioning."

According to stress specialists, this restoration of normal functioning does not necessarily mean that stress must be completely eliminated from our lives. Such a goal is unrealistic. Besides, stress is essential for meeting challenges. Without the stress response we wouldn't be able to perform in a crisis. Perhaps we wouldn't even be here at all, since our ancestors, without their stress responses, might not have been able to survive.

Recently, doctors have come to recognize a personality type that is regularly associated with stress and stress-related illnesses. The *Type A personality,* first identified by San Francisco cardiologist Dr. Meyer Friedman, is distinguished by an intense sense of time urgency and free-floating hostility. Victim of what is called the "hurry sickness," the Type A personality is marked by aggression, competitiveness, and a need to get things done in the quickest possible time.

The Type A personality talks rapidly, often omitting the last words in a sentence—almost as if it takes too long to complete. The voice often is explosive and unpleasantly staccato. The face is taut, and the body exudes an overall impression of tension.

The life-style of Type A personalities regularly displays certain key features. The Type A walks, talks, and eats rapidly and finds it difficult to sit still and just "do nothing." Multiple activities are engaged in simultaneously—dictating memos while driving the car, trying to read while talking on the telephone, and so forth. The Type A personality, because of a feeling of time urgency, thinks about other things even when engaged in conversations. It is as if the person operated on more than one track at once.

Studies have shown that the Type A personality responds differently to stress than someone calmer (*Type B personality*). Male college students challenged to perform mental arithmetic and reaction-timed tasks could be separated into Type A and Type B personality patterns because of the elevated levels of cortisol and epinephrine that the Type A's produced. In addition, blood flow to the muscles of the Type A's was three times as great as observed among Type B subjects.

This heightened "alarm reaction" is taking its toll. The Type A personality is recognized by the American Heart Association as a risk factor in the development of coronary artery disease. It is speculated that the chronic stress response (increases in cortisol and epinephrine) may be causing fat to be released into the bloodstream, where it later settles along the walls of the coronary arteries. Studies show that air force personnel with elevated cortisol levels demonstrate increased coronary atherosclerosis.

The Type A personality, with its heightened response to stress and its tendency to self-impose stressful responses, is among the biggest contributors to the wave of coronary artery operations that are currently being carried out across the nation on men in their forties or fifties. Unfortunately, the Type A personality is very difficult to modify. In Dr. Friedman's words, "The possession of this behavior pattern not only is a source of pride to most of those persons afflicted but its possession also imparts them some sense of security. . . . As a consequence, they fear and will resist any regimen that aims to modify either their sense of time urgency or their free-floating hostility."

The observation that a particular emotional response can exert harmful effects on health was recognized long before the Type A personality was first described in 1959. "Every affection of the mind that is attended with either pain or pleasure, hope or fear, is the cause of an agitation whose influence extends to the heart," wrote Dr. William Harvey in 1628. One hundred fifty years later, a famous British surgeon, Dr. John Hunter, intuitively grasped the connection between his own experiences with angina pectoris and his emotions. "My life is in the hands of any rascal who chooses to annoy me," wrote Hunter. Hunter's exposure to "rascals" no doubt hastened his death. He died while attending a stressful board meeting at St. George's Hospital in 1793.

The typical Type A conflict seems to revolve around many of the goals we have learned to value most: more money, increased prestige, power, and professional accomplishment. No less a figure than Charles Darwin discovered in late middle age that as a result of his quest for fame he had become indifferent to the things that formerly gave him pleasure. Unable to return to reading poetry or enjoying art, he wrote in sadness, "My mind seems to have become a kind of machine for grinding out general laws out of large collections of facts. Now why this should have caused the atrophy of that part of the brain alone on which the higher tastes depend, I cannot conceive.... The loss of these tastes ... may possibly be injurious to the intellectual and ... the moral character by enfeebling the *emotional* part of our nature."

Meyer Friedman agrees that the Type A's marked and prolonged response to stress results from a spiritual deficit. "Type A's must receive specific instruction on how to reconstruct a new mode of living in which such abstractions as friendship, affection, and joy will serve as the new foci for many of their activities." In a phrase, Type A's must be taught to concentrate less on what they possess, or are achieving, and more on developing the compassionate side of their personalities.

Obviously, the treatment of Type A personality has a lot in common with relaxation response. These therapies are all aimed at achieving a sense of control while reducing "driven" behavior that researchers now believe lies at the heart of the stress response. Studies of populations exposed to extremely stressful situations have shown that a sense of community can help people to undergo extremely stressful experiences without breaking down. Nowhere was this clearer than during the German Blitz of London. Stress in London was at an all-time high, but mental disease and stress-related complaints were very low because the whole population was united against a common enemy. Community of purpose helped to cancel out the effects of stress.

Social ties—the sense of belonging to a group—have a significant effect on reducing stress-related illnesses. Among a group of Southern California residents followed over several years, those with few close social contacts died two or three times earlier than those who depended on friends for emotional support. Counselors routinely recognize the value of shared camaraderie. In a sense, misery really does love company. Support groups for alcoholism, obesity, smoking, and gambling are based on the stress relief people get from working together on a common problem.

Social ties are pretty thin in many people's lives today, and as a result, people have few supports in times of stress. Increased mobility, divorce, fragmented families, narcissistic pursuits—all tend toward isolation that makes stress that much harder to bear. Not surprisingly, stress sufferers under these circumstances tend to turn toward drugs and chemical panaceas, which they hope will make up for the loss of social supports and help them to cope. The three most commonly prescribed drugs in the world are all used to combat the destructive effects of stress: an ulcer drug, a drug for hypertension, and Valium (diazepam).

Valium, one of the class of drugs known as benzodiazepines, was discovered through a combination of inspiration, hard work, and just plain luck. Credit for the discovery of the first benzodiazepine (Librium) belongs to Dr. Leo H. Sternbach, of the Hoffmann–La Roche Pharmaceutical Company. In the 1930s, Dr. Sternbach synthesized several new compounds which remained largely ignored until 1954. Over the next year, Sternbach carried out various experiments with these compounds until, during one of the last of his experiments, he decided to make a sudden alteration. The resulting compound Ro 5-0690, later known as Librium, was then returned to a laboratory shelf.

A year and a half later, during a laboratory cleanup, Ro 5-0690 was found and tested for its biological effects on animals. The resulting report marked a landmark in the development of psychochemicals. "The substance has hypnotic, sedative and antistrychnine effects in mice . . . in cats it is almost twice as potent in causing muscle relaxation." The discovery that Ro 5-0690 was biologically active stimulated research on human volunteers. The results were overwhelmingly favorable. In the words of Dr. Irvin Cohen, who carried out an early clinical trial of Librium, "It was effective in controlling tension and anxiety and did so with a minimum of side reaction. Most important, the calming action was accomplished without clouding of consciousness or interfering with intellectual acuity."

In March 1960, Librium was introduced as an antianxiety agent. Within three years, another compound was developed, Valium, which was five times more powerful.

In the past two decades, Valium and Librium have become far more than medications aimed at reducing anxiety; they have also led to widespread abuses. On the streets of our major cities, Valium is peddled at prices ranging from three dollars to five dollars per tablet. From its modest beginnings, Valium has spawned a chemical industry all its own, with thousands of tons being swallowed each year in countries throughout the world. In the city of Copenhagen, for instance, it is estimated that one out of every twelve adults is taking Valium or some similar tranquilizer.

I mention Copenhagen because in that city in 1976 a fascinating discovery was made about Valium. Two young brain researchers in a small Danish pharmaceutical company began thinking about the implications of the known facts about the drug. Most striking to them was the high degree of potency that Valium exhibited. Although alcohol and barbiturates must be taken in large doses to bring about a sedative effect, Valium produces its effect at only a minute concentration. Did this mean, the researchers asked themselves, that the brain contains a specific Valium receptor?

To find out, the researchers ground up a rat's brain to separate out the neuronal membranes. Using radioactively tagged Valium, they discovered that the brain did, in fact, have Valium receptors. Furthermore, the receptors were not spread evenly throughout the brain but were concentrated mainly in the cerebral cortex and limbic structures.

Although gratified with their results and the confirmation that it provided regarding their hunch, the researchers were now faced with a question of a far different kind. Why would the human brain, which can be traced back millions of years, contain receptors for a drug that was discovered—and serendipitously at that—only a few years ago?

At this point you have all the clues available at the time to the researchers. Stop reading for a moment and consider what you would conclude.

Obviously, a likely explanation is that just as opium

imitated the brain's own pain-killer, Valium is mimicking the action of another chemical that occurs naturally within the brain—the brain's own tranquilizer. But how could such a substance ever be located? The fact that Valium exerts such powerful effects in a minuscule concentration suggests that the naturally occurring substance also exists in limited quantities, smaller than the beta-lipotropin Li searched for in camel pituitaries.

Undeterred, the researchers settled on the next best thing to finding the chemical itself: discovering and isolating its breakdown product. To do this, they collected many gallons of human urine from cooperative subjects who could be counted on to avoid the one chemical that could skew the whole experiment: Valium itself.

After collecting the many gallons of urine, the researchers started the tedious task of identifying and separating out the different compounds that are ordinarily contained in human urine, almost five thousand of them. By using mechanically operated filtration devices, they removed all the extraneous compounds. Eventually they isolated a substance which appeared to *cause* rather than *relieve* anxiety. Further research suggested that the chemical was a "red herring." Nevertheless, the finding that small amounts of a chemical could cause fear suggested the possibility that the brain contains not its own tranquilizer but its own fear chemical, which can be blocked by Valium and other drugs that compete for the receptors ordinarily occupied by this fear chemical. It is really very similar to the situation that exists in regard to beta blockers: They occupy sites ordinarily occupied by adrenaline.

When you think about it, why would the brain contain a tranquilizing compound? Certainly from the evolutionary point of view the last thing our prehistoric ancestors required was something that would sedate them. It is hard to avoid predators, for instance, if you are in too "mellow" a mood. Instead of a *tranquilizing* compound, survival would be enhanced if the brain contained an alerting, even a fear-causing chemical. It's likely that Valium occupies the binding site for this fear chemical.

Further modification of the diazepam chemical structure, or perhaps the synthesis of future compounds, may produce tranquilizers without any of the side effects associated with Valium. It is an exciting possibility that has major pharma-

ceutical firms throughout the world scrambling in hot pursuit for the "ultimate tranquilizer." Of course, such feverish
quests leave unanswered some basic questions that extend
beyond the bounds of neurobiology. What is it about the
contemporary world that affects large numbers of people so
adversely that they must seek chemical antidotes? Is the
twentieth-century society so much more stressful than previous ages? If so, why?

5.
Learning and Memory

Do you recall the name of the student who sat behind you in the second grade? What was your telephone number when you were six years old? Who was your favorite grade-school teacher? Most of us have great difficulty with questions like these. Are these memories gone forever? Or are they still stored somewhere in our brain, waiting only for the right stimulus to return once again with all their original clarity?

Over the years, many theories of memory have come in and out of vogue. Scientists once thought our memories functioned like the Library of Congress, with its hundreds of thousands of books. If we wished to get in touch with an event or a person from our past, all we had to do was think back to the appropriate time and date and extract the right memory, like selecting a dusty volume from rarely consulted shelves. Today we have abandoned metaphors that call for shelves in the brain. How *does* memory work? Why do we forget? After years of research, neuroscientists working on the human brain may be very close to answering these questions and, in the process, finally revealing the secrets of memory.

One researcher on human memory is Dr. Gary Lynch, of the University of California at Irvine: "In neuroscience, we have been faced with a phenomenon that seems beyond the possible. For instance, you are sitting here right now,

An inactive neuron. One popular theory of memory suggests that forgetting is a direct result of failure of communication between nerve assemblies.

registering an incredibly modest signal, a word. Somehow that word, which stays in your head as an electric signal for no more than a few seconds, can, if you wish, leave a trace that will last for years. Now in the biological world things do not happen that last for years. Your brain is literally tearing itself apart, if you can imagine this. Somehow the cells and the proteins that constitute cell membranes in your brain are being broken down and replaced, and yet the traces that you stored as a child are still there."

The experience of the French novelist Marcel Proust supports the view that memories are much more enduring than most of us believe. As he grew older, his memory of his childhood remained remarkably vivid. His observations on his own memory provided one of the first clues for subsequent brain researchers on the interrelationship between sensation and recollection.

"One day in winter, on my return home, my mother ... offered me some tea.... She sent for one of those squat, plump little cakes called 'petites Madeleines.' ... And soon after a dreary day ... I raised to my lips a spoonful of the tea in which I had soaked a morsel of the cake. No sooner had the warm liquid mixed with the crumbs touched my palate than a shudder ran through me and I stopped, intent upon the extraordinary thing that was happening to me. An exquisite pleasure had invaded my senses, something isolated, detached, with no suggestion of its origin.... Whence could it have come to me, this all-powerful joy? I sensed that it was connected with the taste of the tea and the cake.... Whence did it come? What did it mean? How could I seize and apprehend it? ... And suddenly the memory revealed itself. The taste was that of a little piece of Madeleine which on Sunday mornings at Combray ... my Aunt Léonie used to give me, dipping it first in her own cup of tea.... And as soon as I had recognized the taste of the piece of Madeleine soaked in her decoction of lime blossom, which my aunt used to give me, immediately the old gray house upon the street, where her room was, rose up like a stage set; ... and with the house, the town from morning to night and in all weathers, the Square where I used to be sent for lunch, the streets along which I used to run errands, the country roads we took when it was fine.... So in that moment all the flowers in our garden and in Monsieur Swann's park, and the water lilies on the Vivonne and the good folk of the village and their little dwellings and the Parish church and the whole of Combray and its surroundings, taking shape and solidity, sprang into being, town and gardens alike, from my cup of tea."

Certainly, without Proust's memory he would not have become one of the world's great writers. In a way, one could say that his memories changed his life. Like Proust, we build our present upon the foundations of the past. And, under appropriate conditions, large patches of that past can be recovered.

In the 1940s and 1950s, Wilder Penfield, the Canadian neurosurgeon we mentioned in Chapter 2, conducted operating room procedures on patients undergoing neurosurgery. After obtaining their permission, he electrically stimulated the exposed temporal lobes of his fully conscious patients. Penfield's patients suddenly experienced vivid recollections from their pasts. For example, after stimulation of a specific part of her temporal lobe, one patient recalled a melody she had heard and sung during her childhood. Subsequent stimulation at the same site caused a repetition of the same experience, an "experiential illusion," as it was called by Penfield.

Everyday experiences like Proust's taste of a Madeleine can by themselves trigger vivid recollections. Other somewhat more artificial catalysts, such as electrical stimulation of the temporal lobes, can prompt equally vivid memories. In both instances memories embedded in the physical structure of the brain can be recovered by physical mechanisms. This is an important breakthrough in our attempts to unravel the mysteries of memory.

If memory is locked within the brain, then perhaps we can understand more about how memory is stored by observing the changes in a person's memory over time. Consider Stanley Holloway, actor and entertainer, in a reflective mood shortly before his death at age ninety-one: "I have had a very good memory. I remember at school playing in Shakespeare's *Henry the Eighth*. I played Wolsey, and I have never looked at it from that day to this, but I can go through Wolsey's speech: 'Farewell, a long farewell to all my prisoners. This is the state of man who puts forth tender leaves of hope. Tomorrow blossoms and bears his blushing honors thick upon me.' . . . I could go through the whole

Marcel Proust, the French novelist who described the evocation of memory by tastes and aromas in his magnum opus, Remembrance of Things Past.

speech today, and I have never seen it since I was about twelve or thirteen. But that is what memory does. It fools you because you think you remember things and suddenly it is gone."

Holloway observed specific problems in his own memory that neuroscientists have discovered typically accompany normal aging. "Things that I did fifty years ago I find I can remember, but things I did five weeks ago I have no idea," Holloway added.

What makes Holloway's memory loss so interesting is that it's patchy. One would think old memories would fade before new ones. However, like Holloway's, our memories vary according to our interests, beliefs, and preoccupations of the moment.

We remember those things, people, and events that interest us. Moods can alter our memories. The most painful aspect of serious depressions are memories of past failures or inadequacies, real or imagined. Therapy for such serious depressions often requires electroconvulsive therapy, which, among other things, lessens the intensity of painful memories. As the mood begins to lift, other memories start replacing the painful ones, and memories that only a short time ago caused distress and anguish undergo a change—things seem not to have been so terrible after all. With further improvement of mood, other more pleasant memories begin to emerge. After a while, the patient recovering from depression no longer reacts with fear to the memories in his or her mind.

On occasion, memories can get so colored by emotion that certain events become too painful to be thought about at all and must be deliberately pushed out of our awareness. Soldiers suffering from "battle fatigue" often are cured when their memories of combat experiences are restored via hypnosis. Within the hypnotic trance they relive their painful experiences, assimilate them into their consciousness, and in doing so, reduce their intensity. There are well-documented examples of important memories, inaccessible to recall under ordinary circumstances, recovered in the twilight state of hypnosis. License-plate numbers, physical descriptions of assailants, childhood traumas—all have been brought to light under hypnosis despite initial memory failures.

Memory researcher Elizabeth Loftus, at the University of Washington, has shown that memory can be contaminated by questions containing hidden suggestions such as, "Did the yellow car run the red light?" when there was no red light, but a stop sign instead. In a court of law, if the witness or legal counsel fails to correct the questioner, this discrepancy between a red light and a stop sign can later be entered into evidence and used to impugn the witness's credibility.

There are also quantitative disturbances of memory. A patient suffering from a severe memory disorder often can't remember what he or she had for breakfast and, if the disturbance is serious enough, can't recall his or her own address or the month and date of Christmas. On the other side of the ledger, a paranoid can remember past events

"Let's see if this refreshes your memory."

down to the minutest detail. His or her hypervigilance and suspicion lead to constant monitoring of the past aimed at detecting evidence of other people's malevolence. If the illness is far enough advanced, long-forgotten events can be dredged up to "prove" the correctness of the distorted convictions. We see milder forms of paranoia every day. Who can't bring to mind the "grievance collector" who never forgets occasions on which other people have been less than totally devoted and committed to his or her welfare?

To confuse the issue, failures of cooperation are frequently camouflaged as a disorder of the memory. "Let's see if we can refresh your memory," says the gangster to his captive, who couldn't "remember" the combination to the safe. But "refreshing" people's memory by means of threat or stress can also lead to false memories.

Thus, failures of memory are intertwined with such seemingly unrelated qualities as cooperation and competence. Memory often is a combination of the intensely personal and the coldly analytic. Like Alice, we often find ourselves slipping "past the smooth, cold surface of the looking glass and finding ourselves in a wonderland, where everything is at once so familiar and recognizable, yet so strange and uncommon." The looking glass, I would suggest, is our memory.

In an international restaurant in downtown Washington, D.C., Jacques Scarella, maître d'hôtel and co-owner, greets hundreds of people during his restaurant's busy lunch and dinner sittings. Each customer will place with Scarella an order for French gourmet food that must be prepared to perfection. After more than forty years in the restaurant business, this dapper, trim man with silver-gray hair can remember specific dinners favored by his customers, some of whom haven't been in the restaurant in several years. The morning after a busy evening during which the occupants of the restaurant's forty-six tables have changed perhaps three or four times, Scarella can close his eyes and recall each of the customers' orders as well as their exact table and place setting. His ability to match face, place, and palate has gained Scarella a deserved local reputation as the possessor of a superpower memory. But by his own admission, his memory has its limitations. For instance, although he does marvelously well with faces, he doesn't always recall names quite as easily. "If you ask me the name of the intersection at our corner at home, I couldn't tell you. Why should I bother to remember it?" he asks. "I know how to get home."

Jacques Scarella's talent has developed in response to the desire to achieve his present status: the owner of a restaurant frequented by the wealthy and powerful. His memory, which he considers a "natural gift," developed in tandem with a desire to succeed. It is also a part of his

professional credo as a restaurateur: The customer's preference is important and, therefore, should be remembered.

Jacques Scarella, restaurateur and mnemonist.

"It is not just the orders that I remember. I can recall a
customer's attitude during the time they were last in here.
When they order, I can help direct their attention to those
things which in the past have given them pleasure."

Scarella doesn't use any of the commonly accepted
memory systems. He does, however, combine "mental
pictures" with an inner verbal recitation. For instance,
forty-five years later he still can recite Victor Hugo's
After the Battle, which he learned while attending a school
in his native Nice. "While I am reciting it, I can *hear* the
words inside my head running along in front by just a few
seconds. I can't see the poem written out. For that reason, I
am very vulnerable. If someone captures my attention, say,
by asking me a question, I lose my place, and I have to start
all over again."

Scarella's memory for faces, his forte, doesn't follow
along the lines of a photograph or a phonograph record.
His brain is able to take into account the changes wrought
in a face over time. In a Washington restaurant where he
was working as a waiter some years ago, Scarella was able to

recognize an American soldier he had seen on a single occasion at age fourteen in the lobby of a hotel in Nice. "Obviously, he was greatly changed. Nevertheless, I knew that it was him, and I had no hesitation in approaching and chatting with him about his stay in Nice."

While Jacques Scarella relies solely on his own natural abilities to combine faces and palates, others with super-power memories, mnemonists, have developed systems. The most famous system of all was also developed in the context of food, in this case a Greek banquet.

According to the Roman orator Cicero, the poet Simonides was asked by a nobleman, Scopas, to chant a lyric poem at a banquet in Scopas' honor. After the poem Simonides stepped outside for a moment. During his absence the roof of the banqueting hall collapsed, crushing Scopas and all his guests beneath the ruins. Later Simonides was able to recall the places at which all of the guests had been sitting, and in this way he helped relatives identify their dead. This experience suggested to the poet the principles of the art of memory:

"He inferred," wrote Cicero, "that persons desiring to train this faculty of memory must select places and form mental images of the things they wish to remember and store those images in the places, so that the order of the places will preserve the order of the things, and the images of the things will denote the things themselves, and we shall employ the places and images respectively as a wax writing tablet and the letters written on it."

This vivid story underscores several important points about memory that remain valid two thousand years later. To memorize a list, it is easiest to form an image mentally of each item on the list. Depending on which "memory system" is used, the objects one wishes to remember may be transformed into images in various ways.

The mnemonist Trevor Emmott uses a code that assigns a letter to each word. He then makes minor modifications in the letters so they form words. For instance, during a public demonstration, Emmott broke down a series of thirty-six computer-generated numbers into six groups of six numbers each. The number 351639 is transformed into an image of a chimp holding a mallet and smashing a lantern. How did he arrive at such a bizarre image?

"Take the numbers three fifty-one and six thirty-nine,

which form the fourth group of six that I am trying to remember. To remember this I use a peg. Four is 'r' in the figure alphabet. I think of the word 'ray'—it starts with an 'r' and gives out rays of light. Three fifty-one converts to the letters 'mlt,' and that is easily remembered as the word 'mallet.' Six thirty-nine converts into the letters 'chm.' I add a 'p' to it to form the word 'chimp.' That leaves me with a lantern, a mallet, and a chimp. These words go together quite neatly. I visualize the chimp holding the mallet and smashing the lantern."

Notice that Trevor Emmott's technique involves the eventual conversion of data into visual images, just like Simonides' conversion of the names of his listeners into the visual images of where they were sitting at the banquet. Jacques Scarella uses visual images, too. He closes his eyes and mentally "sees" his customers arranged at the forty-six tables in his restaurant. This also makes sense from the neurobiological point of view. Of all our senses, sight is the one most likely to involve recall. And the more bizarre the visual image, the more likely we are to remember it. The chimpanzee smashing a lantern with a mallet is considerably easier to remember several days later than the numbers 351 and 639.

Some perfectly reasonable objects of thought cannot be transformed into images. If I tell you that I am thinking of a "woman *not* applying mascara," the phrase may sound strange out of context, but it makes sense. But try to *imagine* a woman not applying mascara. There can't be an image for a negative concept (*not* doing something), despite the fact that we talk in negative concepts every day. "I am not going to work this morning." What image does this bring to mind? Certainly not the kind of specific imagery that accompanies "I am going to work" (for example, a mental snapshot of someone sitting on a bus and reading a newspaper).

However you may feel about the "imageless thought" argument, there is no denying that the formation of vivid mental pictures makes remembering easier. To Aristotle, this formation of mental images was like tracing with a signet ring on wax. Whether a memory results depends on the condition of the wax. This analogy comes quite close to contemporary neuroscientists' ideas: The function of memory does depend to a great extent on the state of the brain.

The figure alphabet used by Trevor Emmott assigns letters with "sounds" to the ten digits; T is 1, M is 3, and so on. Vowels have no numerical value and can be used in any position. Illustrated here is the example discussed in the text.

"Some men in the presence of considerable stimulus have no memory owing to disease or age, just as if a stimulus or a seal were impressed on flowing water. With them the design makes no impression because they are worn down like old walls in buildings, or because of the hardness of that which is to receive the impression. For this reason the very young and the old have poor memories; they are in a state of flux, the young because of their growth, the old because of their decay. For a similar reason neither the very quick nor the very slow appear to have good memories; the former are moister than they should be, and the latter harder; with the former, the picture has no permanence; with the latter, it makes no impression," wrote Aristotle.

To the ancients, this image of wax as the basis for memory extended to everything we see, hear, or think. The ancients also anticipated Proust's discovery of the vividness and longevity of memory. It is said of Appolonius of Tyana, "Even after he had become a centenarian he remembered better than Simonides and used to sing a hymn in praise of the memory, in which he said that all things fade away in time but time itself is made fadeless and undying by recollection."

In the early 1920s, a young newspaper reporter in Moscow was sent by his editor for a psychological evaluation. Although the reporter's personality was nothing out of the ordinary—he carried out his work well enough and got along nicely with the other staff members—his memory went beyond anything the editor had ever encountered. The important but oftentimes trivial details that can make or break a story, the information required for each article (street addresses, names, telephone numbers, and so on)—none of these requirements taxed the reporter's memory in the slightest. In fact, he never took notes.

Upon his arrival at the clinic, the reporter, known forever after in psychological literature simply as S, was examined by Aleksandr Luria, perhaps this century's greatest psychologist. For years Luria had been fascinated with memory, and he was familiar with the few writings existent at the time on the lives of famous mnemonists. Nothing, however, had prepared Luria for S. Within the first hour or so of the testing, S repeated a long series of numbers with unvarying exactitude. Luria was, in his own words, both "embarrassed" and "perplexed" by these results.

Despite the fact that after a while the lists of words and numbers had grown quite long indeed, S's performance never varied. An increase in the length of the series did nothing to delay S's response, nor did it increase his percentage of errors. Years later, Luria wrote of his experiments with S in a book, *The Mind of a Mnemonist,* a small volume of less than two hundred pages. Despite its brevity the work is recognized as a brilliant glimpse into the mechanisms of memory.

"As I experimented, I soon found myself in a state verging on utter confusion," Luria wrote of his first encounter with S. "For it appeared that there was no limit either to the capacity of S's memory or to the durability of the traces he retained." This retention was not limited to the immediate testing situation but, in many instances, carried over to testing sessions that took place thirty years later! Luria's notes are detailed and precise on this point. They leave no doubt that a series of random numbers or letters memorized on a single occasion could later be repeated on request by S. Intrigued, Luria undertook the task of trying to explain S's strange and fascinating memory patterns.

Over the years the methods employed by S changed as he shifted from one occupation to another: from reporter to efficiency expert to financial analyst and, finally, professional mnemonist. In all of these occupational endeavors, S used his memory to a greater and greater extent, culminating in the career in which he literally remembered for a living.

At the time of the first sessions between Luria and S, it was obvious that S not only remembered better than most people, but also, more importantly, he went about the task of memorizing in a unique way. If given a series of numbers, he reported that he could "see" the figures in his mind. It therefore made little difference to him whether he was asked to remember the numbers back to front or front to back. He could even skip around and report on every third or fourth number, depending on the experimenter's fancy.

Most curious of all, however, was a remark that S made to Luria one afternoon concerning interruptions in the routine, which was well established by this time: Luria reading a series of numbers to S in a slow, measured tone.

Aleksandr Luria

Any variation—such as comments or questions from Luria—introduced what S referred to as a "blur" in his mental images. To control for this, he would speak of "shifting" the number series away from the blurred section. He could thus "see it more clearly" and continue to read off the remaining numbers or letters. Further elaboration on this point revealed an important clue: S's memory method was based on a strange interpenetration of sensory channels. In other words, he made no clear distinctions among sight, sound, touch, and taste. All of us possess some rudimentary ability to merge sights, sounds, taste, smells, and feelings. We routinely speak of a "loud" color, a "piercing" sound, a "cold" voice. We even relate colors to the days of the week. For instance, Monday is "blue" if we don't enjoy our jobs. But in S's case, the interpenetration of sensation went far beyond everyday experiences. Voices and speech sounds elicited distinct colors, often in the form of "splashes."

"I can't escape from seeing colors when I hear sounds," S wrote in 1953. "What first strikes me is the color of someone's voice." In instances where the voice sound changed frequently (such as that of a professional actor), variations would produce a different color, an "entire composition," a "bouquet."

Luria's examination of S revealed that this peculiar ability—in fact, compulsion—to remember things in exact detail over many years had more in common with perception than it did with what most of us usually think of when we speak of "memory." For instance, S often took a "memory walk" along a favorite street in Moscow. During this exercise he would mentally "place" those objects he wished to remember in front of certain key houses, store windows, or statues. Later, to recall the items, he would simply picture the street in his mind's eye, with the objects he wished to recall nicely distributed along the way. On occasion, however, his memory failed him, and he omitted an object from a series. Puzzled, he reviewed the matter in his own mind and came up with an unexpected explanation.

In many cases, the objects were omitted because of some physical attribute having to do with brightness or color. For instance, he reported that a white object (an egg) had slipped from his memory's grasp because, unintentionally, he had placed it in front of a fence painted white. On other occasions he reported that the light wasn't strong enough.

"Sometimes I put a word in a dark place and have trouble seeing it as I go by," he wrote in 1932 in the journal he kept for Luria. "In one instance, the word 'box' was placed in front of a gate. Since it was dark there, I couldn't see it."

On other occasions of temporary memory failure, S could trace the problem to an effect created by one sensory channel interfering with another. A sudden noise or voice, for instance, produced "blurs" that precluded S from visualizing his own mental images, much as a blur in a photograph precludes a spectator from recognizing a familiar face.

This ability to envision a word or object in a mental landscape and then "read it off" later is strikingly similar to the memory systems of Simonides and others. In the case of S, however, the process appears to have been natural rather than contrived. The images often arose spontaneously, and it was only when confronted with particularly difficult challenges that S consciously resorted to a construct such as his "memory walk."

"What pointless images come up on account of a single word," he once wrote more out of frustration than self-congratulation. "Take the word 'something,' for example. For me there is a dense cloud of steam that has the color of smoke." For most people a word such as "something" doesn't elicit any image at all.

By this time you may have also concluded that a mnemonist—at least S, the only mnemonist subjected to such thorough neuropsychological investigation—goes about memorizing in ways you could never learn. But this is not entirely true. As we have mentioned, memory experts from Simonides to Trevor Emmott have devised systems to increase memory powers. All of these experts depend to a greater or lesser extent on similar mechanisms: the construction of stark and original images; focused concentration at the moment of memorization; practice; and, probably most important of all, an intense desire to improve one's memory capabilities. Are special abilities required to achieve the levels of a professional mnemonist? Would S have reached such amazing levels of performance without some special gift? Although one can only speculate on such matters, it seems unlikely. Certainly, Luria until the time of his death believed that S possessed unique mental capabilities:

An aboriginal child finds his way in the Australian outback.

"There is no question that S's exceptional memory was an innate characteristic, an element of his individuality, and that the techniques he used were merely superimposed on an existing structure and did not 'simulate' it with devices other than those which were natural to it."

Despite the near universal appeal of systems and methods for improving memory, there are several reasons why it is unlikely that a "perfect memory," or a system for developing it, will ever come about. For one thing, as S demonstrated so well, a superpower memory is a mixed blessing. There are innumerable things one wouldn't wish to recall (telephone numbers of people no longer of interest, tiresome dates and times for appointments that need never be made again). Both natural and contrived memory aids can easily prove burdensome and a liability in everyday living.

"An individual whose conscious awareness is such that a sound becomes fused with a sense of color and taste; for whom each fleeting impression engenders a vivid, inextinguishable image; for whom words have quite different meanings than they do for us—such a person cannot mature in the same way others do, nor will his inner world, his life history tend to be like others," Aleksandr Luria wrote regarding his patient S.

In the barren plains of northwestern Australia, psychologist Dr. Judy Kearins tests aboriginal children for their ability to memorize the position of objects placed on a board. She compares their performance to that of white Australian children. Dr. Kearins places both natural and man-made objects on the board and asks the two groups to remember them. To make things even harder, and in an attempt to eliminate memory by verbal description, she also includes a series of identical stones.

"I have tested children between the ages of six and about sixteen years, and they always performed better than white Australian children . . . about three years ahead. So that an aboriginal child of about seven years would perform about as well as a ten-year-old white Australian child," says Dr. Kearins.

This difference in performance between the two groups existed for all spatial memory tasks and in all age groups tested. Although one can only speculate on the reasons for these differences, it seems likely that the aboriginals' life experience—dwelling in a featureless landscape, which can be traversed only by paying close attention to subtle, positional cues—has resulted in enhanced spatial memory abilities. Would this advantage diminish if the aboriginal children's experiences were less dependent on spatial clues?

Several years ago, in *The Cultural Context of Learning and Thinking,* psychologist M. Cole described vast cultural differences in memory. In one study, Cole compared the performance of different cultural groups when presented with a list of twenty words divided into familiar categories. The subjects were read the list of words and asked to recall them. This was done five times. Among the groups tested were Liberian rice farmers, whose performance was quite limited (they recalled only nine to eleven items). What made the study most interesting, however, was the lack of improvement with succeeding trials: They did just about the same on their last attempt as they had on the first. Offering rewards, demonstrations of the objects to be remembered, breaking the words into categories according to their uses— all these efforts failed to improve the farmers' performance. American groups, in contrast, showed great improvement with repetitive trials, and after a while they organized the words into specific categories, which in time aided recall even further.

At this point the experimenters incorporated the test words into folk stories. The effect on the Liberian farmers was immediate. A vast improvement in memory resulted. Obviously, what was needed was a method of placing disconnected words into cultural context. While memorizing raw data is customary in Western education, it simply made no sense in Liberian culture. Follow-up studies have confirmed that the ability (and perhaps the willingness) to memorize a list of unconnected and unrelated items increases according to education. In fact, willingness to memorize seemingly meaningless data might be taken as a measure of a culture's "sophistication."

One hundred years ago a young German, Hermann Ebbinghaus, first attempted to study human memory psychologically. He memorized long lists of nonsense syllables to a strict rhythm. Since the words had no meaning, the task was formidable: "baf, dak, gel, kim, wauch, fol, hep," and so on. After several repetitions, he timed himself to the tick of his watch, continuing until he had the list memorized perfectly. Ebbinghaus found that there was a mathematical relationship between the number of times he recited the list on one day and how fast he could perform the next. Although this tells us something about memory (practice makes perfect, or repetition increases the likelihood of subsequent recall), it tells us very little about how memory works in the real world. As one experimental psychologist put it, "nonsense syllable learning is probably the archetype of psychological irrelevance."

In a more contemporary study, students in Ghana were compared to students drawn from child development classes at New York University. Both groups listened to a recitation of a story and were asked to recall details of the story several weeks later. In general, the Ghanaian students recalled the stories better than their American counterparts. This result is even more striking when one considers that the Ghanaian students had to hear and later write about the stories in English, an acquired second language. It is speculated that the stronger oral tradition among the Ghanaian students accounts for their ability to recall details about stories that were read to them several weeks earlier. Our own culture, much more dependent on written than oral cultural transmission, is at a disadvantage when it comes to recalling stories from memory that were heard rather than read. Such findings are consistent with similar studies: Memory undergoes a kind of disuse atrophy in cultures that are heavily dependent on written records.

Starting with the Greeks and extending into the Elizabethan period, memory systems seemed to have importance in direct proportion to the unavailability of books. With the advent of printing presses and the widespread distribution of written documents, there was less impetus to develop a superpower memory. Today, memory is not much prized in educational circles. National testing places a low priority on memorization. Although this may be justified by such considerations as discrimination against the culturally deprived, it is nevertheless significant that the capacity to memorize is presently deemphasized, even discouraged. "Don't just memorize it . . . reason it out," says the teacher.

It seems reasonable to suppose that as computers make further inroads into the curriculum of our nation's schools there will be even more erosion of our memory capabilities.

Is memorization soon to be encountered only among trained mnemonists?

Patients with "memory disorders" are encountered by physicians every day, and not just by neurologists and neurosurgeons. Head injuries due to traffic accidents or football mishaps, attacks of *encephalitis* (infection of the brain) or *dementia* (loss of intellectual functions)—these afflictions routinely result in disorders of memory that differ according to the areas of the brain affected.

One of the most common memory disorders, *Korsakoff's psychosis,* is caused by alcoholism continued over many years. The illness, named after the neurologist who first recognized the disorder, usually isn't a psychosis at all. Typically there isn't any impulsiveness, agitation, hallucinations, or bizarre delusions. On the contrary, the patient usually is quiet, fully cooperative, and performs perfectly normally on standard intelligence tests. Only *memory* is affected and in a most bizarre way. New memories cannot be established. If you talk to a patient with Korsakoff's psychosis for five to ten minutes, walk out of the room, and return five minutes later, you will not be recognized. But if you then suggest that you have encountered the patient somewhere else, she or he will immediately describe the circumstances of this fictitious meeting. It is as if the patient uses your suggestions to fill in large gaps in his recollection.

Along with this high suggestibility, the patient affected with Korsakoff's psychosis cannot retain what is learned. New information slips away like water passing through a strainer.

If I ask you to remember three words (orange, pencil, wall) and tell you ahead of time that you will be quizzed regarding your ability to recall these items, chances are you will be able to recite them fifteen seconds later no matter what other task you might be engaged in during the fifteen-second interval. Not the Korsakoff patient. Merely asking him or her to start counting backward from one hundred by twos will completely disrupt recall for the three items. It is as if the processes by which information is encoded within the brain are permanently out of sync. Any competing activity, even something as simple as subtraction, will interfere with the initial step in memory formation.

Examination of the brains of Korsakoff patients reveals

a loss of nerve cells within the portion of the thalamus closest to the midline. Is this then the brain center for memory? Not likely, since other memory disorders have been implicated within quite different areas of the brain. Most disease processes are promiscuous when it comes to the brain areas they consort with. A blazing encephalitis, for instance, will attack the whole brain despite the fact that it may have a special predilection for a particular brain area. But there is one instance where neuroscientists can be certain of the location of the trouble spot simply because of the peculiar circumstances by which it came about: the brain lesion was *deliberately* inflicted.

Over a quarter of a century ago a young man arrived for treatment at a hospital in Hartford, Connecticut. The victim of a seizure disorder since age sixteen, he had been sent to the hospital by his doctors, who by this time were desperate to find *anything* that could stop the seizures, occurring almost daily. Since medications hadn't helped, a neurosurgical operation was suggested, the removal of the anterior portions of both temporal lobes. Although this operation had been carried out on other patients previously, it had always been restricted to only one instead of both temporal lobes. What was about to take place was what we would now call "experimental surgery." In 1953, however, the medical community was less precise in its distinctions. Besides, patient, family, and treating doctors were less interested in fine points of terminology than they were in putting an end to the patient's seizures, which by this time had become life-threatening.

By all accounts, the surgery proceeded uneventfully. It was only later—in fact, within the first few hours following the operation—that it became obvious to everyone that something was terribly wrong. Although the seizures had stopped, H.M. couldn't find his room, nor could he recognize members of the medical staff. If anyone was introduced to him, he forgot the person's name and face within minutes.

In the ensuing thirty years, H.M. has been studied intensively by psychologists and quizzed by eager science reporters. No one can quite believe that this tall, graying man, now in his late fifties, is unable to find his way around his own neighborhood, or to remember faces or telephone numbers, or, on occasion, even to remember his own age. (Usually he has to subtract his birth date from the present date.)

But the most striking aspect of H.M.'s memory disturbance concerns his inability to encode new memory traces. If given a seven-digit number to remember and recite, he can do it perfectly as long as there is no delay between hearing the numbers and repeating them. As the delay between hearing and repeating increases, his performance quickly deteriorates. Even something as simple as reporting whether two stimuli (sounds, colors) are identical or different will prove troublesome if a sufficient time delay is introduced. After a delay of one minute or more, H.M. can only guess about such matters. Similar difficulties are encountered whenever H.M. is asked to trace his way through a maze. He simply can't remember the directions for more than a few seconds, after which he reverts to guessing. Once learned via persistent trial and error, however, any successful maze-tracing performances can be repeated at a later date, despite H.M.'s inability to recall that he was ever previously tested.

Similar discrepancies between performance and recall have been described with other amnestic patients. One patient learned to play a piano melody from memory. He permanently retained this skill despite a total inability to remember the original training sessions. It was as if the performance was encoded within the brain but somehow the experiences leading to the encoding had permanently slipped away.

In 1981, H.M. was subjected to what might have been the most thorough and painstaking neuropsychological examination ever performed. The conclusions of the psychologists follow: "He still exhibits a profound . . . amnesia and does not know where he lives, who cares for him, or what he ate at his last meal. . . . Nevertheless, he has islands of remembering, such as knowing that an astronaut is someone who travels in outer space. . . . A typical day's activities include doing crossword puzzles and watching television." This study has also shown that H.M. can show some improvement in his ability to solve puzzles. But the study's most important contribution to our understanding of memory stems from the evidence it provides that memory is not just one global system but, instead, consists of many subsystems.

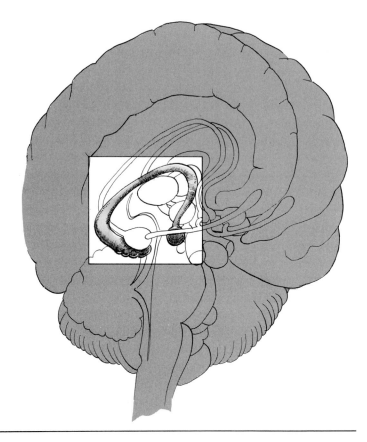

This diagram shows some of the structures of the limbic system, highlighting the hippocampus and its deep-lying interconnections to the hypothalamus.

The tragedy of H.M. convinced neuroscientists around the world of the importance of the *hippocampus* for memory formation. Complementing the experience with H.M. were other observations that brief electrical shock applied near the hippocampal area elicit fleeting memories in wakeful patients. From here further clarification awaited microtechniques that could lay bare the mechanisms of hippocampal functioning. At the basis of this investigation were these intriguing questions: What is so special about the hippocampus? Why is it important for memory?

The hippocampus is named after its curving shape, which reminded early neuroscientists of a sea horse (and others of a ram's horn). The hippocampus is one of the most ancient parts of the brain and is directly linked with fibers conveying multisensory inputs (touch, vision, sound, and smell) as well as with portions of the limbic system.

The hippocampus was one of the first portions of the brain to assume a distinct shape. As the forebrain enlarged during evolution, the hippocampus got shifted around, finally attaching itself to the temporal lobes. (The hippocampus is a paired organ, one on each side of the brain.) As the temporal lobe enlarged further, the hippocampus was pulled along with it, finally settling entirely within the lobe. Neural organization within the hippocampus is also distinctive: Stereotyped microcircuits are laid out in an intricate pattern of excitatory and inhibitory neurons.

The most common cause of hippocampal damage is loss of normal oxygen supply due to a difficult birth and delivery. A brief period of *anoxia* (lack of oxygen) wreaks its greatest damage to the hippocampus. The great majority of patients with *idiopathic epilepsy* (where the cause is unknown) suffered at birth from anoxia that damaged the hippocampus.

The relationship of the hippocampus to memory involves the remarkable hippocampal response to repetitive stimulation. Its synapses, particularly those receiving inputs from the environment, change according to previous experience. For one thing, there is an increase in neurotransmitter release that enhances the synaptic potential of the hippocampal cells. Such functional changes may form the structural underpinnings of memory.

Analysis of slices of hippocampal tissue removed at surgery reveals the neurochemistry of the circuits. The neurotransmitter *glutamate,* for instance, is believed to be the substance responsible for excitation, while another neurotransmitter, *GABA,* is important in governing inhibition. In the event of an imbalance in these neurotransmitters, epileptic seizures or memory disorders—or both—may occur. Epileptics with long histories of "fits," for instance, routinely demonstrate memory problems on being tested.

Investigations into the mechanisms responsible for memory were dramatically advanced by the discovery in the 1960s by Chosaburo Yamamoto and Henry McIlwain in London that slices of the human brain can be prepared after surgical removal and kept alive for a short time. Since that time many parts of the brain, including the hippocampus, have been studied under conditions that mimic those found within the body. By means of microelectrode recordings of the isolated human hippocampus, neuroscientists discovered excitatory and inhibitory circuits as well as the fact that repetitive stimulation leads to increased neurotransmitter release. Such efforts would seem to establish the vital importance of the hippocampus in memory. But the situation is not quite that simple.

The mischief caused by hippocampal removal may result not so much from damage to the hippocampus itself but from damage to tracks closer to the midline that connect with the temporal lobe cortex via the hippocampus. The Korsakoff patients mentioned earlier often have a normal hippocampus on both sides in the presence of severe damage to the midline structures of the thalamus. Animal experiments, too, bear out the hunch of an increasing number of neuroscientists that there is no single "locus" or "site" responsible for memory. Bilateral removal of the hippocampus in monkeys or rats destroys only part of their memory. In some instances, the animals forget how to stop a certain motor act and continue with it long after it has ceased to be purposeful. At other times the animals lose the

In this view, the amygdala is highlighted. Located at the tip of the temporal lobe, it is an important component of the limbic system.

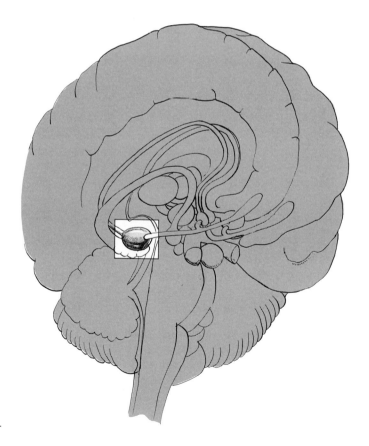

ability to carry out a behavioral sequence such as food gathering. This doesn't negate the importance of the hippocampus, but rather suggests that the hippocampus is one of several structures important in different kinds of memory. Furthermore, even within the same brain areas, different memory functions may be carried out by two areas separated from each other by only a few millimeters.

Not far from the hippocampus is the component of the limbic system known as the *amygdala*. Recent research indicates that the hippocampus may be important for simple recall while the rearrangement of memory images, as in imagination, may be mediated by the amygdala. Both depend on an intricate network of sensory connections.

Dr. Mortimer Mishkin is a memory researcher at the National Institute of Mental Health, where he works with his associate, Leslie Ungerlieder. "Every memory stimulus has a more or less indirect pathway by which it connects with two areas of brain we believe are most important in memory, the amygdala and the hippocampus," Dr. Mishkin points out. All of our sensations—sight, sound, touch, taste, and smell—can evoke memory, but not all of them accomplish this with equal facility. As Proust discovered with his Madeleine experience, taste and smell are particularly powerful stimulants for recollection. Part of the reason for this is that olfactory fibers synapse *directly* with the hippocampus and amygdala, whereas vision requires several intermediate cell connections. A visual scene detected by the receptive cells of the retina undergoes several transformations along many way stations between the retina and the visual cortex. It isn't possible, for instance, to relate the retinal area stimulated by, say, a human face to the emotion produced. There would be far too many connections required, and to do this the human brain would need to be perhaps ten times as large as it is. With such an arrangement we would be so top-heavy that walking would become impossible. Instead, at several points along the way—in areas called the *lateral geniculate,* the *striate cortex,* the *peristriate cortex,* the *temporal lobes,* and, finally, the hippocampus and amygdala— information is organized into a hierarchy. The final product that reaches the memory areas for storage is highly abstract and many synaptic connections removed from the original stimulus. Smell, in contrast, makes an immediate connection with the memory structures, hence its powerful effect in stimulating memory.

"We know that in monkeys and other primates and most probably in man as well there exists a hierarchical model of memory," says Mishkin. "In addition, we have reason to believe that the amygdala and the hippocampus store different kinds of memories."

The amygdala is important for memories that have an emotional component. Scientists speculate that when a perception reaches the cerebral cortex, it will be stored within the amygdala if it arouses emotions: fear at the sight of a tiger, or fond remembrance in the case of Proust looking back on his boyhood town of Combray. If the image's significance is spatial—say, a map of Combray—the memory is stored within the hippocampus. Thus the nature of the memory plays an important part in how it will be recalled in the near future.

Proof of Dr. Mishkin's hypothesis exists in monkeys. Their memory breaks down in two different ways, depending on whether the amygdala or hippocampus is out of whack. Loss of the hippocampus produces a monkey that loses its awareness of its spatial environment. Loss of the amygdala, however, results in a loss of emotional memory— the animal no longer responds with fear to its predators.

Although experiments selectively damaging either the hippocampus or the amygdala haven't been carried out in humans for obvious ethical reasons, there is reason to believe that our memories, too, are stored in different ways. Although it is easy to recall events from our childhood, particularly if we are cued by a family photograph album, it is a lot harder to evoke the emotions that accompanied the events.

I have a picture of myself at age twelve on the occasion of receiving my first bicycle. Although I remember this as one of the happiest days of my childhood, I can't summon up the feelings I had at the time. To do so, it would probably be necessary to see the bike once again, perhaps even sit on it, or somehow re-create as many of the sensory aspects of that occasion as possible.

"For reasons we don't understand, the emotions involved are often far less accessible to our memories than the images we have stored for events in our past," points out Dr. Mishkin.

It is likely that differences exist in people's abilities to reexperience their emotional memories. Creativity, especially the evocative genius of a Proust, may depend on a heightened ability to "get in touch" with the emotions and not just the images of the past. The flip side of this ability may involve painful, haunting memories that can't be forgotten despite strongest efforts. Such memories torture severely depressed patients, sometimes to the point of suicide—they are memories gone awry, memories that seem to have taken on a malevolent life of their own.

In everyday life, memories are also formed in relation to emotionally upsetting events. Can you recall where you were when President Kennedy was shot? Most people who in 1963 were adolescents or older can vividly recall today what they were doing when they first heard that the President was shot. These "flashbulb" memories, as they are called, are sharply etched within our minds because they involve a sudden upheaval of powerful emotions: shock, pity, anger, disbelief, outrage.

Does this mean that "flashbulb" memories are encoded within the brain in different ways from memories of ordinary events? This is almost certainly the case. Our memories for every other day in November 1963 are largely composites: we recall bits and pieces of our life from that period, then combine them into a "typical day" that exists only in our imagination. But November 22 stands out vividly. Some people can even recall the exact words and tones of voice of the persons who first told them of the assassination. There is obviously a powerful link here between emotions and memory. If emotions are muted, memories are less powerful and less enduring. For this reason, it is open to question whether a similar event could ever evoke such a powerful effect on the memories of so many. The public's reaction to the next most serious assassination attempt, that of President Reagan, was, most observers agree, less intense than the reaction to the attempt on President Kennedy. One may speculate that this difference in responsiveness may result from the fact that President Kennedy was killed and President Reagan was not. Even granting this point, however, it will be interesting to see how many people will remember in future years what they were doing when they first heard of John Hinckley's attempt on Ronald Reagan's life. If fewer people recall this event, it may suggest that our

Many people today have vivid memories of November 22, 1963, evidence of the strong link between emotions and memory.

memories are dependent on our capacities for the more profound emotions: to be shocked, to care, to experience life with vividness and intensity. In any case, this relationship of memory to emotion surely is more than fortuitous. We remember best those events that had an emotional impact on us, unless, of course, the events were too upsetting.

Many of the memories elicited by Wilder Penfield from his epileptic patients were accompanied by extremely intense emotional outbursts from them. Although Penfield was stimulating the cerebral cortex in the area of the temporal lobe, neuroscientists are now speculating that he achieved his result on the basis of the effects of his stimulation on limbic structures. The temporal cortex is in two-way communication with the hippocampus and amygdala, and it is likely that involvement of these structures, rather than of the cortex itself, resulted in the emotional component of memory. This theory, if correct, supports the importance of the subcortical areas of the brain, those centers well below the cortex, in memory storage.

"Memory itself must be conceived of as involving rather widespread neuronal connections laid down by experiences and involving widely separated structures, all of which are important in memory formation," says Dr. Mishkin.

By studying the effects of damage to selected brain areas (the amygdala and the hippocampus), neuroscientists are developing new treatment methods. One patient who has been helped tremendously by these new methods is Lori, who is now 20 years old and a patient in Boston of Dr. Nelson Butters, a specialist in the evaluation and treatment of memory-impaired patients.

Three years ago Lori contracted a serious form of encephalitis that attacked her temporal lobes, especially the hippocampus. Upon recovery from the attack, which had hospitalized her in a comatose state for several weeks, Lori couldn't remember anything. She failed to recognize her school friends, even her own mother.

Today Lori is completing an intensive rehabilitation effort involving Dr. Butters, speech therapists, Lori's parents, and her own friends. Most of the therapy consists of painstaking efforts on everyone's part to review with Lori those past events of her life that are now lost to her. She sits for hours with her mother poring over old photograph albums, often having to be told such things as where she lived as a little girl, the names of her friends, even the name of the boy who took her to the senior prom.

During one test session, Dr. Butters administered to Lori a test of his own design, the Famous Faces Test. It consists of a series of photographs of famous people, starting with photos from the 1950s and proceeding into the 1980s, and tests a person's ability to recall events and significant people from the past. Normally a subject without memory problems should be able to identify 80 percent of the faces. Initially, when Lori was tested within the first few weeks after her discharge from the hospital, she could correctly identify only one face from the 1970s. Today things have improved greatly for Lori. Thanks to tremendous efforts from her therapists and family, Lori can recall an increasing number of details from her past.

Dr. Butters believes there are two reasons Lori has progressed so well. First, Lori was a young woman when she contracted the encephalitis. If the illness had occurred at, say, age fifty, there would be less hope for significant improvement. Second, Lori, along with her doctors and friends, has worked hard at retrieving her memory. Dr. Butters feels things already have improved to the point that her ability to learn and retain new information will be close to normal within another year. However, Lori's ability to recall her past hasn't progressed at the same rate.

Patients such as Lori, shown here with her mother, help specialists such as Dr. Nelson Butters learn more about the specific areas of the brain involved in memory.

Dr. Butters says: "Lori, I think, basically demonstrates two very interesting points: One is the separation of what we can call the ability to learn new information vs. the ability to recall the past. Very often it has been believed that these two things go together; that if you could assess a person's ability to learn new information, you automatically knew how bad their ability to recall the past was; that these were, in a sense, two sides of the same coin. Lori demonstrates very nicely that these are actually two separate abilities and that one can improve much faster than the other. This suggests that they are probably mediated by different parts of the brain."

Lori's memory problem differs from H.M.'s in several important ways. Although he can remember events prior to his operation, H.M. is unable to transform present experience into those new memories upon which his identity could be formed. Lori, by contrast, is learning about her past at the same time that her recovering brain is increasing its capacity to form new memories. Although both types of memory disturbances can devastate a personality, the lack of the ability to form new memories is by far the more disabling.

Despite their differences, patients such as H.M. and Lori reveal important similarities in their memory impairments. Their amnesia occurs in striking isolation from other problems. Lori in particular demonstrates all the usual and necessary social skills. She speaks normally, is friendly, and possesses normal intelligence. Only her memory is impaired. H.M., too, has performed normally on intelligence tests and expresses himself in ways that are perfectly clear to his listeners. In both cases, however, but particularly with Lori, it is necessary to employ special tests to reveal the extent of memory impairment. Specialists who administer such tests are a new breed in psychology known as neuropsychologists. They employ the material of traditional psychology—drawings, blocks of wood, pictures of faces and objects—but they utilize these items specifically to conclude which parts of the brain may be damaged in certain patients.

Dr. Neal Cohen is a neuropsychologist at Johns Hopkins University. Testing patients with memory disorders, such as Paul, has convinced him that there are a lot of very basic things we still don't know about human memory. For instance, some patients may be unable to recall the name of the vice presidential candidate who ran with Barry Goldwater in 1964. If they are "cued" by the hint that the candidate's last name is the same as the refrain of a nationally known beer commercial, they may find themselves humming "It's Miller time," which then leads them to the correct identification, "William Miller." In this instance, was the memory of the name "William Miller" intact but momentarily inaccessible? Or was it faded, like the colors of a print dress? If the problem is one of retrieval, then cuing simply made it easier to "reach back" and extract the isolated information. But if the loss of the memory was more like the melting of an ice cube, recovery would require that it be restructured, firmed up through cuing.

For example, imagine a situation in which you wake up one morning having forgotten where you parked your car the night before. Is your memory actually gone, or is it still in your memory system but you can't quite get to it? At the behavioral level, it is almost impossible to tell.

This scene of Menachem Begin and Anwar Sadat embracing as President Carter looks on is one of of many routinely used by Dr. Cohen in his testing for memory loss.

"At the neurophysiological level, we can ask the same sort of questions. We can ask whether changes in synaptic connections that may underline memory are actually still present when one has forgotten, or whether they have actually lost their strength, lost their connectedness. In the latter case, forgetting would seem to be the actual loss of the changes that constituted memory. In the former case—in the case where the changes still seem to be apparent but behavioral memory isn't elicited—we might want to argue that it is a *loss of accessibility* to the memories that are, in fact, alive and well," says Dr. Cohen.

At this point, neuropsychologists don't agree about which of these explanations is correct. Part of their difficulty in deciding between memory-retrieval and memory-renewal theories comes from our failure to distinguish between what Neal Cohen refers to as "knowing what" and "knowing that."

"I think a good example of the difference between 'knowing what' and 'knowing that' can be seen from something such as John McEnroe's tennis skill," states Dr. Cohen. "Despite his obvious expertise in serving the tennis ball, I doubt whether McEnroe can recount where he actually learned the different components of that skill. And I doubt that he can list in any detail the actual knowledge he has about how to serve the ball. In a way, he knows exactly how to do it without being able to tell you how he learned it and what it is that he learned."

Dr. Cohen with Paul, working to overcome Paul's memory loss.

Dr. Cohen suggests that our concept of memory is much too narrow. When discussing memory, most of us think of a situation in which we are questioned about an event in the past. Although such an interrogation is certainly a test of one aspect of our "memory," there is, obviously, much more involved. We have memories for lots of things we can't talk about.

"Memory really pervades all that we do, what we are, our personalities, how we interact with other people, how we drive, how we perform simple motor acts and complicated intellectual acts, and so on. We don't think of them as specific memories, because we don't remember precisely where we acquired this information. Nevertheless, that knowledge guides our performance. It guides our behavior and pervades everything we do," according to Dr. Cohen.

The study of brain-injured patients, such as Lori and H.M., suggests that our sense of identity, our very selfhood, depends on a normally functioning memory.

Learning and Memory

Consider a science-fiction situation in which a brain is transplanted from one person to another. Is the recipient getting a new brain, or is the donor getting a new body? Is the self the brain? Or is the self the body? If forced to choose, most people would argue that the real self is the brain and that the body is only the agent by which the brain brings about certain behaviors. (There are a lot of problems with either answer, problems we will take up in Chapter 8. But for present purposes let's assume a neat division exists between brain and mind.) The one aspect of brain that is most important for the feeling of selfhood is memory. Our experiences, what we have learned, the knowledge we have acquired over the course of our lifetime—these are permanently encoded within our brains. Deprive a person of the ability to have access to his or her past, as with Lori, and you have destroyed part of that individual's personality. Interfere with a person's capacity to encode ongoing experiences into their memory, as with H.M., and you perform an even nastier assault on identity. In a sense, the richness of memory is a reflection of the richness of personality. The more data that can be brought from the past into the present by means of memory, the more enlightened our present behavior, particularly our decision-making. Consider, for instance, the gloom that accompanies severe amnesia.

Dr. Cohen: "Patients with a memory problem appear to get stuck in time, namely, the period when their amnesia began. There are many things about the way they behave, about the way they dress, about the way they look that preserves that time period. New events come and go. The patients take very little note. What they do acquire isn't incorporated in the ways that most people are able to incorporate new knowledge. They live, in short, a very restricted, limited life. They tend to stay by themselves, because making friends is so difficult. They don't know what to say to them. They can't tell you what they have been doing recently. They don't remember what you have been doing recently. From what one can tell from the outside, patients with a memory problem tend to live overwhelmingly in the present. They don't remember the last time they have seen you. So they tend to avoid other people. They tend not to read books or watch TV, because it is so hard to make sense out of it. It is hard for them to keep track of their running story, so it greatly limits their life. They have lots of unfinished business in their life."

Neurobiological investigation into human memory has shed light on aspects of our mental life that, until recently, were exclusively the province of psychiatrists. For instance, the difficulty we all have retrieving memories of earliest childhood has traditionally been attributed to "repression." According to this theory, difficult, negative, or traumatic events were repressed so that painful experiences of the past would not be relived in the present. But now the study of amnesia suggests another possibility: It is likely that during our earliest childhood we simply hadn't yet developed those portions of our brain that would be responsible for recording memory events. As proof I point to Aleksandr Luria's patient S, who retained vivid memories of his infancy and childhood throughout his lifetime. Psychoanalysts could study with great profit some of S's earliest recollections. Let me quote only one:

"This is the sense I had of my mother: Up to the time I began to recognize her, it was simply a feeling—'This is good.' No form, no face, just something bending over me from which good would come. . . . Pleasant. . . . Seeing my mother was like looking at something through the lens of a camera. At first you can't make anything out, just a round, cloudy spot . . . then a face appears, then its features become sharper."

Are such reminiscences "composites" of many different experiences with his mother? Or, instead, does S really remember a particular day and his feelings toward his mother? The only way of deciding for certain would be to discover how memory is encoded within the human brain. At this point a complete explanation is impossible. In the meantime, however, the search for the molecular basis of long- and short-term memory continues.

One promising lead is provided by *tubulin,* a component of cell membranes, particularly synaptic membranes. In the brain, tubulin is arranged in a repeating pattern of long, threadlike polymers known as *microtubules.* During brain growth, tubulin aggregates to form microtubules that convey nutrients to areas of the neurons where they may be used to promote growth or maintain cell processes. It is possible to disrupt the regular pattern of tubulin, thus shearing the microtubules and interfering with the flow of materials. This inhibits nerve cell growth and uncouples one nerve cell from another. Neuroscientists at the University of Manchester postulate that such processes might also interfere with memory.

To prove this hypothesis they trained goldfish to discriminate between a yellow or a blue panel at opposite ends of a fish tank. To avoid an electric shock, the fish soon learned to swim toward the yellow panel rather than the blue. After the initial training period a neutral salt solution was placed into the cavity overlying the fishes' brains. This was done as soon as the fish had learned to discriminate yellow from blue. Retesting two days later revealed that the fish still were capable of color discrimination, a neat demonstration that the fish had succeeded in transferring their learning from short- to long-term memory. But when *colchicine,* a drug that disrupts tubulin, was injected immediately after the training period, the fish couldn't perform the discrimination task when tested two days later. The drug didn't interfere with the fish's ability to learn the task, only the capacity to remember it when retested later.

When colchicine administration was delayed for a little over an hour after the training period, the fish were still able to retain their discrimination ability when tested several days later. Presumably, by the time the colchicine was administered, the process of transfer from short- to long-term memory had already taken place, or at least it was well under way. Finally, when the colchicine was administered a little over an hour *before* the training session, the fish still learned the discrimination task, but they lost their memory over the ensuing two days.

These experiments suggest that colchicine can prevent a newly acquired memory from being transferred into a permanent form (most likely a stable molecular configuration). Although the exact details aren't clear, it seems fair to say that at least in the experimental model microtubules are important in mediating some of the growth and structural changes involved in the establishment of long-term memory. The time sequences are particularly intriguing. It is known from observations of head-injured patients that a critical period is required to switch from short- to long-term memory. For example, a concussive blow to the head wipes out memory for events immediately preceding it. Such findings are consistent with the view that memory must involve some alteration of neuronal connections. If this theory is true, then it suggests, of course, that the converse may also hold true: Drugs capable of stabilizing key molecular components may lead to enhancement of memory. In goldfish this has turned out to be true. Heavy water, *deuterium oxide,* a stabilizer of microtubules, facilitates learning in the fish by accelerating growth of nerve processes in isolated nerve tissue. It is speculated that it does so via the stabilization of microtubules and the enhancement of flow of materials along the nerve cell processes.

Does all this research indicate that memory and its derangement can be understood on the basis of tubulin? Not at all. Alterations in one component within the human brain often bring about alterations elsewhere, so-called *epiphenomena.* This makes it difficult to distinguish the principal event from its consequences, since a disturbance in membrane permeability may bring about alterations in the concentrations of key ions or neurotransmitters. Fluid and electrolyte balance may shift toward new, unstable organizations. In such circumstances the overzealous investigator may base his or her theory of memory on the functioning of a particular neurotransmitter, ignoring the possibility that he or she is really studying *consequences* rather than *causes.*

Furthermore, in a dynamic system, multiple components interact with each other according to various levels of complexity and organization. An increase in a particular *neuropeptide,* such as the hormone *vasopressin,* may result in a conservation of body water. This, in turn, may lead to a dilution of certain ions in the blood. *Hypokalemia* (low potassium) and *hyponatremia* (low sodium) are notorious for their ability to induce neurobehavioral changes (confusion, disorientation, psychoticlike states). In this hypothetical case the culprit isn't the ionic imbalance itself, however, but rather the disturbance in vasopressin release. In short, one must be extremely cautious about accepting oversimplified explanations of complex brain processes. Rarely, with the exception of infectious diseases (bacteria, viruses, and so on), is one agent by itself the sole explanation of why things have gone awry. When it comes to explaining normal as opposed to pathological functions, things are even stickier.

Even granting that a disturbed memory may be due to a distinct imbalance or dysfunction within the brain, this doesn't by any means provide an explanation for how normal memory works. These considerations are important when it comes to proposed methods of chemically improving our memories. For instance, several researchers have noted that memory, both in test animals and humans, can be improved by administering the neuropeptide vasopressin. This substance is manufactured within the hypothalamus and transported along the axons of the nerve cells, where it is finally deposited in the nerve terminals within the pituitary. Activation leads to the release of the neuropeptide into the general circulation, where it eventually acts on the kidney to conserve body water.

Over the past decade, neuroscientists in various parts of the world have independently confirmed that vasopressin enhances memory and learning.

In one experiment rats were taught to avoid entering a dark box by being given an electric shock. They could be trained to avoid the box for a much longer time after training if given an injection of vasopressin. Dr. Floyd Bloom, of the Salk Institute, along with several other neuroscientists, modified this procedure in 1978 and found that injecting vasopressin directly into the ventricles of rats led to doubling the period of time required before the rats "forgot."

Dr. Philip Gold, a psychiatrist at the National Institute of Mental Health, has found disturbances in the vasopressin levels in the spinal fluid of patients suffering from severe depression. This disturbed vasopressin level is accompanied by an alteration of the neuropeptide *oxytocin,* which is also produced in the posterior hypothalamus and conveyed to the pituitary. Could it be, Dr. Gold reasoned, that vasopressin and oxytocin are opposite sides of the memory coin? That vasopressin enhances memory and that oxytocin inhibits it? Although a definitive answer isn't possible at this early stage of investigation, several findings suggest the opposing actions of vasopressin and oxytocin on memory. For example, Dr. Gold's depressed patients improved their memory performance after inhaling vasopressin. (Persons with normal moods also improved their performance.) And manic patients tended toward higher natural vasopressin levels and lowered oxytocin levels. Could this account for the fact that manics are besieged by too many memories that often render them incoherent and disorganized? At this point the evidence for vasopressin's memory-enhancing ability is compelling enough so that major pharmaceutical companies are now investing heavily in the development of "memory drugs." But to what purpose will these drugs be put? Will they provide a kind of chemical surfboard on which the poorly motivated or lazy student can ride the crest of the waves instead of plunging deeply into the depths of academia? And suppose the "memory drugs" enable us to recover long-lost childhood memories. Will this necessarily be a boon? Not everyone's childhood was rosy, and many people will undoubtedly say, "Thanks, but no thanks" to the opportunity to recollect scenes of poverty, emotional indifference, or even abuse.

When it comes to mental health, forgetting is oftentimes as important as remembering. "There is such a thing as too good a memory," cautions psychiatrist Frederick K. Goodwin, director of research at the National Institute of Mental Health. Dr. Goodwin and others suggest that certain fears and phobias as well as obsessions and preoccupations may be examples of memories that are too powerful, exerting an almost demonic influence on our lives. The diary of the mnemonist S is a record of the anguish that can result when a person cannot forget. In a diary entry dated in December 1935, S speaks of a "tremendous amount of conflict" created by his memory powers:

"It becomes difficult for me to read. I am slowed down, my attention is distracted, and I can't get the important ideas in a passage. Even when I read about circumstances that are entirely new to me, if there happens to be a description, say, of a staircase, it turns out to be one in a house I once lived in; I start to follow it and lose the gist of what I am reading. What happens is that I just can't read, can't study, for it takes up such an enormous amount of my time."

In 1950, a psychologist, Karl Lashley, published a paper titled "In Search of the Engram." In it were the results of research that had occupied most of his professional life. He concluded that learning and memory could not be localized to any one structure within the brain but are distributed diffusely throughout the brain. Lashley's conclusions are a strong vote for the view that the investigation of neuronal organization will not yield an answer to where and how memory is stored within the brain. Lashley even went so far as to comment, only half humorously, that after a lifetime of studying memory and learning, he was beginning to doubt that these processes even existed! At the time, Lashley's work had a powerful influence on neuroscientists, many of whom took Lashley's conclusions as the last word on the subject.

At about the same time that Lashley was making incisions in the brains of rats and checking the effect on behavior, one of his students, Donald Hebb, was suggesting that learning and memory must involve changes in neuronal circuits, real physical changes that, given the proper techniques, could be demonstrated. Hebb, in his book *The Organization of Behavior,* suggested that every psychological function, such as memory or learning, must be due to activities in a *cell assembly* in which the cells are connected in specific circuits. He suggested that when a cell is acting, its synaptic connections within the circuits have been modified. This modification may be a relatively short-lived increase in excitability (useful for short-term memory), or it may involve some kind of longer-lasting structural modification of the synapses (useful in long-term memory). Hebb's theory that local circuits and cell assemblies were the foundations for behavior provided a theoretical framework for neurobiologic research. How to define these circuits? What kinds of synaptic change are brought about when memories are established? Where are the circuits and cell assemblies? These questions have occupied neuroscientists in the three decades since Hebb's prophetic work.

Donald Hebb lives in a one-hundred-year-old house in the farm country fifty miles outside Halifax, Nova Scotia. One of the foremost theoreticians on the subject of the human brain, Hebb, at age seventy-nine, is still actively searching for an explanation of human memory. On a lovely spring afternoon he took time out from writing to talk about his concept of the "cell assembly."

"I spent a lot of time trying to think of a way in which the brain could function. All the theories that I knew made the brain out to be completely controlled by the things that were going on around it, by the sensory events that the brain was exposed to. But it occurred to me about 1945 that the brain might be functioning independently of the messages it is getting from the outside. I came up with the idea that brain activity is actually the activity of a number of separate systems that I call cell assemblies. Thanks to these cell assemblies, activity can go on in the brain without any external stimulation at all. For instance, if I sit quietly, as I am sitting here in my armchair, with no noise and no visual stimulation—perhaps with my eyes closed—I still may have an intensely active brain with no messages from the outside coming at all. To this extent the brain is not programmed by the environment, but instead is programming itself. This is possible because brain activity consists of the activity of cell assemblies—little groups of cells influencing each other.''

According to Hebb, cell assemblies collaborate with

Dr. Donald Hebb; below, Dr. Hebb's grandson, Matthew, playing with his mother.

one another "so that one cell assembly, A, will excite another cell assembly, B, which may excite yet another, C." Experiences are built up from combinations of cell assemblies. The sight of an object, for instance, may correspond to one group of assemblies, with the name of the object representing a separate group.

"The development of a child while he is in the stage before learning to speak will consist of the development of cell assemblies for hearing, vision, smell, taste, and skin contact. Each cell assembly corresponds to a particular kind of experience that the child may run into. And the course of the child's development in the first few years will consist of establishing separate systems in the brain, groups of brain cells that will act together and reinforce one another's activity."

Hebb believes in the existence of thousands upon thousands of cell assemblies that become less efficient with normal aging. Forgetting is a direct result of a failure of communication between nerve cell assemblies. Hebb's theory of cell assemblies provides a valuable compromise between those who insist that memory must be localized and those neuroscientists who believe that memory is more widespread throughout the brain. The theory is impartial on this point. Cell assemblies may consist of neighboring cells tightly organized, or, by the same token, the cells comprising these assemblies may be located at various places within the brain.

The cell assembly theory is also consistent with the different ways that memory breaks down. For instance, on occasion we can't come up with the name of an object despite being able to recognize it and explain its use. Presumably the cell assembly for the word describing the object is temporarily functionally disconnected. In dementia this disconnection may be permanent. At the other extreme, creativity may consist of harmonizing cell assemblies in uniquely effective ways. Hebb believes that everyone has the potential to be creative—in fact, cannot help being creative.

"Every normal human being is creative all the time, thinking of new ways to make bread, new ways to serve breakfast, new ways to plant the garden. Creativity is not something that occurs only in the brain of outstanding individuals. It is a normal aspect of human brain function.

And it is accounted for by the almost infinite number of possibilities for new combinations of cell assemblies."

On the day of our visit Hebb was making a boat for his two-year-old grandson, Matthew. We took this opportunity to ask Hebb what cell assemblies might be forming in Matthew's young brain.

"Matthew's experience with boats of any kind is so limited that at this stage in his life he has not yet found a cell assembly that would correspond to the idea or to the experience of seeing a boat. In perhaps three years he will have an idea of a boat very well developed—that is, he will have a cell assembly or cell assembly groups corresponding to the different experiences of a boat as seen from the side, as seen from the front, as seen out on the water sailing, and so on. At present I doubt very much that cell assembly activity has been developed. Instead of seeing a boat taking shape, he is only now seeing me hitting a piece of wood with an ax."

Earlier in the day Hebb had given Matthew a toy rowboat to play with in his bath. Might that not suggest the possibility to Matthew's two-year-old brain that the wood being chopped by the ax would later be turned into a boat?

"In a relatively short time I think that might be the basis of an idea of a boat. It is possible that, thanks to the toy rowboat experience, the word 'boat' would mean more to him in a few weeks than it does now."

Over the next two to three years, according to Hebb, Matthew's brain will be constructing cell assemblies that correspond to the sound of words and other cell assemblies relating to the objects to which the words are applied. At the same time separate cell assemblies will be developing relating to the production of words naming the object. Eventually a rich and myriad tapestry will result composed of all the different sensual and cognitive aspects of boats and boating. It is possible that brain development consists of the appearance of increasing numbers of cell assemblies based on life experience.

When Hebb's novel theory was first published in 1949 in *The Organization of Behavior*, there was little proof for the existence of cell assemblies. To this extent the theory was interesting and, as mentioned a moment ago, was consistent with observations concerning normal learning and forgetting. In the ensuing three decades, however, Hebb's cell assembly theory has been translated into neurobiological terms.

The human brain resists the investigations of neuroscientists intent on understanding memory on several fronts. As we've discussed, the sheer numbers of neurons (nerve cells) involved preclude anyone tracing the neuronal impulses accompanying even the simplest stimulus. For this reason alone, organisms with simpler nervous systems have fascinated neuroscientists for a long time. Some of these organisms, the crayfish, the leech, the cricket, and the locust, have only between 10,000 and 100,000 brain cells, compared to the billions of neurons in the human brain. Furthermore, these cells are gathered together in clusters called *ganglia,* each of which may contain no more than five hundred to two thousand individual neurons. Even more important than the fewer numbers involved, however, is the invariance in position that the neurons display. The ganglia of the primitive worm Ascaris, for instance, contain exactly 162 cells. This means that a neuroscientist in Sydney, Australia, can cut into an Ascaris and encounter exactly the same organization and number of ganglia as a counterpart dissecting an Ascaris specimen in Cambridge, Massachusetts. Such similarities in brain organization aren't found in humans, even between identical twins.

This invariance in cell numbers among *invertebrates* (organisms without a spinal column or backbone) raises two intriguing questions: Does each nerve cell always make the same connection in different organisms of the same species? And if the anatomical organization is the same, do the cells exhibit similar functional properties of either exciting or inhibiting their neighboring cells? The answer to both questions is a resounding yes. Not only is the anatomical arrangement similar, but also the nerve cells in two organisms of the same species exert the identical effect on their target cells. Thus there is a high degree of conformity within the brain of simple invertebrates, a conformity that suggests that Descartes may have had a point when he suggested that animals, other than man, work like clocks. But there is one obvious difference between the workings of a clock, which, after it is wound up, always operates the same whatever the conditions (night-day, winter-summer), and that of an organism, however simple or "far down the scale of evolutionary development."

The living organism must adapt to changes in the environment. The extent to which it can do so successfully will determine the organism's place on the evolutionary scale. To this extent the findings of homogeneity in the nervous system of invertebrates should come as no surprise: the comparative "rigidity" of their neuronal organization is mirrored by the limitations of their behavioral repertoires. Crayfish don't talk. They don't vote. And, insofar as can be determined, they don't ask themselves questions about purpose or undergo crises of identity. In fact, if one concentrates only on those things invertebrates *can't* do (in other words, things we can do and they can't), they seem to offer little to help us to understand our own brains. But if we can overcome our chauvinism, several points of similarity immediately present themselves.

Successful adaptation to the environment requires that an organism be capable of learning. Thus the properties of *learning* (modifying behavior in response to experience) and *memory* (the capacity of storing, retrieving, and acting upon this knowledge) should be shared by neuronal systems all the way from an earthworm to a Rhodes scholar. The important point, of course, concerns whether the nervous systems of earthworms and those of Rhodes scholars go about learning and remembering in ways that are similar enough to enable neuroscientists to establish correlations between them.

Over the past two decades Dr. Eric R. Kandel and his associates at Columbia University College of Physicians and Surgeons in New York City have been studying the nervous system of the marine snail Aplysia. Specifically, Dr. Kandel, a psychiatrist and neurobiologist, has been interested in the learning capabilities of this primitive and—compared to humans—simple biological organism.

To study the learning and memory capabilities of Aplysia, Dr. Kandel concentrated on the ability of the organism to protect itself against unexpected intrusions by withdrawing into its protective shell. In its "relaxed" state, the Aplysia gill extends outward from its respiratory chamber, the mantel cavity. A gill-withdrawal reflex is elicited whenever part of the mantel shelf (a siphon) is stimulated. This is a protec-

Dr. Eric R. Kandel

tive reflex, no different in purpose from something like an eye blink in response to a speck of dust.

By means of repeated stimulation, Dr. Kandel discovered that the Aplysia learns from experience and, after a while, can even ignore repetitive stimulation. For instance, after receiving several innocuous jets of water directed at the siphon, the animal's reflex response will be reduced to one third its original value. Neurochemically, this corresponds to a reduction in the number of chemical packets, *quanta,* released by one set of neurons onto their target cells. This process is known as habituation—the ability to disregard repetitive stimuli that are neither rewarding nor harmful. Thus the Aplysia can learn to ignore certain changes in the environment that experience has revealed to be inconsequential. It can also reassert itself if the stimulus changes. For instance, if a noxious stimulus is presented to a different area of the siphon, the organism is sensitized, and the defensive withdrawal reflex reappears with all its original vigor.

Research on Aplysia has shown that "commonsense" deductions about structure and function actually were errors of the grossest kind. For instance, the finding that the nerve cells of Aplysia are arranged in precise and invariant ways would suggest that its response would be equally invariant. Instead, the organism is capable of learning from experience. Both short- and long-term memory can be established. After a training session of about ten to fifteen touch stimuli to the siphon, the withdrawal reflex decreases. This memory, however, is lost for only a short period. Within an hour the animal begins once again to respond to the stimulus; after one day the response is back to normal.

A different response results if original stimuli are continued over a longer period. Four repeated sessions of ten stimuli each bring about memory of the stimuli that may last for weeks. During this period the reflex is depressed or, in some cases, ceases altogether.

These experiments illustrate that in the Aplysia, memory traces can be short- or long-term. The important question, of course, is whether similar processes are going on when a memory is established within the brains of different organisms. Eric Kandel believes the process may be identical:

"There appears to be no fundamental difference in

structure, chemistry, or function between the neurons and synapses in man and those of a squid, a snail, or a leech."

If Dr. Kandel is correct—and there is a lot of research indicating he is—a study of the mechanisms of learning and memory in the Aplysia may have much to teach us about these processes within our own brains. For instance, take the influence one cell may have on several others. Traditional wisdom favored the view that each cell tended to be either excitatory or inhibitory. Textbooks published less than a decade ago make reference to stimulatory or inhibitory neurons. Actually, the activation patterns of individual nerve cells are much more complex. The cells may mediate actions by different connections. They may excite one target cell while inhibiting another. In some cases they may make a dual connection, both inhibiting and exciting the same cell. Even more important, each of these activities may be mediated by a *single neurotransmitter.*

Dr. Kandel with one of his snails.

Obviously, if the same neurotransmitter (messenger) can elicit different effects, then it follows that the final result must depend on both the neurotransmitter and the nature of the receptor on which it acts. As it turns out, that synaptic activity is controlled by the neurotransmitter's effect on the receptor of the target cells. In one instance, the neurotransmitter may affect the receptor channel important for the passage of sodium (an influence that produces excitation). On another cell, this same neurotransmitter may have no effect on sodium, but instead it may influence the facility by which chloride can pass through the receptor channel of the membrane (an action that results in inhibition). Thus neurotransmitters, like the neurons themselves, cannot be neatly assigned into excitatory and inhibitory categories. Instead, the final expression of a particular neurotransmitter depends on how it reacts with the particular receptors on the membranes of its target cell. A target cell with different membrane characteristics will result in different responses. Think of it this way: If this sentence were written in Italian, it would trigger a response in a reader with a knowledge of Italian, while it would be incomprehensible to someone who didn't read Italian. The sentence by itself doesn't "excite" all readers. A similar situation occurs with a specific neurotransmitter.

"The chemical transmitter is only permissive," Eric Kandel has written. "The instructive component of synaptic transmission is the nature of the receptor and the ionic channels it interacts with."

The most exciting aspects of Dr. Kandel's work are the implications it has for our understanding of the chemical and molecular basis of memory. In the Aplysia, at least, it is now established that learning involves an alteration in the character of the neuron. The quantity of neurotransmitter released varies according to whether the stimulus is novel (an increased amount) or repetitive (a decrease). After repetitive stimulation, the organism has "learned" and can "remember." But after the passage of a certain amount of time, the organism "forgets" and the reintroduction of the same stimulus results in a renewal of the originally robust response. With longer-term memories (the result of stimulation continued for extended periods of time) there is evidence that the structure of the neuron that releases the neurotransmitter may undergo a change in the number of active zones concerned with the release of neurotransmitters.

Could we remember some events for years because our nervous systems have been structurally altered by the original experience? It is an exciting and slightly scary prospect. If true, it does away with strict nature-nurture distinctions. If experience can alter brain cells despite the strong genetic influence on their structure and function, then neither environment nor heredity alone provides a sufficient explanation for behavior.

Although many philosophers have felt intuitively that neither the nature nor the nurture side of the argument was very persuasive, integration was precluded by the fact that no one had ever demonstrated that a "psychological" event could lead to structural consequences within the brain. But Dr. Kandel's work with the Aplysia illustrates that the much-vaunted "plasticity" of the brain is more than mere metaphor. In Eric Kandel's words, "A new dimension is introduced in thinking about the brain."

The connections between brain cells—largely a matter of genetics and presently unknown influences—are enhanced or diminished by experience. Learning and the exercise of memory, perhaps even along the lines of the memory systems mentioned earlier, lead to enhancement of brain functioning. Could it be that the more we use our brain, the more efficient and wondrous an organ it becomes? Certainly this is true in every other part of our body. Why not our brains?

The powerful and formative influences of certain patterns of thought on the mind have been commented on by sages throughout the ages: "All that we are is the result of what we have thought" is written in the Buddhist text *Dhammapada*. Dr. Kandel's work has added another dimension to this matter of the relation of thought, mind, and brain. Eric Kandel in one of his more wide-ranging, free-wheeling essays (remember, he is a trained psychiatrist as well as neurobiologist) has even speculated on the implications of the Aplysia work and psychotherapy. In "Psychotherapy and the Single Synapse: The Impact of Psychiatric Thought on Neurobiologic Research," Dr. Kandel has written:

"When I speak to someone and he or she listens to me, we can not only make eye contact and voice contact, but the action of the neuronal machinery in my brain is having a direct and, I hope, long-lasting effect on the neuronal machinery in his or her brain, and vice versa. Indeed, I would argue that it is only insofar as our words produce changes in each other's brains that psychotherapeutic intervention produces changes in patients' minds. From this perspective the biologic and psychologic approaches are joined."

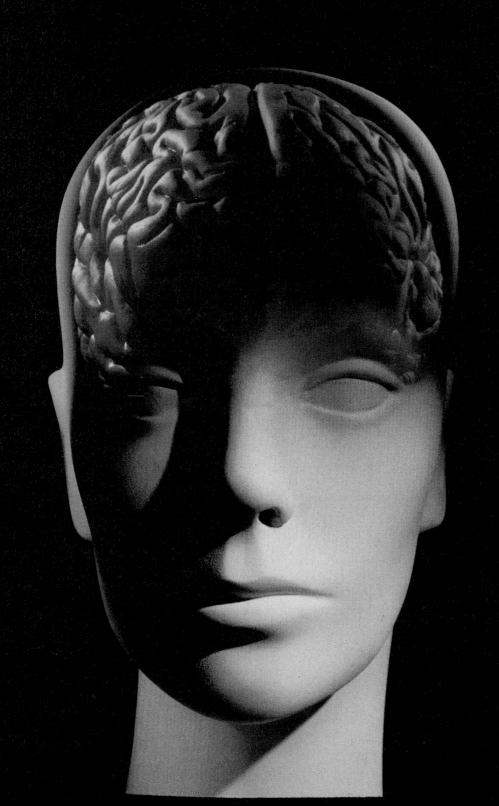

6.
The Two Brains

In 1861, at the start of the American Civil War, a less bloody but no less deeply felt conflict was taking place between two rival camps of brain scientists. The traditional group held that the two hemispheres of the brain were mirror images of each other and that there was, therefore, no reason to assign specific functions to one hemisphere rather than the other. By contrast, the rebel position believed that the hemispheres *were* specialized along certain lines and that such activities as speech and language were "localized" in one hemisphere. Although each side made periodic advances against the other's position, the issues remained largely unresolved until April of that year, when a decisive battle was won by those who favored localization.

At a meeting of the Paris Anthropological Society in April 1861, Paul Broca, a surgeon and neuroanatomist, exhibited the brain of a patient who had suffered up until the time of his death from a severe difficulty in speaking (known as *aphasia*). Broca's patient, a man named Leborgne, was referred to as "Tan Tan," a reference to his inability to say any other words. The patient understood what was said to him, and he could communicate using facial expressions and hand gestures. Only his ability to speak was impaired.

On examination, Tan's brain showed a circumscribed area of damage within the left hemisphere about the size of a hen's egg. Broca convincingly argued to the membership that Tan's speech problem was the result of this damage to his left hemisphere.

Ten years later, a German neurologist, Carl Wernicke,

If our skulls were transparent, our right and left hemispheres would appear as mirror images of each other.

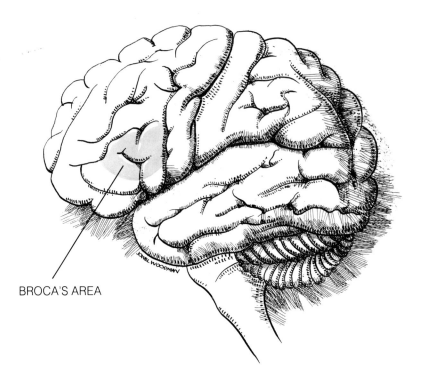

BROCA'S AREA

discovered a different type of aphasia in several of his patients. Unlike Tan, the patients described by Wernicke were positively verbose, but their speech was totally incomprehensible. For instance, a patient with Wernicke's aphasia, when asked, Who is running the store now? might say:

"I don't know. Yes, the bick, uh, yes, I would say that the mick daysis nosis or chipickters. Course, I have also missed on the carfter teck."

Each of the two types of aphasia, Broca's and Wernicke's, corresponded to identifiable areas in the left hemisphere of the brain. Based on this anatomical localization, it appeared that language function resided in one hemisphere, usually the left in right-handed people. It also seemed reasonable that other functions, too, could be localized within certain brain areas.

But despite the battles won by Broca and Wernicke, the debate between localizationists and "holists," who think of the brain as a single, integrated organ, continued. In 1906, Broca's patient's brain was reexamined by a French neurologist, Pierre Marie, who postulated more extensive lesions within Tan's brain than were originally reported by Broca. Although he stopped short of declaring Broca a fraud or an incompetent, Marie didn't hesitate to proclaim boldly that Broca's area "plays no role in the function of language." A reexamination by CAT scan in the early 1980s confirmed that Marie was correct in at least one regard: Tan's brain had more extensive lesions than simply the hen's egg-sized area of destruction in the left hemisphere.

Despite this discovery that Broca's view was slightly simplistic, there was no denying that damage to certain parts of the brain resulted in specific, well-defined disturbances in function. Today, even the most vocal proponents of a holistic brain must admit there are areas in the left hemisphere "associated with" language and speech. However, as such scientists are quick to point out, it is dangerous to try to pinpoint such areas too closely.

If you step outside your home and turn the key in the ignition of your car only to find that the car won't start, is the ignition key the "center" responsible for the performance of your 350-horsepower engine? Of course not. The carburetor may be flooded, the ignition wires may be wet from the heavy rainstorm of the night before, or you may even be out of gasoline. All of these parts—the carburetor, ignition wires, fuel—must work together for the automobile to operate. A failure of any one and the car won't start.

Similar difficulties exist when it comes to locating a "center" for speech and language in the brain. Who hasn't on occasion experienced a failure to come up with the "right word"? This phenomenon can result from just being tired or overworked, or from one of many different kinds of brain damage. If we keep in mind this difficulty in actually pinpointing the "center" for a given activity in the brain, many current ideas on hemisphere specialization may be less confusing.

Within seven years of Broca's discovery of the importance of the left hemisphere in language, another neuroscientist, J. Cotard, used autopsy studies to show that the brains of young children appear to be differently organized than those of adults. A stroke in a young child of six or seven, for instance, often has no effect on subsequent language development. But if the same stroke occurs in an adult, the effect will be devastating: a severe and largely permanent loss of speech function. Why? What could be happening? How could a stroke deprive an adult of speech, yet have little effect on normal language development in a child?

According to one theory, the two hemispheres provide backup systems for each other in the event of damage to only one. Such an arrangement is common in internal organs other than the brain. We have two legs, two arms, two lungs, two eyes, two ears, and two cerebral hemispheres, which makes sense from the evolutionary standpoint: The possession of a backup organ confers a distinct survival advantage.

Before the advent of modern obstetrics, birth injury to the brain was much more common than it is today. In these cases, a healthy hemisphere could take over the function normally carried out by a damaged one. Studies on the long-term effects of *hemispherectomy* (the surgical removal of one hemisphere) early in life support this notion. Infants who have required surgical removal of one of their hemispheres have displayed excellent physical and mental development. But although kidneys and lungs continue to back each other up throughout a lifetime, the brain's hemispheres become so specialized that, beyond childhood, complete recovery from a stroke in one hemisphere is extremely rare.

Some scientists speculate that the roots of adult brain specialization lie buried deep in prehistoric times. While hunting and foraging, particularly among trees, early man found it necessary to use his arms independently of each other. This required an asymmetric arrangement between brain hemispheres different from such symmetric activities as swimming, walking, postural adjustments, and so on. As one arm or hand started being used in preference to another, the hemispheres began to "specialize" further. In this way, specialization and lateralization of brain and hand progressed in tandem over thousands of years.

As it turns out, the asymmetry of our hands and our brains is very much part of the natural order of things. Right- and left-handed sugar molecules differ in their geometry, a quality that can be taken advantage of in a weight-reduction program. Since our body cells accept only right-handed sugars, the left-handed sugars become capable of sweetening our food without burdening us with needless calories. The situation is reversed when it comes to amino acids, the building blocks of proteins, which can be used by the body only if the amino acids are left-handed.

Examinations of the human brain at autopsy show clear-cut asymmetries in the area of speech. In the left hemisphere this portion, the *planum temporale,* is decidedly larger in two thirds of the brains examined. This difference has even been shown in a thirty-one-week-old fetus.

X-ray studies using CAT scans reveal the same kinds of asymmetry in adults. The *Sylvian fissure* (a deep cleft in the outer surface of the brain around which the major speech areas are located) is longer and more horizontally placed in the left hemisphere than it is in the right. In some left-handed people, this tendency for acute angulation on the right hemisphere is less marked, the first demonstration ever of a difference between the brain structures of right- and left-handed persons.

Since the Sylvian fissure leaves a pattern on the inner surface of the skull, it is possible to trace these asymmetries backward in time. Harvard neuroradiologist Marjorie Le May examined the skull of a Neanderthal man thirty thousand to fifty thousand years old and the skull of a Peking man three hundred thousand years old. She found an asymmetry in the Sylvian fissures similar to that in brains examined in the 1980s, an indication that cerebral asymmetry and left-hemisphere dominance for language are not recent events in human evolution.

With the invention of increasingly powerful microscopes and of special stains that can color some parts of the brain while leaving others unchanged, it became possible to examine specific portions of the brain in painstaking detail. Such studies, usually performed by neuroscientists specially trained in interpreting the zigs and zags of neuronal processing, have uncovered some stunning surprises. One such case occurred in 1979, when Dr. Albert M. Galaburda and Dr. Thomas L. Kemper, both of Beth Israel Hospital in Boston, examined the brain of a dyslexic man who had died of internal injuries sustained after a fall.

Dyslexia (a technical term for extreme difficulty in learning to read in an otherwise normally intelligent person) affects about 5 percent of school-aged children. So far its cause has eluded educators and neuroscientists alike. Since dyslexia isn't a fatal disease, the opportunity to exam-

Dr. Frank Duffy of Boston's Children's Hospital, in front of his BEAM scanner. Dr. Duffy has pioneered the use of Brain Electrical Activity Mapping, a sophisticated technique discussed in detail in Chapter 8, in the diagnosis of dyslexia and other brain abnormalities.

ine the brain of a dyslexic doesn't present itself very often. So when Drs. Galaburda and Kemper read about the accidental death of an adult dyslexic, they hastened to obtain permission to examine the brain (it hadn't been directly injured in the accident).

Within the language areas of the left hemisphere they found "disorganized cortex . . . the layers were scrambled and whirled with primitive, larger cells in this part of the brain." These disruptions of normal neuronal architecture were found mainly in the areas concerned with speech and language. In addition, the usual difference in the planum temporale (left side greater than right) wasn't encountered. Both sides were about equal. The Galaburda and Kemper findings were the first demonstration of a difference in the brains of dyslexics. Additional confirmations will be needed before neuroscientists can be certain that the Galaburda and Kemper findings are typical, but their discovery breaks exciting new ground.

Is cerebral hemisphere specialization limited to humans? Neuroscientists have only recently started looking for hemisphere differences, but they have already discovered behavioral and anatomical asymmetries in the brains of apes and monkeys as well as of birds and rats. Fernando Nottebohm, of Rockefeller University, found centers in the left side of the brain of canaries responsible for the development of song. In the rat brain the width of the cerebral cortex varies along sex lines.

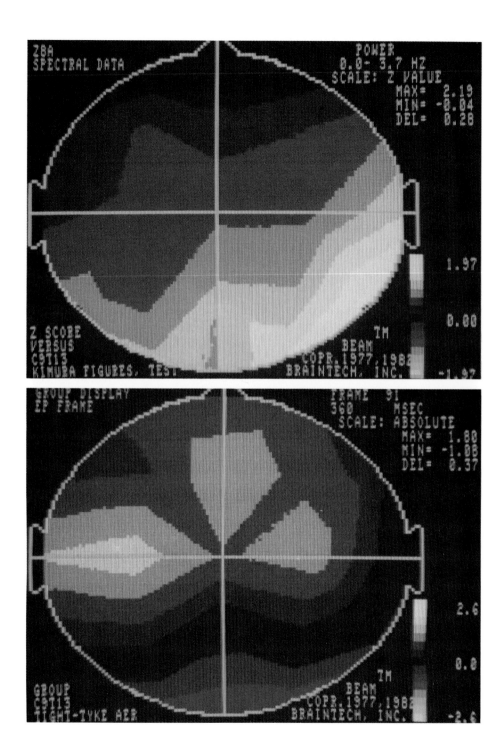

BEAM scans can be combined into a single scan for study. Top, lighter areas indicate where brain electrical activity in dyslexics dif- fers most from that in a group of normal readers; below, the control group.

Brain-Sex Differences: Are They Real?

Men generally have better spatial function than women. This refers to the ability to mentally visualize and maneuver objects within three-dimensional space. But among men who don't produce the male sex hormone testosterone, spatial abilities are poorly developed. According to Harvard neurologist Norman Geschwind, "It is very important to stress that there are women who have absolutely superb spatial function and there are plenty of men whose spatial function is abysmal. But *on the average* men have better spatial function than women." One practical consequence involves the difficulties some people experience in the immediate discrimination between right and left. In one study twice as many women as men reported "frequent" problems in rapidly deciding about right-left issues (turning right at a fork in the road, quickly responding when asked to raise the right or left hand, and so on).

Other areas in which brain-sex differences play a prominent but by no means exclusive role include:

Language facility. Females generally speak earlier, learn foreign languages more easily, and outperform males in tests of verbal fluency.

Fine hand control. From an early age, rapid sequential movements are performed better by girls, who, as a result, exhibit better penmanship than boys of the same age.

Mathematical ability. Studies among mathematically gifted students reveal that males outnumber females among the superior achievers. According to Johns Hopkins researchers Camilla Benbow and Julian Stanley, "We favor the hypothesis that sex differences in achievement in and attitude toward mathematics result from superior male mathematical ability, which may in turn be related to greater male ability in spatial tasks."

Dyslexia, stuttering, delayed speech, autism, hyperactivity—each of these neurobehavioral disorders occurs with greater frequency in males.

Although the above sex differences are well established, no one has as yet convincingly demonstrated an anatomic difference between the brain structures of human males and females. These behavioral differences may be the result of chemical changes in brain function resulting from the influence of sex hormones in early prenatal development.

Although distinct anatomical differences between the brains of men and women are strongly suspected, no convincing proof has been found. However, males *are* more likely to be left-handed and to suffer from dyslexia. Needless to say, the notion of brain sex differences has stimulated heated debate, and the evidence indicates this subject will continue to generate controversy. According to Dr. Elliot S. Gershon, chief of the section on psychogenetics, Biological Psychiatry Branch, National Institute of Mental Health, "Sex differences are well established. It is the ideology of feminism, not the evidence, that leads to calling this area of investigation 'science fiction.'"

The two hemispheres of the brain are connected by a four-inch-long, quarter-inch-thick, pencil-shaped bundle of nerve fibers called the *corpus callosum*. For a long time the function of this connecting link between the two cerebral hemispheres defied explanation. One brain researcher even quipped that the corpus callosum might have no other function than to transport epileptic discharges from one hemisphere to the other. This joke concealed a grim reality: Some patients with incurable epileptic seizures were dying because of the transfer of seizure activity across the corpus callosum. What would be the result, a neurosurgeon named W. P. Van Wagenen asked himself in the 1940s, if the corpus callosum were severed, like cutting the cable connecting two barges?

For one thing, it was certain that the two brain hemispheres wouldn't drift away from each other. The brain is snugly enclosed within three supporting coverings, which are, in turn, locked in position by an unyielding skull. The hemispheres themselves are only the uppermost outcroppings of the brain. Below them the subcortical and brainstem structures are firmly fused.

So, as a last desperate effort to save his patients with incurable epilepsy, Dr. Van Wagenen cut the corpus callosum. It was a daring and highly innovative move, which turned out to have rewards for both his patients and for medical science.

As soon as discharges were no longer able to cross the corpus callosum, the formerly untreatable seizures stopped. Then, to their delight, neurosurgeons found that the surgery resulted in no detectable impairment in mental function.

This discovery, although a godsend to patients and neurosurgeons, posed a vexing puzzle to brain researchers. Common sense demanded that so many millions of nerve fibers must have some purpose. But what was it?

Starting from the proposition that the corpus callosum served no purpose, researchers in the 1940s—including Dr. Van Wagenen and his associate Dr. Andrew Akelaitis—failed to find any change in the patients who had undergone the procedure. It was a classic case. If you start with the proposition that nothing will be found, it is amazing how successful you can be.

Two decades later an experimental psychologist, Dr. Roger W. Sperry, and his colleagues, principally Dr. Michael S. Gazzaniga, demonstrated that the corpus callosum does serve a function. They explored its implications by means of painstaking research on the visual system of a single patient.

According to Dr. Gazzaniga, if you keep your gaze

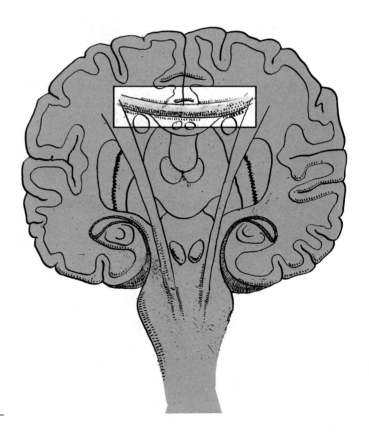

The corpus callosum (highlighted), a "highway" of nerve fibers connecting the two cerebral hemispheres. Cutting these fibers isolates the hemispheres from one another.

fixed on the nose of a person standing in front of you, that half of his or her face to your left projects to your right hemisphere, while that half of his or her face to your right projects to your left hemisphere. Rather than seeing two separate halves of a face, however, you see the *whole face;* this process takes place by means of the corpus callosum, which integrates information from the two sides of the brain, enabling you to build up a complete composite "picture."

In the early 1960s, the researchers studied a forty-eight-year-old epileptic man nicknamed W.J. Dr. Gazzaniga's lab was a far cry from the elaborately equipped facilities one usually associates with brain research: a bare room with a table, a chair, and exposed pipes crisscrossing the ceiling. The initial experimental apparatus also was surprisingly simple: a four-foot-by-four-foot screen suspended from the hot-water pipes, and a slide projector.

Despite the simplicity of the equipment, testing the separate hemispheres was anything but simple and demanded strict attention to detail. For instance, the patient's eyes had to remain fixed on the screen. Second, the visual stimulus, usually a slide of a household object, had to be flashed for only a tenth of a second, before the eyes had time to move.

Prior to W.J.'s surgery, he could rapidly and accurately identify visual objects presented to the right or to the left of a fixed point. After an operation that split his corpus callosum into two unconnected halves, W.J.'s performance was altered in a distinctive way. When a slide of, say, an apple was rapidly presented to his right visual field (which is projected to the left hemisphere, where speech is elaborated), he could rapidly identify it. The same slide when shown off to the left, however, failed to register. In fact, W.J. denied that anything had happened at all.

Michael Gazzaniga's testing of W.J. went on for over a year. (On those occasions when his patient was unable to come to the lab, Dr. Gazzaniga brought the lab to him. He simply piled a portable set of testing apparatus into an old Studebaker and made the trip from the California Institute of Technology to Downey, California.)

On the basis of their findings, Dr. Gazzaniga and his mentor, Roger Sperry, later a winner of the Nobel Prize in Physiology and Medicine in 1981 for the split-brain research, next entered Phase Two of the research—a demonstration

Dr. Roger Sperry

that the two cerebral hemispheres process information differently.

"Phase Two all started rather meekly back in 1961 with W.J.," recalls Dr. Gazzaniga. "I showed that his right hand was unable to arrange a standard set of red and white blocks to a picture design, while the left, nonpreferred hand could complete the task. . . . The claim that we based on those findings was that the left hemisphere is dominant for language processes and the right hemisphere is dominant for visual-constructional tasks."

In the ensuing quarter century since the first testing on hemisphere specialization, neuroscientists have learned a great deal about what each hemisphere does better. In general, the left hemisphere is more important for language and certain motor skills. On the average, the right side of the brain does better with certain kinds of spatial functions such as mentally walking through a maze, understanding and working with maps, visualizing and remembering faces, and other performances that don't depend on verbal descriptions.

But the human brain, like life itself, doesn't break down into neat categories. Remember that the brain is above all a functional organ operating within an evolutionary framework, and its performance can often best be understood as a choice of what is most favorable under the circumstances. Put differently, the same activity may be carried out by different brains according to past experience and present goals. With the advent of the PET scan, which measures cerebral metabolism, the findings of hemisphere specialization along different lines in different people have been confirmed.

For a recent landmark experiment Dr. John Mazziotta and other research scientists at UCLA compared PET scans in people listening to music after having been given some highly specific and unique instructions. The researchers were testing a hunch that the brain responds differently depending on the strategies employed by the listener. As an illustration of the kinds of testing they carried out, imagine my presenting you with two musical chords and asking this simple question: Are they the same or different? If you merely listen and respond reflexively, perhaps by pushing one button if the chords sound the same or another button

PET Scanner (Positron Emission Tomography)

Human brain metabolism varies according to the activities of the moment. The resting brain, for instance, differs from the alert, wakeful brain in its blood flow and glucose utilization. For this reason, measurements of metabolism within the brain provide an indirect indication of what parts of the brain are active at different times. When moving the right hand, for instance, a person's metabolic activity is enhanced in the hand area of the opposite hemisphere.

As a consequence of the development of radioactive isotopes it is now possible to administer a radioactively tagged substance via intravenous injection and then "track" the isotope within the brain by means of instruments that detect and measure the decay of the isotope. For instance, FDG is a positron-emitting compound. Since this compound cannot be metabolized by brain cells in the manner of regular glucose, it tends to accumulate within the brain cells in direct proportion to the brain activity at a given time. For instance, if the visual cortex is active (the person is staring at a pattern), the FDG accumulates in the visual areas. As the radioisotope decays, it emits gamma rays. After detecting and recording these gamma rays, a computer converts the information into a colored biochemical map of the brain. In essence, the conversion of matter into energy within the brain is translated into a colored visual image that corresponds to brain activity.

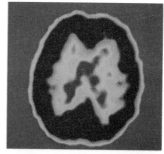
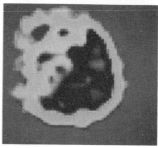

PET scans of a normal brain (top) compared to a brain during an epileptic seizure. Below, a patient enters the scanner.

The PET scan (shorthand for *positron emission tomography*) is presently being used to "map" the brain. Specific brain areas involved in movement, sensation, thinking, and even memory can be pinpointed by means of measured changes in glucose consumption within the brain.

Already, PET scans are proving useful in the diagnosis of schizophrenia, manic-depression, and other psychiatric conditions. The most exciting prospect, however, concerns their usefulness in the study of the "normal" brain. Eventually it is hoped that PET scans or some similar technologies involving short-lived radioisotopes will provide a means of distinguishing one brain from another.

if they sound different, the task is likely to be carried out by the right hemisphere of the brain. You are merely responding according to your perceptions. But if you respond to my question by, say, mentally arranging the chords along a scale (a task that obviously requires some musical sophistication), you have shifted the task to the more symbolic mode of the left hemisphere.

In these experiments the stimulus remained constant (all subjects were exposed to the same musical notes or chords), yet the PET scans confirmed that hemisphere activation differed, suggesting something quite remarkable—that hemisphere specialization is dependent on the strategy employed by the listener. Furthermore, when the experimental subject is taught to graph mentally the sounds heard along a scale, say, from high to low intensity (an analytic strategy similar to ones used by musicians), hemisphere specialization shifts from right to left. This is additional confirmation that the important issue is not so much the material dealt with (music, tones, etc.) but rather the cognitive strategy (mental processing) employed. This suggests that a musically sophisticated subject not only "processes" music differently than his or her naïve counterpart (an insight that is far from original) but also employs different parts of the brain to perform tasks of listening and playing music.

Although it has only recently become possible to carry out studies such as those at UCLA, it is likely that brain metabolic mapping of individuals engaged in other activities will reveal similar disparities. People may not only be of a "different mind" on issues, but they may also use different parts of their brains to do the same thing.

This discovery tremendously enriches our understanding of the human brain. Instead of thinking that the left hemisphere is specialized for language, it may, more accurately, be specialized for symbolic representation. The right hemisphere, by contrast, seems to deal with representations that mirror reality more directly, those large chunks of experience that don't employ language. One example of right-brain specialization is the ability to distinguish one person from another. Police artists are used routinely to help witnesses identify suspects in criminal investigations because language is inadequate in conveying the necessary detail.

Division of the hemispheres into *symbolic-conceptual*

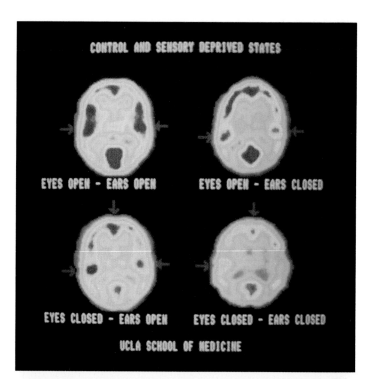

CONTROL AND SENSORY DEPRIVED STATES

EYES OPEN - EARS OPEN   EYES OPEN - EARS CLOSED

EYES CLOSED - EARS OPEN   EYES CLOSED - EARS CLOSED

UCLA SCHOOL OF MEDICINE

These PET scans were made during the landmark UCLA auditory stimulation experiments. These images show the brain as seen from above, looking down onto the top of the skull. The person in question is facing forward (towards the top of the page).

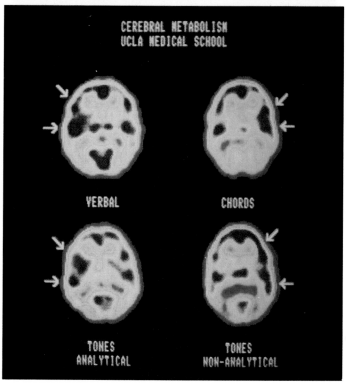

CEREBRAL METABOLISM
UCLA MEDICAL SCHOOL

VERBAL   CHORDS

TONES
ANALYTICAL   TONES
NON-ANALYTICAL

In most people, the left hemisphere is concerned with reading, language, writing, arithmetic, and other "reasoning" abilities. The right hemisphere's functions are geared to spatial, associative, and other "artistic" abilities. These are only general guidelines, however, because the brain operates as a holistic structure, combining all these skills.

(left hemisphere) vs. *nonsymbolic directly perceived* (right hemisphere) avoids many oversimplifications. For instance, it is not totally true that the right hemisphere is completely devoid of language ability. It may be capable, after some practice, of decoding a word such as "horse." It will have difficulty, however, when presented with a more symbolic one such as "faith." It is as if the right hemisphere can most easily derive meaning from a concrete object or event. Notice that I qualified the last two sentences with escape clauses "will have difficulty" and "most easily," both of which imply that the matter isn't completely decided. These qualifications are necessary because evidence exists that the right hemisphere can learn to enhance its verbal-symbolic skills in the absence of any obvious increase in language abilities.

For instance, in an experiment carried out by Dr. Gazzaniga and fellow researcher Margery Pinsley, a male subject was shown pictures projected only to the right hemisphere. Immediately afterward the patient was given four choice cards and requested to point to the card that best related to the stimulus. In some cases the cards were related to the stimulus in ways that required inferences, judgments, or conclusions to be drawn. For example, when the claw of a chicken was projected to the right hemisphere, the subject made the correct choice among the cards, an illustration of an egg. Clearly, the relationship of a chicken claw to an egg is not simply picture matching but also requires the subject to draw an inference. But there is a problem here: Inferences require logic and language, internal reasoning, or "talking things out." Yet the patient cannot name what he has seen; he can only point to one of four cards. If asked why he picked an egg, he can't say, and he doesn't recall that only a moment ago he was presented with the flash picture of a claw.

Such performances present us with a seemingly unresolvable paradox. There is a solution, however, if we can admit one important distinction: Tests of the separate hemispheres may be probing two different selves. Most of us recoil at such a prospect. Our sense of personal continuity seems to contradict such a proposition. We know who we are from day to day (at least most of us think we do). But the truly introspective person also recognizes that on occasion he or she does things for reasons he or she can't always satisfactorily explain. The answers may lie in split-brain research.

Vicki is the divorced mother of a seven-year-old daughter. Several years ago Vicki had a split-brain operation. Today, although she is able to function as a mother and homemaker, she finds some experiences troubling. For instance, when she chooses the clothes she will wear for the day, her left hand often reaches in the drawer and extracts additional items.

"It would reach in and get something that I wouldn't want at all. A couple of times I had a pair of shorts on, and I would find myself putting another pair of shorts on on top of the pair I already had. . . . My hands sort of took control, got that other pair of shorts. . . . I have had trouble like that."

Vicki's strange symptom results from the disconnection between her right and left hemispheres. Ordinarily the two hemispheres engage in cross talk via the corpus callosum. Once this fifty-million-fiber connecting link is severed, however, the two hemispheres are no longer able to communicate. When Vicki strikes a match, for example, each hand is controlled by the opposite side of her brain. But since Vicki can see both of her hands at the same time, she can coordinate them. Blindfolded, Vicki wouldn't be able to tell that her left hand was holding the matchbox. Language resides mainly in her left hemisphere, which only knows about the match in her right hand.

Several times during the year Vicki is tested by Dr. Gazzaniga. In a typical experiment an image is rapidly flashed in the right field of Vicki's vision (handled by the left hemisphere of Vicki's brain). She identifies it immediately. When the same stimulus is projected to the right hemisphere, the difference is dramatic. In one such experiment, Vicki identified a picture of a woman talking on the telephone simply as "woman." At this point, Dr. Gazzaniga advised, "Write what she was doing with your left hand. Close your eyes and just let your left hand go."

When Vicki was finished, Dr. Gazzaniga asked, "What did you write?"

"Skipping rope."

Dr. Gazzaniga: "Let me show you what you wrote."

Vicki: "Telephone."

In this example Vicki's right hemisphere wasn't able to elaborate verbally beyond the recognition that the slide had depicted a "woman." With her eyes closed, she was then asked to write with her left hand, which was controlled by the right hemisphere. It instructed Vicki's hand to write out the other significant feature of the picture, telephone. But when Dr. Gazzaniga took Vicki's written report away and asked her what she had written, she could only guess: skipping rope.

This isolation of one side of Vicki's brain from the other points up the possibility, some might say necessity, of the existence of two separate selves or personalities, one belonging to the left hemisphere and another to the right hemisphere. If you still find this difficult to accept, consider the following.

On a split screen the word "clap" is flashed on the left side and "laugh" on the right side. Vicki immediately both laughs and claps.

Dr. Gazzaniga: "What did you see that time?"

Vicki: (laughs) "Am I supposed to be seeing two words?"

"The left hemisphere controlled the laughing response, and the right hemisphere controlled her ability to clap," states Dr. Gazzaniga. "Yet, when pressed in this kind of situation, the left hemisphere dominates, and she maintains that the only command that had been given to her was, in fact, the command to laugh. What is very important is the independence of these two half brains. They can both be given a command at the same time. They can both organize a movement at the same time. And they can both carry it out at the same time."

Dr. Gazzaniga's work with Vicki and other patients who have undergone split-brain operations has convinced him that within each of us are many selves, not all of whom get along well with each other. For instance, consider this exchange with the right hemisphere of a patient P.S., recorded soon after his split-brain operation:

"Who are you?"

"P.S."

"Where are you?"

"Vermont."

"What do you want to be?"

"An automobile racer."

The same series of questions when presented to the left

hemisphere elicited the same answers, with the exception of the one to the last question:

"What do you want to be?"

"A draftsman."

P.S. is probably the most unusual patient ever tested after a split-brain operation. His right hemisphere, rather than volunteering only crude and unelaborated answers, is capable of intensely personal responses (the "automobile racer" response). What is most interesting is the attitude that P.S. expresses toward the performance of his right hemisphere. For instance, if questions about his favorite food or TV programs are delivered to P.S.'s left visual field (right hemisphere)—with special care that the left hemisphere doesn't see the questions—he answers, "I didn't see anything." But a few seconds later his left hand will pick up a pen and write out an answer to the question. P.S.'s right hemisphere, Michael Gazzaniga postulates, comprises a "separate mental system" capable of expressing its own feelings and preferences. Throughout all this the left hemisphere, with its preference for verbalized, symbolic expression, tends to elaborate reasons, sometimes even spurious ones, for what is going on.

In one test P.S. was shown two pictures, one projected to the left hemisphere (a chicken claw) and one to the right hemisphere (a snow scene). He was asked to indicate from a series of pictures what picture he had just seen. P.S. selected a picture of a chicken with his right hand and a picture of a snow shovel with his left. When asked why he had made these particular selections, P.S. remarked: "That's easy. The chicken claw goes with the chicken, and you need a shovel to clean out the chicken's shed."

In this instance, P.S.'s left hemisphere employed its language superiority to construct a plausible, "logical" explanation for the choices he had selected. But the explanation was wrong, an error that suggests to Michael Gazzaniga that our speech and language systems routinely attempt to interpret rather than simply report our activities. If P.S.'s explanation is at all typical of the rest of us, it suggests that the reasons we give for our own behavior may not be the salient ones at all.

Psychiatrists have always claimed that many facets of our everyday behavior involve rationalizations. Although we may choose plausible-sounding reasons for doing something,

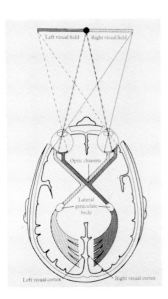

The human visual system causes the right side of the visual field to be processed in the left hemisphere, and vice versa.

our explanations aren't necessarily true. Now neuroscientists such as Michael Gazzaniga are providing proof for the accuracy of the claim that in many instances "our right hand doesn't know what our left hand is doing." Or to be more precise, "our left brain doesn't know what our right brain is doing."

The most compelling objection to Dr. Gazzaniga's work with P.S.—indeed, to split-brain research in general—is that patients who undergo a sectioning of their corpus callosum do not have normal brains in the first place. This is true: If their brains were perfectly normal, they wouldn't be involved with neurosurgeons, operating theaters, and experimental psychologists. Can any of the findings of what Dr. Gazzaniga calls "multiple systems" of the mind be detected in individuals without known brain disease?

One way of testing this hypothesis involves threading a long tube, called a catheter, into the arteries flowing to either the right or left side of the brain. Once in place, one side of the brain can then be put to sleep by using an anesthetic, while the opposite side continues to function. Since the left hemisphere is usually the side of the brain formulating language and speech, an anesthetic delivered to the left hemisphere via the catheter results in a mute patient, who can't say anything for about two minutes. During this time the right hemisphere remains capable of functioning, however, a feature that Michael Gazzaniga took advantage of.

"My idea was to give the right hemisphere something to remember while the left was asleep. After the left woke up, I was going to ask it whether or not it knew about the information I had given to the right." Dr. Gazzaniga discovered that the left brain couldn't talk about information that had been fed into the right hemisphere. But if the right hemisphere was given an opportunity for expression, usually by pointing to an array of possible choices, its response was always right on target.

"In short, we had collected data that revealed that even within the normal brain the right hemisphere possessed knowledge that was encoded in a form that remained insulated from the search process of the left hemisphere's language system," says Dr. Gazzaniga.

Based on experiences with P.S. and other patients with split-brain operations, along with the work with normals described above, Michael Gazzaniga has concluded that the human brain is organized in terms of a "mental society." In other words, alongside our verbal system, there may reside any number of "mental units [that] can exist, can have memories, values, and emotions, and all of these can be expressed through any of a variety of response systems." What makes this whole process so eerie is that these systems may not be in touch with the verbal system at all but rather, have their own existence outside of the areas of our brain responsible for our language and our logic.

Think back for a moment to Paul Broca's discovery of the importance of the left hemisphere in language. As we know, destruction in "Broca's area" renders the speaker incapable of a sentence such as Is that what you really mean? But even a sentence as simple and straightforward as this raises questions that involve far more than language alone. In addition to semantic and grammatical components, all spoken communications employ a third component: prosody, the melodic and stress contours of speech.

Is *that* what you really mean? with the emphasis on the second word lends an entirely different meaning to this sentence than Is that what you *really* mean? Prosody imparts emotional tone and makes subtle shades of meaning possible. Other components of prosody include tones of voice that convey irony, disbelief, or sarcasm: Is that what *you* really mean? might be a way of implying you are merely mouthing someone else's ideas.

On the basis of these considerations, thoughtful neuroscientists have always been slightly uncomfortable with the distinction that only the left hemisphere is important in language. How is prosody encoded in language? Might the two elements of language—semantics and prosody—be encoded differently in the brain?

Recent research carried out by neuroscientists at the University of Texas Health Center in Dallas and at Harvard University reveals that disturbances in the right hemisphere can rob a person of the ability to distinguish important nuances in everyday speech. For instance, normally the "green house" is easily distinguishable in ordinary conversation from the "greenhouse." Nor is the "dark room" likely to be confused with the "darkroom." But individuals who

Popular Questions About the Brain

Q: *Are there foods that can be used to improve the brain's performance?*

A: Certain amino acids in the diet are the precursors of the neurotransmitters —substances released from a nerve cell when it fires. Some brain cells convert tryptophane into serotonin. Others incorporate choline into acetyl-choline. In still other brain cells, tyrosine is the precursor for dopamine, norepinephrine, and epinephrine (collectively referred to as the "catecholamine transmitters"). Among some patients suffering from diseases affecting the memory, the administration of choline has been helpful. The choline can be taken in the form of lecithin (found in soybeans). Unfortunately, most of the lecithin preparations now available in health food stores are very low in phosphatidyl-choline, the only effective source of choline.

At this point the role of amino acids is limited to the treatment of patients suffering from illnesses associated with deficiencies in available neurotransmitters (low acetylcholine is linked to some memory disorders, decreased dopamine is involved in Parkinson's disease). Generally there is little evidence that mental performance in healthy people can be boosted by food supplements.

Q: *Is it true that the older one is, the more difficult it is to learn new tasks?*

A: The human brain exhibits a remarkable flexibility in performance, a flexibility that does decrease with age. For instance, an infant can recover from a severe brain injury that would leave an adult permanently disabled. The young brain is more adaptable and learns such things as languages more easily. But the brain's adaptability is compromised by normal aging processes. CAT scans of older people show changes consistent with the view that even normal aging is accompanied by a measurable loss of brain cells. It is likely that the learning difficulties experienced by the elderly are the consequence of fewer brain cells and less efficient connections. We see the same phenomenon in the animal kingdom. As folk wisdom suggests, it's hard to teach an old dog new tricks.

have suffered damage to the right hemisphere are unable to make such distinctions easily.

In a typical experiment, individuals with right-hemisphere damage are presented with four pictures and asked to select the one that corresponds to a spoken word or phrase. For instance, the "*red* coat," when pronounced with a particular emphasis on red, might represent a picture of an eighteenth-century British soldier. Or if the inflection on red is slightly altered, it would correspond to a coat made of red material. In a similar way, "red cap" can refer to a porter or to a cap that is not green or blue but *red*. Damage to the right hemisphere interferes with the facility of making such subtle but important distinctions.

From experiments such as these, neuroscientists are changing many traditional ideas about human communication, particularly language. Obviously, the purpose of language involves far more than simply the transmission of grammatical information. Additional messages are conveyed by voice modulation, changes in inflection, and alterations in prosody. "He is absolutely unbelievable!" when written in isolation is capable of multiple meanings. But when spoken, it is soon obvious whether the speaker is expressing admiration or the broadest kind of sarcasm.

We all know people who never quite get the point of a joke until it is explained to them. Others can be ridiculed to their face using not so subtle forms of irony. Is it possible that these people suffer from similar disturbances in handling the prosodic components of language?

Although we can only speculate, there is little doubt that vast differences exist among otherwise normal people in dealing with subtleties of language. The construction and appreciation of puns, for instance, demand an ability to alter meaning playfully according to differences in inflection.

The poet T. S. Eliot's famous lines "That is the way the world ends/Not with a bang but a whimper" served as a vehicle for the late jazz alto saxophonist Paul Desmond to describe a woman friend who changed her mind about marrying a struggling artist and selected a wealthy financier instead. "That is the way the world ends, not with a whim but a banker," quipped Desmond. A person with damage in the right hemisphere would fail to appreciate the wordplay involved.

The right hemisphere seems to contribute the color,

the verve, the "firepower" to ordinary speech. In addition to puns and wordplay, it makes possible the expression of enthusiasm, joy, sadness, and despair. Picture for a moment a person who is in the prime of life, successful in his social and occupational relationships, happy, looking forward to his most productive years. Now imagine the effect of a severe stroke leaving this forty-seven-year-old male accoun-

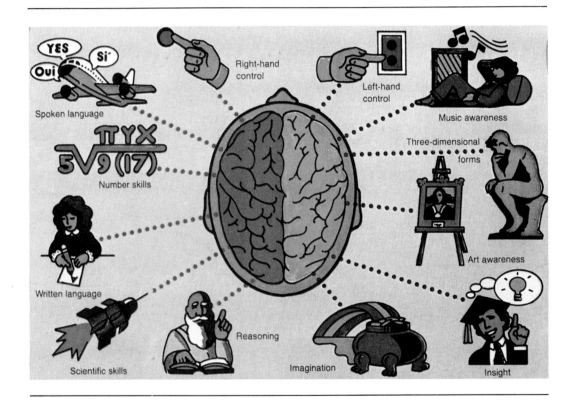

tant totally paralyzed on the left side of his body with his speech slurred to the point that at all times he sounds drunk. No doubt you would expect such a person to be depressed, feeling terribly sorry for himself, perhaps even resentful. In fact, the man I am describing showed little emotion, and in the words of his neurologist, Dr. Elliott Ross, "There was no discernible difference in his voice when discussing his sadness over his illness, his prolonged absence from his family, or his excitement and anticipation about his upcoming weekend pass." Dr. Ross was curious about his patient's reaction and set about testing him.

With the exception of slurring his words, the patient's

comprehension and expression were perfectly normal. But if he was asked to speak an ordinary English sentence in an angry voice, he was unable to do it. Nor could he express exasperation. ("Will you please answer that phone! It has rung fifteen times!") In each case his voice was flat and unemotional. His comprehension of the emotional color in speech, however, was perfectly normal. He was able to detect when other people were experiencing surprise, disinterest, sadness, elation, or anger, as reflected in their voices. Since the patient was able to comprehend emotions but was unable to express them, Ross termed the disorder a *motor aprosodia*. He characterized it by "monotone speech, poor ability to repeat sentences with prosodic-affective variation, and excellent comprehension of the affective components of speech and gesturing."

Left at this, Dr. Ross's observations are interesting but not terribly informative. Why can't the patient express emotion despite the fact that he can comprehend and distinguish a variety of mental states? As often happens in the neurosciences, answers are come by at a price, in this instance the unexpected death of this man, who, on September 23, 1980, suffered a massive blood clot in his lungs. Examination of his brain at autopsy revealed an *infarction* (small stroke) in the right side of the brain below the cerebral hemisphere.

Based on this finding and investigations of other patients, Ross and others have proposed that matching language and emotions takes place within the hemispheres via cross communication over the corpus callosum. The expression of emotion, however, takes place farther down the brainstem. In other words, a disturbance within the right hemisphere would make it difficult for a person to comprehend the emotional context of a spoken sentence. He or she would be likely to remain unflappable in response to the peremptory command "Get the hell out of here!" But if the disturbance is located in an area that receives fibers projecting downward from the right hemisphere, as in the case of Dr. Ross's patient, the difficulty comes in expressing emotion rather than in comprehending it. Regardless of exact location, the main point that emerges from these studies is the predominant role of the right hemisphere in the production and experience of the emotional aspects of speech.

Damage to the right hemisphere also results in another strange condition. A thirty-nine-year-old patient of the famed British neurologist and neuroscientist MacDonald Critchley was paralyzed on her left side and could neither see nor feel objects on that side. Nonetheless, she "denied she was paralyzed and insisted that her left arm and leg belonged to her daughter, Ann, who she said had been sharing her bed for the past week. When the patient's wedding ring was pointed out to her, she said that Ann had borrowed it to wear. When the patient was encouraged to talk to Ann, to tell her to move her arm, she became confused and talked vaguely about Ann being asleep and not to be disturbed. When asked to indicate her own left limb, she turned her head and searched in a bemused way over her left shoulder."

Another patient of Dr. Critchley's "kept wandering about in the blind . . . half field of vision. When the patient wrote, the left hand would wander across and butt in and rest on the right hand. Not recognizing this as his own, he would exclaim: 'Let go my hand!' He would swear at it in exasperation: 'You bloody bastard! It's lost its soul, this bloody thing. It follows me around and gets in the way when I read.' "

Despite such fantastic presentations, the denial of left-sided paralysis by patients with lesions on the right hemisphere isn't rare. Patients who deny or downplay their left-sided problems can be encountered in the neurology wards in any reasonably busy hospital. In fact, if they are not found, it is usually either because the staff isn't aware of the condition of *anosognosia* and doesn't think to test for it, or because the patient's lack of concern for a severely disabling stroke is taken as evidence of fortitude.

Although neuroscientists disagree on the exact reasons for the denial of left-sided paralysis, they do agree on its location, almost always resulting from disease in the right hemisphere, particularly in the parietal region, which is now thought to be responsible for our body schema.

Damage to the right hemisphere also brings in its wake several mental peculiarities that implicate the right hemisphere in our emotional responses. For instance, think back to the response of Dr. Critchley's first patient when the wedding ring on her own hand was pointed out to her. At this moment, the evidence that the hand lying on the bed belonged to no one but her was overwhelming. Yet she continued to deny it and claimed the ring belonged to her daughter, Ann, who she said was asleep and shouldn't be disturbed. Far more is going on in such a situation than mere denial. Rather, it seems that the patient with right-hemisphere damage is unable to experience appropriate emotional orientation, as if the problem belongs to someone else and is of no immediate concern. Often this lack of apparent concern extends beyond the immediate illness or disability and can include a "couldn't care less" attitude about financial problems and personal conflicts.

In the words of Harvard psychiatrist David M. Bear, "The fundamental deficit, of which denial of illness may be only a special case, could be a failure in emotional surveillance. The patient does not detect an important threat and, therefore, does not sustain attention, emotional concern, or initiate adaptive responses." If Dr. Bear is correct, then it should be possible to demonstrate heightened emotional responses from the *intact* right hemisphere in normal people.

In 1977, Drs. Stewart Dimond and Linda Farrington carried out a study "Emotional Response to Films Shown to the Right or Left Hemisphere of the Brain Measured by Heart Rate." As a first step, Drs. Dimond and Farrington fitted their subjects with specially constructed contact lenses that restricted vision to either the right or the left visual field. (Remember, the left visual field projects to the right hemisphere, and vice versa.) Medically naïve subjects viewing films of surgical operations judged the films more disturbing when they were projected to the right hemisphere. Their heart rate also fluctuated more widely when views of a mutilating surgical procedure were projected to the right hemisphere as compared to the left.

The Dimond and Farrington study provided the stimulus for other neuroscientists to test a hypothesis: The right hemisphere is concerned with negative emotions (such as sadness or anxiety), whereas the left hemisphere is responsible for more positive moods (happiness, joy, laughter, and so on) and their expression.

If you study a series of facial photographs carefully, you will find that the left side of the face is more intense in its emotional display. This is particularly true for sadness and depression. Measurements of electrical activity in facial muscles show a similar pattern—more obvious left facial involvement when a person is feeling sad, and greater activity on the right side in the presence of "upbeat" emotions.

Yale psychologist Gary Schwartz has found that even questioning a person about negative feelings brings about an increase in the electrical activity of the left side of their face. If the questions are switched to positive feelings ("Tell me how you felt the day you found you had been accepted into Yale"), the balance shifts, and the right-sided facial muscles become more active. The responses of Dr. Critchley's patients and the findings of Dr. Elliott Ross regarding prosody should now begin to make sense. If the right hemisphere is concerned with providing negative emotional coloring to our experience, then damaging it could result in the denial that anything unfortunate has happened. If the right hemisphere is overexcited, on the other hand, such as with an epileptic seizure originating in that hemisphere, a strong negative emotion would be expected. Indeed, this is what occurs—uncontrolled crying, seemingly for no reason, accompanies right-hemisphere but not left-hemisphere epileptic seizures.

Think of it this way: As far as emotions go, the right and the left hemispheres are two sides of a balanced scale. The left hemisphere is concerned with positive emotions; the right, with negative emotions. Now imagine lifting the weights from one side—say, the right. Immediately the scale tips toward the left. The removal of weights corresponds to damage in which brain tissue is lost. Since the right hemisphere usually is the side that would provide the appropriate sadness and concern, damage to its nerve cells results in lack of concern, even denial.

An epileptic fit that causes an increase in activity is roughly equivalent to putting *more* weight on one side of our hypothetical scale. In this instance an epileptic patient with fits starting in the right hemisphere begins to cry for no obvious reason. If the fits start in the left hemisphere, our hypothetical scales tip to the left, and we have uncontrollable emotional outbursts, such as laughter, that occur for no discernible reason. Even the patient cannot explain why he or she suddenly bursts into laughter.

Although the scale is an effective analogy for right- and left-hemisphere components of emotion, it would be a mistake to assume that emotions are strictly localized in the two hemispheres. As with Dr. Elliott Ross' patient, damage may be located deeper within the substance of the brain. If you open a fan and study its configuration for a moment, you can get a feel for how brain fibers converge as they descend deeper into the brain. The cerebral hemispheres correspond to the wider, top portions of the fan. This narrows into a handle, which corresponds roughly to the subcortical (literally below the cortex) and brainstem areas. A smaller stroke within this area can destroy a huge proportion of cells in the cortex. A stroke of a similar size, if it occurred up along the edges of the fan, would affect only a small portion of the total fibers "fanning" downward.

A similar situation exists for brain cells carrying sensory information from the body and traveling up toward the cerebral hemispheres. The fibers enter the narrow end of the fan and spread out as they ascend to the cortex. This model of a fan is also useful because it serves to remind us that the cerebral hemispheres don't exist in a kind of "splendid isolation" but are linked with areas within the subcortex and brainstem.

It is always helpful to remember that ongoing events within the brain don't always proceed according to common sense. For instance, I mentioned several times that stimulation from the right side of the body winds up registering on the left side of the brain and vice versa. This happens because sensory data cross the body's midline at several sites, depending on the origin of the stimulus. For instance, if you stub your toe in the dark, pain signals from the foot cross over at a region far below the crossover point from pain signals sent by the hand. Pain impulses from the face, such as a toothache, cross over even higher in the brainstem. The end result of all of the crossing over from one side of the body to the other is a bewildering network of interlacing nerve fibers that extends the total length of the human spinal cord. The key question is, of course, what purpose is served by such an arrangement. At this point neuroscientists have yet to formulate a really convincing answer. To put the matter differently: The human brain has yet to discover this aspect of the mystery of its own functioning. There is little doubt, however, that we need both sides of our brain. In fact, one can state with equal validity that we are not just the right and left sides of our brain but simply *we are our brain* and wouldn't want to lose any part of it if we had a choice.

The Japanese Brain

Is left-hemisphere specialization for language universal? Before assuming that the answer is "yes," let's look at some of the remarkable diversity of expression made possible by different languages. English, for instance, is heavily dependent on consonants. Try to compose a sentence, however short, that doesn't contain one or more consonants. It's impossible. Japanese, in contrast, can express extremely complex notions in sentences using only vowels: *"Ue o ui, oi o ooi, ai o ou, aiueo"* means "a love-hungry man who worries about hunger hides his old age and chases love."

Dr. Tadanobu Tsunoda, a specialist in speech and hearing disorders at the Tokyo Medical and Dental University, has investigated patients who have suffered strokes to their left and, presumably, speech-dominant hemispheres. While testing his subjects, Dr. Tsunoda observed that an isolated vowel, such as a single sound "ah," was processed principally in the left hemisphere instead of the right, as would be expected. Exploring further, he began a crosscultural study comparing native-born Japanese with non-Japanese living in Tokyo. These included North and South Americans, Europeans, Middle Easterners, Polynesians, East Indians, Australians, Chinese, Filipinos, and Koreans. He found that all of these diverse groups processed isolated vowel sounds predominantly in the right hemisphere. Only the Japanese handled vowels in the left hemisphere. However, most interesting of all, Americans and Europeans raised in Japan and exposed to the Japanese language since an early age showed the same hemisphere specialization as native-born Japanese. This finding, a smashing surprise to Dr. Tsunoda, immediately disposed of one of the two most likely explanations for his findings: heredity. Obviously, if processing vowel sounds in the left hemisphere is inherited, then Americans and Europeans raised in Japan would retain the Western right-hemisphere dominance for isolated vowel sounds. Instead they resembled native-born Japanese in this respect.

Over the years anthropologists have commented about the unique way the Japanese think about space and individuality, and the importance they place on intuition.

There are also deeply philosophical differences. Perhaps it is not accidental that Zen, with its emphasis on emptiness and the willful relinquishment of "self" during meditation, is a Japanese rather than a Western phenomenon. Certain Zen sounds are untranslatable, such as "ka!" or "ga!," indicating a spontaneous cry at the moment of attaining satori, or enlightenment.

Dr. Tsunoda's findings provide a plausible reason why Zen and other aspects of the "Japanese mind" are so puzzling and frustrating to Westerners. Simply put, the Japanese brain may be organized differently. Dr. Tsunoda speculates that the Japanese preference for indirect, intuitive routes to problem-solving may result from the fact that both capabilities reside within the same hemisphere.

If Dr. Tsunoda's research is correct, the left hemisphere in the Japanese brain is concerned with things that are as important as logic is to a Westerner: intuition, indirection, and the creative use of space and sound. The sensitivity to these multiple components of human communication facilitates judgments about people and events that would be impossible to a person who relies on "logic" alone.

Central to Dr. Tsunoda's thesis is the importance of language as a determinant of brain organization, patterns of thinking, and ultimately culture. While Westerners allocate both their language and logical function to the left hemisphere, with the nonverbal aspect of communication to the right hemisphere, the Japanese brain, in contrast, processes sounds and experiences relevant to emotion in the left hemisphere. The stimulus for the relegation to one hemisphere or the other, according to Dr. Tsunoda, is nothing other than language itself.

"I believe that the mother tongue differentiates the way in which people receive, process, feel, and understand sounds in the external environment," says Dr. Tsunoda. "The mother tongue is closely related to the development of the emotional mechanism in the brain. I conjecture that the mother tongue acquired in childhood is closely linked with the formation of the unique culture and mentality of each ethnic group."

The accompanying figure shows the brain of a monkey treated with radioactively tagged PCP. The *mesolimbic system,* the area of the brain that is the substrate for our emotions, is intensely activated. If this PCP had been given to a human (an unthinkable laboratory experiment that, sadly, is being carried out daily on the streets of our nation's cities), a similar activation would be seen. In this dramatic example, no one can doubt for a moment that behavior and neurochemistry are intimately linked. Scientists believe that some mind-altering drugs exert their primary action on the limbic system, which links up with the cerebral hemispheres where

Receptors "lighting up" in the brain of a monkey given a radio-actively-tagged dose of PCP.

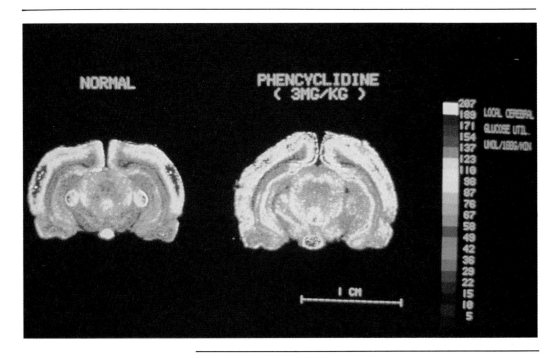

changes induced by these chemicals are elaborated symbolically: visual hallucinations, feelings of grandiosity or paranoia, declarations of unity with the cosmos, and so on. It is likely that the dramatic effects of drugs such as PCP are due to the powerful linkages these drugs form with neuronal receptors within the limbic system and cerebral hemispheres.

The slide of the monkey's brain exposed to PCP illustrates the pervasive effects of this chemical on brain functioning. The slide also vividly portrays the unity between self and brain. As this chemical locks on to the brain receptors, the most important aspects of individual personality are affected, in some cases permanently. That such extensive changes in personality could be brought about by a chemical provides confirmation of what neuroscientists are telling us: *We are our brain.* Are neuroscientists the only ones to feel this way? Rudyard Kipling intuitively came to the heart of the matter in the poem *Kim:*

> *Something I owe to the soil that grew—*
> *More to the life that fed—*
> *But most to Allah, who gave me two*
> *Separate sides to my head.*
>
> *I would go without shirts or shoes,*
> *Friends, tobacco, or bread*
> *Sooner than for an instant lose*
> *Either side of my head.*

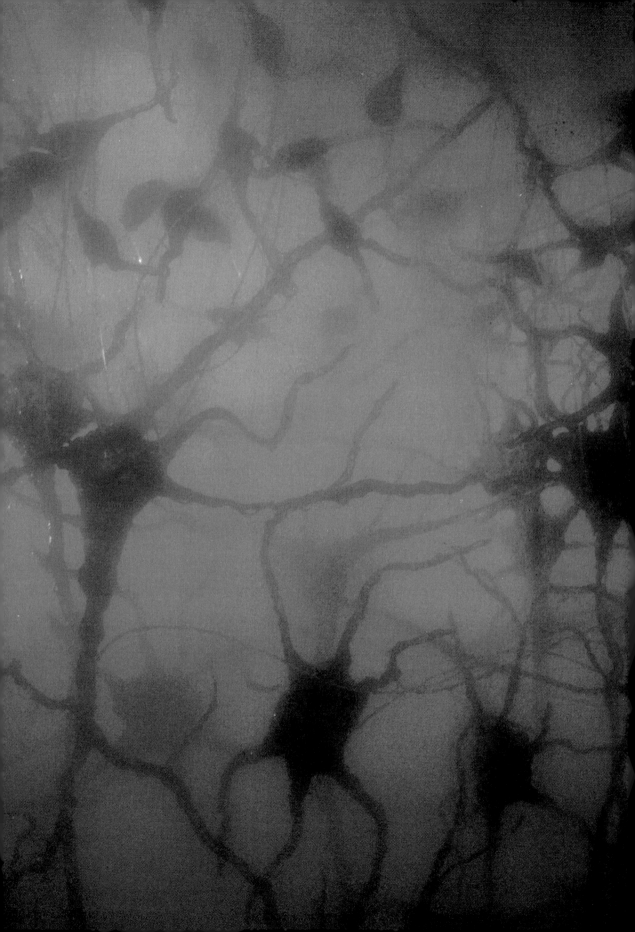

7.
Madness

One late October morning, the doctors, nurses, and psychiatric social workers at St. Elizabeth's Hospital in Washington, D.C., are gathered for Grand Rounds, a weekly conference to review the progress of selected patients hospitalized in the wards.

St. Elizabeth's is one of the oldest mental hospitals in the country. Over the years its wards have accommodated patients of every race, creed, and profession. It once housed the poet Ezra Pound. But on this particular morning the staff is gathered to discuss a much less renowned patient. His name is Jerry, a former policeman who has been diagnosed a schizophrenic.

As the side door opens, a hushed silence falls over the room. Several doctors lean forward in their chairs in order not to miss a single word of the dialogue between Jerry and Dr. Llewellyn Bigelow. Jerry is a dark-haired, muscular young man who greets Dr. Bigelow with an intense, unblinking stare. Within seconds Jerry begins looking off into space and, occasionally, toward the other staff members seated in the audience. Throughout the interview Jerry twists and curls his hair with the fingers of his right hand, twisting it up into a peak and then untwisting it again.

"How are you today?" asks Dr. Bigelow.

"I feel as though people have called me here to electrocute me . . . judge me . . . put me in jail. All because of some of the sins I've committed."

"Is this a new feeling for you?"

"It's not a new feeling. No. I'm scared of people. I'm

In the substantia nigra of a Parkinson's disease victim, we might see the kind of cell shutdown evident in this neural network.

271

so scared that I can tell you that the picture over there on the wall has a headache."

"Tell me about that, 'The picture has a headache.' "

"When a sperm and an egg go together to make a baby, one sperm goes up at once and when they touch at two contact points, they fuse. It's like nuclear fusion, except it's human fusion. There is a mass loss of a proton in the form of a heat abstraction. One heat abstraction goes up, and the electron spins around and comes down into the proton to form the mind, and the mind can be reduced to one atom."

Several days later Jerry is interviewed again, this time in Dr. Bigelow's office. Present are Jerry; Dr. Bigelow; another psychiatrist, Dr. Darrell Kirch; and Jerry's mother. The purpose of this meeting is to convince Jerry that he requires further hospitalization and treatment. Jerry is a "voluntary" patient who has signed himself into the hospital and therefore is able to sign himself out. At this point Jerry wants very much to leave St. Elizabeth's. So far, though, he hasn't any idea where he will go or what he will do.

After some initial sparring between Jerry and Dr. Bigelow on the subject of Jerry's need for further treatment, Jerry declares that he will stay only if his mother remains in Washington rather than returning to her home. At this point his mother interrupts:

"Listen for a minute, Jerry. Do you mean that letting us visit you once a month isn't enough?"

"In comes this dude with green teeth. I couldn't think of what to do, so I just reached up and kicked old Green Teeth right in the knee. . . . If I'm not scared, I won't kill you," says Jerry.

"Jerry, listen to me for a second," his mother says.

"Why? You gonna tell me Snoopy is dead?"

"Don't talk about something else when I'm talking to you," his mother pleads.

"I'm not talking to you at all."

A few moments later Dr. Bigelow breaks in to tell Jerry he needs to remain in the hospital. "You are confused enough and frightened enough; I am afraid you might hurt yourself."

"Let me give it to you a different way," Jerry says, gazing intently at Dr. Bigelow. "How long has it been since

I discovered I was there in Hillbilly Heaven? How long has it been since *Town Without Pity*? How long has it been since *The Man Who Shot Liberty Valence*?"

To a casual listener, Jerry's responses sound "crazy," completely meaningless, irrelevant to the comments and questions of his mother. But to a trained psychiatrist, such as Dr. Darrell Kirch, Jerry's responses are typical of a specific illness: schizophrenia.

"When you see Jerry, I think your reaction might be that you have seen total chaos," says Dr. Kirch. "But if you take some time, you can begin to see some of the cardinal symptoms of schizophrenia. His thinking is disorganized. He has delusional ideas. Some of these delusions are grandiose. Some are paranoid. He has disturbances in his mood. His mood in some cases is almost absent and in other cases, totally inappropriate. And his behavior is disordered.... It is unusual.... His mannerisms [his hair-pulling and twisting] are inexplicable. He has purposeless, aimless behavior around the ward. He is a textbook case of schizophrenia."

In another time and place, Jerry would not be in a mental hospital. His strange behavior would mark him as a medicine man or a shaman. In the Middle Ages or in Salem, Massachusetts, in the seventeenth century, his declarations would have been seen as emanating from "the powers of darkness" and treated accordingly.

Over the centuries, schizophrenics have been burned at the stake, chained in dark dungeons, starved to death, and drowned. All of these excesses were responses to a disorder that to this day confuses, frightens, and mystifies people who come in contact with it. Fortunately, however, things are improving for Jerry and the two million Americans who will suffer from this disease.

In the past two decades neuroscientists have learned quite a bit about what is going on in the brains of schizophrenics such as Jerry. Before exploring these advances, however, let's sketch in some of the things we know about this disorder that affects nearly 2 percent of our population.

Schizophrenia is an illness confined to humans. Although "animal models" of the disorder have been vigorously sought after, no really convincing instance of schizophrenia has ever been encountered in any organism other than man. This isn't totally surprising. Schizophrenia is marked by delusions, hallucinations, and disorders of thought; it attacks the will, clarity of thinking, the emotions—in short, those mental processes that differentiate us from the other organisms in our environment.

A sixteenth-century engraving of a "witch" about to be burned to death. Epilepsy and other forms of brain and mental diseases were often interpreted as an expression of demonic possession, and treated accordingly.

Although schizophrenia is a twentieth-century term (dating to 1911 when Eugen Bleuler, a Swiss psychiatrist, wrote the now classic book *Dementia Praecox or the Group of Schizophrenias*), it is likely that the disorder has existed throughout history. It was not until the mid-eighteenth century, however, that "madness" was recognized as a medical rather than a religious or political problem. As a result of this insight, burning at the stake and imprisonment were eventually replaced by more humane treatments.

Ever since the mid-nineteenth century, the insane—most of whom were suffering from illnesses we would now unhesitatingly diagnose as schizophrenia—have been unchained, released from prison, and generally given care consistent with a medical rather than a penal orientation. Despite this general improvement, schizophrenics still have difficulty obtaining jobs and are shunned by people who act as if the disease were contagious. Overall, schizophrenia is the most misunderstood and unrecognized mental illness in the contemporary United States. This may account for the fact that research into schizophrenia garners only a fraction of the money allotted to cancer, an illness that equals but does not exceed the cost of schizophrenia in terms of workdays lost, hospitalization, costs of medication, and so on.

At least partially to blame for the public's distrust of schizophrenics is the bizarre and off-putting nature of the illness. Although the person with cancer or heart disease doesn't act or talk any differently from the rest of us, the schizophrenic's statements often don't make "sense." Jerry's opening remarks regarding a picture having a "headache" is typical. In addition, he or she may act in frightening or even threatening ways. The schizophrenic appears to live in a "different reality" than the rest of us.

At one time psychiatrists were confident that schizophrenia could be diagnosed on the basis of what they half-facetiously referred to as the "four A's": ambivalence, autism, loose associations, and altered affect.

Ambivalence: Psychiatrists noted that schizophrenics often simultaneously express both positive and negative feelings about other people and events around them, almost as if they can't make up their minds. Jerry's desire to remain in the hospital coexists with an equally strong urge to sign himself out. He can't choose, and he lashes out in rage at his mother and the doctor who are trying to help him make the best decision.

Autism: Schizophrenics tend to withdraw from others. In many instances, schizophrenics exhibit a lifetime history of introversion and shyness. Later, as the schizophrenic process progresses, this withdrawal intensifies and psychic energies are focused on an increasingly disturbing internal experience.

Loose associations: The schizophrenic's statements often don't make sense. It is as if several unrelated or loosely related items were somehow jumbled together. Jerry's comments regarding the death of Snoopy and the movies *Liberty Valence* and *Town Without Pity* fit the definition of loose associations. In his psychosis he may be suggesting that he would be shot like Liberty Valence and that neither his mother nor Dr. Bigelow had any feeling ("pity") for what he was experiencing. But such loosely associated material may have many other meanings. The obscurity of these communications defies analysis.

Said one schizophrenic of his own thinking processes:

A "demented idiot" under restraint in a French asylum, 1883.

"Half the time I'm talking about one thing and thinking about half a dozen other things at the same time. It must look queer to people when I laugh about something that has nothing to do with what I am talking about, but they don't know what is going on inside and how much of it is running around in my head. You see, I might be talking about something quite serious to you, and other things come into my head at the same time that are funny, and this makes me laugh. If I could only concentrate on one thing at a time, I wouldn't look half so silly."

Altered affect: The schizophrenic's reaction to his or her disturbed perceptions may range from a frenzied torrent of emotions to a flat monotone. At one moment the schizophrenic may terrify friends and relatives by the intensity of his or her imagined fear and then, only a few moments later, discuss in an emotionless tone matters that to most people would be distressful, such as the death of a relative, or the illness of a small child.

The schizophrenic is often frightened of the world around him or her. Things and people appear menacing. The world is confusing and unpredictable. Eventually the schizophrenic's terror, coupled with an inability to direct and control his or her own thought processes, brings about an abrupt withdrawal from society. This withdrawal, while it may temporarily ease the schizophrenic's sense of threat from the environment, only serves to deepen the isolation and loneliness. Thoughts become increasingly disordered and confused. "My thoughts get all jumbled up," one schizophrenic wrote of his experiences. "People listening to me get more lost than I do."

The above descriptions of typical schizophrenic experiences end up being nothing more than a laundry list of the various things that can go wrong. The specific disturbances shown by any particular schizophrenic are as individual as his or her fingerprints. There is no single pattern. This heterogeneity provides a clue that schizophrenia may not be one disease but rather a whole spectrum of disorders, a "group of schizophrenias," as they were first described by psychiatrist Eugen Bleuler in 1911.

After studying hundreds of patients, Eugen Bleuler identified certain symptoms (the four A's) that were regularly associated with prolonged, usually unremitting illness. Bleuler's predecessor Emil Kraepelin had postulated that the illness was totally incurable and invariably followed a deteriorating course. Bleuler, however, was slightly more optimistic. He observed that on occasion the illness spontaneously remitted. His observations of patients in a large mental hospital in Zurich prompted him to drop the unwieldy and basically inadequate term dementia praecox in favor of the term schizophrenia, splitting of the mind. This split has nothing to do with the so-called split personality, which we will discuss in Chapter 8. It refers instead to the victim's inability to harmonize feelings and thoughts. This affects the ability to socialize and, by implication, the capacity to care deeply about others. If, as previous chapters have implied, our humanity depends on our ability to think and communicate in complex symbolic forms, schizophrenia is the brain illness most destructive to our humanness. The schizophrenic is "split off" from his or her own feelings and the feelings of those around him or her. This dissonance may alarm people, frighten them with the inappropriateness of the schizophrenic's responses.

Eugen Bleuler, the Swiss psychiatrist who first described the symptoms of schizophrenia.

Jerry and his sixty-eight-year-old father sat in the living room during one of Jerry's visits home.

"I don't know if you are going to kill me and I don't care. . . . Enough is enough," said Jerry.

"Why do you think I'd want to kill you?"

"Because we were getting twenty gunshots a night, and I couldn't figure out where they were coming from, so I went out there and found out. Everybody was shooting everybody. There was a lot of stress in that city. . . . Dad, do you know how you feel? Well, I feel even worse than that. That man [points to his father] is a father complex. He is not a wishy-washy father complex. He is sixty-eight years old, and he can still kick my ass. . . . I don't have any fun at all [said in an anguished tone]. The police department was fun."

Several elements are jumbled together in this brief dialogue. Jerry's fears of his father killing him; the remembered stress of police work; some details of a shooting incident. Then Jerry's loneliness and pain break through as he tells his father in an anguished tone that he can't "have any fun at all anymore." Needless to say, such communica-

Jerry, "a textbook case of schizo-phrenia," with his mother, right, and his father, above.

tions are extremely upsetting to the person addressed by the schizophrenic. Sufficiently upsetting, in fact, that in some instances even the psychiatrist caring for the schizophrenic patient may respond with fear and anger. The schizophrenic's isolation from friends and relatives, even his or her isolation within the mental hospital, is partly due to the difficulties other people experience in communicating with a person who demonstrates a "splitting of the mind."

Jerry's mother described her impressions of Jerry in these words: "To me, it is like the mind is racing like a motor . . . racing continuously . . . and it goes on that way even when he is asleep. . . . When he goes to sleep he has nightmares, so I think his mind is really working the same whether asleep or awake. He says he's in hell whether he is sleeping or awake. One hesitates to compare his situation to hell, because no one really knows what hell is like, although I have often heard him remark, 'I don't have to die to go to hell.' "

The parents and relatives of schizophrenics also inhabit their own special kind of hell.

"To bear a child who is that different is a tremendous load for a family to carry," according to psychiatrist Arnold Scheibel of UCLA's Brain Research Institute. "To learn from the psychiatrist that this awful difference may very well have been due to the way the child was nurtured—a disease of nurturing, if you will—generates an awful lot of guilt. Parents are guilty enough. Raising children is a very difficult thing. To raise a difficult or schizophrenic child is even worse. And then to have the confirmation from the outside that 'this child is schizophrenic because of what happened in the family' is a truly terrible load to carry. I am afraid that very often my colleagues thought this way in the past because that was the frame of reference under which they had been trained."

Fortunately, psychiatrists have largely abandoned the fruitless, painful, and often cruel efforts to find a scapegoat for schizophrenia. As a result of new interest in the search for the molecular and chemical accompaniments of the disorder, no one seriously contends anymore that schizophrenia is a disease of "bad mothering" or "bad parenting." But for a long time they did.

"At the turn of the century, every neuroscientist who was interested in schizophrenia was convinced that this was a brain disorder," says NIMH psychiatrist Daniel Weinberger. "It was only when they couldn't make sense of the findings that they raised the question of a psychogenic cause. They then started to believe that bad mothering caused schizophrenia, or bad neighborhoods caused schizophrenia, or drugs, or some peculiar school experience, or some other major psychic trauma. There is absolutely no scientific evidence for this theory."

The search for a "psychological" explanation for schizophrenia is ironic in light of Sigmund Freud's views on the matter. "Freud felt that schizophrenia was not a disease that was appropriately treated by psychoanalysis," says NIMH psychiatrist E. Fuller Torrey. "However, some of his followers tried to anyway. They had a notoriously poor success rate. They said it was caused by early childhood experiences. There is no evidence whatsoever for this, and, in fact, all of the research evidence to date is distinctly opposed to this view."

Dr. Daniel Weinberger

But what *are* the causes of schizophrenia? What could go wrong in the brain of the schizophrenic to produce such a heartrending dissolution of the normal personality?

The search for a biochemical cause for schizophrenia dates back a hundred years. The biochemist Johan Ludwig Wilhelm Thudicum first suggested in 1884 that schizophrenia ("insanity," as it was then referred to) was the result of "poisons." But despite several initially promising developments, no single substance has ever been isolated within the brain of schizophrenics. The search for a biochemical "cause" has, however, turned up some interesting leads.

It has been reported that administration of *gluten,* a component of cereal grains, has been shown to result in a flare-up of symptoms in patients who have had schizophrenia over many years. It doesn't affect all schizophrenics in this way, only a subgroup. This suggests that within the large population of schizophrenics particular varieties of the disorder may exist that can be helped by a gluten-free diet.

There are also varieties of schizophrenia associated with alterations of the immune system. (Asthma and allergies are much less common among schizophrenics than in the population at large.) Some schizophrenics have larger ventricles (cerebrospinal fluid-containing cavities), while others with slightly different symptoms have ventricles that are no different in size than in persons free of schizophrenia. Overall, the situation is very much like a smorgasbord: A number of possibilities are available that appeal to various palates and tastes. Each researcher picks a particular item that corresponds to his or her previous training, experience, and theoretical orientation. There is absolutely no agreement as to the most likely explanation for the disorder.

To the geneticist, schizophrenia is an "inherited disease" and efforts are directed at pinpointing the pattern of inheritance. To the psychiatrist with biochemical inclinations, the disease is the result of a so far undiscovered chemical in the brain's neuronal pools. To psychiatrists trained primarily along psychoanalytic lines, schizophrenia is a drama with a cast of "villains" (mothers, fathers, and so on) whose failures have somehow precipitated the disorder.

Is schizophrenia inherited? For the longest time such a proposal seemed unlikely, even absurd. Philosophers and psychologists traditionally believed that behavior stems from the operation of the mind. And for centuries the mind was like the "soul," an ethereal substance that remained permanently outside the boundaries of science. But most neuroscientists now believe the mind is actually a term that refers to a set of functions carried out by the brain. For example, when we speak, our language and communication is an activity of our mind. When we think and remember and express emotions, these brain-based activities are also "mind." Mind, in essence, is all the things the brain does. To search for a "mind" existing somewhere outside the brain is something like observing an Olympic swimmer and asking where in the athlete's body the "swim" resides. Swimming is the name we have given to describe the activity of propelling oneself across water by means of coordinated movement of the arms and legs. Mind is the term we favor for certain thoughts, behaviors, and emotions that are made possible as a result of the function of our brains. If mind and behavior are considered functions of the brain, it becomes easier to investigate whether behavior can be affected by genetic factors just as though it were an organ of the body.

In 1938, Franz Kallmann, a psychiatrist, published a study entitled *The Genetics of Schizophrenia.* He found that the incidence of the disease is dramatically increased in the families of schizophrenics. Although Kallmann suspected that was due to hereditary predisposition, he couldn't prove it. Obviously, everything that "runs in families" isn't hereditary. Wealth, a tendency for succeeding generations to take up the same profession, malnutrition as a result of poverty—these things are not genetically inherited.

The most compelling evidence of a hereditary influence on schizophrenia comes from the study of twins. Among identical twins (*monozygotic,* twins possessing the same genes), the likelihood of a second twin developing schizophrenia, if the illness exists in one of the pair, is about 50 percent. In fraternal twins (they share only half their genes, since two eggs were fertilized separately instead of only one, as with identical twins), the risk of schizophrenia in the second twin falls to about 10 percent, the same risk as exists for a sibling or child of a schizophrenic. Among the general population in which no family incidence of schizophrenia can be found, the incidence of the disease is about one percent.

Before claiming that a certain trait or behavior *is*

inherited, it is necessary to control environmental factors. A father with a vicious temper is likely to produce a son with a similar impulse because of the example he furnishes rather than any genetic predisposition to nastiness. But how can environmental factors be controlled? Obviously, children can't be separated from their parents just to answer the age-old nature-nuture problem. Or can they?

In the late 1960s, psychiatrist Dr. Seymour Kety, Dr. Paul Wender, and Dr. David Rosenthal traveled to Denmark to carry out a series of investigations aimed at settling once and for all the issue of whether there is a significant genetic component in schizophrenia. They chose Denmark because it is among the most advanced countries in the world for record keeping. From birth, a record is made of each citizen, and the record is kept current until the time of death. Among the items recorded are admissions to psychiatric hospitals and discharge diagnoses.

Dr. Kety and his cohorts searched the registry in Denmark for adults who had been adopted soon after birth and later developed schizophrenia. They reasoned that adopted individuals who shared their genetic endowment with their biological relatives and their environment with their adoptive family would permit separation of the genetic and environmental influences which operate in schizophrenia and make possible an independent evaluation of these separate influences. After gathering information from records and interviews, they found that the biological relatives of schizophrenic adoptees showed a ten percent incidence of schizophrenia. The adoptive relatives with whom they were reared showed no higher incidence of schizophrenia than is found in the general population. These findings on schizophrenia, published in the past decade, provide compelling new evidence for the importance of heredity rather than environment, and have revolutionized our ideas about the illness.

But none of the studies indicating the genetic factors in schizophrenia rules out the possibility that environmental factors also play a role. For instance, birth complications are thought to increase the risk of schizophrenia later in life. Some forms of schizophrenia may result from viral infections. Genetic factors alone cannot explain the etiology, development and course of the illness. What about the fifty percent of identical twins who don't follow the same course as their sibling? How do they escape the disorder?

Since the genes in identical twins are the same yet only one of the twins comes down with schizophrenia, environmental factors must be important. For example, in many cases the "normal" twin is excessively shy, withdrawn, given to daydreams, and exhibits a tendency toward smoldering suspicions of other people. Among other biological relatives of schizophrenic patients, traits are also found which may resemble those in the schizophrenic. Formerly labeled "latent" schizophrenics, such individuals are now referred to as "schizotypal" personalities.

One also has to remember that the outbreak of any illness is almost always dependent on environmental factors. Stress and malnutrition, for instance, make it that much easier to develop pneumonia or frequent colds. Someone in a family given to ulcers is more susceptible to ulcers if he or she smokes or drinks to excess. In a similar way, scientists speculate that the schizotypal syndrome may represent a mild form of schizophrenia that, given sufficient stress, can break out into full-fledged schizophrenic psychosis. Under favorable circumstances, on the other hand, such individuals may simply impress others as perhaps a little strange, the town eccentric.

"The stress of the environment is a factor in how severe the expression of the illness might be in some patients," says NIMH's Dr. Weinberger. "It determines whether they can be out of the hospital or whether they have to come back in the hospital because the environment outside is too stressful. Stress also determines how long somebody can go before they come to the attention of the psychiatrist. If they have a family that can help them cope, they may go a much longer period of time before they are diagnosed as having schizophrenia."

Weinberger's comments regarding the role of the family in helping reduce stress on the schizophrenic are worthy of elaboration. On the whole, other family members of schizophrenics haven't come off very well whenever a psychiatrist has attempted to understand and explain a schizophrenic breakdown. The psychiatrist's judgments on these matters have ranged from outspoken scapegoating (the *schizophrenogenic mother* who allegedly induced the illness in her offspring as a result of her "cold and distant" mothering) to the postulation of unhealthy interaction, a *double-bind situation* in which the schizophrenic is given a contradictory message: "We want more than anything else for you to stay well but, frankly, I can tell from the way you're acting now that you are going to get sick again."

But in recent years, psychiatrists have given the family of the schizophrenic a second chance. Dr. Ian Falloon and his associates at USC and UCLA have shown that a schizophrenic's chances of remaining well when he or she is outside the hospital are favorably influenced if environmental stresses within the family are reduced by using a family-treatment approach.

As part of Dr. Falloon's treatment, therapists conduct informal sessions within the home. Family members are told during the first meeting that families don't cause schizophrenia but can play an important part in improving the course of the illness. Subsequent sessions are devoted to reducing family tensions while encouraging the expression of feelings and emotions without the turmoil that often occurs in the families of schizophrenics. By their own admission, family members often can't "cope" with the "chaos" and "confusion" engendered by having a schizophrenic within the family. They are taught skills such as attentive listening and how to request behavioral change without resorting to threats or withdrawal of affection.

The results of Dr. Falloon's study are quite dramatic. Family-oriented therapy is associated with stress-related relapses in only 6 percent of patients. In contrast, 44 percent of the schizophrenics treated only by traditional one-to-one psychotherapeutic sessions relapsed. In that 6 percent of schizophrenics who suffered a relapse despite family-centered therapy, the episodes were less severe and lasted a shorter period.

One particularly important factor in Dr. Falloon's treatment consists of reducing the schizophrenic's contact with "high-stress" relatives—those given to making hostile, critical comments about the patient. This was brought about by encouraging the patient to get out of the home environment during the day, perhaps take a job. All of these measures were aimed at bringing about a reduction in stress. The schizophrenic's brain, it seems, has tremendous difficulty handling interpersonal relations and often breaks down from the induced stress of social contacts.

"This is probably related to the fact that the schizophrenic nervous system is not well suited to the subtle adjustments of interpersonal exchange which most people bring to bear when meeting strangers and inspiring their future confidence," according to Dr. C. Christian Beels of the New York State Psychiatric Institute.

Family therapy when combined with the genetic studies of Drs. Kety, Wender, and Rosenthal point to an inherited predisposition to schizophrenia that can be modified and, perhaps, even prevented by reducing stress, particularly the stress that originates within the schizophrenic's family. Nature is thus allied with nurture. Heavy genetic "loading" predisposes some individuals to the likelihood of a schizophrenic breakdown sometime in their lives, irrespective of their environmental experiences. Others with less genetic predisposition to the disease may require an extremely stressful environment to bring on the disorder. The success of Dr. Falloon's family treatment underscores the importance of avoiding too fatalistic an attitude toward schizophrenia. We do not passively respond to the environment; rather, we engage our environment in dynamic interplay. The results of this interplay are partially influenced by our genetic inheritance. But this is only half the story. The other half depends on the degree of support and help we receive from others. To this extent we are all very much our "brother's

PET scans of a normal brain, left, and the brain of a schizophrenic, right.

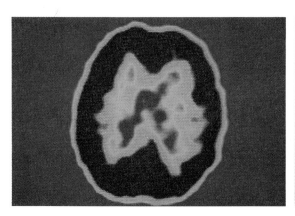 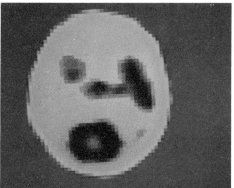

keeper" when it comes to mental health, particularly the mental health of someone predisposed to schizophrenia.

Despite Dr. Falloon's impressive results, the greatest hope for the eventual cure of schizophrenia is likely to come from insights that have emerged in the past three decades regarding the psychobiology of this disorder.

In 1950 Dr. Henri Laborit, a Parisian surgeon, became interested in devising a method for counteracting surgical shock. Dr. Laborit, like other surgeons, routinely encountered patients who died or suffered serious relapses on the basis of "shock." He began to search for a way to reduce, or perhaps even eliminate altogether, the need for powerful anesthetics, the "hammer blows on the skull," as Dr. Laborit now refers to them.

Dr. Laborit was aware of earlier reports that shock resulted from the release of chemical mediators, what we now call neurotransmitters. He searched for something that would reverse the effect of these neuromediators, directing his attention to the antihistamines usually employed as antidotes to allergy and asthma.

Working with several commercially available antihistamines, Dr. Laborit had noticed that the substances "put my patients into a particular psychic state. They became indifferent to the environment. . . . They were no longer afraid, no longer experiencing anxiety." Along with these changes in mental attitude, Dr. Laborit's patients also required remarkably lower doses of anesthesia and, in some cases, no anesthesia at all. "We were at the stage of anesthesia without an anesthetic," Dr. Laborit recalls. "I remarked on their indifference to the environment, and I said to my colleagues, 'It must have an application in psychiatry . . . to induce indifference on the part of individuals toward their social environment.' "

But Dr. Laborit had difficulty testing his hunch that antihistamines, especially a drug called *chlorpromazine,* might be helpful to psychiatrists. "Psychiatrists didn't believe that chemical molecules could have an effect on the human brain, especially when it came to mental pathology."

Undeterred by the initial lack of enthusiasm on the part of the psychiatric establishment, Dr. Laborit invited local psychiatrists to visit his patients and observe their nearly complete absence of anxiety. The psychiatrists were impressed but still uncertain whether the drug could be used with psychiatric patients. Encouraged, Dr. Laborit pressed on—instructing, debating, haranguing anyone who would listen. The turning point came when a surgeon who had attended one of Dr. Laborit's surgical conferences returned home and told his brother-in-law, a psychiatrist, about Dr. Laborit's results. This psychiatrist, Dr. Pierre

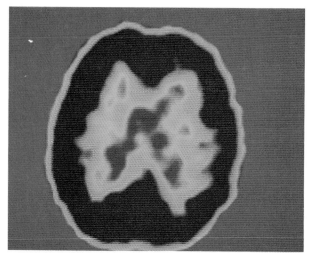

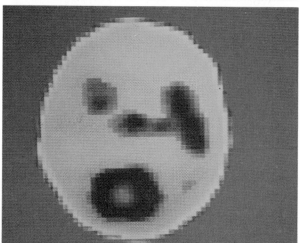

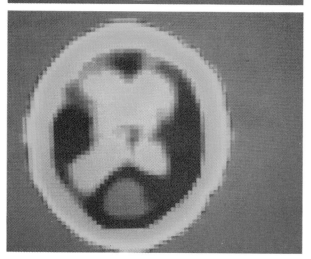

The PET scan on top shows a normal brain, the one in the middle that of a schizophrenic, and, at bottom, the brain of the schizophrenic after a drug treatment.

Deniker, was sufficiently intrigued to order a supply of chlorpromazine and inject it into ten agitated, uncontrollable patients.

"Very quickly you could feel their agitation slowing down," Dr. Deniker recalled, during an interview at St. Anne's Mental Hospital, where the "experiment" was first carried out. "They began to be able to sleep again, and they grew less rather than more agitated." Soon other psychiatrists were trying this new drug, which was promptly dubbed the "chemical straitjacket." Their results were equally encouraging: Patients who formerly required treatment in isolation rooms or straitjackets now were capable of being left unattended.

In the intervening quarter century, antischizophrenic drugs based on chlorpromazine have drastically reduced the population of mental hospitals around the world. The drugs totally eliminated certain kinds of psychoses: the extreme agitation and withdrawal so severe that patients didn't move for weeks at a time. Here is a description by Dr. Deniker of the kinds of patients formerly found in any mental hospital, whose presence there now is almost nonexistent:

"We had immobile patients who remained in the same posture for days, weeks, months at a stretch. We had patients who burned themselves against radiators because they stayed rooted to the spot in front of them without feeling the heat. It is hard to imagine nowadays. The most normal among them fit the standard public idea of Napoleon and Joan of Arc."

UCLA's Dr. Arnold Scheibel recalls a similar situation: "I can remember very clearly having to put patients into restraining baths. They were put into a bathtub of cool water, and a canvas top was put over the tub in order to make the patients stay there. This was done because it was found that this kind of bath had a sedative effect. With the introduction of the antischizophrenic drugs, however, this kind of thing was no longer necessary. For the first time we could do something substantial for these patients. For the first time we could see that they were sick individuals to whom we could now talk."

The incidences of acute agitation, hallucinations, prolonged immobility, sudden outpourings of aggression—all were dramatically improved with the help of antischizophrenic drugs. Throughout all this, thoughtful psychiatrists were asking themselves several pivotal questions. How do the drugs work? What is the biochemical mechanism that explains how madness can be so dramatically ameliorated?

The first clue to the cellular action of the antischizophrenic drugs came from observations of the drugs' effects on motor behavior. Patients under treatment moved slowly; they tended to blink infrequently; their arms didn't swing normally as they walked. If given too much of the drug—a slight overdose—the patients started behaving like caricatures of old age. More precisely, they looked exactly like patients with Parkinson's disease.

In 1817, James Parkinson, an English physician working in London, first described the disease that now bears his name. The patients he observed demonstrated general body rigidity, slowness in initiating and carrying out movements, and a rhythmic tremor at rest. This was exactly the picture presented by schizophrenic patients treated with antipsychotics. Could there be a connection between the naturally occurring Parkinson's disease and a drug-induced condition?

The question was pivotal in the history of the neurosciences. If antischizophrenic drugs produced a picture like that in Parkinson's disease, it just might suggest that the same substance known to be involved in Parkinson's disease, the neurotransmitter dopamine, is involved in both disorders.

In the late 1950s, three Swedish pharmacologists first discovered that 80 percent of the brain's dopamine is located in the basal ganglia, an area that makes up less than 0.5 percent of the total brain weight. From the study of human brains at autopsy, another investigator noted that some of his samples had low amounts of dopamine. All of these patients had also suffered from Parkinson's disease. Furthermore, the *substantia nigra* ("black body"), a normally pigmented area of the brain, appeared desaturated, the dopamine seemingly bleached out of it. Since in the normal brain the substantia nigra contains a large proportion of the dopamine-producing cells, this finding suggested that the reduction of dopamine within a portion of the basal ganglia (the *striatum*) resulted from a degeneration of dopamine-producing cells in the substantia nigra. But what, under ordinary conditions, *is* the function of dopamine? Is it an inhibitory or excitatory neurotransmitter?

If neurons from the basal ganglia are surgically removed and bathed in a solution of dopamine, their activity *decreases,* suggesting that dopamine acts as an inhibitory neurotransmitter. Decreasing the level of dopamine, therefore, leads to a loss of inhibition (disinhibition) and an abnormal discharge of cells in those areas of the basal ganglia that receive input from the substantia nigra. The discovery of the importance of dopamine, along with its inhibitory action, provided a starting point for speculation about the neurobiology of schizophrenia.

Because of its influence on the striatum (highlighted), the substantia nigra is associated with such diseases as Parkinson's.

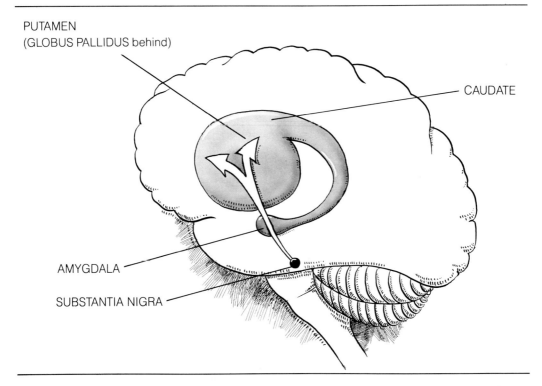

PUTAMEN
(GLOBUS PALLIDUS behind)

CAUDATE

AMYGDALA

SUBSTANTIA NIGRA

Avid Carlsson—the same Swedish investigator who, in 1959, first pinpointed the location of dopamine in the basal ganglia—established a decade later that antischizophrenic drugs interfere with dopaminergic transmission mostly by producing a blockade of dopamine receptors.

In the patient with Parkinson's disease the dopamine is reduced because of a loss of dopaminergic (dopamine-producing) cells. These findings taken together suggest that schizophrenia results from an *excess* of dopamine transmission. There are several points in favor of this hypothesis.

First, as mentioned above, antischizophrenic drugs bind to dopamine receptors. In addition, the effectiveness of an antischizophrenic drug varies directly with its capacity to displace other, weaker drugs from the dopamine receptors.

Second, drugs that enhance the action of dopamine (cocaine, amphetamines, and even L-dopa itself) worsen schizophrenia. In normal individuals, schizophreniclike episodes can be precipitated by these agents. Even to the trained psychiatrist, they may induce states indistinguishable from the onset of a bona fide schizophrenic psychosis.

Third, although there are three principal dopamine-producing systems in the brain, one of them, the mesocortical system, is particularly likely, because of its anatomical connections, to cause emotional disturbances. These dopamine-cell bodies, located slightly above the substantia nigra, project to the limbic system, an area we have mentioned previously as playing a key role in emotional experience and expression. One area in particular, the *nucleus accumbens,* the most prominent of all limbic nuclei, receives transmissions from the hippocampus, the amygdala, the septum, the hypothalamus, and the frontal lobes of the cerebral cortex, areas that are closely associated with our emotions and, quite conceivably, could contribute to schizophrenia in the event of malfunction.

Further support of the hypothesis comes from studies of epileptics suffering seizure discharges in these mesocortical areas. The resulting psychomotor epilepsy can, on occasion, mimic acute schizophrenia down to the smallest detail. Some investigators who have studied schizophrenia via implanted EEG electrodes have even reported abnormal spike discharges in these areas, the distinctive EEG trademark of epilepsy.

From everything we have observed, schizophrenia appears to be the behavorial manifestation of an excess of dopaminergic transmission. Notice that I did not say schizophrenia is *caused by* an excess activity of dopaminergic cells. The distinction is a subtle but important one. At this point neuroscientists are still investigating the factors that may bring about excess dopamine activity within the brain. These influences could conceivably include thoughts, conversations, or fantasies. If such a correlation could ever be made between mental events and neurochemistry, it would, of course, put a permanent end to the artificial division that presently plagues those who seek to understand the human brain: "Mind" would no longer be set apart from brain. So far, though, such correlations haven't been made, and investigators continue to search for abnormalities within the schizophrenic brain that may account for the syndrome.

Currently there are four possibilities most actively being explored. First, dopamine-producing neurons may be releasing too much dopamine. Second, dopamine receptors may become hypersensitive to normal amounts of released dopamine. Third, since dopamine is only one of several often competing neurotransmitters, the real culprit may be an underactivity of an antagonistic neurotransmitter. Finally, there may be a failure in the feedback mechanism, whereby under normal conditions the dopamine receptors signal to the dopamine cells to stop making additional dopamine when the receptors are fully occupied.

At this point, neuroscientists are unable to choose from these possibilities. The situation may even be more complicated, and additional possibilities may yet turn up. A variety of cellular mechanisms are capable of altering neuronal functions, and it is dangerous to settle on one "pet theory" prematurely. In addition, it is difficult to speak of *the* neurochemical disturbance of schizophrenia when at least four possible molecular mechanisms could be at work.

"In the past ten years we have concerned ourselves mainly with the hippocampus," says Dr. Arnold Scheibel of UCLA's Brain Research Institute. "This is a deeper, older part of the brain which is very much concerned with the ways we feel and the ways we relate to the world around us." Dr. Scheibel has discovered unusual patterns of nerve cells in the hippocampus of schizophrenics.

"What we see essentially in the normal individual is an ensemble of nerve cells aligned almost like little soldiers. In the schizophrenic patient the cells are like soldiers who have a discipline problem. There are many different orientations. The nerve cells and their processes are completely awry. We speculate that the connections are also quite different, and it is our hypothesis that the schizophrenic must be experiencing the world quite differently from the way the nonschizophrenic person does."

Despite promising but controversial claims such as this, there remain major conceptual hurdles to understanding schizophrenia. If dopamine is increased in the schizophrenic brain, where is it doing the most damage? Conceivably a disturbance in one small brain region might be sufficient to precipitate the disease—a brain area so small we may not have discovered it yet. There is also evidence that antischizophrenic drugs themselves induce permanent alterations in the schizophrenic's brain: an increase in the binding capacity of dopamine receptors on the nerve cell membranes. Thus the "schizophrenic brain," if there is such an entity, could be discovered only by examining patients who have never been treated with antischizophrenic medications. This raises serious ethical questions. Withholding antischizophrenic drugs from a schizophrenic would be like withholding antibiotics from a patient suffering from an infection or refusing digitalis to a patient with a failing heart.

It is also misleading to imply that the dopamine hypothesis and the current research stemming from it provide a fully satisfactory explanation of schizophrenia. Antischizophrenic drugs are effective in treating acute episodes of schizophrenia but are almost useless helping with the social withdrawal, lack of motivation, and inadequate emotion that are the hallmarks of the disorder. As mentioned earlier, people with mild forms of schizophrenia may live out their entire life without a "breakdown." Obviously, schizophrenia involves more than simply the outbreak of disturbed and disturbing behavior. Initially it appears as a kind of desaturation, a bleaching out of the color, verve, and warmth that is the essence of "personality." Neither the dopamine hypothesis nor any other current theory explains these changes.

Finally, there are logical puzzles. For instance, assume that schizophrenia may result from disturbing a neuronal balance that is normally maintained by a combination of inhibitory and excitatory neurotransmitters. Assume further that dopamine, along with three or four other neurotransmitters (we'll keep the numbers small for the sake of simplicity), provides inhibitory input to a particular brain region. If this inhibition is increased by the overreaction of one of the several inhibitory neurotransmitters other than dopamine, the resulting imbalance may result in schizophrenia. Treatment by reducing the effects of dopamine may be effective (by reducing the *total amount* of inhibition) despite the fact that the actual precipitant for the disorder is an alternative, perhaps as yet undiscovered, neurotransmitter.

The situation is very much like trying to guess changes

in personnel on a football team simply on the basis of the team's win-loss record. If the team starts winning more games, is it because they have strengthened their offense, or is it because they have beefed up their defense and thus stopped the other teams from scoring? A team's performance depends on a combination of offense and defense. The brain's performance, too, depends on a combination of positive and negative influences along with facilitative and modulatory influences. A transmitter may be neither positive nor negative but instead facilitate activity of excitatory or inhibitory neurons. In the football analogy, the coaches, team physicians, and even the water boys facilitate the performance of the game.

In addition, behavioral disturbances sometimes prove irrelevant to understanding and treating the underlying illness. For instance, the psychoses associated with deficiencies of vitamin B_6, syphilis, and inflammations of the brain are indistinguishable on behavioral grounds alone. One patient looks and sounds much like another. The specific diagnosis is reached only by observing the patient's response to medication (an antibiotic to cure inflammations, or vitamin B_6 for the specific deficiency), or his or her reactions to certain tests (a positive blood test for syphilis). In each instance biological measures provide keener insights into the nature of the illness than behavioral observations alone.

The greatest obstacle to the understanding, treatment, and eventual cure for schizophrenia springs from imprecision about diagnosing the disorder. Accurate diagnosis in psychiatry generally is more difficult than in other areas of medicine because the symptoms of mental illness are expressed primarily in behavior, feelings, thoughts, and perceptions. Obviously these aren't as easily measured as pulse, blood pressure, or temperature. The present situation in regard to schizophrenia is very similar to that at the turn of the century about mental retardation. Great emphasis was placed on establishing performance scales. As a result, individuals with a wide variety of brain diseases were forced into the artificial categories of morons, imbeciles, and idiots. Only much later did neuroscientists realize that understanding the brain disturbances responsible for mental retardation was far more important than measuring scores achieved on standardized tests. A similar situation exists for schizophrenia. Some subgroups can be readily detected (schizophrenics with cerebral atrophy and accompanying enlarged ventricles, hereditary forms of the illness, and so on), while other subgroups may have neurochemical imbalances sufficiently subtle that their elucidation may take decades.

Each level of explanation in the neurosciences is like encountering a multilayered Chinese box. Open one box and inside you find another, slightly smaller one. Open that box and you encounter yet another, smaller box. The ultimate question concerns whether there is a final minuscule box, or whether the boxes will continue to decrease in size until they escape our powers of detection. Remember, that is exactly what happened at the end of the nineteenth century. Microscopes and special stains eventually proved unable to distinguish normal brains from impaired ones, with the unfortunate result that investigations into the neurobiology of mental illness halted. The situation is much more hopeful now that we have PET scans and BEAM studies at our disposal, but these techniques also stop far short of resolution on the molecular scale. "In order to discover differences in the brain of schizophrenics, we need some kind of microscope so powerful that it has not been developed yet," according to NIMH psychiatrist Dr. Daniel Weinberger.

Neuroscientists continue to express confidence that given enough time, effort, and brain research we will learn important new things about the biology of schizophrenia. Whether such research will tell us *the* cause of schizophrenia is a question that transcends the discipline of neuroscience. Is there a single cause for war? What is *the* cause of inflation? What is *the* reason for racial tensions and animosities? Obviously, at a certain level of complexity problems can no longer be resolved by a single overriding "explanation." But for the most part, brain scientists are content to set aside such philosophical conundrums in favor of those areas of brain research that intrigue them.

Traditionally, psychiatrists have separated mental illness into disorders of *thinking* and *emotion*. We know now that these distinctions are largely artificial, that the brain cannot be so neatly compartmentalized. Disturbed thoughts produce disturbed emotions, and vice versa. But for purposes of discussion, consider Jerry's delusions and disjointed associations the hallmarks of a *thought disorder*.

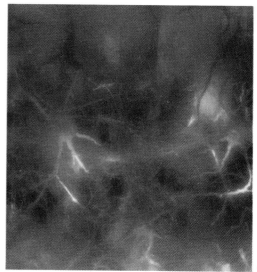

a

b

The Neural Network

This sequence of images is an artist's rendering of the network of neurons in the cortex of the brain. Cells that are inhibitory in their influence are painted red. Yellow/amber cells show excitatory firing. Since current technology is not yet sophisticated enough to reveal neuronal activity at the level of the individual cell, these illustrations provide a dramatic and unusual account, as follows:

In the initial view (*a*), we see the neural network with cells firing inhibitorily. This is a common state of affairs in the cortex, as it is throughout the brain.

In the next image (*b*), we see an inactive neural network. No cells are shown firing.

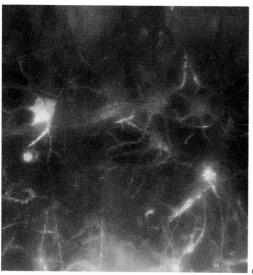

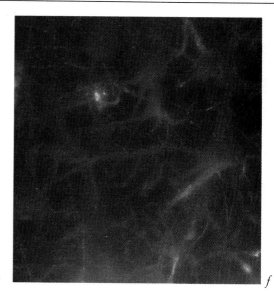

e

f

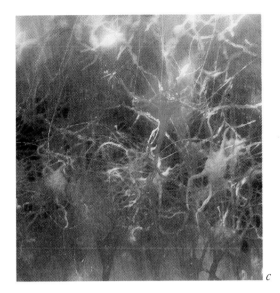

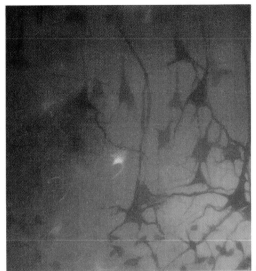

c

d

Now, in (*c*), there is only one active cell, the bright red (inhibitory) neuron slightly to the left and below center.

In the subsequent image (*d*), the neural network is shown in blue, corresponding to the artist's conception of the action of Valium.

Now, in (*e*), there is a balance of excitatory and inhibitory firing.

In the following image (*f*), we see low excitatory activity throughout the cortex, the artist's rendition of a patient with Parkinson's disease.

The shutdown of cells in the neural network (*g*) imitates the substantia nigra of a Parkinson's disease victim.

Last (*h*), we see a close-up of a pyramidal cell at rest in the cortex.

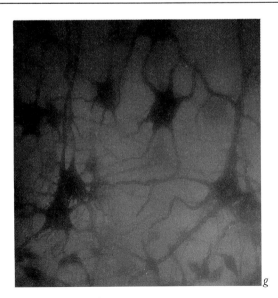

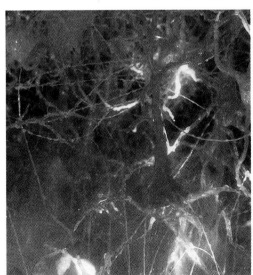

g

h

We are now going to move into an exploration of *emotional disorders*.

At any given time, about 4 percent of the general population cannot maintain an evenly balanced mood. The symptoms of their disturbance may vary. In the case of depression, these may include a pervasive feeling of hopelessness, boredom, and lack of enthusiasm. Sleep may be disturbed (usually tending toward early-morning wakening). Appetite decreases as well as sex drive and general energy level. The depressed person feels guilty, "worn out," often deriving no sense of refreshment after a night spent in fitful sleep. Thought patterns, too, may be slowed down, the answers to routine questions delayed to the point of embarrassment, giving relatives and friends the idea that the depressed person's "mind may be failing." The depressed individual cannot concentrate. If the depression deepens, suicide may be considered or, in the worst cases, actually carried out. As the depression deepens further, thoughts may become disordered, although not usually to the extent observed in schizophrenics like Jerry.

The average age of onset for depression is about forty, with women affected two to three times more often than men. Contrary to popular opinion, depressions do not result from deprivation or unhappy life experiences. In more than half the patients admitted to mental hospitals for severe depression, no precipitating cause can be discovered.

Despite the differences between schizophrenia and depression, they share an important characteristic. Genetic factors are important in both illnesses. In some families the tendency for depression can be traced back several generations. In any particular generation, if one identical twin develops depression, the other twin has a 70 percent chance of developing the illness. In nonidentical twins the figure drops to 13 percent, just about the same as for brothers and sisters.

Apart from the risk of suicide, depression can seriously impair general health. There is a high incidence of alcoholism and drug addiction among the depressed. There is also speculation among psychiatrists that certain impulsive "daredevil" behaviors (such as hang gliding) may be attempts to ward off or overcome symptoms of depression.

Among the more severely depressed, episodes of dampened mood may be followed by overtalkativeness, hyperactivity, racing thoughts, impulsive behaviors, distractability, and a decreased need for rest and sleep. These are the signs of mania. At one time manic-depression was considered a separate illness from simple depression or melancholia. More recent studies favor the view that depression sometimes occurs along a continuum, with milder forms of depression on one end, moving toward the more severe manic-depressive disorders at the other end.

Studies have also revealed strong genetic load for these related mood disorders. Among people who develop manic-depressive illness, there is a higher rate of illness within biological parents than is found in adoptive parents. The incidence of suicide among biological relatives of patients with manic-depressive illness is six to ten times greater than the rate encountered in the general population.

In contrast to many of mankind's earliest ideas on schizophrenia, the earliest concepts regarding depression were formulated in terms that make a considerable degree of sense even today. The Greek physician Hippocrates proposed that normal moods depend upon a balance within the body of four fluid humors: blood, phlegm, yellow bile, and black bile. Although the scientific usefulness of Hippocrates' rather fanciful terms has lessened over the years, his concepts are firmly entrenched in our language. For instance, a person with little natural enthusiasm is commonly described as phlegmatic. A nasty temper is the trademark of a bilious disposition (a reference to yellow bile). In each case, one humor has assumed priority over the others, creating an imbalance.

Although scientists no longer believe that the ardor of a lover or the sharpness of a temper can be meaningfully explained on the basis of humors, they continue to support Hippocrates' view—suitably dressed up in modern neuro-chemicals rather than humors—that mood is the behavioral expression of a shift in balance among various neurotransmitters in the brain.

The naturally occurring substance *rauwolfia* has been used in India as a sedative for centuries. More recently it was discovered that the drug *reserpine,* made from rauwolfia, could lower the blood pressure of patients with hypertension. But it accomplished this with one troubling and inexplicable side effect: Fifteen percent of the patients treated with reserpine became seriously depressed. In many cases the depression was serious enough that if the earliest signs went unnoticed, suicide resulted. This observation of reserpine-related depression was also observed in animal studies. Animals treated with the drug became sedated, lethargic, and poorly motivated, almost as if they were suffering from the same loss of "interest" in their surroundings as depressed patients.

Neurochemical studies carried out at NIMH provided the first clue to what was occurring in reserpine-induced depression. Dr. Bernard Brodie and his associates discovered that reserpine depletes the brain of serotonin and norepinephrine. It does so by releasing these neurotransmitters from their storage granules, where, under ordinary conditions, they await their release via nerve stimulation. Under the influence of reserpine-induced release, these two neurotransmitters are broken down by the enzyme *monoamine oxidase*. Therefore, they are not available at the time of normal nerve stimulation, suggesting that depression may result from a deficiency of one or both of these neurotransmitters.

A second clue pointing to the importance of norepinephrine and serotonin came from observing the effect of an antitubercular drug. *Iproniazid* was initially synthesized to improve the treatment of tuberculosis and eliminate several troublesome side effects often encountered with antitubercular medications. Quite independent of this use, however, the drug brought about an elevation in mood. Many patients, some of whom suffered from advanced forms of TB, reported an increased sense of well-being. They began eating and sleeping normally again. Chemical investigation of Iproniazid revealed that the drug functioned as an inhibitor of monoamine oxidase. Since, under ordinary conditions, monoamine oxidase breaks down norepinephrine and serotonin, inhibition of the enzyme led to an increase in these two neurotransmitters.

Taken together, these independent observations suggest a testable hypothesis: Depression results from a decrease of the neurotransmitters norepinephrine and serotonin. Therefore, an improvement in mood might be brought about by administering drugs that increase the concentration of these two neurotransmitters. This hypothesis was tested when Iproniazid was first administered to depressed,

The Blood-Brain Barrier

The brain is unique among other bodily organs by virtue of a blood-brain barrier. In contrast to, say, the liver or the spleen, the brain receives only some of the many substances in the circulating blood plasma. Other substances aren't permitted entry. For example, many large proteins can't pass from general circulation into the brain while other substances, such as nicotine, are allowed free entry. (This is one of the reasons why cigarette smoking is addicting.) This arrangement whereby the brain exists in a state of splendid isolation is made possible by special structural features in the capillaries (blood vessels) surrounding the brain cells. These brain capillaries are uniquely constituted so that in order to enter the brain, substances must pass directly through the cell membranes rather than through small "clefts" in the walls of the capillaries—as they would throughout the rest of the body.

In general, substances pass into the brain in proportion to their degree of solubility with the lipid (fatty) outer membrane of the capillaries, although other biochemical and biophysical characteristics of the substances (such as ionic charge, the size of the molecule, etc.) are also important. Thanks to the blood-brain barrier, the brain is protected against the unpredictable and oftentimes uncontrollable fluctuations in the content of many blood plasma constituents.

A drug enters the neural network by passing through the uniquely structured outer membrane of a brain capillary. It will go on to alter the chemical messages being transmitted across the nearby synapse.

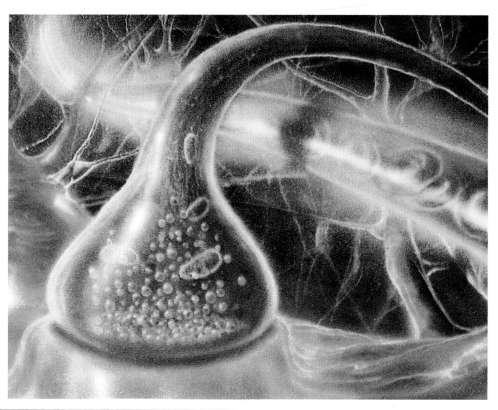

nontubercular patients. The effect was dramatic. Lifting of depression improved over several weeks.

Soon other evidence contributed to the growing case for the importance of *noradrenergic* (noradrenaline-producing) and *serotonergic* (serotonin-producing) neurons in depression. If Iproniazid was given to reserpine-treated animals, it counteracted their sedation and torpor. A similar situation occurred in humans: Reserpine-induced depression responded positively to Iproniazid.

Norepinephrine and serotonin currently are thought to be the principal transmitters associated with depression. Both are synthesized by specific neurons and have amino acid precursors (*tyrosine* and *tryptophane,* respectively). They are packed in storage granules. Upon stimulation, these neurotransmitters are released into the synaptic cleft, where they interact with receptors on the cell membrane of other neurons. Both norepinephrine and serotonin are then taken up, "captured" by the neuron before they are broken down by monoamine oxidase. Inhibiting monoamine oxidase is only one way of increasing the availability of serotonin and noradrenaline. If the reuptake of these neurotransmitters were blocked, prolonging their period of activity, this would have the same effect as inhibiting the enzyme monoamine oxidase from breaking down the neurotransmitters into their component parts.

Investigations along these lines have resulted in a second class of antidepressants: the *tricyclics,* which give the neurotransmitters more time to act within the synaptic cleft.

Since neither serotonin nor norepinephrine crosses from the bloodstream into the brain (both are halted by the blood-brain barrier), these substances cannot be given directly to patients. Instead, *L-tryptophane* (the precursor of serotonin) was tested for its antidepressant effectiveness when combined with a monoamine oxidase inhibitor. It improved the depression.

Other drugs, too, affect depression according to their tendency to increase or decrease the availability of neurotransmitters. *Amphetamine* ("speed") enhances release and blocks reuptake of certain neurotransmitters, transiently elevating mood in both normal and some depressed patients. *Cocaine,* another drug widely known to provide temporary improvement of mood, also blocks the reuptake mechanism. On the other side of the equation, agents that inhibit serotonin synthesis lead to a deterioration of mood and abrupt relapses in depressed patients who previously responded favorably to antidepressants.

Why and how does altering the level of a neurotransmitter elevate a person's mood? So far there is no answer to that important question. One hypothesis concerns the role of neurotransmitters in the so-called pleasure centers within the brain. As discussed in Chapter 4, there are pathways in the brain, particularly in the hypothalamus and limbic system, that involve the perception of pleasure. Test animals will repetitively self-stimulate if electrodes are implanted in these areas. These pleasure or reward centers are heavily "wired" with neurons producing neurotransmitters. It is conceivable that depressed patients experience loss of pleasure as the result of abnormalities in norepinephrine and serotonin, or other neurotransmitters.

The formation of neurotransmitters is part of the process of degradation, breaking down these molecules into simpler substances, the so-called end products. Norepinephrine, for instance, is broken down into the compound *MHPG*, which is secreted in the urine. Serotonin's breakdown product is *5HIAA*. In those cases where either norepinephrine or serotonin is reduced within the brain, the concentration of the breakdown products is decreased as well. This simple measurement forms the basis for a "suicide test."

Patients suffering from severe depressions often show a reduction in the spinal fluid 5HIAA levels. In those patients who have attempted suicide, the reduction is particularly dramatic. The measurement is reliable enough that severely depressed patients undergo periodic examinations of their spinal fluid 5HIAA, and those patients with the most marked reduction are carefully monitored to prevent attempts at self-destruction.

Overall, the so-called *biogenic-amine* (norepinephrine and serotonin) hypothesis has been helpful. It has enabled neuroscientists to relate a subtle disorder of the emotions to disruptions in certain key brain neurotransmitters. But there are perils in applying the hypothesis too literally. A decrease in a certain neurotransmitter within the brain—say, serotonin—can result from several causes. Perhaps not enough of the substance is being synthesized. Or too much is being broken down. Or perhaps it isn't being released from its stor-

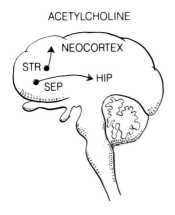

ACETYLCHOLINE

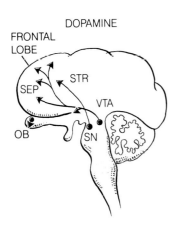

DOPAMINE

age vesicles. Or the reuptake mechanisms may be overworking. Each of these different causes opens up a host of possible explanations.

Furthermore, the measurement of the breakdown products of a neurotransmitter is a measure of the pervasiveness of the neurotransmitter throughout the whole brain or, at the very least, large areas of the brain. The actions of the neurotransmitters, on the other hand, may be limited to a tiny brain area. The only truly useful information, therefore, would consist of an accounting of what is happening neurochemically in a small fraction of the brain. This kind of information can't be gathered from collections of cerebrospinal fluids.

A second problem with the biogenic-amine hypothesis springs from the long-term effects that psychotropic drugs exert on the brain's receptors. As mentioned earlier in regard to the drug treatment of schizophrenia, medications alter receptor sites. The sites may, for instance, increase in number and become supersensitive to medications. To this extent the effects of a drug are far more complicated than simply leading to a decrease or an increase of a particular neurotransmitter. Recent developments in antidepressant therapy bear this out. Several newly synthesized compounds effectively relieve depression but have no discernible effect on serotonin or norepinephrine.

Some feeling for the difficulty facing neuroscientists in relating behavior to neurochemistry can be gleaned from a glance at the diagrams on these two pages. Each of the separate sketches corresponds to the pathway of a different neurotransmitter. Each involves different brain areas and different concentrations of the neuroactive compounds. And the situation in the brain isn't at all like a static sketch. Instead we are dealing with dynamic patterns ongoing at all times, subtly influencing each other in ways that neuroscientists are only beginning to understand.

Recent evidence from immunochemistry indicates that some neurons contain both a "classical" neurotransmitter such as norepinephrine and a peptide transmitter (small chain amino acid). It is likely that both interact to produce chemical transmission. The peptides must amplify or otherwise modify the effects of the "classical" transmitters. On occasion the peptide may serve two functions: as a neurotransmitter in its own right and as a modulator of the effects of other neurotransmitters. It is naïve to think that something as complex as human emotion and behavior could ever be explained on the basis of a variation in the concentration of one or two neurotransmitters. Each exerts an influence on the other to produce the exquisite balance that makes normal brain functioning possible. Any alteration in the balance of neurotransmitters could easily bring about unanticipated disruptions in overall brain functioning. Perhaps the keenest observer of the subtleties involved was the experimental physiologist Sir Charles Sherrington:

"It is as if the Milky Way entered upon some cosmic dance. Swiftly the brain becomes an enchanted loom where millions of flashing shuttles weave a dissolving pattern, always a meaningful pattern though never an abiding one; a shifting harmony of subpatterns."

When the balance of neurotransmitters is disturbed, it is as if the Milky Way were transformed into a maelstrom; order and regularity are replaced by fearful chaos. In all, it is a sobering thought that the contents of our mind and our mental balance are so intimately and permanently linked with the chemistry of our brain.

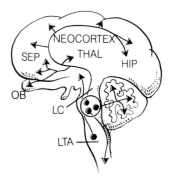

NOREPINEPHRINE

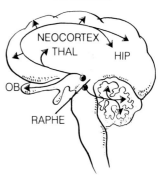

SEROTONIN

These diagrams show the primary locations of neurons containing certain of the neurotransmitters (left, acetylcholine and dopamine; right, norepinephrine and serotonin). Fibers from these neurons project from their source to other areas of the brain, as indicated by the arrows. Abbreviations are as follows: HIP, hippocampus; LC, locus coeruleus; LTA, lateral tegmental area; OB, olfactory bulb; SEP, septum; SN, substantia nigra; STR, striatum; THAL, thalamus; and VTA, ventral tegmental area.

8.
States of Mind

Of all the rituals and traditions that surround the study of the human brain, none is more compelling than dissection. A neuropathologist gathers together a selected group of medical students, nurses, neurologists, and neurosurgeons who meet in a small dissecting room, usually located deep in the bowels of a hospital or medical school. There, set out upon the dissecting table, is a human brain that has been suspended in a solution of formaldehyde to harden it for the surgeon's scalpel.

As the ritual begins, one of the medical students or resident physicians starts reading the case history of the unfortunate individual whose brain is on the table. As the reader drones on with the list of complaints, physical findings, and laboratory test results, the neuropathologist begins cutting into the brain in search of a "neuroanatomical correlation," some explanation for what went wrong within this particular brain.

At one time neuropathologists thought that dissection might eventually be perfected, enabling us to understand the human brain in all its complexity. No one seriously believes that now. Cutting into the brain in search of abnormalities can provide only a rough guideline for particular cases. For instance, a patient who suddenly loses strength on the right side of his or her body along with the ability for normal speech may later provide the neuropathologist with a neuroanatomical correlation: an *infarct* (stroke) in the left hemisphere, in those regions subserving movement and language.

But the demonstration of a lesion—an abnormality in one part of the brain caused by disease—doesn't tell much

These tangles of abnormal dendrites are characteristic of Alzheimer's disease.

Dr. Tom O'Donohue

about normal brain function. Powers of movement and speech, as we have seen, involve many areas of the brain. Besides, it is difficult to understand normal brain functioning on the basis of brains that have ceased to function as they should.

There are also limitations of scale. Brain dissection is limited to structural considerations: something goes wrong within the brain's structure and destroys some aspect of normal brain activity. But structure is only one part of brain activity. There is also function: neuronal impulses are conveyed along axons from one neuron to the next; neurochemicals spurt from the ends of presynaptic neurons and cross the synaptic cleft to the postsynaptic membrane, where they are taken up by the second neuron.

In recent years, therefore, neuroscientists for the most part have given up on the long-cherished belief that an understanding of the human brain will ever come about by means of brain dissections alone. In its place, neuroscientists are concentrating on the brain's chemical coding. If the brain's neurotransmitters and their receptors can be fully revealed, it might be possible to understand how neurons communicate with each other. But experiments along these lines require gathering huge numbers of brains. One neuroscientist who is doing just that is Dr. Tom O'Donohue, of the National Institute of Neurological and Communicative Disorders and Stroke. About every two weeks Dr. O'Donohue and his assistant make the forty-five-mile trip to a Baltimore slaughterhouse.

"We go there to collect hog brains. We use hog brains for a number of reasons. We are trying to isolate a neurotransmitter that exists in very small amounts in brains. In order to isolate enough of the transmitter to learn its chemical structure we have to start with a lot of brains. We take two hundred pounds of pig brain, and we homogenize it in about fifty gallons of liquid. Eventually we end up with micrograms of peptide."

Dr. O'Donohue's research was stimulated by a discovery in 1979. Research teams in New York and Paris reported that year that radioactively tagged PCP (known on the streets as "angel dust") binds to the receptors in the hippocampus and the cerebral cortex. This suggests that receptors in the cerebral cortex may actually exist for binding the endogenous PCP-like peptide and that PCP may exert its destructive behavioral effects by chemically disconnecting the cortex from the limbic system.

"It's generally thought that the cortex, which is a relatively new part of the brain, exerts an inhibitory control on the limbic system," says Dr. O'Donohue. "In the absence of cortical control, it's possible that the limbic system begins to operate on its own."

Violent murders, self-mutilation, bizarre homicidal and suicidal rages—all have been reported as a result of PCP intoxication. "In the PCP state the emotions just run wild," says Dr. Candace Pert of the NIMH.

Dr. Candace Pert

"PCP, like other psychoactive drugs, binds to special receptors, in this case receptors confined almost completely to the cortex," says Dr. Pert. "We believe that there is an *endogenous* [naturally occurring within the brain] *peptide* which normally activates these receptors." In light of the extreme disturbances produced by ingested PCP, what possible function could a natural PCP serve?

The popular view among some neuroscientists is that naturally occurring PCP may induce an altered state of consciousness—not psychosis, but a milder, perhaps even a pleasurable state. Dr. Pert, in a more free-ranging moment, speculated along these lines.

"Perhaps the natural PCP is concerned with a shift of our conscious awareness into more subtle forms. In this state we may be more sensitive to other people, more apt to get new ideas or enter into states of reverie. At this point we just can't be sure."

Could it be that schizophrenia, with its bizarre hallucinations and disordered thought content, is the result of a flood of PCP within the brain? Neuroscientists aren't sure.

One of the ways of finding out more about PCP is to isolate it, chemically characterize it, and describe what it does within the normal brain. Once these goals are achieved, it might be possible to reach conclusions on the nature of schizophrenia, how to treat it, and ultimately how to prevent it.

"At the end of our work with hog brains we typically end up with a sample of PCP which weighs about ten micrograms, about the weight of one human hair," says Dr. O'Donohue. "What we want is to find out what the compound is ... how it works, and ultimately why it is in the brain."

At first glance, the search for a PCP receptor—as well as other neuropeptides and neurotransmitters—seems to have nothing to do with the brain dissection mentioned a moment ago. Both approaches, however, have one thing in common. They are different experimental techniques aimed at uncovering a common mechanism of how mind is somehow embedded into the matrix of the human brain. They are also studies of human consciousness and its transformations. What is the self? What does it mean to be conscious? What is the mind? Consider for a moment the context from which such unanswered and, perhaps, unanswerable questions arise.

The brain resting upon the autopsy table is just a mass of protoplasm. How was it possible for this gelatinous structure to produce, during the deceased's lifetime, conscious awareness? Where in the brain did creativity arise? Love? A sense of belonging to family or community? Certainly to the members of the deceased's family that brain was never thought of as simply a *brain* but as a husband, a father, a person. In this final chapter we will discuss some of the ways neuroscientists are trying to reconcile our ideas about mind with our emerging insights on the structure and function of the human brain. One way of doing this is by concentrating on how variations in brain function result in altered states of consciousness. Literally, what we perceive of the world around us, how we respond to it, our "inner worlds" are all exquisitely dependent upon the state of our brains from moment to moment.

For instance, it is obvious by this time that only a small number of the things capable of capturing the brain's attention actually do so at any given moment. As you are reading these words (depending on where you are), your brain is ignoring a host of sights, sounds, and activities in the environment. Attention is, in fact, a highly directed process. Shift the focus of attention, the area of interest, and totally new sensory data flood in. This shift depends on such things as alertness, degree of concentration, and areas of interest. Beyond these considerations, however, there is reason to believe that the brain directs attention according to a series of rules that remain outside our awareness. We do know that when the brain suffers an injury in certain areas, the normal process of attention breaks down.

A patient with an injury on one side of the brain, for instance, may ignore events at the opposite side of the body. A woman may apply makeup to the right side of her face while ignoring the left side. Another patient may only lift up his right hand in response to the command "Lift up both your hands." Patients with such defects in their attentional powers (known as *neglect*) may perform such bizarre activities as ignoring the food on one side of the plate, or shaving only one side of the face. When writing, they may squeeze all their sentences to one side of the page, leaving an unusually wide margin on the other side. It is important to emphasize that in many of these strange instances, the patients aren't paralyzed. If the examiner helps the patient to get started, it is possible to elicit movement of the arm that a moment before the patient seemed unable or unwilling to bring into action.

In some instances the neglect may be quite subtle, requiring equally subtle methods for demonstrating it. For instance, the patient may be asked to close his or her eyes and report the location of a light touch. When only one side of the body is touched at one time, the patient's identification is correct. But if two sides of the body are touched simultaneously (a light tap of the examiner's fingers on both the patient's cheeks), only one of the stimuli registers.

Artists who have suffered damage to one side of the brain may lose the capacity to depict objects on one side of the canvas over time. In a portrait, one half of a face may be blurred, or objects to one side may be only hazily depicted. With recovery from brain injury, the artist may recover his or her ability. More often, however, there remain subtle deficiencies that may be obvious only to the trained observer or art critic.

On the basis of studies of neglect in patients afflicted with brain lesions, neuroscientists several years ago started piecing together a theory about the normal brain's role in attention. Initially they speculated that a mechanism must exist for regulating attention. But the details of this hypothetical mechanism remained obscure. What happens, for instance, within the brain that causes it to appreciate some events in the environment while ignoring others?

The first breakthrough in our understanding of the brain mechanisms of attention came in the late 1950s when two independent teams of investigators showed that neglect could be induced in monkeys by experimentally placed lesions centered around the inferior parietal lobe. If the animals were stimulated on two sides of their body, they responded to only one of the stimuli, ignoring the other.

With the development of methods of measuring local areas of electrical activity, it became possible to monitor the discharge patterns of individual neurons in the parietal areas. Most intriguing of all are the stimuli that elicit the attention response. If the animal is hungry, neurons begin firing whenever the animal detects, looks toward, or tries to grasp food. If the animal is thirsty, a liquid rather than food

Artist Anton Raderscheidt suffered a stroke that impaired his ability to perceive "reality" in one visual field. In this self-portrait we can see the artist's neglect of one side of his face.

elicits a minor neuronal storm. In short, the animal's "motivational state" at any given moment is crucially important. Since this can vary (the animal may be either hungry or thirsty, both, or neither), the evocative value of different stimuli will also vary according to different times and circumstances. It is reasonable to assume, therefore, that this complexity of internal psychological states requires an equal complexity in neuronal processing: not just one area, but many interconnected brain areas must be involved in attention. One way of testing this hypothesis involves tracing the interconnections between the parietal lobe to

HRP-marked nerve cells enable researchers to trace neuronal connections within the brain.

discover what other brain areas, if any, have defects in attention.

One method for marking cells and tracing their interconnections involves a large plant enzyme, *horseradish peroxidase* (HRP). This enzyme is taken up by the nerve endings and is transported back toward the cell body where the nerve endings originated. In this way it is possible to label a nerve fiber within the parietal lobe and, by means of HRP, discover where the nerve cell is coming from.

States of Mind

Dr. Marsel Mesulam

When HRP was injected into the parietal cortex, nerve cells were discovered that projected far more extensively than any of the investigators originally anticipated. There were connections with motor areas, particularly those areas concerned with eye movements (looking toward the object of attention); extensive two-way connections exist uniting portions of the limbic system (necessary for generating the appropriate emotional drive). There were also cells extending as far down as the brainstem, particularly the reticular system. All these structures may operate to provide the necessary arousal, since attention is impossible in a sleeping or drowsy person.

Harvard neurologist M. Marsel Mesulam, who carried out the HRP experiments, has formulated a hypothesis about how the brain operates in directed attention. First the reticular structures exert an alerting effect. From here events proceed within a tightly interlocked system involving sensation, movement, and emotion. According to Dr. Mesulam, neglect can result from brain damage anywhere within this network. Dr. Mesulam speculates that the degree of neglect may depend on the extent of damage. If all three areas are involved, more severe forms of neglect may ensue (e.g., applying makeup to only one side of the face). If the damage is less extensive, more subtle forms of neglect may be encountered (extinguishing one of a pair of simultaneous stimuli).

Dr. Mesulam has placed on a firm experimental basis what other neuroscientists have suspected for years: Attention is a *distributed process* that involves extensive areas of the brain. Further, each brain area involved in attention makes its own special contribution. Overall, the results are consistent with observations gleaned from both the laboratory investigation of experimental animals and everyday observations of our own fluctuating levels of attention. Our interests as well as our internal states (hunger, curiosity, and so on) determine to a large degree those stimuli in the environment that capture our attention. The aroma of freshly baked bread will appeal to us when we are hungry, whereas that same stimulus may be ignored or even exert a cloying effect after a huge meal. Attention also involves more than pure calculation: We tend to turn our attention to objects and people that are emotionally significant for us. All these factors are correlated within the network of neuronal connections extending throughout large areas of the brain. Although some parts of the brain (notably the right hemisphere) are considered more important in attention than others, there is by no means an "attention center." In fact, research in attention underlines the point made many times throughout this book that complex behavioral activities rarely emanate from a single brain area. Nor should this be surprising. The brain functions as a whole, with each area affecting other areas, even ones widely separated from each other. In our attempt to understand the brain, we tend to isolate certain processes in a way similar to turning off a movie projector to study the film one frame at a time. But more is lost than gained by such simplifying efforts. An analysis of separate frames from a movie can never capture the dynamism of the film played out in the intended rapid sequence. "Stills" of the brain provide us with a similar loss of perspective. Isn't it equally foolish to limit our attention to only one aspect of an infinitely complex process?

A profound alteration in our state of consciousness takes place in each of us every twenty-four hours when we sleep and, particularly, when we dream. As mentioned in Chapter 3, sleep and dreaming occur in regular, rhythmic sequences that can be altered only slightly by our own efforts. In fact, if anyone becomes too cocky about that person's ability to control his or her own destiny, this simple experiment should be tried: Remain awake for forty-eight hours. Most people, unless they are exposed to an unusual stress or excitement, will be unable to meet the challenge. Clearly, the freedom of our consciousness is bounded by cycles of sleep and wakefulness.

Disagreements abound regarding the nature of sleep. Eight centuries before Christ, the Greek poet Hesiod characterized it as "sleep, the brother of death." Shakespeare, perhaps a troubled sleeper, was more impressed with the apparitions that can disturb the peaceful sleeper:

"To sleep: perchance to dream: ay, there's the rub; For in that sleep of death what dreams may come."

Sigmund Freud founded a profession on the meaningfulness of dreams. Today, those who can't afford a psychoanalyst can learn about their dreams through books about dreams, or by sharing information about their dreams with friends.

One of the most intriguing observations on sleep and dreaming was made in ancient times, perhaps by the Egyptians or the Mesopotamians. At that point, somebody noticed for the first time that animals dream, too. A dog will leap up out of a sound sleep barking at the phantoms that troubled the dog's sleep a moment before. Animals were commonly observed to sleep according to a different rhythm than we do. When we doze off for only a few minutes, we are taking a "catnap."

In the 1930s, a Belgian neurologist, Frederick Bremer, became interested in catnaps. In the spirit of a small boy out to discover which block in a tower was responsible for holding it up, he set out to discover what part of the cat's brain was responsible for sleep. Dr. Bremer cut into the brainstem at different levels. He discovered that cutting between the medulla or pons had little effect on the sleep-

Edward Weston, Neil, *1925*

wake cycle. A cut placed a little higher, through the midbrain, produced an animal that was permanently drowsy, if not asleep.

Dr. Bremer was the first neuroscientist to suggest that the brainstem wakes the cortex—that sleep would intervene were it not for some influence propagated from below. On the face of it, this was a curious notion. According to Bremer, if the cortex was deprived of its connectedness with the "lower" brainstem, sleep would set in. Dr. Bremer's research provided the basis for another series of experiments, carried out in the late 1940s, that further elaborated on the concept that sleep was a passive process resulting from a lack of arousal.

Giuseppi Moruzzi of Italy and Horace W. Magoun of Los Angeles delivered a series of electric shocks deep into the brainstem of a laboratory cat. Arousal resulted: The cat sat up, wanted to play, found milk enticing. The site for these shocks was the *reticular formation,* a system of nerve fibers extending from the medulla to the thalamus. Drs. Magoun and Moruzzi discovered that stimulation alerted the animal, whereas lesions, cuts, or electrocoagulations of the area produced a deep sleep. Animals with experimentally induced injuries to the reticular formation were not aroused by hearing their names, the pricks of a pin, or even electrical shocks. This research supported Dr. Bremer's earlier work, rendering it more specific, more "scientific." Simply put, wakefulness was thought to be the product of stimulation conveyed by the reticular formation in its path from the lower brainstem to the thalamus. It all seemed very simple.

But as often happens in brain research, extremely esoteric procedures were taking precedence over obvious everyday observations. As anyone who has spent a night with a bedmate knows, people don't simply descend into a state of deep sleep like a diving bell coming to rest on the bottom of the ocean. They toss and turn, roll about, sometimes even call out. Apparently Drs. Bremer, Moruzzi, and Magoun spent more time observing their cats than they did their wives.

In 1953, two sleep researchers permanently scuttled the notion that sleep results simply from the lack of arousal. Eugene Aserinsky and Nathaniel Kleitman were the first to place on a firm scientific foundation certain observations that could be traced back to the Hindus: Just as there are different levels of alertness, there are also different levels of sleep.

To prove this, Drs. Aserinsky and Kleitman recorded the eye movements of infants. Their reasons for conducting this unorthodox experiment stemmed from a combination of intuition and a firm grasp of brain organization. A disproportionately large cortical area is involved in eye movements. In addition, the precision required for firm motor control of the eyes involves a large number of nerves linking up with the muscles that move the eyes. Finally, the cranial nerves responsible for eye movements are located amid fibers of the reticular formation that slipstream around them on the way to the thalamus.

Sleep laboratories around the world investigate the EEG patterns of normal sleep as well as common sleep disturbances, such as insomnia, night terrors, and sleep walking.

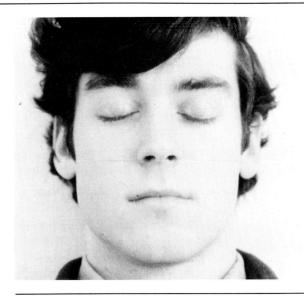

"One is led to suspect that the activity of the extraocular musculature and the lids might be particularly sensitive indicators of central nervous system changes associated with a sleep-wakefulness cycle" was how Drs. Aserinsky and Kleitman explained it in their paradigm-shattering paper, "Two Types of Ocular Motility Occurring During Sleep."

The observations of Drs. Aserinsky and Kleitman weren't new. Mothers and curious relatives had noted over the centuries that a baby's eyes rotate upward and outward during sleep. However, no one had really studied the movements carefully, nor had anyone ever correlated them with the depth of sleep throughout the night. It was another of those experiments that could have been made by Egyptians or by Roman housewives observing their babies during afternoon siestas. But it wasn't performed until Drs. Aserinsky and Kleitman did so. Their work ushered in a period of unparalleled research activity on a brain process as old as mankind.

Sleep researchers found that after falling into an initial period of deep sleep, people go through alternating cycles of light and deep sleep. Light sleep is associated with rapid eye movements regularly accompanied by dreams. Soon researchers around the world were hooking people up to all-night monitors. At the same time, they were advertising in scholarly journals for technicians who could sit up all night watching other people sleep, faithfully recording their subjects' brain waves without falling asleep themselves. Not only did the sleep technicians have to run the recording equipment, but they also had to correlate EEG patterns with rapid eye movement, body movement, and dreaming.

Since several different processes were under observation, the resulting sleep terminology is confusing. Essentially it breaks down like this: Deep sleep involves slow wave EEG activity and is therefore dubbed *S-sleep.* In light sleep, the EEG is desynchronized (similar to what we see in wakefulness), and *dreams* occur, so it is called *D-sleep.* (Since rapid eye movements also occur during light sleep, it is called *REM sleep.*)

The most important change wrought by the early sleep researchers was the recognition that sleep is an active process marked by regular alterations throughout the night of light and deep sleep episodes. Recognition of this pattern was only beginning, however. More important questions loomed, tough questions such as, What purpose is served by such regular cycles of sleep stages? Why do we dream?

Faced with questions such as these, sleep researchers concentrated on discovering the brain mechanisms underlying these observed sleep fluctuations. What is going on in the brain when a subject switches from deep sleep with its slow, synchronized EEG to a REM state characterized by a series of vivid dreams and EEG rhythms similar to those of a waking subject?

In adults, the first REM period lasts only about ten minutes. As the night wears on, more time is spent in REM sleep until, in the early-morning hours, REM sleep lasts about an hour. Infants follow a decidedly different pattern, seemingly finding dreams, or at least REM, more interesting than anything around them. Half of an infant's sleep is spent in the REM state. If infants could talk, what could they tell us of their dreams? Some researchers think they would have little to tell us, since for them REM may serve a different purpose than it does in adults, who spend only about 20 percent of their time in this state. In infants REM may be a stimulus for the brain, an electrophysiological prod for brain growth and development.

Along with differences in REM, people vary greatly

A typical sleep lab's EEG equipment and below, a patient participating in an all-night experiment is not bothered by the EEG electrodes once asleep.

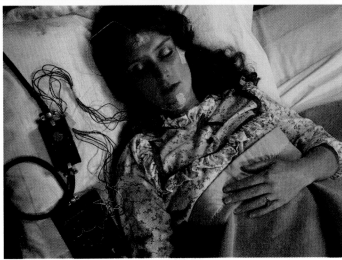

according to their need for sleep. Babies seem to require the most, about sixteen hours on the average. By age three, the infant has dropped to twelve hours, and by age five or six children and mothers are arguing over the need for afternoon naps. Starting in the teens, an adult pattern emerges, somewhere in the range of seven to eight hours, with some people able to make do on five or five and a half, while others can't function at their best on less than twelve. These variations may explain some of the cultural differences in regard to sleep. Even though we have given up formal siestas, there may have been wisdom in the tradition of the afternoon nap. Maybe that is why in the afternoon children

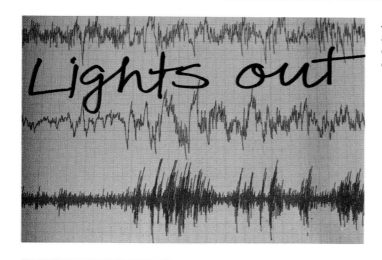

A portion of an EEG tape. A researcher will write the occurrence of any significant event directly on the tape as the night unfolds.

become cranky, young students get glassy-eyed, and large corporations record a postafternoon break in productivity.

Although all primates sleep, there are vast differences in their sleep patterns. The sleep of rodents and smaller mammals and birds involves only two distinct stages: slow wave sleep (the correlate of stage 4, non-REM) and REM sleep. REM sleep doesn't occur at all in reptiles or amphibians, perhaps an indication of the importance of the cerebral cortex in REM. But French sleep researcher Michel Jouvet suggests another interpretation: Since REM does not exist in cold-blooded animals, dreams may not be necessary for life. If Jouvet is correct, we can stop speculating about what fantasies may be disturbing the sleep of crocodiles sunning themselves along the edge of a swamp. They are dreaming, simply, of nothing at all.

Since REM sleep is easily detected by EEG monitoring, subjects can be awakened and the effect measured. REM deprivation experiments produce a shift in the subject's sleep patterns. If, over the course of several nights, subjects are awakened during REM sleep, they spend more time in REM sleep later, when the "experiment" is over. Longer periods of deprivation result in a longer and longer REM "rebound." Freud would rejoice at this discovery. In many ways it proved him right.

In his monumental *Interpretation of Dreams,* Freud claimed that we need our dreams. They help us make sense of our everyday world, fulfill some of our wishes, provide clues to our motives. If we cheat ourselves of REM sleep (or some diabolical sleep researcher does it for us), we rapidly return to our fantasy worlds the moment we fall back to sleep.

Dreams are active. We learn from them, look forward to them, even on occasion respond with terror to them. For centuries, sorcerers interpreted the dreams of kings, and on the basis of these interpretations, expeditions were outfitted and wars fought. On occasion dreams determined who lived and who died. Dreams can give us creative insight not only into our own psychological processes but also on occasion can reveal to us some of nature's secrets. For instance, in one famous case, a dream revealed a secret about the human brain.

In 1903 Otto Loewi, the German physiologist, conceived a theory about the role of chemicals in transmitting nerve impulses. Despite his confidence that his theory was correct, Loewi could think of no way of testing it. He pushed it to the back of his head until the night before Easter 1921, when Loewi had a dream:

"I awoke, turned on the light, and jotted down a few notes on a tiny slip of thin paper. Then I fell asleep again. It occurred to me at six o'clock in the morning that during the night I had written down something most important, but I was unable to decipher the scrawl. The next night, at three o'clock, the idea returned. It was the design of an experiment to test whether or not the hypothesis of chemical transmission that I had uttered seventeen years ago was correct. I got up immediately, went to the laboratory, and performed a simple experiment on a frog heart according to the nocturnal dream." The experiment was a resounding success (as described in detail on pages 163–165).

Although many cultures have accepted that dreams are meaningful, they have nevertheless disagreed on the interpretations of particular dreams. Sigmund Freud believed that dreams represent censored versions of unconscious desires. Within the dream are concealed, according to Freud, those ideas and emotions that the conscious mind is unwilling or unable to entertain during states of wakefulness. When asleep, however, the mind performs its "dreamwork" and disguises these forbidden impulses, which reappear in the form of symbols and improbable narratives. Freud's theory also provides an internally consistent but, as we shall see, inadequate explanation of why dreams are forgotten: Once the sleeper is awakened, the curtain of repression descends once again.

For Freud, dreams performed the function of a kind of safety valve. With the buildup of unconscious forces, the mind required a means of discharge. The dream was a compromise: The impulse is given partial expression, but outside of awareness. Presumably this prevented the further buildup of energy from the unconscious, which, thanks to the dream, could now stop short of precipitating a mental breakdown.

Notice that Freud's theory of dreams very much followed along the lines of nineteenth-century physics, with the brain functioning as a kind of steam engine in which powerful forces are generated. Unless these forces are somehow contained, dreadful "explosions" might result: madness, violence, and so on. There is also nothing in Freud's dream theory to suggest that dream formation has a physical basis. Everything is psychological.

Neuroscientists no longer believe that dreams represent simply a transformation of everyday conflicts, a kind of costume party in which the unwanted and the distressing are outfitted in acceptable symbolic representations. Two Harvard researchers, Dr. Allan Hobson and Dr. Robert McCarley, believe the brain is a "dream state generator." According to their experimental results, dreams result from basic brain processes rather than from disguised fears and wishes. Dreams are in fact the brain's attempt to impose meaning on an array of electrical signals that arrive at the cortex from the lower brainstem during REM periods.

Drs. Hobson and McCarley have isolated cells in the pons that are more active during sleep than waking. At the onset of REM these cells begin firing and forwarding information to higher cerebral cortical centers. The brain then tries to make sense out of this data, doing its best to construct a plausible explanation for what is going on. The way in which the brain assembles and integrates the burst of neuronal impulses from the pons depends on the unique life experiences and personality of the dreamer. The mismatch between the disparate signals arriving from the pons and the brain's previous waking experience accounts for the bizarre nature of many dreams. The dreams represent the brain's best possible interpretation under the circumstances. Notice that there is nothing disguised or repressed. Instead the brain is trying to construct a story out of disparate and unrelated data.

Although the theory of Drs. Hobson and McCarley is intriguing, it is not likely to be the final word on the nature of dreams. Despite what anybody says, some dreams are Freudian in their structure and meaning. Who hasn't experienced a prophetic dream, achieved an important insight about another person in a dream, or suddenly discovered a solution to a confusing daytime dilemma via a dream? It is difficult to imagine how such a process could result from the brain's attempt to improvise a story line on the basis of random data.

If you wake up 100 people during a REM period, 84 of them will remember a dream. Half of them will report an emotion accompanying that dream. Ninety percent will speak to you of a visual scene. More important than any of this, however, half of the awakened subjects will be able to make sense of their dream in terms of recent experiences. Such statistics not only support Freud's assertion of the importance of dreams, they also raise bothersome questions: Why do we remember so few of our dreams? Wouldn't it be nice to be able to use our dreams more?

Sleep researcher William C. Dement believes that creative people are able to employ their dreams to solve problems and to construct novel solutions for puzzles. On one occasion he gave five hundred undergraduate students at

Stanford University a problem to dream about. The problem was: "The letters *o t t f f* form the start of an infinite series. Find a simple rule for determining all successive letters. According to this rule, what would the next two letters be?"

Two of the students were able to solve the brain twister in their waking state. Seven of them solved it during a dream. Here is one dream: "I was standing in an art gallery, looking at the paintings on the wall. As I walked down the hall, I began to count the paintings; one, two, three, four, five. But as I came to the sixth and seventh, the paintings had been ripped from their frames. I stared at the empty frames with a peculiar feeling that some mystery was about to be solved. Suddenly I realized that the sixth and seventh spaces were the solution to the problem!"

Have you solved the puzzle yet? To do so, you may have to try dreaming about it. The solution is deceptively simple: *o t t f f* are the first letters of one, two, three, four, five. The next two letters are *s* and *s* for six and seven, the two letters requested by Dement. The dreamer counting the pictures in his dream gallery was already onto the solution of the problem. He had only to translate what transpired in the dream: *counting* is the key to the puzzle.

Such an experiment illustrates the difficulties inherent in dream interpretation. If the subject knew the solution to the problem, why couldn't he or she articulate it in the waking state? If the subject didn't know, how could he or she learn it in a state of unconsciousness? Who figured it out? Certainly not the waking subject, since even when reviewing the dream in the morning, he or she still didn't know the answer but had only been provided the clue: counting. To this extent, the dreamer both knew and didn't know the solution to the puzzle. One is reminded of Samuel Taylor Coleridge's haunting question, "What if in your dream you dreamed, and what if in your dream you went to heaven and there plucked a strange and beautiful flower, and what if when you woke you had the flower in your hand?"

Despite our confidence to the contrary, the issue of whether one is awake or asleep at any given time isn't really as clear-cut as it first appears. Nineteenth-century philosopher Ernest Mach once realized he had fallen asleep during a reverie only because he noticed an unusual pattern to the movements of some twigs in the dream. Some dreamers regularly have "lucid dreams" in which they become perfectly aware, while asleep, that they are dreaming. To some extent they can even control the content of their dreams and, like a movie director, have quite a bit to say about the narrative, dialogue, and action. There are even some claims by dream researchers that people can learn to control their dreams, learn to increase the likelihood that their dreams can be helpful by exploring their inner worlds in ways not possible during ordinary waking consciousness.

No one knows for sure why we sleep or what benefit it bestows. It doesn't seem to be essential for health. Every sleep center has on its roster one or more people who sleep only one or two hours per twenty-four hours yet don't seem any worse for such a brief period of sleep. Nor does sleep simply recharge the energy lost during the day. If a person stays up late one night, the person discovers at about 3:00 or 4:00 A.M. (the exact time differs according to the subject) that he or she is less sleepy than two or three hours before.

"Since you start to get less sleepy as you approach the early-morning hours just before dawn, it indicates that people don't get sleepy simply on the basis of missed sleep. If that were true, you would get sleepier and sleepier the longer you stayed up. Instead, the pattern is typical of a cyclic internal program," says Dr. Thomas Wehr, acting chief, Clinical Psychobiology Branch, National Institute of Mental Health, and researcher on biological rhythms and sleep.

Studies over the past 20 years have revealed a complicated internal structure to sleep and dreaming. As mentioned earlier, it includes periods of partial arousal (REM) that share some properties of arousal in the waking state. It is now almost certain that this arousal pattern is produced by coordinating centers in the brainstem. First the brain patterns revert to the normal active pattern seen in Stage 1. (Stage 1 REM sleep can be distinguished from Stage 1 non-REM sleep only by monitoring eye movements and muscular tension.) This active brain pattern is associated with increases in heart rate, blood pressure, and breathing. The muscles of the neck and shoulders are actively inhibited. The only muscles registering activity are those of the middle ear and the eyes (REM). Obviously such a precise orchestra-

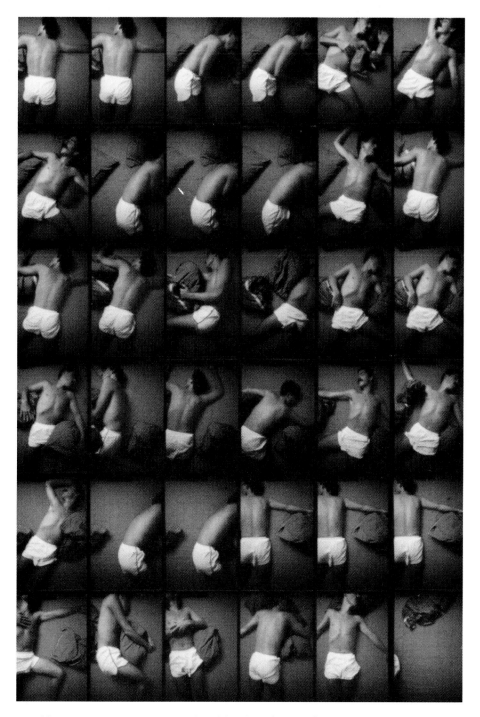

*In addition to EEG measurements, sleep labs often photograph
the sleeper at regular intervals to look for
patterns of movement during sleep.*

tion doesn't just "happen." There must be some coordinating mechanism within the brain capable of altering our blood pressure in tandem with inducing relaxation of the muscles of our neck.

Recordings from the brainstems of animals reveal a phasic burst of electrical activity from the pons, the nuclei of the nerves subserving eye movements (*oculomotor*) and two-way stations along the visual tract (the lateral geniculate nuclei of the thalamus and the visual cortices). These sharp waves—called *pontine geniculate occipital spikes* (PGO)—are the primary triggering mechanisms for the rapid eye movements of REM sleep. Proof of the importance of PGO spikes comes from "spike deprivation" experiments.

If cats are awakened at the first sign of PGO spikes, they will need more REM sleep over the next several nights (*REM rebound*). The same thing happens, but to a lesser extent, if they are awakened a few moments after the PGO spikes, at the moment of the first rapid eye movements. PGO spikes may induce REM at the same time as they inhibit motor activity elsewhere in the body.

The insight that sleep is an active process instead of a mere decrease in vigilance stimulated researchers to search for "wakefulness" as well as "sleep" centers. In 1958, a wakefulness center was discovered just a few millimeters below the area of the midbrain cut by Bremer over a quarter century earlier. Instead of remaining permanently asleep, these cats couldn't sleep at all. This paved the way for the theory that sleep and wakefulness result from the interaction of neurons involved in wakefulness as well as other neurons, slightly lower in the brainstem, important in inducing sleep.

The search for "sleep-inducing areas" has revealed a collection of serotonin-producing cells in the midline of the medulla. Destruction of these cells produces temporary insomnia in cats followed by the almost total elimination of REM sleep. These lesions also depress serotonin levels within the brain to a degree correlating nicely with the length of insomnia. For a while it seemed that sleep induction might result from an increase in the levels of brain serotonin, while wakefulness depended on just the opposite: a reduction in the levels of available serotonin. But things aren't that simple. The repeated chemical inhibition of serotonin formation results in an initial period of insomnia followed

Popular Questions About the Brain

Q: *How does a drug like cocaine act in the brain?*

A: As a general rule, all drugs which affect behavior and mood do so by altering neurotransmitters within the brain. Danger arises from the unpredictable effects these alterations may take.

Cocaine is a local anesthetic that alters the permeability of the membranes of nerve cells. For this reason it has been used for years in surgery on the nose and mucous membranes. It also prolongs the life span of neurotransmitters within the gap ("synapse") between nerve cells. Neither of these effects, however, is believed to be the cause of the euphoria induced by cocaine. It is likely that this effect is directly related to the concentration of the drug within the brain. Smoking or injecting cocaine leads to a faster rise in the drug's concentration within the brain than occurs with eating or snorting the drug. This difference is believed to be responsible for the high consumption and drug-seeking behavior so destructive to normal life routines. Although cocaine is not formally classified as an addictive substance, its prolonged use, particularly by means of "free base" snorting or ingestion, leads to serious dependence. Sudden deaths and brain hemorrhages also have occurred as a result of the temporary elevation of blood pressure produced by the drug.

Q: *Why do some stroke victims recover while others do not?*

A: The brain doesn't "break down" the same way as a mechanical device. Instead, the end result of a "stroke" depends on the brain's ability to reorganize itself after sustaining damage.

A "stroke" is a cerebral vascular accident: brain damage resulting from a disturbance in the blood supply to some part of the brain. Some blood vessels serve crucial brain areas responsible for movement, sight, and language. Destruction of these areas leads to serious, often permanent disabilities. Other blood vessels supply less critical areas and, when affected by a stroke, the damage is less disabling. In addition, there are differences in brain organization between the young and the old, men and women, left-handers and right-handers. For instance, women in general recover quicker and more completely than men from a stroke within the cerebral hemispheres. For some reason, the female brain and the brain of a left-hander exhibit less lateralization: both hemispheres can share in language and spatial tasks rather than one hemisphere specializing to the exclusion of the other.

by the return of almost normal sleep patterns. This recovery occurs despite the fact that brain serotonin levels remain below normal.

Other components of sleep also deviate from normal. For instance, REM events, notably dreams and rapid eye movements, shift into periods of non-REM sleep. Cats will jump, arch their back, and hiss at ghostly visitants that exist only within their dreams. Serotonin may have some role to play in restricting PGO spikes to REM sleep. With a decrease of available serotonin, the spiking may shift over into non-REM periods and produce a series of "waking dreams."

Overall, neuroscientists now believe that sleep and wakefulness result from the interaction of a distributed system of centers within the brain. Differences in anatomic location and neurochemical secretion determine whether a particular center contributes to wakefulness or sleep. Some researchers suggest that arousal is associated with noradrenaline secretion while deep sleep results from serotonin influences. These various alertness and sleep-inducing centers and neurotransmitters are thought to interact according to an internal clockwork pattern. After a period of alertness different areas concerned with sleep intervene. Sleep and wakefulness tend to occur in regular cycles, but these cycles aren't etched in granite. In some instances sleepiness gets out of control and can't be resisted despite the most valiant efforts.

About 250,000 Americans suffer from *narcolepsy,* an embarrassing, mysterious, and, on occasion, dangerous sleep disorder. Narcoleptics can't remain awake during the day no matter how much sleep they have had the night before. Despite his or her best efforts, the narcoleptic remains permanently susceptible to "sleep attacks": the sudden, overwhelming requirement for five to twenty minutes of sleep. To an observer, such people behave like sleep addicts: they can't be reasoned with, cajoled, or threatened into wakefulness. They fall asleep in the midst of a conversation, while talking with their boss, even while making love. In one study of narcoleptics over 40 percent admitted that, at least on one occasion, they fell asleep at the wheel of a car.

Along with these "sleep binges," narcoleptics are subject to sudden, abrupt loss of muscle tone. They may suddenly fall to the ground, especially when they are emotionally excited. (Medically this behavior is known as *cataplexy*.) As a result, narcoleptics often are the target of pranksters who get their kicks out of sneaking up behind them and shouting. The resulting scare sends them plummeting to the ground, sometimes suffering broken bones. Two other signs of narcolepsy are sleep paralysis (a brief loss of muscle tone in the period between wakefulness and sleep) and hallucinations, dreamlike images during the same period.

The cause of narcolepsy is only partially understood. The narcoleptic may suffer from an inability to inhibit REM sleep. Within the first few minutes after falling asleep, the narcoleptic enters directly into the REM state. Normally the transition from wakefulness to REM takes over an hour. In addition, narcoleptics are able to fall asleep quicker than the average person, even when free of narcoleptic attacks. On the average, it takes about fifteen minutes for a person to fall asleep if he or she has chosen to take a nap at an unaccustomed hour. Not so the narcoleptic. Within two minutes the narcoleptic can fall asleep regardless of the time of day or how much sleep the person had the night before.

Narcoleptic symptoms—inappropriate sleep onset, cataplexy, hallucinations, and sleep paralysis—lend support to the theory that sleep is correlated with muscle tone and visual imagery. Speculating for a moment, the sleep paralysis of cataplexy may result from the intrusion into wakefulness of the inhibition of muscle tone usually seen only in REM sleep. The hallucinations may correspond to dreams in the twilight state between waking and sleeping.

"The current consensus is that cataplexy, sleep paralysis, and hallucinations are dissociated manifestations of REM sleep," according to Stanford University sleep researcher William Dement. Dr. Dement's work on narcolepsy took on a new dimension with the discovery of an animal model for the disorder. In some Doberman pinschers narcolepsy is genetically transmitted. Analysis of the brains of these narcoleptic dogs reveals involvement of several neurotransmitters, which provides support for the theory that REM sleep results from such an interaction.

"Our results support a proposed theory linking the initiation and maintenance of REM sleep to a critical balance between serotonergic, adrenergic, and cholinergic neuronal networks of the pontine area of the brainstem," according to Dr. Dement and his coworkers.

Some support for this hypothesis comes from the study of narcolepsy's mirror image: *chronic insomnia.* New evidence indicates that this, too, may result from a mixup in the body's normal sleep rhythms. For years, standard treatment for insomnia has involved barbiturates. With the advent of all-night recordings, it became possible to monitor the effects of these habit-forming drugs. It turns out that rather than enhancing REM sleep, barbiturates severely suppress it. After a few nights of use, barbiturates actually become part of the insomnia problem rather than contributing to its solution.

Alternative methods of treatment are based on considering insomnia a disturbance in the body's biological clock. Patients with insomnia get out of "phase" with their own sleep-wake cycles. As a result, they toss and turn for hours before falling asleep and then wake up the next morning utterly worn out. The treatment, pioneered by Harvard University's Charles Czeisler, is *chronotherapy:* The sufferer's day-night schedule is gradually shifted until the internal sleep clock beats in time with the rhythms of the outside world. Occupations that demand erratic changes in sleep-wake patterns are thought to predispose individuals to delayed sleep-onset insomnia.

Researchers have also undergone a change of mind in the ways they think about insomnia. It is no longer considered a disease all its own but rather a symptom of some other disease. In a study of insomniacs carried out several years ago, over 70 percent were discovered to be suffering from emotional problems, notably depression. Some depressives have improved when they have skipped a night's sleep. Others respond favorably to being awakened each time they enter REM sleep. These patients are likely to improve on an antidepressant, another suppressant of REM. One means of monitoring improvement in depression is to observe the patient's sleep patterns. Medications that are likely to prove effective may initially do so by restoring a normal sleep rhythm.

In sleep centers throughout the United States researchers are employing a vast array of electronic equipment to improve the sleep, mental health, and well-being of a host of people suffering from sleep-related disorders. Analysis of the timing, length, sequence, and internal organization of sleep cycles is permitting better diagnosis and treatment of many sleep-wake disorders.

It is obvious from the study of sleep and dreaming that the brain has a great capacity for utilizing alternative channels. At one moment the brain may be in a state of deep sleep, followed a few minutes later by REM periods of dreaming, followed still later by a period of full conscious alertness. This shift in conscious awareness is mirrored by differences in the strategies the brain may use to accomplish its goals. To take an example during full conscious awareness, if I want to hand you a copy of this book, I can use my right hand or my left. I can even restrict my muscle activity to the movement of my lips and tongue and ask a companion to hand the book to you. The task is the same (conveying the book from me to you), but the methods differ markedly.

Recent research indicates that differences in brain specialization may provide a clue to a disorder that has mystified and confounded psychiatrists for centuries. So-called *multiple personalities*—two or more separate personalities existing within one individual—may represent two or more separate brain states.

Dr. Frank Putnam, a psychiatrist at the National Institute of Mental Health, has discovered that brain-wave tracings—specifically, evoked potential studies—can be used in many cases to distinguish the separate personalities that may coexist in a "multiple." Multiple-personality patients may enter into unique neurophysiological states in each of their separate personalities. To an extent, several personalities coexist within one brain: as the brain function alters toward a different pattern, the personality alters with it.

For years, psychiatrists who have studied patients with multiple personalities have noted that the switch in personality often is accompanied by subtle variations in body posture and tone of voice. Within a minute or two, the transformation is complete. The new personality talks, walks, and postures differently. There may even be alterations in values, behavior, and the expression of ideas. Speech may be accelerated, or it may exhibit other variations in rate, tone, or emphasis.

Although professional actors are able to accomplish similar alterations, they cannot do so with the facility of the true multiple personality. In addition, evoked potential stud-

The Multiple Personality

Tony

Meet Tony, a 58-year-old carpenter, with at least thirty different personalities. Many of these personalities see and experience things which the others don't know anything about. Because of this, Tony, in common with other "multiples" throughout the world, suffers from frequent memory lapses. "I have no memory. If the different selves don't tell me 'we did this' or 'we did that,' I am lost. I have no recollection of what happened." On one occasion, Tony attended a wedding or, to be more correct about it, one of Tony's other personalities attended, the one he calls "the imposter." "I had no memory of it. The imposter took over, blanked me out the whole night. And there I was a couple of days later going around asking people, 'Did you see me there?' "

In an effort to understand his multiple selves, Tony traveled to the National Institute of Mental Health to be tested by psychiatrist Frank Putnam. By measuring Tony's evoked potentials (the brain's electrical response to a series of repeated sounds or light flashes), Tony was discovered to be harboring three totally unique personalities, each with its own distinct evoked potential. "These differences in the evoked potentials among three or more different personalities in Tony suggest that there may, in fact, be some real bodily changes that occur when the alternative personalities take over and are out. It suggests, too, that we are seeing a psychological condition that also affects the body," says Frank Putnam. Dr. Putnam has confirmed his evoked potential findings by testing other people with multiple personalities. As a group they exhibit differences in evoked potentials according to which personality is dominant at the moment.

People who pretend to have multiple personalities do not exhibit the kinds of differences seen in these PET scans of Pam (another patient) and Tony.

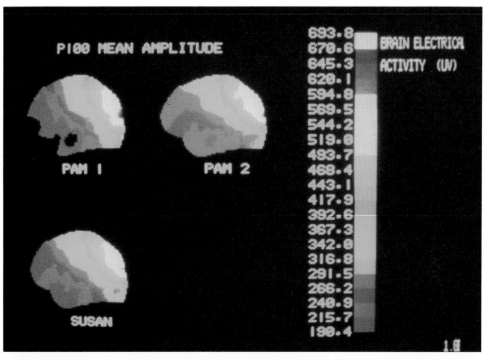

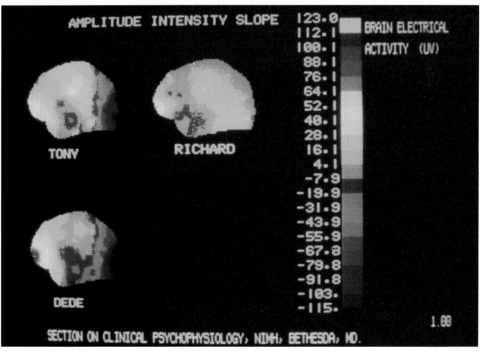

ies of actors reveal no change in their basic brain patterns. Multiples, by contrast, may shift their evoked potential patterns when each of the different personalities appears.

From studies of multiple personality, neuroscientists are beginning to change some of their traditional ideas about altered states of consciousness. Multiples may represent extreme examples of things we all do every day. For instance, faced with a difficult or stressful situation, we often try to "put it out of our minds." When bored, we tend to lapse into reverie and daydreams. Our conscious awareness alters under the influence of drugs, alcohol, and even the amount of sleep we have had the night before. This doesn't imply that we are all "multiples." But it does suggest that our everyday personalities aren't nearly as coherent and integrated as we like to believe. Changes in our brain wave patterns often accompany these changes in our mental state. Drowsiness and reverie, for instance, are marked by a slowing in the background rhythm. Full alertness, in contrast, is marked by a well-organized, sharply defined background rhythm.

From studies of the evoked potentials of multiples, we may soon learn more about the neurobehavioral mechanisms underlying normal personality. Do our brain electrical patterns differ according to mood? Do these patterns alter across substantial periods of time—say, five or ten years? So far, no one can answer these questions. Standard EEG's are too insensitive for such an investigation. The EEG samples too widely and is altered by too many extraneous factors. Evoked potential recordings may someday be capable of demonstrating subtle changes within a person's brain under different psychological conditions. So far, though, the necessary experiments haven't been carried out.

But other altered states of consciousness have been the subject of research in laboratories throughout the world. Zen meditators, for instance, have been found to alter their alpha frequency according to their depth of meditation. Experienced meditators can almost immediately enter Stage IV meditation, which is marked by the disappearance of a normal alpha rhythm and its replacement by the slower theta activity.

"Levels of experience in meditation are to an extent revealed in brain-wave patterns," according to Dr. Tomio Hirai, a leading Japanese research specialist in neurophysiology and the author of *Psychophysiology of Zen*. In some of his more recent experiments, Dr. Hirai has even correlated brain-wave patterns with a Zen practitioner's success in finding answers to *koans* (metaphysical riddles) presented to him by his Zen master.

"We found that Zen masters never accepted the answers of trainees who had been emitting beta waves at the time their solution was reached. To produce an answer acceptable to the master, the trainee had to reach Stage IV or at least Stage III." (In Stage III meditation alpha waves slow down and slower theta rhythms appear.) This alteration in brain activity is more than a simple shift toward slower rhythms such as those corresponding to drowsiness or light sleep. "Zen meditation is not merely a state between mental stability and sleep, but a condition in which the mind operates at the optimum," writes Dr. Hirai. "In this condition the person is relaxed but ready to accept and respond positively to any stimulus that may reach him. This, in turn, suggests that the operation of consciousness can be interpreted as an alteration of the brain waves."

But not every alteration in states of awareness is accompanied by changes in the brain's electrical activity. Hypnotized subjects, for instance, have normal brain-wave patterns in their trance states. The usual forms of autogenic training and transcendental meditation are also typically accompanied by EEG's of normal drowsiness. Overall, current neuroscience research suggests that the brain's electrical activity and its responses to internal and external stimulation can be modified by some practices but not others. It is not clear why some practices can produce alteration in brain activity while other seemingly similar approaches have no effect. We do know that perfectly normal people regularly experience dramatic changes in their consciousness. As Dr. Frank Putnam puts it:

"I think that there is a great deal to suggest that normal people exhibit quite striking changes in state, and these may be accompanied by physiologic changes. The hard thing is to be able to demonstrate these changes. I see multiple personalities as a strong expression of normal processes. The multiples are not strange, alien creatures but merely exhibit an exaggerated form of a process which occurs in all of us."

If the brain is what makes us human, then disruptions and distortions in normal brain functioning can be expected to impair our humanity. A damaged brain produces, according to the area of damage, a damaged mind. For instance, as we have seen in earlier chapters, memory is affected as a result of diseases in the hippocampus or amygdala. Awareness of one side of our body may go awry if the parietal lobe on the opposite side of the brain is injured.

But the most destructive effect on our humanity comes from brain disorders that are more widespread in their effect. Dementia is one of the most feared and most devastating aspects of aging. It is the principal reason for the confinement of the elderly in nursing homes. About 5 percent or more of persons over sixty-five years of age suffer from severe forms of dementia, with an additional 10 percent exhibiting mild to moderate impairments. Altogether, dementia accounts for six billion dollars a year in nursing home costs. More important, however, is the toll that this pernicious illness inflicts on its victims.

In its earliest stages, dementia induces sufferers to forget events that happened in the recent past. He or she can't recall names, addresses, and important bits of information that formerly required little or no effort. Generally, the affected individual's recall of events in the distant past is far better than for things that happened only moments earlier. As the illness progresses, the victim loses the ability to read, write, add, subtract, or even speak coherently. Accompanying this deterioration are a host of emotional symptoms: irritability, emotional instability, hallucinations, even paranoid fears that relatives and friends may be contributing to the disease. In the final stages, the patient with dementia is a pitiful sight: totally confused, often unable to control bowel or bladder, frequently incapable of recognizing loved ones and friends.

Examination of the brain of persons suffering from dementia, specifically a form of the disorder known as *Alzheimer's disease*, consistently reveals that the cerebral cortex and hippocampus contain twisted tangles and filaments and abnormal *neurites* known as *neuritic plaques.* The symptoms of Alzheimer's disease are thought to result from these strange developments in the cerebral cortex and hippocampus. In fact, the density of these abnormal components varies directly with the severity of the mental disorder.

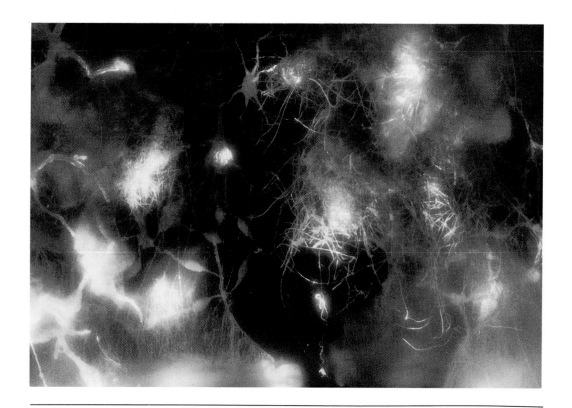

Until recently, neuroscientists had few clues about how Alzheimer's disease might be prevented or treated. In lieu of treatment, patients were warehoused in mental hospitals and nursing homes. Experiences in the past decade, however, are justifying a cautious optimism that Alzheimer's disease may someday be treated, perhaps even prevented. Treatments presently under investigation involve neurotransmitters, and one of the most promising avenues of research concerns the effects of the neurotransmitter *acetylcholine* on memory function. Drugs that block brain acetylcholine induce amnesia in normal volunteers. This amnesia is highly selective: Only recent memory is affected. A further indication of the importance of acetylcholine in recent memory formation comes from studies on the effects of drugs that augment brain acetylcholine. Altering the balance of neurotransmitters to enhance acetylcholine content improves a person's memory. Conversely, failures of the acetylcholine system may underline some of the disturbances encountered in Alzheimer's disease.

But the detection of a specific neurotransmitter defect—

This model depicts the damage Alzheimer's disease inflicts: plaques and dendritic tangles clog the neural network, disrupting the normal functions of the brain.

acetylcholine—provides only a partial insight into the mechanisms of Alzheimer's disease. What causes the decrease in acetylcholine? Is there a deficit in acetylcholine production or storage? To answer these questions, neuroscientists have examined the brains of patients who have died of Alzheimer's disease. In the cerebral cortex they found a 60 percent to 90 percent decrease in the enzymes that synthesize acetylcholine. At the same time, they have focused their attention on an area in the forebrain, near the *optic chiasm* (where the optic nerves cross) that projects to the cerebral cortex. Destruction of this area, the *Nucleus basalis* of Meynert, named after its nineteenth-century discoverer, W. Meynert, results in reduced cholinergic activity in the cortex similar to that in Alzheimer's disease.

A PET scan of a normal brain, right, is in dramatic contrast to one of a patient with Alzheimer's disease.

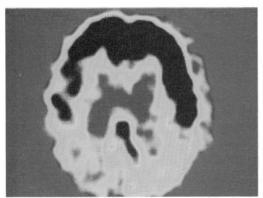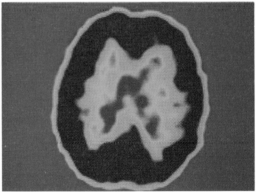

It is presently believed that the initial abnormality of Alzheimer's disease may involve a slow dying off of the cells of the Nucleus basalis. This failure may account for the formation of senile plaques, since the cells in the Nucleus basalis can no longer provide sufficient acetylcholine. As a result, the nerve processes—which extend from the Nucleus basalis to terminate in the cortex—begin to malfunction. The axons start to turn into plaques, and neurotransmission breaks down. This situation suggests that the Nucleus basalis may stimulate the cortex to respond to events in the environment. Certainly the effects of recording from the cells in the Nucleus basalis are consistent with this hypothesis: the cells are most active when the animal is attending to events in the environment or seeking rewards.

In humans, the acetylcholine system is believed to activate whenever a person is intently involved with the environment: automatically memorizing the facial details of a new acquaintance, or following the quick wit of a scintillating conversationalist. The patient with Alzheimer's disease, on the other hand, is relatively unconcerned about people and events in the environment. Interest, enthusiasm, and memory are severely stunted.

The importance of acetylcholine in memory formation is stimulating a series of brain grafts in experimental animals that may be the forerunners of similar surgery for patients afflicted with Alzheimer's disease. According to Anders Bjorklund, of the University of Lund, Sweden, it is likely that in the future, grafts of acetylcholine-producing brain areas may provide the acetylcholine needed to maintain or restore normal mental functioning. Experiments on rats have already shown that a rat's performance in maze running can be enhanced when it is given a graft of acetylcholine-producing brain tissue from another rat.

Dr. Bjorklund's transplant experiments are an extension of the work described earlier on patients with Parkinson's disease, in which dopamine-producing cells in the patient's own adrenal gland were transplanted to the brain to provide the missing dopamine. Grafts involving acetylcholine, however, are more complicated. For one thing, there is no equivalent of the adrenal gland to supply acetylcholine. Second, neuroscientists now believe that dopamine and acetylcholine perform very different functions within the brain. Dopamine exerts its effect by a connection between the substantia nigra and the striatum, acting as a kind of hormone that keeps the striatum functioning at the proper activity levels. "It's like the output from a thermostat, the substantia nigra, controlling overall levels of striatal activity . . . it's not information as we think of it . . . it's simply juicing up the striatum," according to neurobiologist Miles Herkenham. Acetylcholine, on the other hand, is more like a message sent from one part of the brain to another. It is involved in symbolism, information, meaning. Injecting acetylcholine into the brain and expecting an overall improvement in mental functioning is like placing a dictionary in a playpen and expecting a three-year-old child to compose an essay on child-care practices.

"This information is one of the great drawbacks of the

supposed cure of Alzheimer's disease," according to Dr. Herkenham. "Acetylcholine neurons projecting to the cortex have a message which they're giving to the cortex. Before 'curing' Alzheimer's disease, we have to learn more about what this message is, how it is composed, and how we can decode it. It is only when we are able to do these things that we will have any real hope of doing anything very dramatic about Alzheimer's disease."

Alzheimer's disease, with its devastating and widespread impact on both the brain and the behavior of its victims, brings up an age-old question once again: What *is* the relationship between the brain and the mind? Is the mind simply the brain? Certain insights provided by modern research bear on the question. For instance, many philosophical speculations of the past lost their relevance in the light of new and innovative techniques for studying the human brain. For instance, with PET scanners it is possible to observe patterns of glucose use while a subject is listening to a symphony. Does that mean that the symphony is "nothing more than" the activity of certain neurons? Such an assertion, far from being demonstrable, doesn't even make sense. A symphony isn't a configuration of neurons; it exists in its own right and cannot be "explained" or "equated" with brain activity. It seems to me that part of the mind-brain difficulty stems from the insistence that there is something else lurking within the shadows of our mental landscapes. For example, while I am at a concert my brain may be responding to the music in ways that a neuroscientist could document by a PET scanner. But his PET scan can't demonstrate the existence of anything other than my-brain-responding-to-a-concert. Why is it necessary to postulate that there is a separate me who somehow exists independently of the experience of listening to the concert? If I become bored with the concert and wish to leave, there is a brain-bored-with-the-concert. When leaving, there is a brain-bored-with-the-concert-intent-on-leaving.

There is no separate and overseeing "me" as I write these words. Instead, there is the me-now-writing-the-words. This me corresponds to my brain, which is engaged in a constant and ever-changing activity. The "I," or the mind, is a fiction that gives the illusion of permanence to my ever-changing perceptions. The use of "my" and "mind" in the previous sentences is part of this fiction. There is simply nothing to prove that anything exists other than the brain interacting with some aspect of external or internal reality. For this reason it should not be surprising that brain scientists haven't yet discovered the "seat of the mind." It is not likely that they will.

The concept of mind originally evolved to fill certain purposes. Prior to the discovery of the electrochemical nature of the brain, it was necessary to describe how thoughts and emotions could occur. Since the earliest brain scientists knew so little about brain activity, they assumed that "something else" must be at work—the "Ghost in the Machine," as it was called by the philosopher Gilbert Ryle. With the dawning of the Industrial Revolution, the brain became identified with the operation of a complicated machine. The legacy of this metaphor is still with us. "My mind isn't sharp today." "My mind's a little rusty." "He was under so much stress his mind finally broke down." But still the mind was considered a mysterious force at work in the machinery of the brain.

The disciplines of neurology and psychiatry are based on a dichotomy created by the "mind is different from brain" metaphor. If you have a mental illness (disturbance of "mind"), you go to a psychiatrist. If you have a brain disease, you see a neurologist. Only recently have the two disciplines been united. Behavioral neurology is based on the insight that the brain is responsible for all behavior and that behavior emanates from a functioning brain. What is now needed is a new metaphor, a new way of making sense of the world without recourse to the outmoded concept of a "mind." Mind is nothing more than a term we employ to describe some of the functions of the brain. And further brain research isn't going to define further the matter of "mind" any more than turning over all the turf in Ireland is likely to turn up a colony of leprechauns.

One of the criticisms against the above point of view was leveled by brain researcher Sir John Eccles. He calls it a form of "promissory materialism." But neuroscience, rightly understood as an aspect of the biological and not the social sciences, doesn't make any promises about such things as mind. The term "mind" is used in the same way as terms such as "inflation," "peace," "progress"—useful concepts about processes. One cannot locate inflation anywhere within a department of economics. One can't travel to the United Nations to interview "peace." These terms aren't *things;* they are convenient terms for processes too complex to be described adequately in a few words. When our brain is at full alertness, operating at its most efficient, we are *mindful* of all relevant circumstances. When our brain isn't operating efficiently and we don't function at our best, we are operating *mindlessly.* There is nothing wrong with the use of this metaphor. It's like a variation of the Santa Claus myth: everybody can have a lot of fun as long as no one starts believing that Santa Claus really exists.

Science is concerned with observable, or at least describable, phenomena. It can tell us nothing about the kinds of questions that have intrigued thinking people over the centuries. To ask, "Is there a soul?," for instance, is not the same thing as asking about the existence of mind. Soul is a religious concept that concerns such things as salvation, eternal life, communication with a deity, and so on. Mind, on the other hand, refers to consciousness, memory, and behavior as well as a host of other manifestations of a functioning brain. While many artificial intelligence experts are claiming that certain advanced computers may possess a "mind," no one has ever had the temerity to suggest they possess an immortal soul. Put slightly differently, to deny that a mind exists separately from a brain doesn't imply any position at all on the existence of a soul, God, a hereafter— these are within the bailiwick of theologians and the religiously committed. Neuroscience cannot and should not bolster or undermine these beliefs. There is another reason for maintaining a reasonable degree of humility about readily dismissing the claims of religious thinkers throughout the ages: Our understanding is limited by the organization of our brains. "We now see through a glass darkly," as one mystic put it. Certainly it cannot be denied that the organization of our brain places limitations on what we can and cannot know by perception or reason.

On the basis of our brain's organization, we are able to perceive certain aspects of "reality" while we remain oblivious to others. Errors inevitably creep in that are as much products of our brain organization as they are of anything in the external world. For this reason I am not confident that we will ever be completely successful in "making up our minds" on the question "Is the mind the brain?"

To appreciate some of the problems involved, imagine yourself in the following experiment.

You are looking at a PET scan while the radiologist who took the scan is sitting with you. Together you are discussing the activity depicted on the scan. Assume that the PET scanner is slightly advanced over anything presently available and depicts glucose utilization in real time. (State-of-the-art scans require a thirty- to forty-five-minute lead time, but in the near future this time lag will be significantly reduced.)

As you are staring at the PET scan, the radiologist points out that the most active areas of the scan are the left hemisphere, particularly the language area and the visual areas toward the back of the brain. At this point some relaxing music comes on in the background. Almost immediately the activity pattern of the PET scan changes. Now there is a focus of activity in the right hemisphere as well. You call the radiologist's attention to that change.

"That's somewhere in the region of the music appreciation center," he responds.

A few minutes later the radiologist asks you, "Do you have any comments on this PET scan?"

"What do you mean?" you respond.

At this point you notice another change in the PET scan: The auditory areas as well as the frontal areas are lighting up on both sides. You look toward the radiologist and notice that he or she is slyly looking at you. You both break out into laughter—you finally realize that the PET scan is depicting *your own brain activity!*

Now consider the following questions: Is this an example of your mind studying your brain? Or can we adequately explain it as your brain studying itself?

Several people whom I have asked regarding the hypothetical situation described above felt that it makes a good deal of difference whether you knew that you were looking at a PET scan of your own brain. Up to that point many respondents were comfortable that the situation was an instance of the brain studying the brain. Their discomfort begins at the point that you became aware that the PET image depicted your own brain. They prefer to think of this as an example of mind, or awareness, or consciousness, or, in any case, *something special* studying its own brain. If you agree with this assumption, then I have a further question:

In this hypothetical situation, are you studying one thing or two things?

If you are studying one thing, then I assume you would agree that you are studying the brain. If not, then what is the multicolored object depicted on the PET scan?

If you are studying two things, then you must admit that throughout the earliest part of the experiment your mind wasn't aware that it was studying itself. It operated on the assumption that it was studying somebody else's brain. But suddenly it realized that what it had taken as another person's brain was actually none other than its own brain. This is a curious situation, isn't it?

It seems that whether one is studying the brain or the mind depends very much on one's point of view. According to this line of reasoning, your study of a PET scan was the study of a brain until it became obvious that it was a PET scan of your own brain. Presumably at this point your mind became aware that it was studying *your brain.*

But suppose that in the above hypothetical situation you were dull and not at all clever that day and failed to recognize that you were looking at your own PET scan image. You would have left the viewing room convinced that you had seen a glucose utilization scan of somebody else's brain. Would that mean that your mind had been studying your brain but didn't know it? Or was it studying itself and didn't know it?

Whenever the brain is conscious of itself (looking at its own PET scan via a visual image conveyed along the optic nerves), we introduce the word "mind." Prior to the knowledge that the PET scan was actually of your own brain, the study clearly involved a study of a brain rather than a mind. All of this leaves unanswered the basic question of what the "one thing" is we are studying from two different aspects. If we are emphasizing brain, then we point to the PET scan image. If we want to emphasize mind, then it would only be necessary to decide to turn off the background music and point to the disappearance of activity over the musical appreciation center: "See my mind brought about a change in my brain activity." But solving the dilemma in this way can be done only at a great price. Emphasizing the control that mind can exert over brain (changing the PET scan pattern by altering thoughts or intentions) places one in the position of an idealist who claims that mind and not matter is the preeminent reality. If this is true, then how is this "mind" related to the brain activity depicted on the PET scan? In other words, how can something immaterial influence something material? And what do we mean when we speak of the "immaterial"? A force?

Let me suggest an alternative solution to the above dilemma. In all instances we are studying *brain*. While looking at the PET scan, your brain was simply studying itself. After you were made aware of this, nothing significantly changed other than the fact that your brain was now aware that it was looking at itself. This realization, incidentally, had no immediate effect on the PET scan. It didn't make any difference in the appearance of the PET scan whether or not you realized the scan was depicting your own brain. This leads to another point we have been making throughout this book: there is no center concerned with self-recognition, no tiny area of the brain in which resides the mind. In other words, mind is nothing more than *yet another property of the functioning brain*. In some cases you are less aware of it (early in the scenario when you and the radiologist studied the unfamiliar PET scan), while on other occasions, more (at the point when you realized you were studying a PET scan of your own brain). Mind, consciousness, and "self-awareness" represent increasing degrees of complexity in the structure and operation of the brain. Some brains (humans, perhaps some higher primates) are sufficiently complex in their structure to result in the formation of mind and consciousness; others are insufficiently complex (bees, lizards), while with still others (dogs, cats) the issue isn't totally resolved.

The appeal of dualism—the belief that there is a mind that exists apart from a brain—springs from our improper understanding of everyday states of consciousness. Until the advent of PET scanners and evoked potential studies, it was possible to maintain the fiction that thoughts can occur independently of bodily processes. "I think, therefore I am," as the philosopher Descartes formulated it in 1637.

But since the development of appropriate technologies, it has become obvious that thoughts, emotions, and even elementary sensations are accompanied by changes in the state of the brain. Glucose, oxygen, and other nutrients and metabolites vary according to mental states and the circum-

Mind vs Brain: The Other Side of the Argument

It would be unfair to imply that all neuroscientists are in agreement that the mind doesn't exist independently of the brain. In order to provide "equal time" for this alternative opinion, the following brief essay is presented from the point of view of the confirmed dualist. Contrast this with my argument developed on pages 342–351. Which do *you* find more convincing?

Two years before his death at age eighty-four, neurosurgeon Wilder Penfield was writing his final book, *The Mystery of the Mind.* During moments away from his desk Penfield continued to ponder the theme of his book: the relationship of mind, brain, and science.

One weekend while at his farm outside of Montreal, Penfield took up a small basket containing old cans of house paint. Proceeding to the slope of a nearby hill, he began painting on a huge rock. On one side, he painted a Greek word for "spirit" along with a solid line connecting it to an Aesculapian torch, which represented science. The line continued around the rock to the other side, where he drew an outline of a human head with a brain drawn inside, which contained, at its center, a question mark. At this point, Penfield was satisfied: brain studies, if properly conducted, would lead inevitably to an understanding of the mind.

But as Penfield progressed with his book, he became less certain that the study of the brain, a field in which he had done pioneering work earlier in his career, would ever lead to an understanding of the mind. Finally, six months before he died, he reached a conclusion.

Donning six sweaters to protect himself from the harsh Canadian wind, Penfield returned to the rock and with shaking hands converted the solid line connecting the spirit and brain into an interrupted one. This alteration expressed, in a form for all to see, Penfield's doubts that an understanding of the brain would ever lead to an explanation of the mind.

Among neuroscientists, Penfield is not alone in undergoing, later in life, a change in belief about the relationship of the mind to the brain. Sir John Eccles, a Nobel Prize winner, has teamed up in recent years with philosopher Karl Popper. Together they have written *The Self and Its Brain,* an updated plea for dualism: the belief that the mind and the brain are distinct entities. Roger Sperry, a Nobel Prize winner in medicine, is deeply engrossed in studies on the nature of human consciousness. Brain researcher Karl Pribram is currently collaborating with physicist David Bohm in an attempt to integrate mind and consciousness with ideas drawn from quantum physics. Together they are searching for a model capable of integrating matter and consciousness into a holistic world view.

Why should these brain researchers have a change of heart late in their careers about the adequacy of our present knowledge of the brain to provide an "explanation" for mind and consciousness? What compels them toward a mystical bent?

For one thing, the human brain is unique among body organs. "There is nothing like a brain," writes neurosurgeon Irving Cooper in his autobiography, *The Vital Probe.* "Given the opportunity to study the tissue that sees, thinks, hears, feels, fears, desires, creates, how could one choose anything else?"

Interest and enthusiasm regarding the brain can't be the only explanations why neuroscientists are susceptible to a mystical bent, since only a small number of them end up waxing philosophical. But the nature of their research and the kinds of questions asked undoubtedly contribute to later "conversions." Penfield's work involved neurosurgical explorations into the temporal lobes. In response to Penfield's electrical probe, his patients reported familiar feelings and vivid memories. In essence, these patients reported experiences that did not correspond to actual events in the operating theater, but rather were the result of direct stimulation of neural tissues. Does this mean that our conscious experience can be understood solely in terms of electrical impulses? Penfield's speculations along these lines led him, over the next fifty years, from the operating theater in the Montreal Neurologic Institute to the final expression of agnosticism he so vividly portrayed in his rock painting.

Researchers like Wilder Penfield and Roger Sperry are examples of brain researchers who have become disillusioned with claims that the mind can "be explained" in terms of brain functioning. They have revolted against what another neuroscientist calls the "Peter Pan School of neuroscience" with its "bloodless dance of action potentials" and its "hurrying to and fro of molecules."

Common to all these brain scientists is a willingness to adapt innovative attitudes as well as pursue unorthodox lines of inquiry. They have also been open to transcendental influences. Eccles, for instance, had a "sudden overwhelming experience" at age eighteen that aroused an intense interest in the mind-brain problem. He attributes his choice of career in the neurosciences to this experience.

Brain researchers with a "mystical bent" have also been comfortable sharing their findings and ideas with specialists in other fields. Penfield's book, *The Mystery of the Mind*, was encouraged by Charles Hendle, professor of philosophy at Yale. It was a much-needed encouragement, since the other neuroscientists to whom Penfield had shown his early draft discouraged him from proceeding with the project. To them, Penfield's speculative leap from neurophysiologist to philosopher was "unscientific." At Hendle's urging, Penfield proceeded to detail "how I came to take seriously, even to believe, that the consciousness of man, the mind, is something not to be reduced to brain mechanisms."

Why should it be surprising that the study of the human brain often leads to mysticism? Consider the paradox involved: The inquiring organ, the brain, is itself the object of its own inquiry. The brain is the only organ in the known universe that seeks to understand itself. Looked at from this point of view, one might expect an even greater number of brain scientists to turn toward mysticism. After all, are not our brains part of the same physical universe whose essential nature remains, after years of research and speculation, essentially mysterious?

stances of the moment. To this extent, a thought without a change in brain activity is impossible. In a very real sense, thoughts have neuronal consequences. In many instances the reverse is also true.

Drop a tab of acid, snort some cocaine, take a few puffs from a joint—in all these instances mental activity (or the mind) is transformed by altering brain chemistry. Thanks to research on memory, certain forms of mental illness, and dementia, neuroscientists are approaching the day when *all* mental activity will be formulated in terms of brain activity. The exact degree of correlation, however, remains to be determined. It is not likely, for instance, that all thoughts will ever be directly translatable into neuronal activity patterns or shifts in the tides of neurotransmitters. For this reason, "thought reading" on the basis of brain activity is very unlikely. Unfortunately, this failure to correlate mind with brain in a one-to-one fashion probably will provide the basis for continued claims for the existence of a mind independent of a brain.

Studies on readiness potentials, the preparatory adjustments in the cerebellar and basal ganglia prior to an act of "will," the prefrontal discharges that occur prior to any motor activity, however trivial—some people see these discoveries as proof that the mind exists independent of a functioning brain. But where is the mind in states of unconsciousness? When the brain writhes in the throes of an epileptic seizure, or is plummeted into an alcohol or drug stupor? Or even when the brain is put under the hammerlock of a powerful anesthetic? It is puzzling why well-informed people continue to hold out for the existence of a mind independent of the brain. Let me speculate for a moment on some of the reasons.

First, the correlation of mind with brain often is mistakenly considered a form of reductionism, one of the "nothing but" arguments that so pervade much of our current culture. "Patriotism is nothing but thinly disguised chauvinism and imperialism." "The love of a husband for his wife is nothing but possessiveness." In each of these assertions something lofty and desirable is reduced to the level of a primitive urge. Hidden in these assertions is the assumption that the person making the assertion is himself or herself operating from a superior position—i.e., on the basis of these "insights," only he or she is really enlightened.

Everybody else is confused, suffers from delusions, remains narrowly confined, and so on. But consider the consequences that flow from the insight that the mind is a convenient shorthand for the brain: *all mental states,* whether they be the ecstasy of the mystic, the hatred of an Eichmann or a Hitler, the genius of a Michelangelo or Dante—all are expressions of the functioning brain. "There is not a single one of our states of mind, high or low, healthy or morbid that has not some organic process as its condition," stated William James at the turn of the century.

The mind-equals-brain equation isn't a form of reductionism at all, since nothing is being reduced to anything else. Instead, mental activity is recognized as emanating from the functioning brain. To understand the "mind," therefore, it is necessary to understand the brain—how concepts are arrived at, the mechanisms underlying perceptions, memory, the neurochemistry of our emotions, and so on.

If our brains were organized differently, we would experience a different reality. We would have different psychological needs. A slight change in our brain could almost be guaranteed to alter our psychology and our sociology. We would be convinced by new kinds of arguments (or perhaps we wouldn't require convincing at all).

What are we likely to discover about the human brain in the near future? The answer depends to a large extent on the development of new technological probes as well as new uses for those presently available. One of several promising areas already being explored is *brain electrical activity mapping,* or BEAM.

Despite the daunting name, BEAM is nothing more than a way of enhancing the amount of information available on a standard EEG. Ordinarily, reading an EEG demands that the doctor perform a statistical and spectral analysis of the "brain waves" displayed on the recording. With BEAM, all of this information is automated not by creating new data but by making it possible to interpret the massive amounts of data already available. Through conversion of the squiggly lines of an EEG into a color-coded map, all available information is made more meaningful, more likely to be assimilated and understood. It is similar to what happens when someone converts a column of numbers into color graphics. In this way the brain can intuitively grasp the significance of the numbers, converting them into a meaningful, recognizable pattern that is more likely to be remembered afterward.

A closely related technique, *significance probability mapping* (SPM), relies on a computer-driven statistical analysis that compares, point by point, whether a given EEG pattern deviates from the normal. With each imaging, abnormalities can be easily defined and studied. Both BEAM and SPM are already proving highly reliable in clinical diagnosis. BEAM and SPM are correct 80 to 90 percent of the time when diagnosing dyslexia in ten- to twelve-year-olds. Brain tumors can also be detected by BEAM with an accuracy at least 10 percent better than relying on standard EEG's.

BEAM also promises to provide a noninvasive, highly sensitive way to diagnose schizophrenics. Schizophrenics with their eyes open in the alert state show a BEAM increase in slow wave activity over the entire cortical surface. In the eyes-closed alert state the pattern changes: Slowing extends over both frontal regions. In the near future, differential diagnosis of troublesome cases may be possible by "hooking the patient up" to a BEAM unit. Eventually the diagnosis may even be made when the patient isn't actively schizophrenic. For instance, there is already evidence that schizophrenics in remission tend to show different BEAM and PET scan patterns in the frontal regions of their brains. Decreases in metabolism in the left frontal area often remain even when the patients are in clinical remission. This suggests that the PET and BEAM studies may provide a marker for the schizophrenic trait irrespective of whether the patient is actively schizophrenic at the time of the testing.

Additional information can be obtained by making alterations in techniques. For instance, combining PET scans and BEAMs leads to an increase in diagnostic accuracy. Changing the radioactive tracer in a PET scan is similar to changing the filter on a camera: we get new and different pictures of the same event. Repeating the PET scan later is similar to taking a photograph of the same object from several different poses. Combining the diagnostic tools (BEAM plus PET) is like converting a series of static black-and-white snapshots into a full-color movie. Since brain activity never ceases except at death, no still picture or measurement of one specific moment can lead to an appreciation of the living brain. At all times, the brain is functioning as a whole. The goal, of course, is somehow to capture the brain in all its dynamism. Future interpretation of PET scans and BEAM studies, therefore, can be expected to be complex and multidimensional.

At this point in our technological development, PET scans cannot reflect brain activity from moment to moment but need thirty- to forty-minute spans for processing information. Although BEAM and evoked potential techniques operate closer to "real time," they have their own limitations. Although the time frame is compressed by a factor of a million (milliseconds as compared to minutes or even hours for PET scans), the localization is less precise. It is limited to seven or eight relay stations starting from the peripheral nervous system and extending to the cerebral cortex. Although abnormalities may be detected anywhere along this pathway, this information reveals little about what may be causing a given problem or, even more importantly, what might be done about it.

In time it is likely that new technological advances will resolve some of these difficulties. In a recent step forward, the distribution of dopamine receptors was visualized by PET scan. The initial experiment in this area was first carried out on May 25, 1983, when Dr. Henry N. Wagner, Jr., of Johns Hopkins Medical School, volunteered to be injected with a drug known to have a high affinity for dopamine receptors in the brains of experimental animals. Images at 40 to 60 minutes after injection and 70 to 130 minutes later revealed high activity in the basal ganglia compared to the rest of Dr. Wagner's brain. This experiment marked a revolution in the study of the human brain: localization of a neurotransmitter receptor within the brain of a living human subject. Based on this technique, it will soon be possible to evaluate the effects of psychotropic drugs in schizophrenia, Parkinson's disease, and Huntington's chorea—three diseases known to be associated with disturbances in dopamine or its receptors.

Neuroscientists may soon be able to perform biochemical "dissections" on the human brain. Thanks to radioactive tagging, it will be possible to administer a drug and then follow it to its final destination on a particular receptor. Based on such information, a series of maps of neurotransmitter receptor sites will emerge. Neuroscientists are hoping that additional research along these lines will soon make it possible to relate regional brain biochemistry to behavioral observations. They hope that correlations will then be possible between disturbed behavior and biochemical changes within specific localizable areas of the brain. This is an exciting and daring hypothesis, as close as neuroscientists have ever been to correlating a disordered thought with a disordered molecule.

Further advances may enable neuroscientists to reach conclusions about ongoing cognitive processes on the basis of increasingly sophisticated brain-imaging techniques. For instance, in the past year Dr. Niels Lassen and his associates at the Bispebjerg Hospital in Copenhagen, Denmark, achieved the first image of a human thought. In their PET study, the subject began by moving his right hand. This activated the frontal and motor areas of the opposite side of the brain. Next, the subject was instructed merely to "think about moving the hand." In this instance the motor components dropped out and the PET image revealed the basic neuronal activity pattern of the thought minus its motor components!

In another study, Lassen has captured the difference between a person listening to his native language and one that person doesn't understand. The native language activates the association cortex, while the unintelligible language fails to generate the same "recognition patterns." Such studies may tell us a lot about learning and why some people have learning "disabilities." They may also provide a shortcut on the way to assessing functional patterns of brain activity, even in instances where the subject cannot or will not cooperate. For instance, a spy could be unmasked by the brain-wave patterns produced when he or she is exposed to language that person understands but claims not to comprehend.

Lassen's studies are moving us closer to the time when brain-imaging techniques can be substituted for traditional methods of information gathering (interviews, the subject's spontaneous responses, and so on). But at this point, the outer limits of such techniques depend, first, on the ingenuity of the experimenter and, second, on the brain's ability to carry out the same task via multiple channels.

As we have stressed throughout this series, the brain is

not limited in its responses. Since the brain is always purposeful in its orientation, the same task can be done in many different ways and involving various neuronal channels. Such variability makes it extremely unlikely that neuroscientists will ever be able to "read thoughts" from the analysis of brain-wave patterns. The privacy of our own mental processes is unlikely to be disturbed. Detecting that an individual may actually understand a language he or she claims not to is light-years away from actually determining what that person is thinking at any given moment.

Dr. Martin Reivich, of the University of Pennsylvania School of Medicine in Philadelphia, has discovered that PET scans can be used to measure anxiety. As patients become more anxious, the metabolic activity in the right hemisphere is altered in comparison to the left. Another application of the PET technique by Dr. Michael Phelps and Lou Baxter, of the UCLA School of Medicine in Los Angeles, points to changes in PET-scan images that correspond to improvement in the patient's clinical state. For instance, a depressed patient given *Ritalin* (a psychic activator) showed an increase in the metabolic rate on the PET scan, which corresponded to clinical improvement. Another patient, a concert pianist with a rapidly cycling manic-depressive illness, showed regular variations of PET-scan activity that corresponded to her clinical state: low-metabolism during depression, heightened metabolic activity as she shifted into the manic state. On the basis of such studies, psychiatrists soon will be able to make reliable diagnoses about mental illness on the basis of brain-imaging techniques. This promises to take much of the guesswork out of psychiatric diagnosis.

Forecasting future neuropsychiatric diagnoses also will become possible. Already, Drs. David Kuhl and Michael Phelps at UCLA have demonstrated that patients with Huntington's chorea show a decrease in glucose use in parts of their basal ganglia (the caudate and putamen). This loss occurs early and precedes any change in tissue bulk. Even more important, they have has demonstrated that these changes in metabolism within the basal ganglia precede any clinical demonstrations of the disease. This technique promises to provide a way of predicting who will get the disease among family members equally at risk. But at this point neuroscientists are busy pondering the social implications of

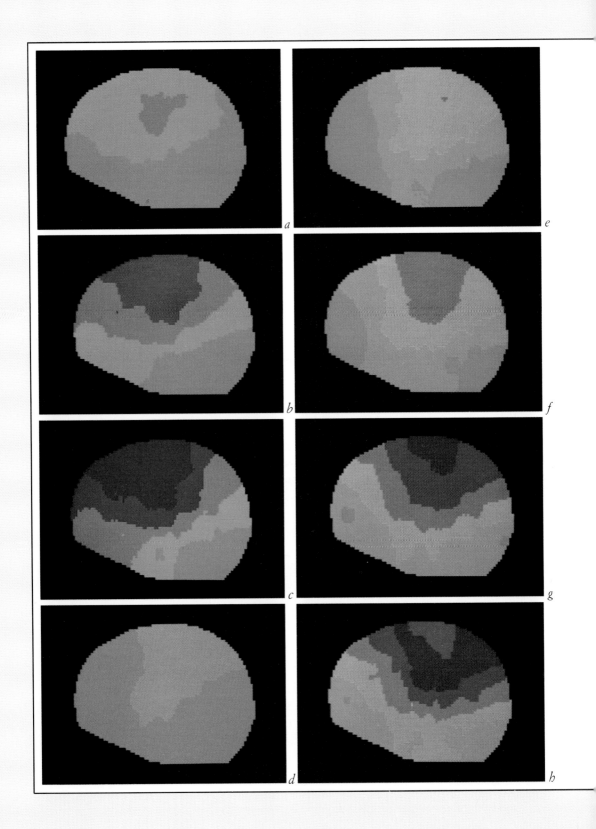

The Brain Images
of Jesse Salb

The image sequence on the opposite page is the work of Jesse Salb (Diasonics, Inc.), who has developed a system of visualizing brain activity. Jesse Salb describes the process:

"CAT scans show us the *structure* of brain tissue. PET scans show the pattern of brain biochemistry and metabolism, but give only a single, static image. An EEG amplifies and records brain electrical signals, the basis of the method used here, but an EEG is comparatively insensitive. In the system represented on the opposite page, a large number of electrodes are placed at predetermined positions over the entire scalp. The electrical activity is monitored, and a computer processes this activity and generates moving images on an anatomical map of the head. This allows a more precise localization of brain activity than has been possible using the older EEG techniques. Furthermore, these maps are made in such a way that we can show the brain's electrical potentials in real time, that is to say, as quickly as they are occurring in the subject's brain.

"All sensory stimuli have electrical potentials connected with them. The different colors represent levels of electrical potential, with the red colors representing positive voltages, the blue negative. The image sequence you see opposite represents the response of the subject's brain to an unexpected *audio tone.* Frames (a-c) and (d-e) represent the initial sensory processing of the tone stimulus by the subject's brain. Frames (f-h) represent the cognitive recognition of the unusual stimulus by the subject's brain."

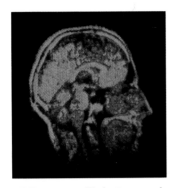

*NMR scans enable brain research-
ers to see very fine details inside
the brain without the need to
perform surgery.*

a technique that may be able to tell people more about themselves than they care to know.

Along the same lines, new methods for studying patients with brain tumors are already in use at NIH. Oftentimes after surgery, it is difficult to differentiate a recurring brain tumor from the aftereffects of surgery and irradiation. A correct diagnosis may take months, even with doctors who have years of clinical experience. But a PET scan now can make this diagnosis within minutes. A recurring brain tumor uses more glucose than other surrounding areas, and as a result the tumor shows up as a bright spot of activity in contrast to the surrounding area of low glucose utilization. Armed with this information, the brain surgeon can diagnose a recurrent tumor at an early stage and plan appropriate measures.

New surgical approaches to epilepsy will also become possible thanks to newly developed imaging techniques. Studies from the Reed Neurological Research Center at UCLA reveal that during epileptic seizures, the brain demonstrates an increased metabolic rate within the epileptic focus. Later, when the seizures have ceased, the metabolic rate in this area dips below normal. These changes inaugurate an era of increasingly specific surgical approaches to selected epileptic patients. It is now possible to delineate the precise extent of an epileptic lesion, a necessary prelude to excising it. This will also help in evaluating seizure control through medications.

Another diagnostic tool, nuclear magnetic resonance (NMR), measures the response of hydrogen protons within brain tissue to applied radiofrequency pulses. The hydrogen atoms emit electrical signals when the pulses are applied. These signals are then processed by a computer for conversion into a colored picture of the brain.

Further advances in the understanding of the brain await the development of suitable models that mimic brain function in important ways. Computers have some answers. But there are problems with trying to understand the human brain by computer simulation. As we have seen throughout this book, the brain is, first of all, an organ heavily dependent on meaning and context. Even at the level of primary sensation, a filtering process is constantly sorting out what seems to be important at the moment. For instance, out of the background of dozens of simultaneous cocktail conversations, we focus on one exchange simply on the basis of our interest in one of the speakers or the subject under discussion. This selection has nothing to do with linear processing. It concerns the *meaning* that one conversation has for us compared to others.

Although one could cite dozens of arguments why computers aren't likely to overtake the performance of the human brain, my favorite concerns the brain's ability to

Will computers ever be able to think in the manner we human beings do? Not until a computer learns to ask itself "In what way is my brain different from a human brain?"

perform at *less than its best*. Computers generally can't do that. At every moment they do the best they can. Our brain, however, sometimes is most efficient when it is idling. Think of how many creative ideas have occurred while a person is relaxing or daydreaming. Computers don't daydream, they don't idle at a bare percentage of their efficiency. They aren't whimsical. They do poorly understanding puns or jokes. They also don't become inspired, don't give up in discouragement, don't suggest better uses for their time. There has never been a computer capable of radically reprogramming itself. This can be accomplished by changing the computer's program, but someone with a *brain* has to do this.

This isn't to imply that computers haven't already achieved important breakthroughs. In the areas of rapid computation, information storage, and retrieval, computers can be expected to eclipse further the powers of the human brain. (A simple hand-held calculator already can outperform the computational powers of all but the most extraordinary humans.) In the future, computers can be expected to store more information as well as demonstrate increasing facility at retrieving and collating data. Present-day chess computers already are taking chess masters to task simply on the basis of the computers' ability to compute hundreds of thousands of moves in microseconds. So far, though, no computer has beaten one of the dozen or so highest-rated grand masters in the world. Why? Because in many situations in a chess match, there are very few really good moves. The capacity to compute hundreds of thousands of foolish or inappropriate moves is less important than selecting the one or two best. Once again we are speaking of inspiration, creativity at the highest level, the capacity to detect meaning and purpose.

Another difference between brains and machines concerns the role of inhibition. The brain exerts most of its power through inhibition rather than excitation. Despite this, artificial intelligence devices continue to be designed along lines that emphasize excitation. Consider the effects of destroying part of the brain. The result isn't simply a total breakdown but rather an internal reorganization of the remaining brain tissue. The same thing winds up being done in a different way, although in the process behavioral sequences may appear that were previously "suppressed": primitive reflexes, emotional responses, and so on. This

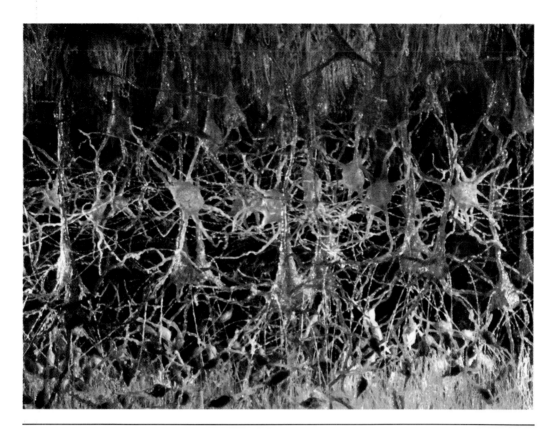

reorganization is internally controlled and proceeds fairly automatically.

I believe artificial-intelligence devices are unlikely to overpower the human brain simply because the brain's basic unit, the neuron, has specific physical and chemical properties. Simply put, neurons are alive while computers are not. To this extent, brains are as different from computers as starlings are from stars. Unlike the components of a computer, no two brain cells are ever exactly alike. They differ in degrees of responsiveness: they don't simply respond in an on-off manner; they demonstrate gradations of sensitivity to the neurochemicals that impinge upon them.

" 'The brain is wet.' Behind that simple statement is concealed a universe unlike anything remotely possible in the world of computer circuitry," according to NIMH neuroscientist Miles Herkenham. He continues, "The brain transmits messages across a wet terrain onto receptors which are floating on the membranes of cells. At all times, peptides are exerting a modulatory effect on the neurons quite

The neural network. Within this intricate pattern, chemical and electrical signals work together to produce a miracle: the conscious brain.

independent of the effect at the synapse brought about by classical neurotransmitters." Dr. Herkenham believes, and many neuroscientists agree with him, that the order of complexity in the brain is so vast that we will never be in a position to use a computer to re-create anything as complicated as human consciousness.

Dr. Herkenham adds, "When you consider all the billions of cells within the human brain, with each one affected by an unknown number of transmitters, peptides, and other 'messenger substances,' the amount of information quickly escalates to a figure approaching the number of particles in existence. It is simply inconceivable that a computer could be constructed along similar plans, which would then manifest a "mind." To this extent, no matter how much we learn about the brain, we can never learn it all. There will always be something to astound us, to amaze us, to keep us humble, while at the same time stimulating us to greater efforts toward understanding the brain. The human brain is simply the most marvelous organ in the known universe."

Bibliography

Blakemore, Colin. *Mechanics of the Mind.* New York: Cambridge University Press, 1977.

Brown, Hugh. *Brain and Behavior: A Textbook of Physiological Psychology.* New York: Oxford University Press, 1976.

Frisby, John P. *Seeing: Illusion, Brain and Mind.* New York: Oxford University Press, 1980.

Globus, Gordon G., Maxwell, Grover, Savodnik, Irwin, eds. *Consciousness and the Brain A Scientific and Philosophical Inquiry.* New York: Plenum Press, 1976.

Granit, Ragnar. *The Purposive Brain.* Cambridge: The M.I.T. Press, 1977.

Harth, Erich. *Windows on the Mind: Reflections on the Physical Basis of Consciousness.* New York: William Morrow & Co., Inc., 1982.

Heilman, Kenneth M., Valenstein, Edward, eds. *Clinical Neuropsychology.* New York: Oxford University Press, 1979.

Luria, A.R. *The Mind of a Mnemonist: A Little Book About a Vast Memory.* Chicago: Henry Regenery Co., 1968.

Luria, A.R. *The Working Brain: An Introduction to Neuropsychology.* New York: Penguin Press, 1973.

Kandel, Eric R., Schwartz, James H. *Principles of Neural Science.* New York: Elsevier–North Holland, 1981.

Marks, Lawrence E. *The Unity of the Senses: Interrelations Among the Modalities.* New York: Academic Press, 1978.

Ottoson, David. *Physiology of the Nervous System.* New York: Oxford University Press, 1983.

Restak, Richard M. *The Brain: The Last Frontier: An Exploration of the Human Mind and Our Future.* New York: Doubleday & Co., 1979.

Rose, Steven. *The Conscious Brain.* New York: Alfred Knopf, 1973.

Shepherd, Gordon M. *Neurobiology.* New York: Oxford University Press, 1983.

Spillane, John D. *The Doctrine of the Nerves: Chapters in the History of Neurology.* New York: Oxford University Press, 1981.

Taylor, Gordon Rattray. *The Natural History of the Mind.* New York: E.P. Dutton, 1979.

Yates, Francis A. *The Art of Memory.* Boston: Routledge and Kegan Paul, 1966.

Index

Credits

The author wishes to thank the many sources of illustration for their cooperation and assistance during the preparation of this book. Each is listed below following the page number upon which their illustration appears.

6: Model created by John Allison Company, photographed by Laura Van Dorn Schneider; 8–16: Research & Design by Juanita Gordon, Illustrated by Jowill Woodman; 21: The Bettmann Archive; 22–23: The Granger Collection; 24: Reproduced from Thomas Willis, *Cerebri Anatome,* London: J. Flesher, 1664, courtesy of the New York Academy of Medicine Library; 25: The Granger Collection; 26: The Bettmann Archive; 27: Research & Design by Juanita Gordon, Illustrated by Jowill Woodman; 28: Manfred Kage from Peter Arnold, Inc.; 31: The Bettmann Archive; 32–39: Paintings by John Allison; 43: W. Maxwell Cowan, "The Development of the Brain" © 1979 Scientific American; 46: Research & Design by Juanita Gordon, Illustrated by Jowill Woodman; 50: Model created by John Allison Company, photographed by Laura Van Dorn Schneider; 52: © Beeldrecht Amsterdam/VAGA New York, Collection Haags Gemeentemuseum, The Hague, 1981; 53 (top): American Journal of Psychology, v.42 p444; 53 (bottom): Courtesy Dr. David Hubel; 55: The Granger Collection; 57: The Bettmann Archive; 60: Research & Design by Juanita Gordon, Illustrated by Jowill Woodman; 61: Marr, David, 1976, "Early processing of visual information," in Philosophical Transactions of the Royal Society of London, Series B, v.275, pp483–524, and Mrs. David Marr, MIT, Dept. of Cognitive Science; 63: WNET; 66: from The Human Brain by Dick Gilling and Robin Brightwell Orbis Publ. Ltd, London; 68: Illustration by Bethann Thornburgh; 69: from The Human Brain by Dick Gilling and Robin Brightwell Orbis Publ. Ltd, London; 72: Witkin Gallery; 74: Courtesy of Jesse Salb; 77: Reprinted with permission of Macmillan Publishing Company from *The Cerebral Cortex of Man* by Wilder Penfield and Theodore Rasmussen; 79: Modified by Juanita Gordon and Jowill Woodman from *Neurobiology* by Gordon M. Shepard, © 1983 by Oxford University Press, Inc. Reprinted by permission.; 82: Courtesy Dr. Norman Leeds; 87–89: Peter L. Bull; 92: Bob and Clara Calhoun/Bruce Coleman, Inc.; 94: Sygma; 100: Model created by John Allison Company, photographed by Laura Van Dorn Schneider; 102: Jan and Des Bartlett/Bruce Coleman, Inc.; 103: Bruce Coleman, Inc.; 104: Courtesy of Joseph Fanelli, Clocks & Things, New York City; 106: Joe McDonald/Bruce Coleman, Inc.; 107: Jeff Foott/Bruce Coleman, Inc.; 108: Research & Design by Juanita Gordon, Illustrated by Jowill Woodman; 110: Phillipe Plailly; 115–125: Peter L. Bull; 126: Courtesy Mitchell Heller; 129: From the James Arthur Lecture on the Evolution of the Human Brain (1965): Evolution of Physical Control of the Brain, Jose M. Delgado, p.33; 132: Courtesy Dr. Allan Siegal; 134: Elliot

Erwitt/Magnum; 137: Courtesy Dr. Paul D. MacLean; 139: Courtesy of Dr. Joe Tupin; 146: Model created by John Allison Company, photographed by Laura Van Dorn Schneider; 149–150: Warren Anatomical Museum, Harvard Medical School; 157: WNET; 158–159: Model by Kip Thompson, John Allison Company, photographed by Laura Van Dorn Schneider; 162: Woodcut by Elaine Grove; 164: Reprinted by permission from *A Dozen Doctors* by Dwight J. Ingle, University of Chicago Press; 166: G. Schaller/Bruce Coleman, Inc.; 170: Courtesy CIBA Pharmaceutical Company; 177: Courtesy of Dr. Herbert Benson; 179: Black Star; 180: Manny Millan/Sports Illustrated; 188: Model created by John Allison Company, photographed by Laura Van Dorn Schneider; 191: The Bettmann Archive; 193: Culver Pictures, Inc.; 195: Max Hirshfeld; 197: from The Human Brain by Dick Gilling and Robin Brightwell Orbis Publ. Ltd, London; 199: Reprinted by permission from *Mechanics of the Mind* by Colin Blakemore, Cambridge University Press; 202: David Moore/Black Star; 208–210: Research & Design by Juanita Gordon, Illustrated by Jowill Woodman; 214: Wide World Photos; 216: Peter L. Bull; 218: Wide World Photos; 219–227: Peter L. Bull; 232–233: Rosalie Poznachowski; 236: Model created by John Allison Company, photographed by Laura Van Dorn Schneider; 238: Research & Design by Juanita Gordon, Illustrated by Jowill Woodman; 242–243: Rick Friedman/Black Star; 246: Research & Design by Juanita Gordon, Illustrated by Jowill Woodman; 248: Courtesy of Dr. Roger Sperry; 249: Dan McCoy/Rainbow; 251: Courtesy of Dr. John Mazziota; 256: BBC; 260: Reprinted by permission from The Brain: *Mystery of Matter and Mind,* Torstar Books, Inc.; 268: Courtesy of Dr. Richard M. Restak; 270: Model created by John Allison Company, photographed by Laura Van Dorn Schneider; 274–275: The Granger Collection; 277: The Bettmann Archive; 278: Courtesy of Jerry's parents; 279: Courtesy of Dr. Daniel Weinberger; 285–287: Dan McCoy/Rainbow; 290: Research & Design by Juanita Gordon, Illustrated by Jowill Woodman; 296–297: Model created by John Allison Company, photographed by Laura Van Dorn Schneider; 301: Painting by John Allison; 304–305: Research & Design by Juanita Gordon, Illustrated by Jowill Woodman; 306: Model created by John Allison Company, photographed by Laura Van Dorn Schneider; 308–309: Kerry Herman; 312: Courtesy of Mme. G. Raderscheidt/ Photograph by Phillipe Plailly; 313: Courtesy of Dr. David Hubel; 314: Kerry Herman; 316: Witkin Gallery, New York City; 318: Ted Spagna; 320 (top): Dan McCoy/Black Star; 320 (bottom): Charles Moore/Black Star; 321: Charles Moore/Black Star; 327: Ted Spagna; 335: Courtesy of Dr. Frank Putnam; 334: Kerry Herman; 339: Model created by John Allison Company, photographed by Laura Van Dorn Schneider; 340: Dan McCoy/Rainbow; 356–357: Courtesy of Jesse Salb; 358: Dan McCoy/Black Star; and 359: P. Goldberg/Sygma